From

The Women's Press Ltd
34 Great Sutton Street, London EC1V 0DX

Sheila Jeffreys is a lesbian and a revolutionary feminist who has been active within the Women's Liberation Movement since 1973. She has been working in Women's Liberation campaigns against pornography and male violence since 1978, and was a founding member of London Women Against Violence Against Women (WAVAW) in 1980. She is author of *The Spinster and Her Enemies: Feminism and Sexuality 1880–1930* (Pandora Press, 1985) and editor of *The Sexuality Debates* (Routledge Kegan Paul, Women's Source Library Series, 1987). She has contributed many articles on feminist theory and lesbian sexuality to journals including *Trouble and Strife, Gossip, Lesbian Ethics* and *Women's Studies International Forum*. She was a founding member of the London Lesbian Archive and the London Lesbian History Group, and contributed to *Not A Passing Phase: Reclaiming Lesbians in History 1840–1985* edited by the Lesbian History Group (The Women's Press, 1989). She teaches in further education and has also taught the history of sexuality on women's studies courses in adult education, for the Open University and for university extra mural departments.

Sheila Jeffreys

ANTICLIMAX
A Feminist Perspective
on the Sexual Revolution

The Women's Press

First published by The Women's Press Limited
A member of the Namara Group
34 Great Sutton Street, London EC1V 0DX

British Library Cataloguing in Publication Data
Jeffreys, Sheila
　　Anticlimax: a feminist perspective on the sexual
　revolution.
　　1. Sex relations.　　Theories, history.
　　I. Title
　　306.7'01

　　ISBN 0–7043–4203–0

Typeset by Input Typesetting Ltd, London
Printed and bound in Great Britain by Cox & Wyman Ltd,
Reading, Berks

CONTENTS

Introduction

For Anne Rowett with the greatest thanks for her patience and support and with my love

Acknowledgments

I would like to thank my friends for the concern and affection with which they have helped me through the four years of writing *Anticlimax*. Much of which I have had to read and work with has been distressing, the demands of my teaching work and political crises have often intervened and I have needed much succour. Particularly I would like to thank Alix Adams and Cherry Potts, Rosemary Auchmuty, Elaine Miller, Margaret Jackson, Lis Whitelaw, Janice Raymond. New friends like Trishar Butcher and Tracey Kennedy help me keep focused on why all this has to be done. I have depended on them in the past against the slings and arrows of outraged sexual libertarians and I know I can do so in the future. The work of feminist and lesbian scholars like Suzanne Kappeler, Sara Lucia Hoagland, Celia Kitzinger, Janice Raymond as well as many other lesbian and separatist thinkers has provided me with inspiration throughout my endeavours.

I am grateful to Cynthia Enloe and Lois Brynes who invited me to be the Fullbright scholar-in-residence in Women's Studies at Clark University in 1985–86. This gave me time to think about my project and I was able to gain encouragement and greater clarity from teaching wonderful students, in particular Stephanie Uluhogian and Monica Schneider.

I would like to thank Gill Hanscombe for her encouraging editing and her belief in the project, Jen Green of the Women's Press for making the whole process of publication painless and Maggie Christie for the indexing.

INTRODUCTION

Historians of sexuality see the 'sexual revolution' of the 1960s as a very positive development for women. They accept the sexological view that the 'sexual liberation' offered by that supposed revolution was a necessary component in the liberation of women. This 'sexual liberation' was the freedom for women to take pleasure from their own eroticised subordination. Sexologic, this book is designed to show, is the idea that sex is and should be a way of expressing and maintaining male dominance and female submission. The sexologists of the twentieth century have been the high priests who have organised the worship of male power.

Anticlimax takes a very different approach to the sexual revolution. In my first book, *The Spinster and Her Enemies*, I showed how the sexologists before the Second World War believed that they would ensure women's subordination by eliciting a sexual response to men.[1] Compulsory conscription into heterosexuality and the performance of the orgasm with a man were seen to ensure woman's submission to her husband and the death of feminism, lesbianism, manhating and spinsterhood. A Freudian psychoanalyst of the 1920s made this clear when he wrote: 'To be roused by a man means acknowledging oneself as conquered.'[2] Throughout the history of sexology the focus of concern has been the resisting woman. The incitement of women to respond sexually to men continued after the Second World War. This becomes clear in a consideration of the politics of sex in the 1940s and 50s, when the future of male-dominant marriage was seen to hang on curing women's frigidity. At this time sexologists

1

showed no self-consciousness about asserting the connection between woman's sexual response and her subordination.

In the 1960s women were enjoined to respond in more varied positions and situations and single women were conscripted into active heterosexual sex. The language of liberation was so loud in connection with the new sexual prescriptions for women that commentators have assumed some obvious relationship between the 'sexual revolution' and progress in women's condition. There is no good reason to suppose that the sexologists changed step and started believing, contrary to all their previous ideas, that women's sexual response to men would actually liberate women. As we shall see the rules of sexologic remained unaltered. Behind the baloney of liberation, the naked power politics of male supremacy were being acted out. The high priests of sexologic, helped by the pornographers, progressive novelists and sex radicals continued to orchestrate woman's joyful embrace of her oppression through the creation of her sexual response. Sexologists have for a hundred years dedicated their lives to eliciting orgasms from women in order to prevent our liberation. The 1960s was a period when greater opportunities were open to women and the 'sexual revolution', rather than being liberating, helped to defuse the potential threat to male power.

Anticlimax is a study of the works of the sexologists and therapists, the pornographers, novelists and sex radicals who took part in the construction of heterosexual desire in the period since the Second World War. Their views of sex and women will be carefully examined so that the political function of sex in maintaining the oppression of women can be clearly understood. Heterosexual desire is defined here as sexual desire that eroticises power difference. It originates in the power relationships between the sexes and normally takes the form of eroticising the subordination of women. In heterosexual desire our subordination becomes sexy for us and for men. Heterosexual desire can exist also in same sex relationships, because women and men do not escape the heterosexual construction of their desire simply by loving their own sex. We all grow up in the political system of heterosexuality. A large section of *Anticlimax* is devoted to showing the extent to which the eroticising of power difference dominates male gay culture and sexual behaviour.

Considered, too, are the ways feminist ideas about sexuality have developed in the most recent wave of feminism. It is clear that feminists were influenced by sexologic in the late 1960s and early 70s. Feminist analyses of male violence and pornography led to a much more critical and less celebratory approach to 'sexual liberation'. In response a libertarian backlash developed, of women inspired by sexologic and the ideas of gay male theorists, which attacked feminists as prudes and puritans for their failure to embrace a male-constructed sexual liberation. In *The Spinster and Her Enemies* I showed how a similar lobby of sexual progressives attacked feminist campaigners against abusive male sexual practice in very similar terms before and after the First World War. In both waves of feminism sex has been seen to occupy a pivotal role in the oppression of women. In both waves of feminism the male apostles of sexual liberation – psychoanalysts, gynaecologists, sex radicals, male gay theorists – have reacted with rage and contempt towards a feminist analysis of sex. They have sought to browbeat women into acceptance of the male view of our 'liberation' and each time there have been women who have embraced the male sexual agenda and sown seeds of confusion within the feminist movement. In the 1980s women's liberation has been hijacked by the sexual libertarians who are devoted to persuading women that the enthusiastic celebration of our oppression in sadomasochism is the same thing as liberation. The language of sadomasochism is based upon the inversion of values as in 'only when bound am I really free' and 'slavery is freedom'. Now the practice of that very bondage and slavery is being interpreted as freedom itself and female power.

The sexologists have traditionally seen heterosexuality as 'natural' and lesbianism as pathological. The sexual liberals see the choice between lesbianism and heterosexuality as a matter of simple preference as in a choice between tea and coffee. In *Anticlimax*, heterosexuality is seen as a political institution through which male dominance is organised and maintained. Sex as we know it under male supremacy is the eroticised power difference of heterosexuality. As a political system heterosexuality functions more perfectly than oppressive systems such as apartheid or capitalism. In heterosexuality what we have been accustomed to see as the wellsprings of our pleasure and happiness, love and sex, are finely tuned to depend on the maintenance of our oppression. As a result, a world of freedom beyond heterosexuality cannot be envisaged because it appears to require the abandonment of 'love' and 'sex'.

The last chapter considers how we can move beyond heterosexuality as a political institution and the form of desire, heterosexual desire, which derives from it. No liberation is possible for women in a world in which inequality, and specifically the inequality of women, is sexy. We need to envision, and start to build, a world in which the connection of power difference and aggression to sexual feelings will be unimaginable. The crucial question on which *Anticlimax* ends is how to construct homosexual desire. This is desire which eroticises equality and mutuality, a form of desire not even recognised as sex by many theorists of sexuality in the present. It is attacked as 'vanilla' or 'bambi' sex by libertarians, and those who practise it are derided as anti-sex prudes. When equality is exciting, not just at the level of theory but in love and sex, then the liberation of women becomes a real possibility.

Chapter 1

THE FIFTIES

Marriage guidance and marital sex illustrate a central premise of *Anticlimax*: that the heterosexual couple embodies a relationship of power and control, rather than representing a consequence of nature, biology or sexual preference. The setting up of the Marriage Guidance Council, the work of sexologists and the development of sex therapy are all instances of how men's power over women was to be supported and managed through the regulation of marital sex.

Sex, in this scheme of things, was not a natural and spontaneous seeking after pleasure by men and women, but a regulatory mechanism designed and constructed to enforce male dominance and female submission. In the 1950s sex was hard work and sometimes an onerous duty. The job of keeping women in their place was not necessarily seen as fun. An examination of the 1950s shows the purpose that male-supremacist ideologues intended for sex without all the hype with which sex has been surrounded since the 1960s. The sexual revolution was to introduce a new language of liberation and pleasure which can befog the observer and make the political function of sexual intercourse less easy to spot. The joy of reading the sexological works of the 1950s is that they do reveal the naked power politics involved in marriage and sex. The Marriage Guidance Council was an organisation set up just after the Second World War with the task of regulating the political relationship of marriage and upholding men's power within it. The writings of its founders are particularly helpful to an understanding of the political function of marriage.

MARRIAGE GUIDANCE

The Marriage Guidance Council was created in 1938, according to its first Secretary David Mace, when 'doctors, psychologists, parsons, social workers, teachers and others' came together because they thought 'there was something going wrong with marriage'.[1] In 1942 Mace became Secretary and in 1943 three rooms were acquired in the West End of London. It wasn't until after the war that Marriage Guidance Councils began to proliferate around the country and marriage guidance as a phenomenon really got off the ground. Whatever concern there had been for the state of marriage before the war was amplified greatly afterwards. One source of anxiety was a sharp increase in the number of divorces.

In 1913 there were 577 divorce decrees granted in England, in 1936 4,000 and in 1945 20,000. H. E. Norman, formerly Secretary of the National Association of Probation Officers, writing in the 1949 book *Sex in Social Life* put together by Sybil Neville-Rolfe of the Social Hygiene Council, attributed the rise partly to changes in the law which had facilitated divorce and separation.[2] When we look closely at the legislation it is clear that these were changes which enabled women to obtain divorce and separation more easily.

The 1857 Matrimonial Causes Act had made it possible for men to obtain a divorce more easily, i.e. simply on the grounds of the wife's adultery. The Act was no great help to women, who had to prove bestiality, incest or some other 'unnatural' practice as well as adultery to get a divorce. The logic behind this discrepancy was stated to be the fact that adultery in a woman was more serious than in a man. An adulterous man, it was argued, would still know he was the father of his wife's children, but if a wife was adulterous there was no way of knowing. In 1923 divorce was made possible for wives simply on proof of adultery and as a result the number of applications for divorce shot up.

Between 1895 and 1925 what were called the Married Women's Acts gave power to magistrates to make separation orders and orders for maintenance. In 1937 two amending Acts widened the grounds and improved the facilities for divorce and set up special magistrates' courts with a simplified procedure for hearing applications for maintenance and separation orders. Every reform was followed by an increase in applications. It is clear that these reforms allowed women the possibility of getting out of abusive marriages and that women were swift to take advantage of them. Thus any lamentation by the male authorities about the breakdown of marriage in this respect must be seen as anxiety at women escaping the prisonhouse of marriage, and the resulting threat to male privilege.

But, Norman tells us, it was not just these legal reforms which accounted for the number of 'broken homes'. There was also an increase in population, and the unsettlement of the war which led to problems for women and men who had to adjust to partners they had not seen for years and may even have married in the romantic flush inspired by posting and never really known. Norman concludes:

> ... a great many marriages are not fulfilling their proper purpose and ... family life for a very large percentage of the rising generation must be so defective that the time is ripe for serious action to prevent further drift and hurt to the social health and security of the nation.[3]

The Foreword to *Sex in Social Life* explained that the conditions of the Second World War had resulted in a serious breakdown in morality which led to the need for effective sex education: during the war 'there has been an exhibition of sexual incontinence and shameless conduct in our streets and lanes which must have shocked many more than just the old-fashioned Christians.'[4] David Mace explained in his book *Marriage Crisis* that the war had made 'a havoc of family life'.

> It was a pretty painful business – the evacuation of children, the life in the shelters, the black-out, the separation of husbands and wives, the frantic embarkation leave marriages, the have-a-good-time-tonight-because-you-may-get-bumped-off-tomorrow atmosphere.[5]

Mace's *Marriage Crisis* is written in what was meant to be a popular style and has the tone of a friendly vicar giving a fireside chat to rather disillusioned parishioners about the necessity of keeping up the wartime spirit. It is genial and uses what he probably imagines to be a working class idiom. His other writings about marriage and Christianity are far more formal. The genial banter sometimes goes a little too far and strikes an entirely inappropriate note of levity as in this comment on Hitler, who is represented as a kind of naughty teddy boy.

> Take Hitler, for instance. What a whole heap of trouble and misery he and his crowd caused! We all knew he was half mad. But why was he like that? . . . some people say it was his bad upbringing that made him such a fanatic, and that he might have been a better man if he had been brought up in a normal happy home. The same thing could be said about all the other little Hitlers who make life so awkward for many of us.[6]

This was an appeal hard to resist. The importance of stable marriages was clear if they could help prevent genocidal dictatorships.

In 1948 the Family Discussion Bureau was set up to do social casework in marital problems, after an approach to the Tavistock Institute by the Family Welfare Association. The reasons given for its inception once again stress the disruption caused by the war to marriage and morals. But even before the war 'the nation was becoming increasingly anxious about the number of homes broken by separation and divorce'. This situation was exacerbated by 'wartime stresses' and the answer was an expansion of the 'national social services' which were concerned with 'maternal and emotional well-being'.[7]

Also in 1948 a government body, the Harris Committee, recommended a grant for marriage counselling services to go to the Family Welfare Association, the Marriage Guidance Council and the Catholic Marriage Advisory Council. The government and the burgeoning social services were now to take a direct role in keeping marriages stable, a task which appears on close examination to mean making sure the wife remains obedient as a servant and handmaid to her husband and children and does not think of making a break for independence. The state is here involved directly in the maintenance of male dominance and privilege at the domestic level.

Through all the sound and fury about weakened morals and marriage breakdown during and after the war there is a clear note of fear about women's independence. It was women, after all, liberated from individual husbands while the men were away, and endowed often with financial independence from war work whether single or married, who were in a position to exercise their new freedom in 'immorality'. The theme of hostility to women's emancipation is clear and strong in the early literature on marriage guidance.

Joseph Brayshaw of the Marriage Guidance Council cites a great list of reasons for marriage breakdown such as decline in religious observance, separation in the war years, shortage of homes, the false values of films, but concludes that there is one underlying reason behind all of these. The reason is the 'equality' of women.

> I shall probably court misunderstanding if I state my thesis bluntly; but in truth it is the new equality of women with man that has led inevitably to the disruption, for the present, of stable marriage and family life. Lest this sound as if I were some old buffer in side-whiskers and drainpipe trousers lamenting that things are not what they were in Queen Victoria's day, let me say that I believe strongly in the essential equality of the sexes. It has, however, far wider social implications than have so far been generally recognised.[8]

What was it that kept marriage stable in the time before women's equality? According to Brayshaw it was the unquestioned dictatorship of the husband and father in the home. Brayshaw invites us to look at 'Grandfather's day' when the father was the clear dictator in the family and the wife had few choices because she could not just go out and get a job. The problem for marriage in the 1940s was that women would openly disagree with their husbands. 'Husband and wife, as equals, must somehow agree upon scores of matters that were not open to discussion by their grandparents . . . obviously there is far more chance of disagreement when there are far more things to be settled jointly.'[9] He states that achieving 'a democratic sharing of responsibility' in place of 'dictatorship' in the family 'can only be achieved by the attainment of a certain level of education and responsibility'.[10] He proposes a general theory that: 'Whenever you get the equality of women emerging in law or in custom, there you get increased breakdown of marriage.'[11]

So what was the solution? If the problem was men being unable to cope with women challenging their authority then an answer might have been to educate men to their role as equals – to reconcile them to their loss of power. This is not the solution that the MGC opted for. To Brayshaw the new equality of women was a fairly unmitigated disaster as he makes clear in this comment on the Roman Empire.

> The only other time in the whole of history when women enjoyed equality with men was in the later days of Rome; and there it may well have contributed to their disasters. The rich ceased to have children, and standards of loyalty and morality decayed. The equality of the sexes may be a means to good or ill; it is not an end in itself.[12]

It does not seem that he had any real doubt as to whether good or ill might result. This fascinating myth, whereby women's equality or sexual promiscuity is supposed to have led to the downfall of Rome, is frequently reiterated by men who tremble before the possibility of women's emancipation. They could think of nothing to compare with the aftermath of the end of male supremacy save the downfall of what they regarded as civilisation and centuries of 'dark ages'.

David Mace also sees the problem of marriage breakdown as being caused by women's equality. Like Brayshaw he sees 'patriarchal marriage' as being under threat.

> What it all comes to is that men and women are now to count as equals. The idea that the man is superior and the woman inferior has had to be scrapped. Women are entitled to the same rights and privileges as men . . . This is all very well; but it has been bad for family life.[13]

10

He uses the word 'family' here as a euphemism for men's power and privilege. The fact that women were no longer seen as 'inferior' was doubtless not a bad thing for women so the family clearly meant men and perhaps children. This is a common use of the word family by sexologists, sociologists and the legal system. How was the Marriage Guidance Council to help? The MGC was to construct a new workable pattern for marriage because: 'It's a particular pattern of marriage and the family that is breaking down. And the reason we're in such a mess is because we haven't yet worked out another pattern to take its place.'[14] The way this worked in practice becomes clear when we look at case studies of marriage guidance. We can then see how counselling could tinker with the husband/wife relationship so as to bolster the man's power and subordinate the woman.

The case studies that follow are taken from the Family Discussion Bureau. One woman was sent by a hospital complaining that her husband's emotionally abusive behaviour had damaged her health. Her husband 'sometimes didn't speak to her for weeks and had built up unbearable barriers between them'. The counsellor's response was to undermine the woman's sense of reality by manipulation so that the woman came to admit that she was actually to blame for her behaviour towards her husband.

The worker suggested that the client felt very uncertain about herself, and was really very worried and unhappy about her behaviour towards her husband. She replied immediately, 'I know I am making him feel inferior and that I get at him whenever he says anything.' And with that, she looked for the first time fully at the worker and became friendly and co-operative.[15]

The counsellors simply did not hear women's reasonable complaints about male behaviour. The women were directed to blame and change themselves in every case. One young woman complained of her husband's offensive sexual behaviour including his 'perverted and inordinate sexual demands when he was drunk, his enuresis, his "dirty-mindedness" . . .' The counsellor described the woman as having 'poured out a tearful story' and clearly did not believe it. Instead she sought to 'show her [the client] ... how anxious she seemed for the worker to recognise the positive side of her attachment to her husband'.[16]

In another case the worker adjusted the husband and the wife to a stereotyped version of heterosexuality, i.e. fetishised masculinity and femininity. The wife became more submissive and the husband's authority was restored. Here it seems the husband may actually have married his wife for her spirit or 'boyishness' but once married wanted his privilege of unquestioned power.

> [Mr C] ... a rather disturbed person with homosexual tendencies. He had married a very boyish girl ... Mrs C seemed to be very immature as well as boyish, humiliated by her feminine position, and unable to accept it, sulky and resentful towards her husband ... Mrs C made astonishing moves towards femininity. She began to make clothes for herself and her child, to have her hair permed and generally to look prettier ... [17]

The restoration of a male-supremacist status quo seems to have been achieved in each case through therapeutic techniques which the wives were not sufficiently familiar with to resist. Sex was the secret weapon for these new marriage counsellors. They understood that woman's pleasure in sexual intercourse facilitated her subordination, and sex advice and sex therapy became important tools in their struggle to maintain male power.

WOMEN'S NEW EQUALITY

The marriage guidance counsellors, sexologists and all those writing sex advice literature in the postwar world, used the rhetoric of women's equality. They spoke as if women's emancipation had been achieved and it was their onerous duty to clear up the few little inconveniences this had caused, and help adjust society to the new situation. What was the new equality that these writers had in mind? The new equality was an ideology of separate but 'equal' development, a kind of sexual apartheid.

Women and men were said to have entirely different roles in society because they were different physically and mentally. David Mace expressed it thus:

> ... although men and women are equal as persons that doesn't alter the fact that there's a lot of differences between them. The woman may be able to turn out as much work as the man. But just because she's a woman, she won't feel the same way about it as the man does ... [18]

The popular sexologist, Eustace Chesser, explains the equal-but-different line in terms of woman's reproductive function:

> Few rational commentators would find it difficult to agree that, in general, the sexes should be regarded as equal, but different. It is impossible to arrive at any other conclusion than that woman holds a much more important position than man, has higher functions to perform, and is, indeed, Nature's chosen sex for the carrying out of her purposes in the world. [19]

Promoters of the separate-but-equal ideology were inspired to fury by the actions of what they called the 'extreme feminists' who proclaimed women's right to do exactly the same jobs, and have the same education and opportunities as men.

> For the sexes are not alike. They never have been, and — let us hope — never will be alike. Recognising that men and women are equal is by no means the same as saying that they must be treated exactly alike in everything ...
> Extreme feminism definitely has an element of childishness. The male has certain toys: the woman must have them. [20]

The differences between the sexes, according to these ideologues, all stemmed from woman's important role as mother.

Motherhood was receiving great attention in the postwar world. There was alarm at the birth rate which had reached an all-time low point in 1933 and only began to rise in the early years of the war. Alarm on another front, problem families and juvenile delinquency, was directed into scapegoating of the

13

mother. Poor mothering was an easier focus of blame for worrying behaviour, particularly that of teenage boys, than social and economic ills which might indicate the need for political change.

The panic about 'problem families' was considerable. C. P. Blacker writing on this theme in the *Eugenics Review*[21] suggests that mothers in problem families are 'subnormal mentally'. He favourably quotes a Professor Crew who asked: 'Do the principles of freedom and the rights of man require that subnormal adults should be allowed to contaminate a neighbourhood with their sordid, filthy houses and to bring into the world children for whom they have no care or affection?'[22] Richard Titmuss, who has a reputation as a benevolent architect of the welfare state, was worried that the undeserving poor were reproducing themselves at a disproportionate rate with the threat of social ruin.

> It cannot be regarded as wise or healthy if a considerable section of the future population is being recruited from a number of very large and very poor families. Is this the position in England today? Are we, or are we not, confronted with a situation in which the economically under-privileged are producing a disproportionately large number of babies while those more favoured with a good environment are unduly restricting the size of their families?[23]

Elizabeth Wilson, in *Women and the Welfare State*, suggests that the alarm at problem families stemmed from the reactions of an unsuspecting and complacement British public to the experience of evacuation.[24] For the first time middle-class folk were able to observe the lifestyle of the very poor and sought an explanation for the ills of poverty in family pathology. A vast expansion of the social services, and a rapid acceleration in the development of the welfare state were expected to deal with 'problem families' through concentrating on the mother.

Underlying the scapegoating of the mother lay much more than anxiety over such social problems. The deepest source of anxiety was the challenge to male authority offered by feminism and the development of what Chesser called 'economic women'. The antidote was to be the reinforcement of motherhood as the primary role for women. Feminist commentators have pointed out the central role played by John Bowlby in the creation of the ideology of motherhood with his development of the theory of maternal deprivation. According to this theory children who failed to receive enough quality attention from the mother, for whom there could be no substitute, would develop emotional problems and would be socially disruptive.

> Proper care of children deprived of a normal home life can now be seen to be not merely an act of common humanity but to be essential for the mental and social welfare of a community. For when their care is neglected, as happens in every country of the Western world today, they grow up to reproduce themselves. Deprived children, whether in their own homes or out of them, are the source of social infection as real and serious as are the carriers of diphtheria and typhoid.[25]

How much attention was necessary for the child? So much attention in fact that one does wonder when mothers would have found time to go to the toilet, let alone commune with their thoughts.

> Just as a baby needs to feel that he belongs to his mother, a mother needs to feel that she belongs to her child, and it is only when she has the satisfaction of this feeling that it is easy for her to devote herself to him. The provision of constant attention night and day, seven days a week and 365 days in the year, is possible only for a woman who derives profound satisfaction from seeing her child grow from babyhood, through the many phases of childhood, to become an independent man or woman, and knows that it is her care which has made this possible.[26]

But the sexologists played a very considerable part in the promotion of motherhood too. In the process they produced some comic gems. The most remarkable has to be the book by Eustace Chesser named *Sexual Behaviour: Normal and Abnormal*. Chesser decided that a lack of enthusiasm in women for motherhood was a hitherto little-recognised 'sexual perversion' which was in fact the 'greatest perversion of them all'. It was feminists, according to Chesser, who had suggested that motherhood should not be all-consuming.

> Finally, this book has been written in order to provide an answer to the demands of the more extreme feminists who advocate a course which must inevitably set women at war with their own nature and which, indeed, cannot be carried to its logical conclusion unless women deliberately turn their backs upon their maternal instinct. If this occurs, 'emancipation from thraldom to man' will leave women face to face with a much more dangerous enemy than man is or ever could be – Nature herself.[27]

Chesser, who clearly hoped that he had stumbled across a new psychological ailment that would be accepted by the medical establishment, invented a name for his discovery. Rejection of motherhood was 'auto-matricidism', i.e. killing of the mother in yourself. This colourful and alarmist language suggests that feminists and all who were less than wholehearted about motherhood were a kind of terrorist with guns pointed at their wombs. How was the auto-matricide to be recognised? That was tricky, according to Chesser, because the 'abnormality' revealed itself in 'varying forms and degrees' and could take the form of 'a dislike of sexuality, fear of motherhood, distaste for domestic duties etc'.[28] Apparently, women who partially 'repudiate feminine sexuality' were most potentially dangerous because they tended to marry and then damage their children. An example of such partial repudiation was a woman's desire to combine work outside the home with being a mother. 'There may be two breadwinners in the family, the mother as well as the father, with the result that, so far as emotional relationship is concerned, the children have no mother, but two "fathers". They never really know a mother's love.'[29]

In the climate of that time, Chesser could reasonably have expected considerable acclaim for having explained, in such a neat and helpful way, all the behaviour by women which most threatened male authority. Feminists and other women who failed to embrace their oppression could be labelled as suffering

16

from a sexual abnormality, like the sadomasochists and homo-sexuals also included in Chesser's book. The lesbian was in fact identified as one variety of auto-matricide. But Chesser's propaganda exploit was not a success. The idea of auto-matricidism does not seem to have caught on and we hear nothing of it in subsequent sexological literature. Why did Chesser's theory fail? Perhaps it's like the development of new roses, some catch on and some don't. Auto-matricidism lacked subtlety. There were plenty of psychoanalytical theories similarly damning of woman's right to exist as an independent and self-respecting human being which had the advantage of being less blatant and fitting into Freudian orthodoxy. Chesser was not disheartened and continued his successful sexological career.

Chesser offered a plan to cope with the damage being wreaked upon the nation by auto-matricidism. It was in his chapter entitled 'Re-education for Total Living'. He wanted to impress the vital importance of marriage and the family on all adults and children. The state should not encourage women to work. Surprisingly he felt there was a need to 'establish, not as an interesting theory or speculation, but as a fact, the essential equality of the sexes'. This was necessary so that 'women can be helped to accept, naturally and as a matter of course, the position which Nature has allotted to them', i.e. a separate sphere designed by men.[30]

The sexologists played a pivotal role in readjusting the relations between men and women in order to repair the damage to male power caused by the strong feminist movement of the late nineteenth and early twentieth centuries and the social and economic changes which were allowing women better opportunities for self-determination. Chesser, in the 1950s, was taking up the mantle of that daddy of all sexologists, Havelock Ellis, who, before the First World War, invented a 'new' kind of feminism which was simply a glorification of motherhood and a development of the different but equal ideology. He opposed this to the ideas of the 'extreme' feminists of the period who wanted complete equality with men.[31] This tendency by sexologists to promote or latch on to a form of feminism which serves their interests and to represent effective feminism as 'extreme' is still prevalent today in the work of the sexual libertarians,

17

and must be regarded with extreme suspicion. One can be fairly sure that the kind of feminism derided by a male sexologist is that which threatens the maintenance of his privilege.

Chesser and the sexologists of the 1940s and 1950s were responding to new challenges by women to male power. All sexological work from the 1900s through to the 1950s can be seen to some extent as a shifting of ballast in response to the first wave of feminism, an adjustment to maintain male advantages. But the war and its aftermath provided some fresh stimulus to the misogynists of the period.

According to the feminist Gertrude Williams, author of *Women and Work* published in 1945, there had been a 'wartime revolution'. During the last few years the public had grown accustomed to 'seeing women taking fares on buses, carrying bags at railway stations, collecting tickets, fixing gas fittings or mending pipes'.[32] Williams argued that those kinds of work were not 'out of women's province'. She explained very straightforwardly how social pressures to conform to sex roles influenced the work women felt able to do:

Girls and boys grow up in a society which assumes that men do one type of work and women another and most people accept what they are used to. If your earliest memories of travelling in a bus are associated with men conductors you take it for granted that busconducting is a man's job . . . [33]

The male sexual experts cannot complain of having lacked access to feminist ideas in this period. Feminists like Williams wrote eloquently of the iniquity of women's oppression and the way that this was perpetuated by the practice of keeping women in a separate sphere.

There is no need for little girls to be taught that their place is a lowly one; it is part of the air they breathe. Wherever they look they see an overwhelming preponderance of men in positions of trust, responsibility and prestige.[34]

The number of married women employed in 1945 was 2.5 million, five times the number employed before the war.

18

Williams calls them the double job women and attributes sex inequality in wages to woman's dual role as well as to the hostility of men in trade unions. Williams was well aware of what happened to women's jobs after the First World War when three-quarters of a million women 'voluntarily retired', and she says the same thing could happen again. In fact efforts were made to ensure that it did.

THE EROTICISING OF THE HOUSEWIFE

WHAT IS SEX?

Postwar sexologists, like their predecessors in the late nineteenth and early twentieth centuries, had a clear idea of what 'sex' was. Sex was the act of coitus in which a man penetrated a woman's vagina with his penis. It was the job of the sexologists to inculcate this knowledge into the resistant or inadequate multitude. Coitus started with the man looking at a woman and getting the idea that he wanted to penetrate her and ended with his ejaculating into her vagina. Kenneth Walker defined the 'physical act of love' thus:

> By this is meant the series of events which starts with the initial stirrings of sexual desire in the man and the woman and ends with the ejaculation of the sexual secretions (semen) within the genital passages of the female.[35]

It was not a woman's arousal which started this sequence of events. The woman was seen as sexually passive, only capable of response, and sometimes not even that. Maxine Davis, in *The Sexual Responsibility of Woman*, explained that a woman 'does not experience intense sexual desire spontaneously' because 'it is an acquired taste like caviare'. Sexual desire was not natural in a woman since 'She was not born with it as her husband was . . .'[36] If she was not born with it then she had to learn it, and this gave the sexologists a difficult task.

Popular sex-advice writers like Davis took their ideas from Freudian psychoanalysts who saw sexual desire as 'masculine'

19

by its very nature. According to a female Freudian disciple, Marie Bonaparte, in her definitive 1953 book *Female Sexuality*, it was the masculine part of woman which allowed her to have an interest in sex. Bonaparte saw woman as an immature male suffering from arrested development.[37] Accepting, as Freudians tended to, that there was something bizarre about the female genitals, she decided that human females actually possessed cloacas. Fish have cloacas which allow the passage of both waste and eggs. Women are seen as some kind of fish. But as well as being a kind of fish they possessed an inferior imitation of the penis.

> In woman the external sexual organs, or, more correctly, the erotogenic organs, appear to reflect her twofold nature. A woman, in fact, possesses a cloaca, divided by the recto-vaginal septum into the anus and the specifically feminine vagina, the gateway to the additional structure of the maternal apparatus, and a phallus, atrophied in comparison with the male penis – the little clitoris.[38]

Freud admitted that he found women a puzzle. Bonaparte was clearly in deep confusion. Woman's masculinity which gave her the only active sexuality she possessed, was seen to reside in her clitoris. To escape a masculinity complex or homosexuality a woman was expected to transfer her eroticism from the clitoris to the vagina. Not surprisingly Bonaparte's introduction to her work is entitled 'Woman's Frequent Maladaptation to the Erotic Function'. She explains:

> Nature does not always succeed in adapting organisms to function perfectly in their environment as we may clearly see from the far greater frequency of defective adaptation to the purely erotic function in woman than in man.[39]

We can see why sexologists have had their work cut out this century attempting to adapt women to the male sexual function despite their inherent inadequacy. Sex, for the woman, had to be constructed from scratch.

Many women seemed unable to appreciate the aesthetic

attractions of the penis. Davis tells us that a woman 'is not always greatly stimulated even by the sight of her husband when he is obviously about to make love'.[40] Some sexologists advised the husband to hide his erect penis from his wife lest she run from the room in revulsion!

It was recognised that even supposing a woman wanted sexual activity with a man she was likely to prefer everything but sexual intercourse. Davis explains:

> She probably likes the petting, the love-making preliminary to intercourse, very much indeed and never seems to have enough of it. But she must not lose sight of the fact that although this part of sexual activity is going to be increasingly enjoyable . . . it is nevertheless only the physical and psychic preface and build-up to the complete sex act. She must learn how to attain complete enjoyment as soon as possible.[41]

Women had to be convinced that 'complete enjoyment' resided in that practice they wished to avoid, rather than in those they actually wanted. This made the sexological task particularly difficult. As 1920s sexologists had not flinched when faced with the realisation that possibly as many as 100 per cent of women had indifference or distaste for sexual intercourse, so forties and fifties sexologists set themselves diligently to the task of constructing the sexual practice of coitus as 'sex' for women and men in the face of women's determined resistance.

Women's lack of enthusiasm for sexual intercourse has been the dominant problem of sexology throughout the twentieth century. In the 1890s feminist theorists stated that sexual intercourse should take place only for the purposes of reproduction. They considered that once every few years would suffice.[42] They saw sexual intercourse as being contraindicated for women because it led to unwanted childbearing or the necessity for 'artificial' contraception which made them feel like machines. It led to various ailments and venereal diseases. Despite the ministrations of sexologists over the last hundred years, who have sought to persuade women that sexual intercourse is a delight, or at least a duty, women remain unenthusiastic in large numbers in the 1980s. A survey by the American agony aunt

Ann Landers in 1985 found that 60,000 women were prepared to write at length about how they preferred cuddles to sexual intercourse.[43]

Feminist theorists of the 1890s used evidence from other cultures which was being produced by contemporary anthropologists to support the idea that coitus should only take place for procreation. In some societies today sexual intercourse is by no means the compulsory and primary sexual practice that it is under western heteropatriarchy. An example of the effectiveness of twentieth-century sexological propaganda, which defines sex as sexual intercourse, is the comment by Leni Riefenstahl in her photodocumentary on the Nuba of the Sudan. Riefenstahl explains that the Nuba believed that sexual intercourse should not take place during lactation.

> Ancient Nuba custom prescribes that children be suckled for that length of time [three years] because a long spell of breastfeeding is thought to make them stronger and more healthy. For the women this represents a considerable sacrifice. The Nuba believe that a child may be harmed by sexual intercourse during pregnancy and lactation.[44]

It clearly did not occur to Riefenstahl that sexual intercourse might be seen as undesirable by Nuba women as it was by many in the West, and that the prohibition might serve women's interests.

Susan Cavin's book *Lesbian Origins* is an anthropological survey of human societies from data available over the last 100 years which sets out to assess the ways in which male supremacy comes to be established in different societies. Cavin suggests that male dominance is constantly in the process of development and that in some societies it may not be as pronounced as in others.[45] She uses the existence of taboos on sexual intercourse as an indication that patriarchal takeover is not complete in societies where these exist. Once taboos on sexual intercourse have been eliminated women's power to control conception, and therefore their own childbearing, is drastically reduced. Sexual intercourse is the only purely reproductive sexual practice and if it is engaged in by women only when they wish to procreate then reproduction is under women's control. Once sexual intercourse is established as compulsory then women have recourse only to artificial contraception, abortion, and infanticide, to control reproduction and childbearing.

FRIGIDITY AND IMPOTENCE

Postwar sexologists admitted that they had a problem in selling the practice of sexual intercourse to men and women. Edmund Bergler in his book *Neurotic, Counterfeit Sex* defined frigidity as 'the incapacity of woman to have a vaginal orgasm during intercourse. It is no matter whether the woman is aroused during coitus or remains cold, whether excitement is strong or weak.'[46] Frank Caprio in his book *The Sexually Adequate Female* defined frigidity in precisely the same way: 'A woman can be passionate and still suffer from lack of orgasm during coitus, also referred to as orgasm-incapacity.'[47] According to Bergler 90 per cent of women suffered from this kind of frigidity.

In order for the woman to have a vaginal orgasm during sexual intercourse the act had to last for more than a second or two and that was a real problem. Sexual intercourse might indeed be the preferred sexual practice of men, but prolonged sexual intercourse seemed to be beyond the powers or desire of most. To explain this phenomenon and provide themselves with a way of worrying men into trying to achieve prolonged sexual intercourse the disease of premature ejaculation had been invented. Bergler quotes Kinsey as pointing out that premature ejaculation was so common in men as to be normal.

Premature ejaculation is a wonderful example of an invented disease. If sexual intercourse were practised only for the purposes of procreation then the depositing of semen in the vagina was all that was needed. For most sexual activity, even within heterosexuality, premature ejaculation would then not exist because there would be nothing to be premature to. Since a man could give a woman perfectly fulfilling sexual pleasure without penile penetration, it would make little difference if a man ejaculated before he walked in the room.

The absence of vaginal orgasm was seen as so serious that women suffering from the complaint were recommended to acquire prompt psychiatric assistance. Sexological tracts gave frightening lists of the ailments that resulted from lack of vaginal orgasm, to encourage women to take their failure seriously. Maxine Davis' list includes 'fatigue, insomnia, backache, headache, including migraine, respiratory infections, indigestion, constipation, dizziness, pain in the back of the neck, gall bladder symptoms, many kinds of skin trouble, rheumatic diseases including arthritis, and all sorts of stomach trouble, including gastric ulcers, and many other complaints.'[48]

The result of constructing the disease of frigidity was that women had no choice but to seek vaginal orgasms. A distaste for sexual intercourse was illegitimate, as was a desire for any sexual practice in preference to sexual intercourse. Caprio's chapter 'The Causes of Frigidity' made clear that many women had a distaste for sexual intercourse but found that it was compulsory. A distaste for stamp collecting or football might be tolerated without a rigorous search for causes, but sexual intercourse was a male hobby with an important political function. Caprio's interpretation of the causes of frigidity provides insights into both sexological ideology and women's experience.

Distaste for sexual intercourse was seen as 'rejection of the penis'.[49] The most serious form of frigidity was said to be vaginismus, in which the muscles of the vagina went into spasm, making sexual intercourse impossible or very painful. Rather than it being accepted that such strong evidence of distaste for sexual intercourse was an indication that the practice should be discontinued, women exercising this form of resistance were submitted to brutal operations. This is the frightening treatment one of Caprio's patients was subjected to:

A week following the honeymoon she consulted a gynecologist who incised the hymen surgically and dilated the vagina. However, when her husband attempted intercourse, the vagina would contract each time and she complained of severe pain. She returned to the gynecologist who subjected her to an operation consisting of making the vaginal passageway larger. But she still had difficulty . . . it required extensive analysis to overcome her fear of sexual intercourse.[50]

Other reasons which emerge in the case studies for women failing to have enthusiasm for sexual intercourse or to achieve vaginal orgasm are all quite reasonable from the woman's point of view, i.e. experience of male sexual violence, a preference for loving women, a disinclination to become pregnant. But these sensible reasons for preferring to avoid sexual intercourse are for Caprio things to be got over in therapy.

Women who disliked or were indifferent to sexual intercourse would sometimes engage in imaginative forms of resistance.

Other women make the serious mistake of engaging in distracting activities during the sex act. One husband complained that his wife was so unresponsive that she continued reading her book while he had intercourse with her. Another told me his wife kept on applying nail polish to her finger nails during the sex act rather than be interrupted in what she was doing. These bedroom mistakes sound fantastic but psychiatrists are not surprised to hear the many ways in which some wives manifest their frigidity or indifference to sexual lovemaking.[51]

It would not have occurred to Caprio that these women deserved medals for their courage and ingenuity. Like all the sexologists quoted he shows a monumental seriousness towards his subject. Sexual intercourse is treated like religious communion. Caprio could no more be amused at a woman painting her fingernails during sexual intercourse than a priest might be at a communicant doing this in church.

Attitude was terribly important. As faith is an individual responsibility in religious experience so the correct attitude, adopted by the wife, would lead to the ecstasy of the vaginal orgasm. Caprio explains it thus:

. . . the ability of a woman to attain an orgasm is dependent upon her attitude toward intercourse, her power of concentrating, her willingness to cooperate, the extent of her wanting

25

to enjoy sex relations and her ability to abandon herself completely to the pleasurable sensation of the sex act.[52]

Eustace Chesser also emphasised the importance of the wife's attitude. He told women that, 'Joyous anticipation is the right mental attitude' and that women might acquire it by 'preparing themselves mentally for the act of union'.[53] If technique, therapy and all other methods failed then the woman was expected to fall back on faith or joyous anticipation.

WOMAN'S ROLE

Supposing that the problems of indifference had been overcome, the sexologists were full of serious advice for women on how to play their role in sexual intercourse. The advice was complicated and often contradictory. The role of woman in sexual intercourse in the postwar world was to be slightly more active than in the 1920s. She was not to initiate 'love play'. That was for the man. Once he had started she was to reciprocate with caresses of her own. Caprio expresses it thus: 'As for a sexual partner, men prefer a wife who is aggressive sexually after he has once initiated the advances.'[54] But she had to be very careful and like Havelock Ellis before him, Kenneth Walker believed that woman's innate modesty or coquettishness was part of her role in sex:

In woman a certain diffidence or modesty may sometimes be evinced. She retreats as well as advances; an element of coquetry may play an important part during the stage of love-play. The husband should act as a courtier for his wife's favours, and she does not necessarily yield immediately to his advances. Desire is stimulated by a temporary refusal, for with many lovers the chase adds relish to the final capture.[55]

This was quite complicated. A woman had to be careful not to get carried away, so that she could achieve precisely the right mix of withdrawal and advance. It was a confusing role, fraught with difficulties and with lots of room for mistakes.

26

One serious mistake, according to Caprio, was the attempt to receive sexual stimulation during sexual intercourse.

> ... there can be no mechanical intensification of arousal of the clitoris through friction during coitus, and the transfer of the arousal from the clitoris to the vagina is purely psychological ... Women know this, as their substitute techniques prove. They try to maintain the illusion of enjoying sexual intercourse vaginally by holding the thighs together, thus establishing artificial contact between penis and clitoris, or they pretend to be highly excited, producing acrobatic movements only to achieve the same aim of penis-clitoris contact ... If a woman, as an adult person, maintains erogeneity only of the clitoris, she is neurotically ill.[56]

This is a terribly cruel prescription. The woman was to be monitored, presumably by the husband, to ensure that she was not nurturing her clitoris and getting too much pleasure.

Another mistake that a wife could make was to reciprocate too enthusiastically so as to make the penis drop out. Walker reminded the woman that her movements should be 'slighter' then those of the man. She should participate by 'bringing forward the whole pelvis and swinging it back so as to increase friction' but 'there is the danger if these movements are too vigorous of breaking the link'.[57] With no intentional irony or sympathy for the mental torment all these complex and contradictory instructions would induce, Walker states as his golden rule that 'love-making must be spontaneous'.[58]

An important component of woman's role was enthusiasm, and if she did not feel it then she was advised to simulate it. Davis considered that the 'virgin bride' who was 'serving her apprenticeship', i.e. learning a job, on honeymoon, would not be likely to enjoy sexual intercourse. But she must not 'make him think she is not enjoying it as much as he wants her to'.[59] An important part of her job was to learn early how to simulate pleasure.

A wartime spirit of the Second World War infused the literature on sex well into the 1950s. Not only was marriage something which the wife, and to a much lesser extent the husband, had to work hard at, but sex was too. Walker saw sexual intercourse for the woman as part of her housework. Here he is writing about sex after childbirth.

> Many women return to their household duties three weeks after their confinement, and there is no reason in this case why intercourse should not be resumed then very gently and carefully so that it becomes normal a few weeks later.[60]

There seems to be a fear here that if sexual intercourse was not resumed very fast the wife would not care to resume it at all. The woman was written about by the sexologists as a machine for the husband's use and a swift resumption of sexual intercourse could be seen as keeping the machinery oiled. Chesser recommends husbands to see their wives as cars:

> The first essential is to devote as much thought to one's wife as to the mechanism of one's car. How does *she* work? What is there to be learned about her mechanism?[61]

Davis uses this theme in a slightly more complicated way – the wife is both an apprentice learning a trade and a machine which can break down and need repair:

> If she does not enjoy her marital relations fully after a reasonable apprenticeship she ought to take stock of the situation. There is nothing to be gained by accepting it, wishfully thinking that time will take care of it . . . She then owes it both to herself and her husband to find out exactly which part of her emotional clockwork is out of gear, have it repaired and put into smooth running order as soon as possible.[62]

The sexologists recommended oiling the machine with lubricant if the woman was not enthusiastic enough to produce her own

vaginal secretions. Davis recommends the wife to 'have an artificial lubricant that she can apply to her sexual organs when
she needs it'. This may be because her glands are inefficient or
'the wife's desire is not sufficiently aroused'.[63]

Sexual intercourse was not seen as entertainment or as leading
to transports of ecstasy for the woman or even the man. This
was a very different spirit from the hedonism which infects
sexological advice in the 1960s and 1970s. It is difficult to
understand why this joyless and difficult activity had to be
performed, and why it was required that the wifely machine
show enthusiasm.

WHY SEXUAL INTERCOURSE AND VAGINAL ORGASM?

In the 1920s sexologists were unambiguous about why women's
sexual enthusiasm was necessary. It was assumed that for a
woman to have sexual pleasure with a man she had to surrender
herself to him and that such surrender would not be confined
to the act of sexual intercourse but would percolate through to
other aspects of her relationship with the man. Her surrender
would affect her whole relationship with the world. Wilhelm
Stekel and other experts on women's frigidity argued that feminism, manhating and the threats to male dominance and 'civilisation' that spinsters, lesbians and resisting women provided,
would be abolished if most or all women could be subjected to
sexual 'pleasure' with men.

In the 1940s and 1950s the political dimension was not
expressed quite so blatantly, but the idea that woman must
surrender to have sexual pleasure was still very much alive.
Eustace Chesser explained that the wife really must surrender,
submission was nowhere near enough. She must surrender her
will, her integrity, her very soul. He writes that a girl may:

> . . . find it impossible to surrender herself completely in the
> sex act. And complete surrender is the only way in which she
> can bring the highest pleasure to both herself and her hus-
> band. Submission is not the same thing as surrender. Many
> a wife submits, but retains, deep within herself, an area which

29

is not conquered, and which, indeed, is in fierce opposition to submission.[64]

There was a clear conviction that pleasure in sexual intercourse would make a woman compliant in other areas of her marriage. She wouldn't nag, complain or assert her own will if she surrendered in sexual intercourse. Davis explained that sexual pleasure would cause a woman to see 'the inevitable annoyances and even major troubles as a normal part of life'. When her husband was 'sexually distasteful' then she would build up 'smouldering resentment' about 'everything'.[65]

There is another reason why woman's sexual response was seen as so important. Woman's pleasure in sexual intercourse enabled the man to feel dominant. Davis explained the husband's need to feel dominant thus:

> For he *is* a man. The pulses throbbing in his veins are the pounding of the elemental male reproductive instinct. He is alive with sexual desire and his organs must respond and express it in intercourse or he cannot feel himself a man. The male need to dominate in the sexual relationship is the wellspring of the species.[66]

If the man saw the woman's pleasure as surrender and was performing a practice which symbolically and actually can be seen as one in which he is 'on top' and in charge, then the vaginal orgasm could be expected to reinforce the individual male's sense of power. Her pleasure would reassure him of the rightness of male dominance in general and his power in particular. Besides, the sexological literature makes much of the fact that woman was, by the 1940s, emancipated and the equal of man. In such a context it would not have been possible to retain the idea that men were the only ones who should really enjoy sex and that they should use the woman simply as a spittoon. This would have looked too obviously unfair. What was important was to engineer the correct sort of response.

Historians have tended to see the eroticising of the housewife as a form of emancipation which was to woman's benefit and in her interests. The sexological literature does not support this contention any more in the 1940s than in the 1920s. Men's sexual satisfaction and their preferred mode of sexual practice remain primary and unquestioned. Women were to be trained to have orgasms in response to this practice, not just because this would be slightly less unfair for women, but because it would reinforce male dominance and women's subordination.

SEX THERAPY

An analysis of sex therapy in the late 1950s illustrates the function of sexual intercourse in enforcing male power and shows clearly the male-supremacist philosophy which lay behind the aims of the practitioners of sex therapy at that time.

Sex therapy is treatment for what is seen to be an illness or medical condition requiring remedy. The illness that sex therapy treats is called sexual dysfunction. The idea of sexual dysfunction is based upon a concept of correct sexual function. If we accept that sexual behaviour is socially constructed, then it is clear that sex therapy, rather than curing a life endangering illness, or even one which causes serious ill health, is a force for social control. Sex therapy constructs correct sexual behaviour for those seen to be falling short of it. Certain forms of behaviour are labelled 'ill' or 'diseased' by the practitioners of sex therapy so that they have something to cure.

It will be no surprise to discover that healthy sexual behaviour is seen by the sex therapists to be penis-in-vagina sexual intercourse. With the mounting concentration on female orgasm in the fifties rather more was expected of men. Where they had previously only been expected to enter the vagina for a brief period, they were now required to remain erect in the vagina for slightly longer after insertion. Correct sexual behaviour for the female was to have a lubricating vagina which welcomed the penis and to have an orgasm, preferably whilst the penis remained in the vagina.

From such specifications the illnesses that required treatment in sex therapy were created. For a man the main illnesses were defined as impotence or failure to achieve or maintain erection, and premature ejaculation. Ejaculation was seen as premature when it took place before penis-in-vagina sexual intercourse had

31

been achieved, or immediately after penetration. Such an illness would not exist if prolonged sexual intercourse were not prescribed for health. It would not make sense in a society in which other forms of sexual interaction were prized more highly than sexual intercourse.

For women the main illnesses were seen as frigidity or failure to become aroused, disinclination to sexual intercourse, dyspareunia or pain during intercourse, vaginismus or muscle spasm which prevented intercourse, and failure to achieve orgasm during sexual intercourse. In the absence of the prescription of sexual intercourse most of these illnesses would simply be inconceivable.

VIRGIN WIVES

In 1958 the Family Planning Association started a 'training-cum-research' scheme for doctors who were working in their Special Clinics for Marital Problems. The doctors, who were all women, worked on various problems under the guidance of a man, Michael Balint. One problem they worked on was that of nonconsummation, i.e. marriages in which sexual intercourse did not take place. Though they agreed that men might in some cases be responsible for nonconsummation they preferred to look at the responsibility of women. In 1962 their work was written up by another man, Lawrence Friedman, in a book delightfully titled *Virgin Wives: A Study of Unconsummated Marriages*. Ten women doctors under the direction of a man worked on the problem of women who did not wish to have sexual intercourse, and their findings were then written up by another man from the Tavistock Clinic.

Virgin Wives is a wonderful book. In the rather naive and straightforward way common to sexologists before gender became an issue in the 1960s, the author and contributors reveal the naked power politics of sex therapy. The book shows us really clearly why sexual intercourse was deemed necessary. It was seen as crucial to maintaining male dominance in marriage. The women seen as cured in the book did not grow to like sexual intercourse, they merely agreed to accept it. Later the female orgasm was to be seen as important to the maintenance of male dominance; here the performance of the act of penetration was seen to suffice.

Michael Balint sets out the political context and purpose of the sex therapy in his Foreword to the book. Balint states that he wishes 'to stress one surprising finding of our research'. This was that the virgin wives were powerful and even dominant in their marriage. He describes the finding thus:

> This concerns the immense power that a number of these women apparently exert over their menfolk. True, often enough this power is hidden behind an impressive façade of sweetness and fear, weakness and despair; nevertheless, it is there. This does not mean that we think that all women are powerful and dominant. What we would state is that in the field of unconsummated marriages power and domination play a very important part.[67]

Power and domination by men in marriage would have been normal and not worthy of any comment, but anything apart from submission by wives was an upsetting of the patriarchal applecart which required not only comment but therapy. What is more, the doctors each saw on average 25 to 30 virgin wives yearly in their practices. This 'power and domination' by women was not an uncommon problem.

A review of the literature gives an idea of how other sexologists had seen the problem of nonconsummating wives. Two studies described wives with vaginismus as having 'hostility toward men' combined in one case with 'dread of the penis'.[68] They were seen as sadistically taking revenge upon their husbands.[69] The women were described as 'hostile, nervous patients'.[70] Another stated that vaginismus was caused by a phobia which was 'aversion to the husband'.[71] One researcher found that virgin wives were often 'psychopathic'.[72] Another described the wife with vaginismus as an independent woman unable to submit herself to her husband and therefore, by sexological logic, 'masculine'.

The masculine character type, very widespread these days, incites the young woman to express her independence and

33

seems to prevent her from passively giving herself to her partner . . . Vaginismus expresses their aggressiveness and serves as a revenge for their day-to-day enslavement. This illustrates what the analysts call their 'castration' tendencies.[73]

The FPA study starts from the basic idea that the wife who resists sexual intercourse is unreasonably avoiding submission to her husband. The case studies are arranged according to a typology of virgin wives. One variety is covered in a chapter entitled 'Awakening the Sleeping Beauty' another is called 'The Queen Bee' and the third 'Gentling Brunhild'. The 'Brunhild' variety of virgin wife is named after the German folktale heroine in *Das Nibelungenlied*. She is the archetype of the 'masculine' woman, i.e. a woman who does not wish to accept subordination to men.

The legend is very clear in its description of the aggressive, masculine woman whose competitive feelings towards men drive her to fight them, whose sexuality is thoroughly mixed up with destructiveness. At another level, she desires to be overpowered by a heroic man, a man who must be superpotent to succeed, since she makes ordinary men impotent. Only then can she become submissive; to submit to a man, to want to give herself to him out of love, is not possible for such a woman, because, to her, submission implies admitting inferiority. Relationships between the sexes become a power struggle for her.[74]

Having described the problem of the resisting woman, the sex therapists conveniently invented a desire on the part of such a woman really to be overpowered and made to submit by a strong man. This was a necessary fiction. Since the therapists were going to arrange her submission it was in their interests to believe that they were doing what she really wanted despite all evidence to the contrary.

But it is not just women in the 'Brunhild' category who are seen as having great power over men and having to be forced to submit. One 'Sleeping Beauty' wife was seen as having this problem. In the case studies generally, going out to work is seen as dominant behaviour by the wife which the therapists are anxious to end. This is ironic considering that all the doctors were working women. One 'Sleeping Beauty' voluntarily gave notice at her work at the same time as 'accepting' first sexual intercourse.[75] In another 'Sleeping Beauty' case the doctor reports: 'I asked whether she really needed to work.' The woman who gave up her work in order to be penetrated had a husband who was too polite and kind and 'incapable of taking his wife by force'.[76] Marital rape was clearly the preferred method of therapy for resisting wives. The husband was put off his natural aggression apparently because his wife had another health problem: 'She can't allow people to be angry or aggressive towards her.'[77] Balint comments:

> Women have a very great power over a man's potency. There is no question that if the woman allows her husband to be aggressive, and even enjoys it, it might give more to him than any psychological treatment . . . [78]

The main approach in treatment for this woman was to encourage her to 'enjoy her husband's aggression' and to 'encourage her husband to be aggressive'.[79] She was, then, to facilitate her own subjugation in sex by her husband. The result was that the husband 'found his wife quite easy to penetrate now and he was enjoying intercourse thoroughly'. The wife does not seem to have enjoyed it.

The virgin wives rarely came to the doctors because they wished to consummate their marriages. Generally the marriages were of long standing, in several cases as long as 10 and in one as long as 17 years. The doctors would identify that the woman had a problem whilst examining her for gynaecological complaints, infertility and so on. Sometimes in vaginal examinations the woman would have a muscle spasm and the doctor would enquire about vaginismus. The virgin wives frequently had no desire to be cured. They were quite happy not engaging in sexual intercourse and in some cases had worked out perfectly satisfying sexual alternatives. One couple who had 17 years of nonconsummation were reported as being 'good friends, very much in love'. They engaged in 'heavy petting and mutual masturbation' and the wife had orgasms through having her breasts stroked. This pair are described as being in 'neurotic collusion' because they did not see the nonconsummation as traumatic.[80]

One virgin wife said that she was only having intercourse because the doctor told her to. The doctor asked her how she felt about her husband's body and whether she ever looked at him. The wife made her absence of erotic feeling towards her husband quite clear.

Mrs Lowe replied, 'Oh, I couldn't!' She had seen a little boy's penis; 'That was soft and sweet. But don't ask me to talk about my husband's – I shall be sick if I do.' At this point the patient retched quite a lot and the doctor did not pursue the topic further.[81]

Later she reported to the doctor that she was having intercourse:

. . . for the baby and for my husband. I don't like it but I see I ought to accept it in the marriage, and my husband says I am getting to be more of a wife. I'm beginning not to need your orders.[82]

With one of the 'Queen Bee' case studies, the doctor had a difficult job working out how to defeat the wife's evasive strategies and get her penetrated. The 'Queen Bees' were women who sought artificial insemination so that they could bear children without doing sexual intercourse. One remarkable woman had already borne one child and was after another when she mistakenly chose to visit one of the FPA study doctors in search of insemination help. The doctor homed in on the problem. She realised that if she refused insemination and tried to persuade the patient to do sexual intercourse instead she would simply visit another doctor. On the other hand if she helped her with the insemination the patient might never return and would never be 'cured'. The doctor decided reluctantly to go along with the patient's wishes in the hope that she might influence her along the way. The patient reported that she had started doing sexual intercourse with her husband 'but only with me on top, not any other way'.[83] This got the doctor very worried and she felt forced to interrogate the patient severely on the extent of her 'domineering quality' in the marriage.

> Dr Jones said, 'You can only do it when you are on top, in the commanding position.' The patient agreed. When asked whether she took the lead in everything in her marriage, she denied it; then she said, 'Perhaps I do make the decisions.'[84]

It is clear from the logic of the doctor's questioning that submission in sex was not the only kind of submission that was to result from sexual intercourse. The woman's submission in that act was meant to spread to all other aspects of the relationship. So a woman who subverted the norms and engaged in sexual intercourse in a position which did not so clearly subordinate her was threatening the power of her husband in other areas.

The FPA doctors favoured psychotherapy as treatment for nonconsummation. This seems to have been just as effective and much less brutal than the physical and surgical forms of treatment available. Surgery was resorted to by some sexologists for vaginas that they considered too tight or unreasonably painful. They worked on the theory that the woman had simply been wrongly constructed by nature and had to be adjusted so that her body would work properly. The right of the woman to avoid sexual intercourse was unimaginable to such doctors. One form of surgery carried out for dyspareunia was a 'perineostomy' or cutting of the perineum.[85] Some doctors favoured operations on the muscles in the vagina.[86] Rather less drastic was dilation of the vagina under anaesthetic to stretch it. The commonest physical approach was and is the use of dilators. The woman is given a set of glass dilators of different sizes and instructed to practise inserting them into her vagina on a graduated scale of size until she is sufficiently loosened up to take her husband's penis.

A more recent example of the surgical approach is contained in an article in an American reader called *The Sociology of Sex*, published in 1971. The chapter is entitled 'Dramaturgical Desexualisation: The Sociology of the Vaginal Examination'. This piece of writing analyses the vaginal examination and shows how the patient is turned into a passive and compliant object so that she will be putty in the hands of the doctor. There is apparently no value judgment here. The article's authors, Henslin and Biggs, seem, in fact, to have assumed that there is nothing worthy of comment in the fact that women need to be turned into objects for vaginal examinations. They include the case of a young woman who had vaginal surgery as an example of 'role failure'. The woman refused to accept 'the depersonalised role of object' and complained and cried in the examining room. In including the interview Henslin and Biggs unwittingly give us an example of the brutality of vaginal surgery. The woman had had a hymenotomy, or removal of the hymen prior to marriage, to facilitate first intercourse. The doctor examined the patient with a speculum in the presence of a nurse and her mother to see if she was yet big enough to accept her husband's penis. The doctor treated her like a farm animal and the patient objected.

> Patient: 'My God! You're tearing me apart! Give me something to bite on! Mom! Give me some gum!' (Patient is shaking her head from side to side very rapidly.) The mother reaches into her purse, removes some chewing gum, unwraps a piece and places it in the patient's mouth. The patient rapidly chews the gum. The nurse moves up to the abdominal area of the patient . . . 'He's ruining me! I can't stand it!' She continues to shake her head from side to side.
> Doctor: 'Gerry, I'm just trying to help you. This will be very helpful to you after you get married.'
> Patient: 'I don't see how. It hurts too much.'
> Mother: 'I'm sorry, doctor.'
> Doctor to Mother: 'She's in good condition now. She'll take a normal sized speculum without difficulty.'[87]

The preparation of this young woman for her role as an efficient hole for her husband seems to have taken place in direct opposition to her will.

THE SINGLE WOMAN

In the 1950s single women were expected to be sexually inactive. Sex-advice books assumed that only married women could be sexually active, and then only with their husbands; lesbianism was condemned on the rare occasions on which it was mentioned. Single women were in limbo, allowed only to be perpetual maiden aunts. They were pitied because they were assumed to be lonely and desperately unhappy, but no crumb of comfort was offered nor any alternative to the lone celibate life. The 1950s was the last decade in which the 'spinster' was seen to be a problem.

The plight of single women in the 1950s stands out in stark relief, however, when contrasted with their situation in prewar Britain. As the result of a powerful feminist movement and changing social and economic forces, single women had grown greatly in numbers and independence in the 1920s and 30s. They had been a force to be reckoned with. Though pilloried by the sexologists of the period, who were hostile to any women not sexually engaged with a man, they retained some of the self-respect and status won for spinsters by a generation of feminist struggle. This self-respect and status disappeared in the postwar world which gave status only to the married woman and pathologised the unmarried. To understand the change in attitude by which the spinster was transformed into the pitied and despised single woman, it is necessary first to look at some of the more affirmative literature which emerged in the 1930s.

Two works from the 1930s are particularly interesting because of their remarkable approach to single women which is extinct by the 1950s. One is Esther Harding's *The Way of All Women*, first published in 1933 and referred to with respect in the literature of the 1950s. Harding was a Jungian psychoanalyst. Born in England in 1888, she studied under Jung in Zurich and practised in New York. The other work is Laura Hutton's *The Single Woman and Her Emotional Problems*, first published in 1935 but republished with revisions right up to the 1960s. Hutton was a physician at the Tavistock Clinic in London in the 1930s. She contributed the section on 'The Unmarried' to the Neville-Rolfe anthology, prepared before the war and finally published in 1949, which was cited in the section on the eroticising of the housewife.

Both Harding and Hutton stressed the unique situation of the single woman in the 1930s when certain social and economic forces had come together to create a large class of strong, independent women. Harding writes:

> But times changed. Women were forced out into the world. Marriage no longer offered the only career for them. Many women, and those by no means only the failures and the 'left overs', remained unmarried for a part of their adult lives, in many cases for the whole. These women far from being the weaklings, the stupid or unattractive members of their generation, may be the most vital and enterprising, the ones with the greatest intelligence and initiative.[88]

Hutton explains that the 1931 census showed there to be 244,500 more women than men in the 40–44 age group. The total 'excess' of marriageable women over men numbered half a million. She saw two factors as having brought about the situation: the development of education, including university education and the professional training of women, and the European war of 1914. These, and the development of wage-earning occupations for women with the opening up of professions and expansion of the white-collar sector, have 'brought into existence a new class of women almost unknown two or three generations ago – women who have left home to take up careers and manage their own lives.'[89] The war led to potential mates being killed and sent 'many women into the ranks of the professional and wage-earning class who might otherwise have remained at home . . .'[90] The historical phenomenon to which Harding and Hutton addressed themselves was new and dramatic. Working-class women had left home for independent working lives in the nineteenth century, but probably not with the idea of remaining single. In the early twentieth century middle-class women were doing the same and were remaining single and independent. Harding and Hutton are both very positive about single women. In this way they fit into a long feminist tradition of which Christabel Pankhurst and Cicely

Hamilton before the First World War are examples; a tradition firmly opposed to the traditional male disparagement of any woman whose life energies were not ploughed into a man.

The most startling aspect of the work of these writers is their enthusiasm about friendship between women, even friendship of a passionate variety. Whereas single women after the Second World War were expected to remain without serious emotional attachment, Harding and Hutton applauded and encouraged the formation of strong bonds between women.

In the current wave of feminism the importance of women's friendship has again become a strong theme of feminist theory, particularly in the recent work by Janice G. Raymond, *A Passion for Friends: Towards a Philosophy of Female Affection*. Raymond defines hetero-reality as 'the world view that woman exists always in relation to man'.[91] She explains that 'Hetero-reality has conferred social and political status only on hetero-relations (woman-to-man relationships)', and has seen female friendship as only a 'personal association' whereas hetero-relations such as marriage and heterosex are 'given public status and are sustained by the laws, ceremonies, rituals, pacts, and informal consistency of hetero-reality'.[92] She advocates that:

> ... women come to recognise in our friendships with each other the implications beyond the personal nature of this bond so that we ourselves do not underrate its social and political power, a power that, at its deepest level, is an immense force for disintegrating the structures of hetero-reality. The empowering of female friendship can create the conditions for a new feminist politics in which the personal is most passionately political.[93]

Women's friendships were given an importance by Harding and Hutton which seems to have been unparalleled between the 1930s and the current wave of feminism. Harding recognised that love between two women was very likely to encompass an erotic element but that there were many reasons why the friends might not choose to recognise this or to act upon it. But Harding

41

gave no disapprobation to the idea that they might sexualise their relationship.

> The very word *homosexuality* is such a bugaboo that it may hardly be mentioned in polite society . . .

> The emotional involvement in a friendship may be intense in its character and yet be without physical expression. For love between women does not necessarily involve physical sexuality. Viewed from one angle such a friendship would not be called homosexual. Yet for women who have no sexual expression in their lives the repressed instinct is bound to colour their major relationship and give it that quality of emotionality which is the earmark of erotic involvement even though no overt sexual acts, nor even conscious sexual impulses are present . . . In other cases the love between friends may find its expression in a more specifically sexual fashion which, however, cannot be considered perverted if their actions are motivated by love.[94]

She concludes that in judging any relationship 'the quality of the emotion involved is the criterion of value rather than the nature of the accompanying physical expression'.[95]

Hutton saw herself as being more positive towards sexual expression in women's friendships than Harding. She calls Harding's assertion that such expression could not be considered perverted if 'motivated by love', a 'sound general principle' but 'somewhat negative'.[96] It is important to understand that these women were writing at a time when lesbianism was receiving savage censure such as in the *Well of Loneliness* prosecution which took place only a few years before. Though there are evasions and ambivalences in their work about lesbian sexuality the positive tone is quite exceptional for any sex-advice writings before the impact of contemporary lesbian feminism. This is particularly true of Hutton. She agrees with Harding that the sexual element of the friendship should be discussed because failure to recognise it was fraught with problems

> The results of such *unrecognised* sexual stimulation are bound

42

to be unfortunate. Tension and irritability will follow, on a substratum of perplexity, resentment and vague guilty feeling, the last particularly if the sexual nature of the emotional-*cum*-physical excitement is dimly divined. The first prerequisite for the management of the sexual element in any friendship is its frank recognition and acceptance.[97]

But Hutton does not recommend repression. She explains how physical affection between friends can lead to sexual expression and sees this as quite reasonable. Hutton describes lesbian sex as 'masturbation, but by another'.[98] It was quite harmless so long as there was no 'excess' and prolongation of stimulation, without climax. This may not sound very exciting but it is a vast improvement on the outrage of male sexologists. Hutton's general approach to sex for the single woman has a girl guide feel to it. She was not hostile to masturbation as long as it was treated a bit like brushing your teeth and you didn't get too carried away. She stood out from fellow sex educators by stating that the much vaunted physical ills supposed to result from masturbation in fact stemmed from a quite wrong sense of guilt and not from the activity itself.

'Get it over and forget about it' is, it has seemed to me, the advice that may be given to those women who periodically feel the need to give themselves sexual relief. 'Let the orgasm come, and turn with ease of mind and increased energy to the matter you have in hand.' The whole thing is *unimportant*, and it is unnecessary and unwise to demand an ideal of complete abstention.[99]

Hutton wanted any sense of guilt over lesbian sex to be eliminated too, because, as in the case of masturbation, it was the guilt which caused the problem and not the activity itself.

The question of 'sexual morality' in respect of lesbian sex was disposed of in a similarly businesslike fashion. Hutton saw the moral objection to lesbian sex as being based on the idea that sex should exist for the purpose of reproduction and her answer is neat and simple: 'It is absurd to say that all heterosexual caresses are intended to lead up to the act of reproduction.'[100]

In the sphere of social morality, Hutton argues, there is no immorality because there is no marriage and lesbians are breaking no contract. The one reservation is that an older woman should not 'initiate a girl, or a woman without previous experience, into homosexual intercourse – i.e. mutual sexual stimulation – for this experience may arrest such a girl's psychosexual development and make it difficult for her to become receptive to heterosexual appeal'.[101] So there was a limit to Hutton's positive feelings about lesbianism. Marriage and a family was still seen as the desirable destiny for a woman who was not a 'real' invert. But in the case of two mature women engaged in a sexual relationship Hutton is totally affirming.

> These conditions – love and tenderness, and freedom from conflict and guilt about the matter based on self-knowledge and mutual respect – are stringent, but where they are fulfilled, a sexual relationship as part of a true friendship may contribute, in a way that is entirely useful and constructive, to the solving of the problem of the unmarried woman's frustrated biological fulfilment.[102]

Such relationships would even, she believed, 'play quite a useful part in society at the present time'.[103]

The sections on 'emotional friendships' and 'sexual inversion' are the central core of Hutton's book. She explains that it was a frequent criticism of friendships between women that 'they are so constantly overheated in emotion, full of exaggerations and upsets, and very frequently unstable and impermanent'.[104] She agrees that women's friendships are often 'marred' by such things but goes on to suggest why that might be. One reason was that conflict might arise from unexpressed sexuality. What she calls the 'characteristic transitoriness of women's friendships' she explains in terms of the pressure put upon friendships which receive none of the societal acceptance and support accorded to heterosexual relationships. This is a political explanation for what hostile sexologists would see as part of the pathology of lesbianism.

When two women decide to set up house together, they lack

all social support, and their proposal is of significance only to the friends themselves. There is, of course, no contract of mutual obligation; no sympathy, approval or even interest is expected. There is no social recognition at all ... Such partnerships in living, then, get nothing comparable with the hopeful start of every normal marriage, although they may, and often do, represent what has been called the 'major relationship' of two women's lives.[105]

What is most surprising before the birth of lesbian feminism is the understanding of the impact which the attempt to survive in a hetero-relational world hostile to women's love for each other, has on women's friendships.

The writings of Harding and Hutton seem extraordinary in the context of what was to be written about the single woman in the postwar years and beyond. Margery Fry and Blanche Marie Smith, writing about the single woman in the 1950s, both paint a gloomy picture full of the problems and none of the joys of a single woman's life. Friendship between women and lesbianism are scarcely mentioned, let alone given the serious space and attention we have seen earlier. It is assumed that the life of the single woman will be lonely and loveless.

Margery Fry was an ex-principal of Somerville College, Oxford. Her *The Single Woman* of 1953 is the published text of a radio talk. The talk stresses the sad plight of the single woman who suffers loneliness and absence of the great satisfaction of motherhood. She demonstrates the importance of her subject by pointing out that there were 4.5 million single women and 25 million widowed and divorced women. She showed her attitude to single status by including a very maudlin poem about the child who is the unborn fruit of the unused womb of the spinster who longs to have been fruitful.

The spinster, according to Fry, missed having a family and being a homemaker. She tended to live at a 'lower standard materially, as well as emotionally ...' than married women.[106] The book was not positive towards women finding love with each other, though she does mention that they can find a home with a relative or friend. Fry says of herself that she is an old maid who has had a full and interesting life, yet throughout she shows that she sees the married state as happier and much superior. She does not mention any advantages stemming from spinsterhood but does warn against the 'crankiness' which the single, she believes, are likely to develop, such as worrying about 'a spot of ink on the carpet, or the milkman's calling late'. Single women are warned to look out for this and 'check its beginnings'.[107] Apparently family life would 'brush away' these 'small oddities'. This is a rather humiliating self-depreciation and does support the most hostile of anti-spinster stereotypes.

Youth was apparently most unkind to the single woman because that was when she most sharply missed marrying. Middle life was kinder because 'the emotional life was less insistent' and she often had a satisfying career. In old age widows were often worse off than spinsters because they had not built up a circle of friends. Perhaps the gloomiest part of the talk is the conclusion in which Fry tells us about one small happiness she has discovered in age:

> Perhaps we all grow a little childish as we get older. There is one good point in this; it seems to me that a pleasure in small things does come back to one; the beauty of the outward world and of people, the satisfaction of warmth in sunlight or fire or even in a hot bottle, the friendly gesture of a child or the ripe juiciness of a plum – it is good to savour these things as they come. Shall I admit to you that sometimes as I wait for a bus on a wet, London winter's night – and we have had plenty lately – when no very obvious gratifications are present, I say to myself, 'Well, anyhow I'm alive and I can see the other people and the play of lights reflected from the pavements and even the posters.'
>
> But alas, I know it is no good pretending that the black moments won't come.[108]

If this was a consolation then the rest of her life must have been depressing indeed.

Hutton and Harding paid lip service to the idea that family life was more fulfilling than spinsterhood, but their belief in the joys of the single state was very obvious. Those joys were based upon the love and companionship of women. Fry is locked within an entirely hetero-relational mould in which a woman is automatically 'lonely' and 'cranky' if she doesn't belong to a man.

Blanche Marie Smith, whose *The Single Woman of Today* was published in 1951 was equally a victim of the constraints of hetero-reality, i.e. the inability to conceive of woman except in relation to man. In her Dedication Smith bemoaned the frequency with which the desirable woman was 'committed to the ranks of the surplus, whilst the less worthy is chosen in marriage'; the book was dedicated to these 'desirable women'. In her writing she seems to seek an understanding of the unkind fate which has relegated her to the surplus. She states that the book is not an 'anti-male treatise' but it does deplore man's 'degeneracy' in his choice of a mate. Men were apparently choosing undesirable women to marry. The grave disadvantages of a single life included the risk of death from the illnesses attendant upon spinsterhood. She lists the diseases caused by disuse of the female organs of reproduction. The death rate from cancer of the ovaries and the fallopian tubes was twice as high as in married women.[109] The single woman was subject to serious mental disturbances too, including 'hysteria, epilepsy, obsessional neurosis, depression, manic schizophrenia, and nervous breakdown . . .'[110] Moreover the inability to attract a man was likely to denote mental illness in itself. If a protesting spinster reader disclaimed any of the physical or mental ills she could always be shown to be ill by the very fact that she was single.

> The traumata of babyhood, repressed from the consciousness, though still active within the psyche, may well lead a woman to refuse, subconsciously, the duties and obligations of the mature state of married life. Analytical psychotherapy may trace in ever-deepening progression the causes of the inability of some otherwise perfectly eligible women to attract a man as a marriage partner.[111]

Whilst celibacy on an individual scale might only lead to the mental illnesses listed above, on a social scale it might lead to 'war and destruction'.[112] This was a worrying thought indeed.

47

One might have thought that the pressures within hetero-reality upon women to attach themselves to a man, such as isolation and stigma, were sufficiently strong already, considering the gloom and despair women like Fry and Smith felt at their failure, without threats of death and destruction. Smith wanted these pressures to be considerably increased. She wanted re-education so that 'the suitable woman would find a man a necessity, and not look upon the search for a mate as humiliating to their ego'.[113] The savagery of such assaults on the integrity and self-respect of the single woman here is as severe as in the male anti-spinster literature of the 1850s and 60s which was a response to the sudden revelation of spinster numbers in the 1851 census. There is no suggestion in these 1950s writings that a woman might choose not to marry. Such a thing was unthinkable. That women might engage in passionate friendships with each other was even worse because this might interfere with their chances of marriage:

> Helene Deutsch, in a masterly analysis of hundreds of cases of women suffering from neurosis, shows how women can, being segregated from men, put off the heterosexual relationship until it is too late. They become unconscious homosexuals. The love given and returned is more sensitive, tender, and passionate than the love given to man, by the very fact that it is denied the sexual satisfaction. Such a relationship, in which two single women are violently and passionately bound to each other, often postpones a normal marriage relationship.[114]

Rather than being a solace, or even an advantage of spinsterhood, such friendships are seen simply as an obstacle to heterosexuality. Smith dismisses the evidence of one woman sexologist that passionate friends were healthier and happier than married women by stating that the Freudian psychiatrists disagree.[115]

How can we account for the very dramatic change that takes place in the literature on the single woman? In the 1930s two writers were able to see strong single women and the superior loving relationships they had with each other as capable of transforming the world in women's interests. The writers of the 1950s are sunk in gloom and despair about the misery of being a single woman. Friendship between women is seen as dangerous despite the terrible loneliness that the writers bemoan. The single woman is seen as suffering from an anti-social disease which prevents her from attracting men. In quite practical terms the failure to suggest that women might love each other, or the condemnation of such a possibility, when the specific problem being addressed is the loneliness of 'surplus' women, i.e. surplus to men's requirements, suggests an extreme fear of lesbianism. That women should get so enmeshed in hetero-reality that they are unable to envisage love or happiness for themselves without being able to serve men and children should not astonish us when we take into account the fact that many heterosexual women who see themselves as feminists today, have a similar problem.

What was it about the 1950s which made it such a bleak decade for the single woman? In the 1930s Harding and Hutton were writing at the tail end of the massive social transformation caused by the first wave of feminism and social and economic forces which had enabled women to leave home, to work and to be independent of men. They could still see the world-changing possibilities which a body of strong independent women who loved and relied upon each other presented. They did not foresee that there was to be a change of step on the part of patriarchal ideology which would nip this challenge in the bud, nor that the sex ratio would become less favourable to women from the 1940s onward.

The imposition of compulsory heterosexuality by determined sexologists was under way by the 1920s with its concomitant construction of women's sexual pleasure with men, but in the 1940s and 50s there was a considerable acceleration of this process. The work of social workers and sexologists in promoting women's selfless service under male authority within marriage, combined with the stigmatising of lesbianism, provided no room or hope for the single woman. She was a pariah on the edge of the world of happy patriarchal families which was the sexological fantasy. Hutton explains that in the 1930s one result of the sexological categorising of homosexuals was that persons of the same sex could not have 'innocent' friendships without inviting the suspicion of sexual inversion which now bore considerable stigma.

> A self-consciousness has appeared on the one hand in the victims of this abnormality, so that there are a large number of conscious, and fewer 'innocent', homosexuals than there were; and at the same time friendly couples of the same sex are now much more readily suspected of homosexual tendencies than would have been the case, say, twenty years ago.[116]

By the 1950s this homophobia had an even more restricting effect upon the possibility of women's friendship according to Smith:

> Households in which two unmarried women live together, however, are still regarded with a tolerance that includes some of the last century's pity and absolution from blame of the woman who did not marry, but this tolerance is markedly decreasing. Young women today who work and share a household have to draw heavily on the housing situation or considerations of economy to justify their continuing such an arrangement . . . Many men who live together have to fend off very heavy social suspicions as to their homosexuality. So have some single women.[117]

In the 1960s the single woman was no longer to be put in the situation of a pariah. She would be found a niche in the hetero-relational universe as she was eroticised for men in books such as *Sex and the Single Girl*. But in the 1950s this had not yet happened. Women were to be sexual only with men and only in marriage. The single woman was an embarrassing anomaly.

ANTI-LESBIANISM

The postwar decade was a particularly bleak period for lesbians and gay men. Hatred of lesbians in sexological literature peaked at this time whilst sexological prescriptions for the housewife became more rigid and limiting. This was to be expected since the stigmatising of the lesbian goes hand in hand with concern about the enforcement of heterosexuality. The greater the paranoia of the sexological high priests about the threats to male dominance, the greater their condemnation of the lesbian. Sybil Neville-Rolfe explained this threat in eugenic terms in her chapter on 'The Homosexual'. She saw the welfare of 'the race' as being 'based on the family' and on 'society devising customs which will select the fittest in character, physique and intelligence as the parents of the future'. To this end 'each generation' must 'protect society from damage from its crop of abnormalities'.[118]

Danger to the family was seen as danger to the state since the male-supremacist state was based upon the subordination of woman in the family. One sexologist describes the danger posed by homosexuals in terms reminiscent of 1950s horror movies about invasion by aliens who threatened cuddly, gender-stereotyped nuclear families:

Homosexuality is to a very large extent an acquired abnormality and propagates itself as a morally contagious disease. It tends to build up a society with even a kind of language of its own, and certainly with practices foreign to those of normal society. It tends to bring about more and more unfruitful unions that withdraw men and women from normal family life, the development of homes, and the procreation of children. The growth of a homosexual society in any country is a menace, more or less serious, to the welfare of the state.[119]

The American literature is more paranoid and brutal than the British literature. Samuel Steward, in his introduction to a modern edition of James Barr's 1950 novel *Quatrefoil*, explains the peculiar viciousness of the 1950s as a reaction to the Kinsey report. Kinsey's 1948 report on male sexual behaviour showed that homosexual experience was relatively normal for the American male. Sexologists leapt to deny this and a battle raged throughout the 1950s between those, like Edmund Bergler, who were horrified by the findings and those who were prepared to accept them. Steward points out that before Kinsey the American public was completely ignorant about homosexuality. This ignorance he describes as a 'protective umbrella' under which gay men went about their lives without too much persecution because no one really believed that they existed. After Kinsey this would never be true again. Suddenly there was a moral panic about homosexuality.

> [The publication of the report] . . . although it did much good for our cause, also stripped away the last tatters of silk, to leave only the metal ribs above us. It remained then for Senator McCarthy with his rumours and accusations to shatter everything and to send us scurrying deeper into our closets than ever, to escape utter destruction.[120]

Frank Caprio, author of the remarkable *The Sexually Adequate Female*, wrote the only full-length study of lesbianism in this period. Literature on lesbians before the birth of lesbian feminism has been very scarce. The word 'homosexual' has been interpreted almost exclusively to mean male. Lesbianism has generally been covered only in the context of warnings to women in standard sex-advice literature not to depart for a moment from the feminine ideal. Caprio was in a panic, apparently caused by the changes in the relations between the sexes resulting from the war. He was frightened that women were becoming 'defeminised' by their desire for emancipation and that this led to lesbianism. We can understand the word 'defeminisation' as meaning an unwillingness to accept a totally subordinate role.

> Female sexual inversion is therefore becoming an increasingly important problem. It is believed by some that women are becoming rapidly defeminised as a result of their overdesire for emancipation, and that this 'psychic masculinisation' of modern women is causing them to become frigid . . . [121]

It is interesting to speculate what an 'overdesire for emancipation' could possibly consist of. He produced what he saw as conclusive evidence of the masculinisation of women. This

consisted of wearing 'masculine-tailored clothes' and the 'smoᵢ
ing habit' which were signs of 'psychic masculinity'. He commented that it might only be a coincidence 'but a significant one' that the lesbians he interviewed were 'for the large part excessive smokers'.[122] General defeminisation could lead to 'the susceptibility of many women to a homosexual way of thinking'. All of this was contrary to a woman's best interests because whether they were aware of it or not, Caprio knew that, 'Women unconsciously prefer to fulfil their maternal role and to be loved by a man.'[123] Such sexologists knew much better than women themselves what they really wanted.

This confident hatred of lesbians was based upon the total dominance of Freudianism in sexological thinking. It was in the postwar decade that Freudianism swept the board in sexology and came to dominate the thinking of the 'caring' professions. Lesbianism was explained in terms of relationships with parents. Edmund Bergler, in 1951, tells us helpfully, 'What lesbians really act, unconsciously, is the passive baby–active Giantess game.'[124] Mothers are referred to as Giantesses throughout the book. This, according to Bergler, is the way the child sees the mother. More likely it is evidence of Bergler's hostility to women despite his fashionable assertion of the importance of woman's mission of motherhood. It could well be that a little boy with a strong awareness of his inherited power as a male might feel really hostile to a woman who had power over him by her sheer size. It doesn't seem a helpful way of thinking about women and lesbians except for those locked into the irrationalities of the Freudian religion of the 1950s. According to Bergler:

Psychoanalytical experience teaches us that the unconscious reason for female homosexuality is to be found in an unsolved oral-masochistic conflict of the pre-Oedipal child with the mother.[125]

Freudian disciples like Marie Bonaparte offer us similar explanations. She writes that lesbians 're-enact to infinity the primary scene of the active-passive alternations of the mother's ministerings to the babe'.[126] The mother was focused on as the source of lesbianism just as she was seen by the psychoanalytic industry as the source of almost all those forms of behaviour they found alarming, from vandalism by teenage boys to rape and indecent exposure.

Puzzling though it seems, the psychoanalysts were able to blame mothers for both male and female homosexuality. This seems hardly fair and even inconsistent. Kenneth Walker tells us that 'the predominance of female influence in the home' is the influence 'most conducive to the development of homosexuality [male]'.[127] Male homosexuals are apparently often youngest sons whose mothers abuse them thus: 'They are often tempted to cling to the youngest and to keep him in babyish clothes and to retain his long hair, 'as charming as that of a girl'. The solution was a 'virile upbringing for boys and the proximity of a revered father'.[128] Close relationships between children of either sex and their mothers were likely to lead to trouble. Lesbians were girls who, as a result of unresolved penis-envy, remained emotionally too attached to their mothers. The strong mother/child bond being required by sexologists elsewhere for the sake of their children could easily turn the children into either lesbians or male homosexuals. This must have caused insuperable difficulties for women who conscientiously sought to follow sexological prescriptions about childrearing. It was a no-win situation. On the other hand weak fathers could produce both lesbians and male homosexuals. Chesser describes the father of one lesbian thus:

> Her father was a country solicitor completely dominated by his wife, who was twelve years younger. He seemed fairly content to remain in the background and to leave the upbringing of the child to his wife. 'Anything for peace' was his maxim.[129]

Other explanations were sometimes advanced. Caprio suggested such additional causes as 'various environmental traumatic influences during childhood and adolescence (broken homes, sexually maladjusted parents, a sadistic feeling attitude toward the opposite sex, death of a parent, predisposition to masculinity and precocious sexuality)'.[130] It is clear that Caprio did not see lesbianism as a positive choice for women. He described it as 'a form of co-operative or mutual masturbation at best', and stated that lesbians were likely to commit serious crimes or even be psychopaths. He explained that when crimes by women were investigated it was often revealed that 'the women were either confirmed lesbians who killed because of jealousy or were latent homosexuals with a strong aggressive masculine drive'. Some lesbians, he stressed, 'manifest pronounced sadistic and psychopathic trends'. They were also likely to be kleptomaniacs. The vast majority were 'emotionally unstable and neurotic' and yet, Caprio stated with amazement, 'Many of them become quite disturbed at the thought that psychiatrists regard them as "sick individuals" in need of treatment.'[131] So one form of the 'neurosis' of lesbians seems to have been a righteous anger at being labelled 'sick'. But Caprio reassures us that 'lesbians would not be healthy persons even if they lived in a society where sexuality with their own sex was socially acceptable'.[132] For this assertion he adduces no 'scientific' evidence. It is simply his own unretouched prejudice.

Postwar sexologists were kind enough to identify the characteristics of the lesbian so that she could be recognised. The sexologists believed that lesbians came in two varieties, the masculine and the feminine. The 'butch' lesbians were seen, by those who believed in biological explanations for lesbianism, to be innately lesbian. The lesbianism of 'femmes' was seen as psychologically determined. The British sexologist Kenneth Walker describes the masculine type thus:

In the first group are those who display pronounced masculine traits. The secondary sexual characteristics in them are poorly developed, the breasts small, the voice low in timbre, the hair distribution approximates to that of the male, and the deposits of fat over the thighs and buttocks, characteristic of femininity, are absent. Many of these masculine women accentuate their already masculine appearance by keeping their hair short, by walking and moving like men and by dressing in male attire. They are often highly intellectual and also extremely able, as is also the case with the male invert.[133]

The second group was larger and 'feminine in both appearance and behaviour'. This group learned to be lesbians. They were led astray by the butch lesbians and could be more easily cured.

In the 1950s the acknowledgment, under the influence of Freudianism, that homosexuality was a disease, led to some confusion for the sexologists. Their clear hostility to homosexuals wrestled with a realisation that a certain tolerance was necessary since it was not the habit of doctors to recommend prison and dire punishments for those who were ill and could not help themselves. The 1940s and early 1950s in the USA were such a savage time for lesbians and gay men that the psychoanalysts found it harder than did their contemporaries in Britain to be sympathetic. Jeffrey Weeks explains that 'with the Korean War a searing memory and McCarthyism burning like a bush fire in the United States, homosexuals emerged to the fore as scapegoats and victims of the Cold War'.[134] In 1950 the State Department forbade government employment to homosexuals, a paranoia which reached Britain. Indeed Weeks cites a London correspondent of the *Sydney Morning Telegraph* in 1953 unearthing a plan urged on the British government by the US government to 'weed out homosexuals as security risks from prominent positions'.

The late 1940s and early 1950s in Britain witnessed an increased persecution of male homosexuals inspired by the appointment of a new and ardently Roman Catholic Director of Public Prosecutions in 1944 and two Home Secretaries hostile to homosexuality, Herbert Morrison and Sir David Maxwell-Fyfe. Prosecutions reached a peak in 1953. While prosecutions for indecent assault, for example, had been 82 in 1938, they were 3,305 in 1953. But this witchhunt led to a revulsion in public and sexological sentiment. Kenneth Walker railed against the retention of any laws against homosexuality and against this use of terror.

It was formerly asserted that homosexuals were only prosecuted when their behaviour became so scandalous that it was impossible for the police to refrain from taking action. This is no longer true for a directive has obviously gone out to the effect that the streets must be 'cleaned up', and as a result the courts are full of these unfortunate cases.[135]

It was not true, he explained, that homosexuality was on the increase. It was just that 'at one period it has been recognised and regarded as permissible and at another discountenanced and driven underground'.

It might have been expected that the 'sexual revolution' of the sixties would be liberating for lesbians and gay men. In some ways it may have been so, but the sexual revolution was a heterosexual revolution and any impulse towards gay liberation was a purely accidental offshoot. Many of the supposedly most progressive prophets of the new sexual freedom remained afraid of or hostile to homosexuality.

Chapter 2

DECENSORSHIP

Norman Mailer is an American novelist notorious for his misogyny whose writing was critically analysed in Kate Millett's *Sexual Politics* in 1971. He describes the battle of publishers and their legal representatives against the obscenity laws in the late 1950s and early 1960s as being like the American Civil War. The publishers were the fearless generals likened to Sherman and Grant who 'are determined to take a hill even if it takes all summer and chews up half their resources'.[1] Charles Rembar, the lawyer who defended the publishers, was 'one of Lee's lieutenants'. He was also Mailer's cousin. Mailer, writing of their boyhood relationship, says, 'I worshipped him . . . because he was a hero.' This opening to Rembar's account of his campaign against the obscenity laws has all the pomp and circumstance of the introduction to a life of Alexander the Great. But the basis on which Rembar is accorded heroic status is rather different. He didn't fight confederate generals or Persians but he did, apparently, win a war.

> A war has been won. Writers like myself can now in America write about any subject; if it is sexual, and we are explicit, no matter, the American writer has his freedom.[2]

The same war was being waged in England at this time. John Sutherland, author of a study of decensorship in Britain from 1960–82, also uses the terminology of warfare to describe this epic conflict. He writes that 'the road to freedom from censorship over the period 1960–1977 is best conceived as a series of rushing advances, encountered by stubborn rearguard and backlash actions.'³ Who were the enemy? In Britain, according to Sutherland, they were Mary Whitehouse, Lord Longford, Raymond Blackburn, David Holbrook, the Festival of Light. On both sides of the Atlantic they were seen as conservative and retrogressive, as the forces of darkness which were deservedly vanquished by the bearers of sexual freedom. Eberhard and Phyllis Kronhausen, whose book *Pornography and the Law* was a piece of campaigning literature for the anti-censors, describe the motivation of the censors thus:

> Those who advocate censorship of erotic materials . . . are either overtly – as in the case of Christian orthodoxy – or tacitly subscribers to the Pauline doctrine of Carnal Sin, whether they realise this connection or not. They cannot regard the natural manifestations of the sexual drive as something quite 'beyond good and evil'. Instead, they are conditioned to feel – by the strength of their inner convictions, instilled by religious and other educational processes of one kind or another – that sex is inherently evil, dirty, and dangerous, or at least potentially so, if not carefully checked and circumscribed by a number of social prohibitions.⁴

So the antagonists were the heroic progressives versus the reactionary prudes. This is the standard interpretation of writers on the sexual revolution, who all see decensorship as a vital component of the revolution. A basic building block of the supposed liberation that was to sweep the West in the 1960s was the right to write about sex without falling foul of the censorship laws. At first sight this does not look controversial, but when we look at the battle in more detail it looks less and less like a jousting match between the knights of darkness and the defenders of freedom.

The much-vaunted great works of literature and sexual openness that the contest centred upon were, according to their admirers, simply telling the truth about sex. Those who opposed such work, they averred, simply objected to and were afraid of sex. This was in the days before the development of a feminist critique of pornography. The books, which were all by men, included D. H. Lawrence's *Lady Chatterley's Lover*, Hubert

Selby's *Last Exit to Brooklyn*, Vladimir Nabokov's *Lolita*, and William Burroughs' *The Naked Lunch*. When we look at the sexual values portrayed in the books we discover female submission and male aggression, male sexual abuse of female children, sadomasochism. The 'truth' about sex that these books reveal does not seem to be anything to do with relationships of equality and mutuality between adults of any gender or sexual orientation. The script laid out in them was, I suggest, the script that was largely followed in the 'sexual revolution' that was to follow. Attention paid to deciphering the sexual script set out here helps to clarify how 'sexual liberation' failed to be the liberation of women.

Rembar, that lionheart of defence lawyers, believed that breaking down obscenity law would allow 'truth' to prevail. As an American he argued on the basis of first amendment rights, i.e. the right to freedom of speech enshrined in the US constitution. The anti-censors have always argued that their fight for sexual literature was a fight for the freedom to speak about socialism too. So long as there was the true mixing of tongues that would result from freedom of speech, they claimed, then truth would out. The message that the public chose would be what they genuinely wanted and what was good for them. To explain this point, Rembar quotes a judge on the issue of truth.

In the free interchange of ideas, the truth will emerge. 'The best test of truth,' said Justice Holmes, 'is the power of the thought to get itself accepted in the competition of the market.'[5]

If we accept this idea then we are forced to accept also that the sexual values currently promoted by the massive porn industry are the 'truth' about sex. They have won undoubtedly. Through the defence of certain dubious books the market was opened up for the truth to be victorious. The free-market argument does of course have some serious flaws. It rules out any grasp of the politics of oppression. Not all groups in society have equal access to the resources, influence and power to saturate the environment with their 'truth' so that the people get a chance to be converted. Moreover, in systems of oppression it is in the interests of those who benefit that the oppression continue, so even should the oppressed by some miracle gain real access to the media, there are good practical reasons why the beneficiaries might fail to be converted.

The Kronhausens were convinced that books such as *Lady Chatterley's Lover*, *Lolita*, etc. represent the 'truth' about sex. They describe such works as 'erotic realism' and distinguish them from pornography which they see as being about fantasy. One might be excused for thinking that this was a rather moot distinction. Could it mean that the situations described in *Last Exit*, such as the gang rape of Tra-la-la, are documentary, and simply replicate events known in detail to the author? No one has claimed such verisimilitude. The contentious works were seen as works of fiction and indeed it was put forward in their defence that they were great works of literature, rather than journalism. Since the Kronhausens believed that these novels simply told the truth, then we must assume that the books' content closely corresponds to the prejudices that this husband and wife team hold as to what sex 'is'. They see this truth about sex to be good and healthy and they recommend that all the books in question be used to teach children what sex 'is'.

> ... the ideal supplement to what the average enlightened home or school offers in the form of sex education would be books of erotic realism, such as Lawrence's *Lady Chatterley's Lover*, Wilson's *Memoirs of Hecate County*, or autobiographical works like *The Life and Loves of Frank Harris*. These books would connect that which the young person has learned in the way of sex anatomy and physiology with the lust mechanism and the appropriate emotional states which accompany sexuality under a variety of conditions.
>
> We have no doubt that this will be the type of complete sex education which good homes and schools will offer in the not-so-distant future.[6]

Decensorship was a necessary preliminary step on the way to the 'sexual revolution'. The battle was won on the territory of books which were comprised of sexual values hostile to women's interests, and this value system became the understood 'truth' about sex for the succeeding decade. The mythology of the decensorship battle, i.e. that it was waged in the interests of truth, freedom and justice for the good of all humankind, is very pervasive and provides a solid barrier against feminist challenges to pornography. Any criticism of the wholesome world of pornography that decensorship brought us is seen not only as ingratitude but as potentially threatening to the rights and liberties of all peoples. Decensorship opened the floodgates for the porn industry. Without the potent propaganda tool that pornography provided it is possible that the ruthless woman-hatred of 'sexual liberation' could not have taken root. Works like *The Naked Lunch* do not have a very wide circulation compared with mass circulation pornography. It was inevitable that those men not keen on reading would demand a less esoteric pornography, and that entrepreneurs would see the opportunities for profit that lay before them. Some of the publishers and defence lawyers were quite cynically aware that using the defence of literary merit to justify novels would form a wedge that would let in a wide range of other pornographic material. Some of those same lawyers now make good money defending material for which literary merit would be an inappropriate defence, i.e. stories and tapes about incest, bestiality, sadomasochism and Nazi death camps and the whole rich variety of womanhatred.

The British Obscene Publications Act of 1857 empowered magistrates to order the destruction of books and prints if, in their opinion, their publication would amount to a 'misdemeanour proper to be prosecuted as such'. The designers of the Act assured their critics that it was not intended to cover works of acknowledged literary or artistic merit. No definition of obscenity was offered at the time. In 1868 what became the standard test of obscenity was formulated in the judgment of Chief Justice Cockburn in the Hicklin case. He stated:

I think the test of obscenity is this, whether the tendency of the matter charged as obscenity is to deprave and corrupt those whose minds are open to such immoral influences, and into whose hands a publication of this sort may fall.[7]

The Cockburn test remained the basis of English obscenity law until the Obscene Publications Act of 1959. It was adopted in the US 11 years after it was formulated in Britain.

It was in the 1950s that the obscenity laws came under attack. Pressure groups of publishers and authors banded together to demand a change in the law. In the early 1950s prosecutions were mounted on many books in what appeared to be a crusade and this stimulated the demand for change. The arbitrary nature of laws which allowed action to rest on police initiative and depended upon the political complexion and sexual politics of chief constables seemed inappropriate in the postwar world.

During the 1950s books which could not have been published in Britain because of the political climate were produced in English language editions in Paris by the Olympia Press of Maurice Girodias. The Press was founded in 1953 to 'see how far I could go, single-handed, in a deliberate attempt to destroy censorship as a moral institution, as a tradition, as a method of government'.[8] Girodias published books which he considered to have literary merit as well as straightforward pornography. The books considered to have literary merit were by men who wrote odes to the practice of aggressive male sexuality, several of which became the subject of obscenity trials in Britain or the US in the 1960s. They included the works of Henry Miller and Jean Genet, Lolita, and The Naked Lunch. The Olympia pornographic titles for which no defence of literary merit was made included Who Pushed Paula?, White Thighs, The Chariot of Flesh, The Story of O, Whipsdom and The Sexual Life of Robinson Crusoe. The result of Girodias' personal crusade to 'rehabilitate sex and eroticism' was that the books which were to form the core material of the anti-censorship platform were perfectly familiar to their male defenders despite the British censorship laws.

The 1959 Act retained the 'likely to deprave and corrupt' definition of obscenity but liberalised the previous law in several ways. One was that the book must be looked at as a whole and not just acted against on the grounds of passages taken out of context. Another was that the book must be seen as likely to deprave and corrupt not just any schoolgirl but the average person. The publishers were provided with the defence of 'innocent dissemination' and publishers and authors the defence of literary or other merit. It was this last change which was deemed most useful and tested immediately with the publication of *Lady Chatterley's Lover*.

LITERARY MERIT

The 'erotic realist' works of the 1950s and 60s which were to be defended against accusations of obscenity with the defence of literary merit included two books we will look at in detail here. These are William Burroughs' *The Naked Lunch* and Vladimir Nabokov's *Lolita*. An analysis of the books shows us that no real distinction can be drawn between 'pornography' and works of literary merit when the values demonstrated in such literature and in pornography about women and sex are identical. The defence of literary merit allowed books containing such values to be published and, not surprisingly, ushered in a massive pornography industry.

It was a matter of accident that the first prosecution under the new Act was of Penguin Books, the publishers of *Lady Chatterley's Lover*, rather than of Weidenfeld and Nicolson who published *Lolita* in hardback in 1959. In 1928 D. H. Lawrence had sought, unsuccessfully, to get *Lady Chatterley* published in Britain and had been forced to self-publish in Florence. Penguin's 1960 paperback edition was the first British publication. Sutherland suggests that the Lawrence novel was picked upon because the language was more scatological, and the price cheap. The English ruling class considered that erotic literature might be viewed without harmful effect by ex-public schoolboys, but should not fall into the hands of the working classes.

Penguin produced a first run of 200,000 and sent a dozen copies to the Director of Public Prosecutions, inviting him to rule on the obscenity of *Lady Chatterley* and being prepared to fight against a prosecution. The DPP decided to prosecute and the defence counsel collected 35 witnesses to testify to the 'public good' of the novel. These witnesses included eight literary academics, and respected novelists such as E. M. Forster. T. S. Eliot waited outside the court, as did many others, but was not called. The defence concentrated on proving that Lawrence's novel was clean and good, a kind of literary Epsom salts, rather than on literary merit. This may be because literary critics saw *Lady Chatterley* as a rather embarrassing book, not up to the standard of Lawrence's usual work. F. R. Leavis was the literary critic most responsible for constructing Lawrence's reputation as Britain's foremost twentieth-century novelist. He declined to testify at the trial because he did not think the novel was great literature. But the appearance of academics and writers of 'great' literature as witnesses ensured that literary merit was added to the other social reasons for seeing *Lady Chatterley* as not obscene. The defence of *Lady Chatterley* in the us, by Charles Rembar, was based solely on the idea of literary merit.

Kate Millett has written an excellent analysis of *Lady Chatterley* in *Sexual Politics* and it is not necessary to go into detail about its contents here. Millett explains that the book is 'a quasi-religious tract recounting the salvation of one modern woman... through the offices of the author's personal cult, "the mystery of the phallus" '.[9] Millett gives a clear feminist analysis of the values implicit in the sexual activity which takes place in the novel.

> The scenes of sexual intercourse in the novel are written according to the 'female is passive, male is active' directions laid down by Sigmund Freud. The phallus is all; Connie (Lady Chatterley) is 'cunt', the thing acted upon, gratefully accepting each manifestation of the will of her master.[10]

The section of the book in which Connie becomes a 'woman' demonstrates these values particularly well. During an act of sexual intercourse Connie felt unable to love Mellors and was unable to feel any respect for his penis. This was because she felt 'inward resistance'. But suddenly she gave in emotionally and was able to experience, with appropriate awe, an act of penetration. As she gave in she felt 'small' (the adjective is much repeated), she melted, she 'yielded with a quiver that was like death, she went all open to him... open and helpless'.[11] The penis was experienced like a 'thrust of a sword in her softly opened body' and she found herself in 'peace' because she 'held nothing' and had 'dared let go everything, all herself, and be gone in the flood'. The high point of her orgasm in response to this sword thrust is described as having her innermost being touched, in Lawrence's rather quaint wording the 'quick of all her plasm'. Lawrence tells us 'the consummation was upon her, and she was gone. She was gone, she was not, and she was born: a woman.' What has happened? In this religious experience Connie has given up her separate human existence, her Self, individuality and independence in order to become a worshipper of the phallus and of an individual man. Loathsome though such masochism may be when it appears in religion, at least it is required of men too. In this phallic religion only women died as human beings in order to be reborn as 'woman' defined as a submissive worshipper.

Such sentiments are not the stuff of pornographic writing alone. Sexological writings at the time of the original publication of *Lady Chatterley* were even more blatant than later sexology in dictating that sexual intercourse should properly lead to the destruction of the woman's separate existence as a whole human being and create her into a submissive handmaiden. In 1926 the analyst Wilhelm Stekel's two volumes on frigidity in women were published. He defined dyspareunia or the failure to achieve orgasm in sexual intercourse thus: 'Obstinacy cancels the will to submission and reopens the struggle for the maintenance of the feeling of personality.'[12] In the *Lady Chatterley* episode described above, Connie's struggle to remain a personality ended.

This theme is common to pornography and forms the story of that famous Olympia Press classic *The Story of O* which was first published in Britain in 1970. This book describes the chosen and willingly embraced annihilation of a woman's self and personality through sexual violence and humiliation, to the point where she is willing to embrace death. It has recently been hailed by sexual libertarians as a work of literature and a liberating book for women's sexuality. This was the response of sexual libertarians to the publication of *Lady Chatterley* in the US. The Kronhausens were ecstatic about the accuracy of Lawrence in describing what sex was and should be about for women. About the passage quoted earlier they comment:

> The above passage from *Lady Chatterley's Lover* is unsurpassed in the beautiful and entirely correct interpretation of what occurs – psychologically – when a female in her association with a real man truly becomes a woman.[13]

These are the writers, we should remember, who congratulate all the works that were controversial in the 1960s as 'erotic realism'.

What then is the difference between 'art' and pornography? The Kronhausens do not use this vocabulary though they spend some energy on the problem. They distinguish between 'erotic realism' and 'obscene' books but they do seem to have the age-old game of distinguishing between art and porn in mind. They explain that 'obscene' books have a 'general structure by which they can be distinguished from other types of writing'.[14] This structure is as follows:

> A book which is designed to act upon the reader as an erotic psychological stimulant ('aphrodisiac') must constantly keep before the reader's mind a succession of erotic scenes. It must not tire him with superfluous non-erotic descriptions of scenery, character portrayals, or lengthy philosophical expositions.[15]

Erotic realist literature on the other hand, contained material which was not just directed to arousal. Also, they say, it 'attempts to portray life as it is, or as it appears to the author, whereas "obscene" books are products of sheer fantasy'.[16] In erotic realist literature, the build-up to sexual arousal may be interrupted by what they describe as 'anti-erotic' material. These are such matters as 'pregnancy, venereal disease, illness in general, death, economic distress, and similar concerns'. The Kronhausens do not seem deeply worried by a concept of 'art' *per se*, which is refreshing.

Those who do worry about 'art' and try to define the difference find themselves in great difficulties. Bernard Williams was

Chair of the Williams Commission on Obscenity and Film Censorship. He recognised that some forms of literature could be considered sexist, but such literature was not 'art' because it was popular literature. He concluded that 'there is some truth, if only some, in the idea that mass-circulation soft-core pornography is sexist primarily because anything mass-circulated is sexist'.[17] Suzanne Kappeler cuts through the hypocrisy of such thinking in her book *The Pornography of Representation*. She comments:

> There is something 'sexist', certainly faintly (softly) pornographic in the idea of mass circulation. It makes MacDonald's hamburgers distinctly less palatable than those of some other restaurant. It means above all that private, individualistic pornography, in the privacy of your home or in the limited luxury edition of some publisher of taste, may be rescuable from the assignation to 'mass pornography' as a phenomenon of 'popular culture' ... The quality of 'obscenity' or the pornographic is thus not located in the representation itself, but in its distribution.[18]

On this basis Williams was able to judge that *Inside Linda Lovelace* was not in itself a work of 'literature'. Another distinction that Kappeler identifies between what is classified as art and what is classified as pornography, is the status of the director or author. Work with nothing but sexual content by an unknown might be classified as pornography but similar work with nothing but sex would be seen as art if it was by 'anyone one has heard of', in the words of a Frenchman struggling with this difficulty.

Kappeler analyses the critical reception of D. M. Thomas' novel *The White Hotel*, published in 1981, in order to show how these distinctions are made. This novel contains material which is accepted as pornographic by the critics, straightforward descriptions of abusive and objectifying sex, written from a woman's viewpoint. Thomas sandwiched his sexual description in material which was not just about sex. In fact, as Kappeler makes clear, he did this quite deliberately. He set out to build a book around a pornographic poem he had already written so that the erotic material could be published and accepted as a novel and a work of art. His work was accepted as a work of art and received critical acclaim. Its acceptance as 'art' was facilitated by the fact that he was someone that the critics had heard of.

The process of promoting pornographic writing as art can be clearly seen in discussion and argument elicited by Burroughs' *The Naked Lunch*.

THE NAKED LUNCH

William Burroughs' *The Naked Lunch* was not the subject of a prosecution in Britain but suffered what Sutherland calls 'trial by *TLS*'. It was particularly indigestible because it concerned not 'just sex' as *Lady Chatterley* might be seen to do, but pederasty, cannibalism and necrophilia. *The Times Literary Supplement* reviewed the book when there was no hint of it being published in Britain, apparently as a preemptive strike which would express outrage and warn against publication. In Boston in the US it was banned until 1966 when the ban was reversed on the grounds that the book was a work of art. Michael Goodman in his 'case history' of *The Naked Lunch* describes these events. He sees the book as 'the last work of literature to be proscribed in this nation's struggle between its belief in free expression and its Puritan heritage'.[19] *The Naked Lunch* was Burroughs' second book. His first book *Junkie* was published in New York in 1953. *The Naked Lunch* was offered to Maurice Girodias of Olympia Press in 1957 and published by him in 1959. In 1962 it was published by Grove Press in America and was first published in Britain in 1964.

Burroughs has gained a considerable reputation as a writer since then though, as his editor John Calder laments, he has been most highly regarded in countries in continental Europe where there is a tradition of experimental art, and regarded with some suspicion in insular Britain and puritan America. His main enemies in Europe, Calder explains, have been Marxists who resented his attacks on targets 'as much of the left as of the right'. Norman Mailer described Burroughs as the only living

American writer of genius.[20] Calder describes his achievement thus:

> A master of dialogue, a creator of character without a contemporary equal, a humorist who gets funnier as his subject-matter gets blacker, and a first-class storyteller, he belongs to that small circle of writers who improve on continued acquaintance and have the ability to extend our awareness of the world in which we live and all its possibilities, good and bad.'[21]

Certain details of Burroughs' life are relevant if we are to understand how he came to be something of a cult figure. He was born into a family which had made its wealth through industrial machines, in St Louis, Missouri in 1914. He went to Harvard in the 1930s. He was rejected from the army in the Second World War as a 'schizophrenic-paranoid type'. He was arrested as a material witness in a New York City homicide case in the 1940s, busted for drugs in New Orleans and fled to Mexico City where he killed his wife. The killing of his wife is called an accident by all commentators and he was released from police custody after only a few days for what Calder calls a '*crime d'imprudence*' with no charges being pressed. The 'accident' happened during an incident which Calder describes thus: 'They were in the habit of playing William Tell and shooting apples off each other's heads.'[22] He was a junkie, a friend of beat heroes like Kerouac and Ginsberg. In 1954 he went to live in a male brothel in Tangier. Later he flew to London seeking a cure for drug addiction. The writing of *The Naked Lunch* was the result of his cure.

Burroughs, then, had a perfect pedigree to be a particular type of American cultural hero. He was and still is obsessed with guns and violence and keeps a large collection of weapons in his bedroom. He has killed a woman. He has lived an appropriately decadent lifestyle with drugs and use of prostitutes. He is homosexual and his main interest is in boys. That does not fit so well into the notion of the hero and Burroughs does not show pride in his homosexuality. Therefore Burroughs, according to Calder, 'is no apologist for militant homosexual causes, keeps his private life strictly private and writes to put over a world view that has no partisan bias other than sounding warnings and revealing the world that he sees around him'.[23] Though homosexuality figured largely in the lives of the beat heroes like Ginsberg and Kerouac, this was in the days before gay liberation when homosexuality was not celebrated. Indeed the beat phenomenon was aggressively macho and organised around an exclusively masculine and apparently heterosexual ethos.

The Naked Lunch does not correspond to commonsense understandings of what novels should be. There is no story. There is not even a consistent subject under discussion. The manuscript was put together 'by chance ... with pages from earlier work occasionally falling into it by accident'.[24] It is easy to see why it is called experimental. It consists of scenes which are each quite unrelated to any other and have neither beginnings nor ends. It starts with a 'junkie's first-person narrative'. Then as Calder describes:

> Many of the sections that follow show highly unconventional, imaginative and sadistic sexual activity, some of it more erotic to homosexuals than heterosexuals, but all intended to stress the connection, now well known to psychiatry and to anthropology, between sex and death and sex and cruelty.[25]

The sexual scenes do not have a story either. The sadistic sex which takes place is simply written according to the rules of pornography, i.e. no characterisation or plot. *The Naked Lunch* was the last of Burroughs' books to contain heterosexual as well as male homosexual activity. Subsequently Burroughs wrote only about sex between males. The following example should give a fair impression of the tone of this writing.

> She locks her hands behind Johnny's buttocks, puts her forehead against him, smiling into his eyes she moves back, pulling him off the platform into space ... His face swells with blood ... Mark reaches up with one lithe movement and snaps Johnny's neck ... sound like a stick broken in wet towels. A shudder runs down Johnny's body ... One foot flutters like a trapped bird ... Mark has draped himself over

71

a swing and mimics Johnny's twitches, closes his eyes and sticks his tongue out ... Johnny's cock springs up and Mary guides it up her cunt, writhing against him in a fluid belly dance ... Mark reaches over with the snap knife and cuts the rope, catching Johnny as he falls, easing him onto his back with Mary still impaled and writhing ... She bites away Johnny's lips and nose and sucks out his eyes with a pop ... She tears off great chunks of cheek ... Now she lunches on his prick.[26]

Hanging is a dominant theme of Burroughs' writing. Generally it is youths who are hanged to delight audiences of adult males who ejaculate as the boys die. In Burroughs' most recent book, *Cities of the Red Night*, 1981, hanging is still the dominant theme.[27] In that book nearly everyone moves around with the mark of a noose round their neck from previous hanging sessions. Hanging is a sexual activity not uncommon among sadomasochists. The custom is to cease the strangulation just after the tremendously enhanced orgasms which are supposed, for the men who practise it, to result from this activity. Stephen Adams, in *The Homosexual as Hero in Literature*, suggests that Burroughs' fascination with hanging derives from guilt about his homosexuality, which drives him to mortify the flesh in order to achieve sexual pleasure and even to seek the destruction of the guilty body.[28]

Burroughs' writing indicates a horror of sexuality. Sex is associated not just with death but with defecation, disability and disease, the female genitals, everything which it seems that Burroughs found most horrifying. In another sequence there is hanging, physical disability, faeces and disease.

Aztec priests strip blue feather robe from the Naked Youth ... A waterfall pours over the skull snapping the boy's neck. He ejaculates in a rainbow against the rising sun. Sharp protein odor of semen fills the air. The guests run hands over twitching boys, suck their cocks, hang on their backs like vampires. Naked lifeguards carry in iron-lungs full of paralysed youths. Blind boys grope out of huge pies, deteriorated schizophrenics pop from under a rubber cunt, boys with horrible skin diseases rise from a black pond (sluggish fish nibble yellow turds on the surface).[29]

Lest any readers find themselves gagging at this material, Calder tells us how we should be reacting to it. He explains: '. . . it must be stressed that reading Burroughs is not only a fascinating, if alarming, intellectual adventure, but also a very enjoyable one.'[30] Not all readers were enchanted, despite Calder's instructions. *The Times Literary Supplement* reviewer entitled the review 'Ugh', and described Burroughs' work as '. . . glug, glug. It tastes disgusting . . . pure verbal masturbation . . . vomit . . . unspeakable homosexual fantasies'.[31] Edith Sitwell wrote in that she did not wish to 'spend the rest of my life with my nose nailed to other people's lavatories'.[32] Victor Gollancz, publisher of the thirties Left Book Club, described Burroughs' work as 'bogus-highbrow filth', as 'life-denying; spiritually as well as physically disgusting, and tasteless to an almost incredible degree, it offends against value of any kind (including intellectual value) every bit as much as against public decency'.[33] Unlike contemporary feminists Sitwell and Gollancz did not have a political language in which to express their objections to *The Naked Lunch*, so the language of personal disgust could be easily dismissed as bourgeois moralism.

But at least they were prepared to say that the Emperor had no clothes on while Burroughs' literary reputation was promoted. Those who objected to Burroughs' work were described by his apologists as puritan America. Usually the battle between the puritans and the sexual liberators is portrayed as a polarisation between those who are anti-sex and those who are seen as pro-sex. When we look at what Burroughs was saying about sex then this distinction seems quite inaccurate. There seems to be an area of common ground between the two teams. Whatever Burroughs was liberating, it wasn't sex, and he seems to have been about as anti-sex as it would be possible to get. Like many of the supposed sexual liberators of the 1960s and 70s he seems to have been unable to associate sex with anything but lavatories, shit, death, or disease.

Those who, like Calder, contend that *The Naked Lunch* is indeed a work of art, rather than simply the exposition of

Burroughs' sadomasochistic fantasies have invented a sophisticated social purpose for Burroughs' obsession with hanging. It was to 'make readers aware of the connection between the urge to kill or torture and sexual desire, in order to stop cruelty through self-awareness in the same way as Swift advocated eating babies to cure the Irish famine . . .'[34] Could it be that Burroughs' collection of guns and the killing of his wife were all intended towards the same purpose of stopping cruelty? It seems a strange way to go about it. Similarly, writing about cruelty in a way which arouses his readers seems a rather odd way to stop it. Ginsberg, in his evidence at the trial, explained that Burroughs wrote about his sexual fantasies so that 'by becoming conscious of his own fetishistic stimuli he becomes free of his obsessional imagery'.[35] This does not explain why he needed to foist his fantasies on the reading public. Presumably he could have kept a secret diary for this therapeutic activity. Moreover it does not explain why he has continued to write down exactly the same fantasies for 30 years. It does not seem an effective form of therapy.

According to his publisher, Girodias, Burroughs was his ideal writer because he was a 'visionary whose books could arouse sexually as well as change the way we view the world, a genius maudit in the tradition of Sade'.[36] If this genius wanted to change the world, what was his project? Apparently he wanted to sever the connection between sex and love. Love, he claimed, was 'a fraud perpetrated by the female sex' and sexual relations between men were not to do with love but 'what we might call recognition'.[37] Burroughs was astute in recognising that women required more of life and relationships than simply constant cruising with the object of sadomasochistic sexual encounters with strangers. He may have been dimly aware that women recognised that such a form of sexuality in men was damaging to their interests and continued existence, as in the case of Burroughs' unfortunate wife, Joan Volhere.

Burroughs devised a solution to the problem of women's opposition to his grand plan. Women had to be eliminated. Burroughs explains the problem of the existence of women thus:

In the words of one of the great misogynists, plain Mr Jones, in Conrad's *Victory*, 'Women are a perfect curse.' I think they were a basic mistake, and the whole dualistic universe evolved from this error.[38]

Women were unregenerately anti-sexual by their very nature and poisoned society with their baleful influence, particularly in those societies he saw as matriarchal such as America. They were, he decided, responsible for the control of consciousness through suppression of eroticism and the supremacy of the family. Women were not just responsible for making the world anti-sex by inventing love and thus making men's lives miserable, they were even responsible for racism!

The whole Southern worship of women and white supremacy is still the policy of America. It's a matriarchal, white supremacist country. There seems to be a very definite link between matriarchy and white supremacy.[39]

Burroughs had plans to ensure that boy children never had contact with women because 'boys who have never had contact with women would be quite a different animal' and would therefore never be contaminated into thinking that sex could be anything other than what he intended. This was to be achieved by cloning of boys from cells in men's intestines to produce 'identical twins of people [i.e. men] gifted with exceptional ability or beauty'.[40] All these themes appear frequently in Burroughs' books. *The Naked Lunch* is full of diatribes against matriarchy, which is held responsible for creating hostility to homosexuality. *The Wild Boys* (1972) presents a Burroughs fantasy which, in an interview in May 1972, he is prepared to call both a desirable scenario and a prediction. In this fantasy boys are parthenogenetically created via anal intercourse, and grow up uncontaminated by women, to live in violent gangs dedicated to killing each other in different ways. *The Soft Machine* (1968) proposed the separation of the sexes in childrearing and education until women became unnecessary.

The interview in which Burroughs so enthusiastically expressed his womanhatred appeared in *Rolling Stone*, one of the new papers of the alternative culture which came into being in the heyday of the 'sexual revolution'. Burroughs was revered in magazines such as *Oz* and *International Times* as the father of the sexual revolution. At a time when women's liberation was already under way as a movement on both sides of the Atlantic, alternative magazines found it unproblematic to promote as a liberator a man who sought the elimination of women. The importance of Burroughs' work lies not just in the fact that it was one of the most notorious to fall foul of obscenity legislation in this period, but in its centrality to the sexual revolution. Burroughs was the darling of the counterculture. The beat writers in general were recognised as progenitors, but Burroughs was picked out for special reverence. It was not an accident that Burroughs was chosen for this acclaim. The values represented in his work, of fear and hatred of women and sexuality, were central to the 'sexual revolution' which the counterculturalists saw themselves as carrying out in his name.

LOLITA

Vladimir Nabokov's *Lolita* is a book which benefited from the 1959 Act and was able to be published in Britain without prosecution. It was first published by Girodias' Olympia Press in 1955. Copies were seized by the British customs. The book was denounced in the Press. John Gordon of the *Sunday Express* wrote: 'Without doubt it is the filthiest book I have ever read. Sheer unrestrained pornography.'[41] In 1959 *Lolita* was published in Britain by the eminently respectable Weidenfeld and Nicolson. Similarly, in the US copies of the Olympia Press edition were seized but then the work was cleared and ran into no further difficulty. Though the book did not have to be defended in a court of law, it was sufficiently controversial to call forth the enthusiastic testimonials of critics and novelists.

The Kronhausens were, as we might expect, sure that *Lolita* was a good example of erotic realism. They describe the novel as a 'realistic tragedy'.[42] The book describes the sexual use by an adult man of a twelve-year-old girl. Whose then was the tragedy? The tragedy was that of the abuser who was 'compulsively driven to pre-pubertal girls by psychological forces beyond his conscious control from within, and harassed by exploitative and intolerant forces from the social environment without'.[43] So the abuser suffered a tragedy because he suffered uncontrollable urges and wasn't able to express them with complete impunity. The Kronhausens expressed the hope that the book would make readers more sympathetic to this 'not too uncommon sexual deviation'.

The girl does not get the same kind of sympathy from the Kronhausens because they see the whole affair as her fault. The abuser was actually the unfortunate victim of her wiles.

> Nabokov's novel also correctly conveys the idea that in spite of the man's fixation on young girls, it was really Lolita herself who teased and seduced him into the affair, and that it was not her adult lover who corrupted the morals of this minor. This is a significant aspect of Nabokov's story, because sexological research bears out the fact − contrary to public opinion − that Lolita's case is more often the rule than the exception.[44]

The Kronhausens are correct in suggesting that sexological writing on the sexual abuse of girls has always blamed the child survivors of abuse as seductive, precipitating, willing and so on. For a profession whose role was to justify and uphold men's sexual prerogative this was entirely logical. The idea that men who abuse children are in fact the victims of those children might seem bizarre at first sight and the Kronhausens are at pains to use the 'scientific' research to back them up because they know that 'public opinion' is likely to take a commonsense view. Pro-pornography lobbyists have long claimed that pornography has no effect on the formation of people's opinions, and that it therefore did not matter if some books contained rather inaccurate or unfortunate ideas abut sexual abuse. The Kronhausens, who are defenders of pornography, tell us that Lolita will definitely change and form attitudes. It will cause the public to feel sympathy for abusers and to realise that the abused children cause their own abuse and victimise adult men.

It seems likely that the Kronhausens were right about the book's effect. Its main legacy seems to have been to spread the sexological orthodoxy of the 'seductive' child among a broad public. The book and the film have made the name Lolita a household word for the seductive child. It seems that the message the Kronhausens hoped would be learned from the book has been learned very well. A 1966 book by Russell Trainer entitled *The Lolita Complex* demonstrates the effectiveness of this learning. It is a work of popular sexology which provides a vehicle for the author to describe the sexual abuse of children all over the world and in history, presumably for the titillation of his male audience. Russell Trainer claimed that 'Lolitaism' was spreading in American society. The sexual abuse of girls is here transformed into 'Lolitaism'. The agency is removed from the male abuser who is indeed scarcely mentioned, to become a problem caused by and consisting in sexually active young girls. This sleight of hand is reminiscent of the way in which male writers on prostitution have traditionally written as if women performed prostitution all on their own to themselves. The male abuser disappears in such work too, and prostitution becomes a problem created by women.

Trainer did not rely on the evidence of *Lolita*. He quotes psychiatrists to support the idea that girls are seductive. Dr Linus Foster explains:

> Young girls who become sexually involved with men are different from other girls. They almost signal their desires. They're flirtatious. They actually sometimes tease. Signs like these aren't easy to ignore, especially for the man who has a low threshold for girls. A clinician recognises the signs of a young girl's seductiveness immediately.[45]

It is easy enough to understand how a clinician can reach such conclusions. Presumably he feels sexually attracted to the girl. Unable to take responsibility for his own sexual interest in children, because it makes him feel uncomfortable and not as objective as he should be, he decides that the girl is seductive. Even psychiatrists, some of the most powerful males in a male supremacist society, find it convenient to give young girls, arguably the least powerful group in any society, total responsibility for how the adult male feels and acts.

Trainer proceeded to articulate many of the other myths which have enabled men to hide or excuse sexual abuse. Children lie, he argued, and 'almost always' cannot be relied upon in court. 'Children,' he says,'are given to fancying and imagining, it has been stated authoritatively.'[46] He saw children who were murdered by their abusers as responsible for their deaths. One murdered child, who was physically disabled, is described as having an inner quality of attractiveness. In a chapter entitled 'Who are the Lolitas?' Trainer tells us how to recognise them: 'Lolitas pout and primp. They giggle. They cry. They're shy and introspective or bold and noisy . . .'[47] He covers all bases here. Just about any child then, can qualify as a Lolita. All that is required is that she be abused by a man and then her personality characteristics can be used to classify her as a Lolita. In *Lolita* the narrator describes the 'nymphet' as having 'certain mysterious characteristics . . . the fey grace, the elusive, shifty, soul-shattering, insidious charm that separates the nymphet from such coevals of hers'.[48]

The hero of *Lolita*, Humbert Humbert, comes to lodge in the house of a woman who has a twelve-year-old daughter. Humbert develops a sexual passion for the girl. The mother proposes marriage to the hero. He has no real interest in her because he is unable to stand adult women, but marries her because it would assure him of access to the girl. The wife he married in Europe before emigrating to the US is described as becoming, immediately after marriage, 'a large, puffy, short-legged, big-breasted and practically brainless baba'.[49] Sex with Lolita's mother is described thus: '. . . I bayed through the undergrowth of dark decaying forests.'[50] Whilst Lolita's mother was alive Humbert did not have direct sexual access to the child. He was forced to get his satisfaction indirectly, through, for example, getting her positioned on his lap in such a way as to occasion erection and ejaculation. He describes this as managing to 'attune' 'my masked lust to her guileless limbs'.

The frotteurist scene is written in the classic pornographic style of the nineteenth century. Lolita is called the 'little maiden'. His erection is described as 'the hidden tumour of an unspeakable passion' and a 'gagged, bursting beast' and contrasted with the 'beauty of her dimpled body in its innocent cotton frock'. The whole scene is described as a 'self-made seraglio' in which a 'robust Turk' enjoyed 'the youngest and frailest of his slaves'.[51] Nabokov uses the word limbs instead of legs and athwart instead of across. The style is coy and the language archaic, perhaps to confuse the reader into thinking he is reading something much more artistic and subtle than straightforward porn. Such famous Victorian pornography as *My Secret Life* by 'Walter' makes use of similar contrasts between beauty and lust and gives endless accounts of successful male 'importunity' winning out against female resistance in a vein very similar to that of Nabokov. It seems likely that Nabokov was influenced by such texts. Male intellectuals seem to favour Victorian pornography over contemporary versions because material enriched with the patina of age can seem more learned and less vulgar.

The mother dies in a road accident when Lolita is at summer camp. Humbert goes to pick her up and takes her on a trip telling her her mother is ill in hospital. They stay at a hotel and Humbert drugs her with sleeping pills intending to 'pursue my policy of sparing her purity by operating only in the stealth of night, only upon a completely anaesthetised little nude'.[52] His efforts are thwarted the first night because the sleeping pills are not efficient. Then in the morning, according to Humbert, Lolita seduces him. Nabokov writes 'I am going to tell you something very strange: it was she who seduced me.'[53] Lolita is described as orchestrating the whole event and organising a passive Humbert into an act of sexual intercourse on the basis of her previous experience and knowledge. Lolita had had sexual experience, we discover, with a girlfriend and a boy of 13. But the act with an adult man, we are told, proved unexpectedly difficult because of the size of Humbert's penis. Humbert asserts that Lolita was 'eager to impress' him with 'the world of tough kids', but was in difficulties when she discovered 'certain discrepancies between a kid's life and mine'. She continued because 'pride' would not allow her to give up.[54] Nabokov describes Lolita as complaining on the next day of pain from having been damaged. Doubtless the idea that the child should be in pain is a particularly titillating detail to the pornophile. It adds a sadistic frisson to the eroticised dominance and submission scenario. Humbert feels relieved of responsibility for the event because Lolita is not a virgin. He comments 'Did I deprive her of her flower?' and tells 'gentlewomen of the jury' that he was not 'even her first lover'.[55]

From this point on in the novel, it is clear that Lolita is enslaved to Humbert and forced into sex. She becomes reluctant after the first night and wants to call her mother in hospital. Humbert tells her her mother is dead. Thereafter she is entirely dependent on Humbert and in no position to refuse sex. Humbert explains that they had separate rooms at the hotel and Lolita came into his room in the middle of the night sobbing. They made it up very gently because 'she had absolutely nowhere else to go'.[56]

For the next two years Humbert takes Lolita around America as his prisoner. Eventually she is able to escape. It is astonishing that Lolita has become a generic term for a sexually willing and seductive girl when the girl in the novel was so clearly forced to submit to unwanted sex with the hero. Humbert describes her frequently as a slave, and that is precisely what she is. Various kinds of threat, force or persuasion are used to get Lolita to allow Humbert to use her body. On one occasion Humbert complains that it would 'take hours of blandishments, threats and promises' to make her 'lend me for a few seconds her brown limbs' in the hotel room before she was allowed to do anything else she might want to do.[57] Humbert threatens Lolita that she will be sent to a reformatory if she tells anyone what is going on. This is described as 'terrorising Lo'.[58] He prepares coffee for her and will not give it to her until she submits to sexual intercourse.[59] He makes promises and withdraws them as soon as he has used Lolita, at which point she ends in tears.[60] He pays her and then gets worried that she will save enough money to run away from him, so he uses physical force to get Lo to show him where she hides the money. He forces her into sexual intercourse when she is ill with bronchitis, 'though it was a very languid Lolita that moaned and coughed and shivered in my embrace'.[61] Humbert is irritated that Lolita should be so determinedly sexually resistant. 'Never,' he complains, 'did she vibrate under my touch.'[62] He called her 'My Frigid Princess'.

This callous and brutal slave owner is the tragic hero towards whom apologists like the Kronhausens tell us *Lolita* will make us sympathetic. This abused and resisting girl is the archetype of the seductive nymphet. It is time to look at the critical comment that greeted *Lolita* in 1959 to see how the great arbiters of art classified the novel. Lionel Trilling tells us that the book is about 'love'.

> Lolita is about love. Perhaps I shall be better understood if I put the statement in this form: Lolita is not about sex, but about love. Almost every page sets forth some explicit erotic emotion or some overt erotic action and still it is not about sex. It is about love. This makes it unique in my experience of contemporary novels . . .

> In recent fiction no lover has thought of his beloved with so much tenderness . . . no woman has been so charmingly evoked, in such grace and delicacy, as Lolita; it is one of the few examples of rapture in modern writing.[63]

It doesn't sound as if he is writing about the same book but it seems that he is. This ability of a male critic to translate the sexual enslavement of a young girl into a great fiction about love is a warning to us. It is the chilling truth that the male literary establishment is in no position to comprehend feminist arguments about pornography and sexuality because to the dwellers in that establishment the enslavement of children for sexual abuse really can be seen as love. The author and the male reader are communicating with each other about what they see as love. This is a private conversation. Women are not expected to question the terms. Enslavement is a common motif in pornography, so we must assume that the idea of women or young girls made totally helpless so that they may be sexually abused must provide a particular satisfaction. The reluctance of the victim adds to the arousal.

Other male commentators were impressed by the humour of the book. Bernard Levin tells us that Lolita is 'enormously funny', and Terence Rattigan says it is 'very funny'.[64] Philip Toynbee says it is 'pervasively and continuously funny, with a humour which is both savage and farcical'.[65] Charles Rolo in *Harper's* magazine explains:

> Above all *Lolita* seems to me an assertion of the power of the comic spirit to wrest delight and truth from the most outlandish materials. It is one of the funniest serious novels I have ever read.[66]

There was some disagreement though about just how funny the book was. The Kronhausens, though they loved the book, were not amused by it. They say that it 'certainly is not' the ' "comedy" it is reputed to be'.[67] We must assume that those who find the book too horrific to laugh at have a poor sense of humour.

The critics were quite sure that *Lolita* was a great work of literature and not pornography. Thomas Karl wrote: 'Nabokov writes literature of a high quality. Influenced by Poe and Baudelaire, he writes as an artist and a poet of cosmopolitan irony.'[68] *Lolita* was, he said, 'certainly . . . not pornography'. Terence Rattigan describes the book as 'a very high literary achievement'.[69] Meyer Levin calls *Lolita* 'the most exciting reading experience in the modern novel since Joyce's *Ulysses*. You have to go all the way back to *Ulysses* for a comparable feeling of newness and validity.'[70] François-Régis Bastid was clearly bowled over. He writes: 'We live such petty lives that it takes us some time to get used to it when a book of this power appears.'[71]

The critics also were determined that the book had a serious moral intent and effect. Kenneth Allsop described the book as 'dreadfully moral' because the hero Humbert did not prosper, but ended up in prison for the grisly murder, lovingly reported in the novel, of the man who took Lolita away from him.[72] Terence Rattigan said *Lolita* was a book of 'the highest moral purpose'. Considering the legacy of the book in softening up attitudes to sexual abuse of children and blaming child victims, 'moral' is a strange adjective for it, but this is yet another example of the peculiar reversal which the ruling male establishment is able to perform to justify its prerogatives and women's enslavement.

In his afterword Nabokov explains why Lolita is indeed a work of art and not pornography. Pornography, he says, follows 'old rigid rules'. In his afterword Nabokov explains to us why Lolita is indeed a work of art and not pornography. Pornography, he says, follows 'old rigid rules'. These rules decree that 'action has to be limited to the copulation of cliches'. The reader's sexual response should not be diluted by having to concentrate on 'style, structure, imagery'. A pornographic novel must contain an 'alternation of sexual scenes' and these scenes must build up to a crescendo'.[73]

According to his own definition of pornography Lolita was not pornographic, although as he explained, it very nearly was. Some readers were misled, he admitted, in the early chapters by some of the techniques of pornography to 'expect the rising succession of erotic scenes' but were disappointed and stopped reading when the erotic scenes stopped. Lolita is not pornographic, therefore, because a whole section of the book contains no erotic scenes. This defence is reminiscent of the expert judgments as to why The White Hotel is not pornography, which are so satisfyingly taken apart by Suzanne Kappeler. In that book it is the existence of some non-erotic padding which is supposed to transform what started out as a privately titillating fantasy into a work of art.

But there is another reason why Lolita is a work of art, according to its author, and this is the feeling he gets from it. The feeling is 'aesthetic bliss' which he describes as 'a sense of being somehow, somewhere, connected with other states of being where art (curiosity, tenderness, kindness, ecstasy) is the norm'. Nabokov bewails the fact that there are 'not many such books'. Most books were simply 'topical trash' or the 'Literature of Ideas'.[74] Nabokov is not modest. His achievement is, he implies, pure art. It is the product of pure inspiration for which he need take no responsibility. He was visited by his muse to produce this work. The form taken by his muse is described as a throbbing, 'the first little throb of Lolita went through me late in 1939 or early in 1940 . . .'[75] and, 'Around 1949, in Ithaca, upstate New York, the throbbing, which had never quite ceased, began to plague me again.'[76] It is presumably pure coincidence that Nabokov's muse sounds so much like a desire to masturbate. Since the book is not pornographic his language here is puzzling. The 'throbbing' is evidence that the book is a work of art. A force greater than Nabokov, we are expected to believe, caused this work to be born. It has now become an interesting task to find out what causes a book to be labelled a work of art by the literary establishment.

In *The Pornography of Representation* Suzanne Kappeler demonstrates that feminists have made a mistake in thinking the creators of pornography are innocent about the way in which their products degrade women. Such feminists believe that if they could only point out 'in stark irrefutable ways the mechanics and structures of the pornographic plot' then the porn producers would admit the error of their ways. In fact, she explains, the producers know very well what they are producing and are perfectly sanguine about it. The dispute, she writes, is not about whether certain literary works degrade women but 'whether there is anything wrong with the systematic degradation of women, the wholesale cultural objectification of women'.[77] In other words, does the degradation of women matter?

Indeed when we look at some of the books which were hailed as works of art in the late 1950s it is hard to avoid the conclusion that they are classified as 'art' and accepted into 'literature' precisely because of their pornographic content. The great works of that time that have entered the canon achieved both their notoriety and their status from their portrayal of sexuality. The adulation heaped upon Nabokov did not stem from the fact that he wrote a wonderful novel which just accidentally happened to have some pornographic content. The novel was about the abduction and penetration of a young female; there was no other plot. It is difficult to believe that the male critics of the time were genuinely innocent of the fact that *Lolita* is about rape. They defined the rape of a child as great love, and the book which described it became great art because of and not despite its content.

Kappeler sets out to explain the process by which works of art are placed in the canon. Literary critics, she explains, 'discuss literary productions in terms of Texts that are given as rocks are given by nature'.[78] They do not ask why a book exists or how its existence affects the world. A book is seen as becoming a work of art by some mysterious but entirely natural and inevitable process, and once it is accepted it is treated with religious reverence, like scripture.

The author of literary scripture exists only in such a rarefied sense as God exists behind his Scripture . . . There are, it seems, new literary productions in the world as there is renewing rain coming out of the sky, an inexorable law of Nature, a natural law of Culture and History.[79]

Kappeler demystifies the process of canonisation. She brings into the picture the 'economic infrastructure which underpins the literary establishment'. Publishers, she points out, do not publish books out of the 'goodness of their hearts' or out of 'genuine enthusiasm for the literary culture' but out of the desire to make a profit.[80] This throws some light upon the decision of respectable publishers in the late 1950s and early 1960s such as Penguin, Heinemann and John Calder to publish the banned books. It is after this stage that the critics become involved.

It is clear that people (men) have been actively involved in this process, reviewing books and choosing them, attributing values to them, or not reviewing them and thus leaving them unvalued, unevaluated.[81]

How do the critics recognise 'the literary'? Kappeler explains how the publishers Picador construct the literary credentials of the books they seek to promote. Picador, in common with other publishers, use two basic techniques. Either the book must be 'chosen or valued by an authority' who is already accepted by the literary élite, or it must be judged to be 'similar to or like . . . another literary work' which has already been accepted. Comments which establish these credentials are placed on the back covers of books or on advertisements. At no stage in this process does anyone seek to define what literary quality is, except in the vaguest terms. With respect to *Lolita* we see this process under way. *Lolita* was recommended by famous authors and critics and compared by them to James Joyce's *Ulysses*, Flaubert's *Madame Bovary*, the works of Aristophanes, Evelyn Waugh, and Aldous Huxley. Burroughs' publisher, Calder, compares him with James Joyce as well, and also with Hieronymous Bosch, the Marquis de Sade, Marcel Duchamp, Tristan Tzara and Georg Grosz.

We can see how the book is constructed into literature, but what is not so clear is *why*. The respectable publishers wanted literary pedigrees for their products lest they be seen as just publishing pornography and thus prosecuted. The 1959 Act provided them with the mysterious and entirely subjective defence of literary merit which encouraged them to prove that their products were works of art. But the tremendous excitement created amongst the male literary establishment around these 'banned' books needs to be explained in its own right. Literary works have been canonised before but not with so much relish.

I suggest that the cause for the excitement lay in the sudden realisation that they could at last have, out in the public sphere, what they had previously had to purchase covertly, or fantasise about in private. This was the degradation of women, or of those reduced to the object status of women.

But where many of these banned books were concerned, the degradation of women was quite a lofty value compared with some of the other aspects that caused the critics to give tongue. There was much enthusiasm about simple dirty talk, the language and subject matter of the boys' changing room. Talking dirty, particularly talking about excretory functions, drew forth a particular reverence. Burroughs was obsessed with this topic and could not be restrained from talking about it. In a Radio Three interview Burroughs remarked in an aside to his fan Eric Mottram: 'Did I ever tell you about the man who taught his asshole to talk? His whole abdomen would move up and down and, you dig? farting out the words. It was quite unlike anything I ever heard.'[82] A salient aspect of the *Lady Chatterley's Lover* trial concerned Lawrence's use of four-letter words. The prosecutor listed 30 'fucks' or 'fuckings', 14 'cunts', 13 'balls',

6 each of 'shit' and 'arse', 4 'cocks' and 3 'piss'.[83] The witnesses defended the book as clean and noble and Richard Hoggart defended it as a 'working-class' novel.

The male literary establishment gloried with prurient relish in the opportunity to speak and write dirty words and read and write dirty thoughts under the guise of great art and total respectability. Words like 'fuck' and 'cunt' are weighted rather differently for women. In a culture in which what is sex is defined as men's dominance and women's degradation, these apparently straightforwardly dirty words carry quite different loadings. Women's less enthusiastic response to the opportunity to say 'fuck' or 'cunt' reflects this.

If male-supremacist values were not so firmly in control in the literary establishment, one might have expected that the canonising of the banned books on the grounds of their pornographic and 'dirty' content would discredit for ever the process by which the literary is constructed. In fact the effect of decensorship was the burgeoning of mass-market pornography. John Sutherland describes how the pornography industry developed in Britain subsequent to the 1959 Act and the great trials.

> Meanwhile, in the shadows behind these spotlighted censorship spectacles, 'pornography' was growing steadily from a hole-in-the-corner specialist supply service to a multi-million pound, efficiently organised industry.[84]

There was no machinery in Britain to mass-produce pornography for the new market opened up by the 1959 Act. At first Britain was mainly supplied by the US, then Europe and Scandinavia. As evidence of this new flood of material, Sutherland tells us that customs seizures of pornographic materials rose between the late 1950s and mid 1960s from 2,000 items annually to a million or more. By the late 1960s as part of a change towards boutique-type retailing, sex shops were established which provided a 'wholesome and hedonistic' environment for the sale of porn, unlike the seedy but traditional truss shops and newsagents that men might feel uncomfortable to be seen walking into. A generation of young publishing entrepreneurs emerged, such as Bob Guccione, to take advantage of a booming market and to use new pictorial techniques to sell women to their audience.

Sutherland connects the growth of the pornography industry directly to the 1959 Act. But some of those involved in the defence of the banned books as art in the 1960s, and in promulgating sexual liberalism, claim to be shocked by the way things turned out. They could not have known, they say, that decensorship would lead to the free availability of sadomasochistic porn. The implication is that something sex-positive and of high quality gave way unaccountably to a hideous pornographic avalanche. Any serious analysis of the banned books should give the lie to this notion. Kappeler argues that the separation of high art from pornography is false and misleading. Rather than there being great works of literature which deal with sex in an irreproachable way, and a quite separate and reprehensible smut industry, she argues that pornography develops its values from art: '. . . responsibility for the dominant modes of representation . . . needs to be sought in "responsible" art and "high" culture, rather than in its waste products.'[85] This makes sense. Those who defend the social value of great art speak of its role in creating noble attitudes. It seems at least as likely that pornographic great art will spawn a pornography industry. The 'art' we have been looking at here is indistinguishable in its portrayal of sex from the less respectable kind of pornography sold in sex shops.

Kappeler defines the pornographic scenario common to both 'high' art and *Hustler* magazine thus:

The pornographic scenario is but a stark representation of the cultural position of the male gender vis-à-vis the female gender. It is extremely limited in scope, revolving around the sadistic act of sex/violence . . . there is a plot: the cultural archeplot of power. There is power on the side of the agent (hero), and there is powerlessness incarnated in the victim-object, and the verb is transitive, always.[86]

The victim-object was not always female in the banned literature. In the novels of Genet, Burroughs and Selby it is likely to be male, but the structure of the pornographic scenario remains

89

the same. The pornographic revolution of the early 1960s was democratic where sexual orientation was concerned, democratic in the old Athenian sense, of equal male citizens. Genet, Burroughs and Selby created pornographic scenarios equal to those of heterosexual pornographers such as Henry Miller, Norman Mailer and Nabokov. Sometimes their productions, as in the case of Burroughs and Selby's *Last Exit to Brooklyn*, are incomparably brutal, and include large amounts of necrophilia and accounts of gruesome death during rape or in the pursuit of sexual satisfaction.

Sexual liberals like the Kronhausens laud the educative value of 'erotic realism'. Witnesses and defenders of the banned books, particularly of *Lolita*, stress that the reading public will learn much that is positive from such material. In this sense decensorship was a vital ingredient of the sexual revolution. Pornography, whether 'high' art or 'trash', was going to educate a generation in what sex was. The sex of the sexual revolution was constructed to follow the pornographic scenario described above. The banned books and their progeny provided the propaganda of the sexual revolution, and they provided the plot.

Chapter 3

THE SEXUAL REVOLUTION

The most famous sex advice book of the sexual revolution was Alex Comfort's *The Joy of Sex*. At first sight this book looks very different from a classic of 1950s sexology such as Eustace Chesser's *Love and Marriage*. Chesser condemned women's attempts at equality for undermining the family and recommended a feeling of surrender in the missionary position. *The Joy of Sex* asserted that women were equal now and that this gave them the right to full participation in bondage, anal and oral sex. A difference in approach to sex is evident here. The work ethic was gone and sex was supposed to be fun. There were fewer references to the family or even to marriage, and group sex was seen as an acceptable activity. This looks like a revolution in sexological thinking and has generally been accepted as such by historians. This 'revolution' has been seen as emancipating women and allowing them equal sexual rights.

It is necessary, however, to look at this revolution with a critical eye. When analysed from a feminist perspective the much-vaunted revolutionary changes can look merely cosmetic. At first glance it could look as though a real revolution in attitudes has taken place between books which saw coitus alone as an acceptable sexual activity and those which promoted oral and anal sex and were heartily tolerant of necrophilia. The difference looks considerable because of the way that the sexologists and the sexual experts of the twentieth century have trained us to look at sex. We have been encouraged to see sex as a range of practices, so that according to this analysis the wider the range of practices, the more liberated the sex. Sexologic has apparently eschewed politics. When we introduce a feminist analysis it becomes clear that little actually changed. A feminist analysis causes us to look not just at techniques but at the power relationship in which those techniques are practised.

A variety of changes in legislation and sexual practice which constitute the 'sexual revolution' of the 1960s can be identified. These changes include the group of legislative reforms carried out by the Labour governments in Britain in the late 1960s, changes in abortion law and in the law on homosexuality. They include changes in the rate of marriage and in attitudes to, if not practice of, premarital sex, a more liberal approach to sex education and a greater freedom in talking about sex. However, rather than focusing on such changes in law and practice, it is necessary to look at the ideas of the 'sexual revolution'.

Historians have offered explanations for why the changes they describe took place in the 1960s. The most common form of explanation is economic. Jeffrey Weeks argues that the revolution resulted from the postwar boom and the greater affluence associated with it.[1] The boom led to a greater orientation of the economy to domestic consumption. The creation of a mass market led to democratisation, a greater flexibility in attitudes and the eroticising of social life. Weeks sees the development of a newly independent and monied youth as an important factor. In 1960 there were one million more unmarried people in the age range 15–24 than 10 years previously. This constituted a 20 per cent increase. These young people had an unprecedented economic power as average real wages rose by 25 per cent between 1938 and 1958 and those of adolescents by twice this. A vast new consumer market was created. The age at which young people reached sexual maturity fell while the school-leaving age rose. Young people experienced a long period in which they were sexually mature but not supposed to be sexually active.

Another important factor, according to Weeks, was that women had become a more influential group in the population, not just because as the holders of the family purse strings they were now in control of far more money than before, but because they were entering the workforce after a much smaller number of years spent in childbearing. Women took part in the new upsurge of higher education and made use of their opportunities to enter well-paid jobs. Women were therefore, some historians would argue, in a more powerful position to make their needs felt and to pursue their pleasures in the area of sexuality. The greater influence women were able to wield is likely to have affected sexology. Women could not so easily be relegated to the role of passive and uncomplaining object when they had more financial independence.

But the increasing independence of women provided a direct threat to the maintenance of male power and privilege. That no such threat did materialise, it will be argued here, owes a great deal to the success of the sexual revolution. The sexual revolution was a counter-revolution and constituted a timely adjustment to the fine-tuning of the heterosexual institution. I argued in *The Spinster and Her Enemies* that it was women's increased independence and opportunities in the late nineteenth and early twentieth centuries that precipitated the birth of sexology as a science. Sex was constructed to be the new binding ingredient in marriage which would compensate for the decreased efficiency of legal and economic constraints. The 1960s was a new time of crisis for male supremacy and a new adjustment had to be made.

The science of sexology was founded on the assumption that sex played a crucial role in maintaining women's subordination. Sexologists believed that women's sexual pleasure did subordinate them, not just in their relationships but in their lives. The conscription of women, not just married women but now single women as well, into male dominant/female submissive sex in the 1960s is part of this tradition. While promoted as 'liberating' for women, it was clear to anyone who read the small print of sexology literature that women's participation in this revolution was not intended to liberate them from anything but their common sense and instinct for self-protection. But at the time no one was reading the small print.

Rather than posing a threat to traditional patriarchal marriage the sexual revolution strengthened the institution. Neither heterosexuality nor marriage were under challenge in this period. Marriage actually became vastly more likely for women. Weeks points out that whereas 552 women in every thousand aged

21–39 were married in 1911 and only 572 in 1931, the figure was 808 in 1961. By the mid 1960s 95 per cent of men and 96 per cent of women were married by the age of 45. Feminists before the First World War attributed the strength of their movement to the strength of the class of spinsters. They saw spinsters as independent and strong, capable of acting to change the world in a way that married women who had to service and obey husbands could never do. If this were true then we might expect the feminism of the 1970s, when marriage was so much more the norm for women, to be a frailer reed than its predecessor. Certainly the marriage rates do not indicate that the 1960s revolution was likely to favour women's liberation.

THE IDEOLOGY OF SEXUAL LIBERALISM

The sexual revolutionaries of the 1960s set themselves the task of reconstructing western morality. The sex reform movement of the early twentieth century and particularly the 1920s saw itself as sweeping away the fog of Victorian morality which had decreed that sex was shameful and to be hidden. The sex reformers stated that sex was positive and to be enjoyed. The 1960s sexual revolutionaries saw themselves as having pretty much the same mission. The earlier onslaught on Victorianism had clearly not been successful. Who had stood in the way of the progress of sexual enlightenment? Women. As women in the first wave of sex reform were seen as slow to appreciate the joys of sexual intercourse with men, if not mainly frigid, so 1960s woman was seen as the fly in the ointment of sexual progress.

The source of sexual enlightenment in the early 1960s was located in Sweden, Denmark and Holland. The denizens of these countries were seen as years ahead in terms of the sexual revolution and their books were published in Britain to great excitement. One such work, published in Britain in 1963, was Inge and Stan Hegeler's *An ABZ of Love*. They identified traditional morality as the source of sexual problems.

The cause of our sexual anxiety is our still fairly strict moral code which makes upbringing anti-sexual and places obstacles in the way of quite sensible enlightenment on sexual questions. Any alteration in sex morals takes several generations because upbringing is of such importance to the personality and therefore retains such a firm hold on people's minds.[2]

They made it clear that the problem was particularly acute amongst women.

THE INHIBITION

The concept of the 'inhibition' was a powerful weapon in the armoury of 1960s sexual revolutionaries. The Hegelers define it as 'a hindering, suppressive activity in the mind'.[3] Not surprisingly we find that women were most likely to be possessed of 'inhibitions'.

Inhibitions may often be of a moral nature, in other words acquired ... Many women (and a number of men) are able to ruin things for themselves by believing these inhibitions to be things they were born with and therefore of divine infallibility. It is not unusual for an inexperienced and uninformed woman to believe that a number of the approaches made by a man are immoral and wrong, because she has learned that this is so – it was always somehow in the air during her childhood and youth, ergo the man in question is a pig.[4]

The Hegelers give examples of approaches that women might have inhibitions about. These are fellatio and cunnilingus. Through the concept of the 'inhibition' we can see that the possibility of sexual choice for a woman was removed. If a woman did not like a sexual activity, whatever the basis of her objection, whether personal, political or aesthetic, she was considered to have had some problem in childhood which constructed for her an inhibition.

Inhibitions were wrong, i.e. they 'prevent a person from developing reasonably' and as they were socially constructed, so therefore they could be removed. It became the personal responsibility of women in the 1960s to work at removing their inhibitions. To be accused by a man of having inhibitions was a serious matter, the implication being that the woman was old-fashioned, narrow-minded and somehow psychologically damaged. Not surprisingly women enthusiastically entered self-improvement programmes, usually at the hands of the men who pointed out their problem. They may not have learned real enjoyment of the required practices but they managed to tolerate them and to avoid guilt and blame.

The Hegelers, like other 1960s sexual revolutionaries had a traditional male-supremacist understanding of sex. Under the heading 'Court, courting, courtship' they point out that, 'To pay court to a woman, to woo, lay siege to, admire, etc. are all exciting things for most men as long as they form part of a planned conquest.'[5] They stated categorically that, 'The majority of women like a little old-fashioned gallantry because it makes them feel more attractive and feminine.' An example of gallantry was that a man should provide a 'little box of chocolates to cheer one up at menstruation time'. The Hegelers were aware of the existence of feminism but saw nothing wrong with such role playing. They decried 'women who deny their femininity and cannot accept these things in the same generous spirit'. They felt that 'feminists could permit themselves to be feminine'.[6]

In such a context of male dominant/female submissive sex, it would not be the least surprising if women had reservations based on a simple understanding of the politics of what was happening to them. Women do know when they are being patronised or humiliated. The concept of the inhibition encouraged them to interpret their unease as a character defect.

The Hegelers sought to reassure women that erotic fantasies in which they are sexually abused are quite normal and healthy, lest some women might develop inhibitions about these too.

Completely normal and healthy women can tell how they have found themselves imagining scenes featuring incest, prostitution, rape, homosexuality, exhibitionism, masochism, sadism and many other isms . . . None of these mental images or fantasies need cause anybody any concern.[7]

Apart from homosexuality, all the fantasy activities seen as harmless here show women in an object or victim role in relation to male sexuality.

MORAL RELATIVISM

Sexual liberalism was based upon a moral relativism. The sexual revolutionaries sought to legitimise sexual practices against which there had been cultural taboos before the 1960s or against which women had had inhibitions. These activities were proclaimed to be really quite 'normal', or at least normal to some people or in some societies. They were prepared to go quite far in their attempts at validation. Some of the sexual revolutionaries did not seem to draw the line at any form of sexual practice. The Hegelers applied moral relativism to the sexual abuse of children. To the Hegelers this was really not a problem at all and often pleasurable and desired by the children involved. It was only a problem if damage to the child's body took place.

> In very rare cases there is a question of actual attempts at intercourse with the child. In such cases it is obvious that there may be a question of physical harm, i.e. of the child's body suffering damage.

> The mental harm produced by these sexual acts towards children depends to a certain extent on the sexual upbringing the child has had and the enlightenment the child has been given.[8]

Sexual enlightenment then, the *raison d'être* of the sexual revolutionaries, could lead to the disappearance of child sexual abuse. The enlightened child would not feel abused. Adult men would continue to use children as objects for their sexual satisfaction but the children would not object. The attitude towards children here is similar to the attitude towards women in the book. Enlightenment was expected to eliminate inhibitions, reservations, and feelings of disquiet on the part of women and children about their experience of male sexual behaviour.

The Hegelers' tolerant attitude to the sexual abuse of children is justified by the use of arguments of moral relativism. We are

97

told that, 'There are things that are punished severely as sexual crimes in one country but not at all in another.'[9] They furnish as examples the prohibition of sexual intercourse between black and white in South Africa, and of 'seduction to masturbation' in some American states. They have selected here examples of sexual practices in which no abuse of power occurs to compare with a practice, child sexual abuse, in which abuse of power is axiomatic. This insensibility to the abuse of power in the area of sexuality is fundamental to sexual liberalism. All sexual practices are seen as equally morally neutral. Power differences between men and women and men and children are not recognised. Sex is seen as fun and games without exception. Abuse is relabelled as the prudery of the victim. Unenlightened women and children were the only ones who would see abuse in a sexual situation at all and they could be educated out of such bad manners. Under the heading 'Indecency' the Hegelers again compared a practice of mutual sex with an abuse of power in a way which made the abuse disappear.

> Indecency: Means any action which offends a sexual prejudice. It may be a grown-up fondling a child rather intimately (see Crimes, sexual), or two lovers embracing on a haystack. In other words, it means what we want it to mean.[10]

In other words sexual abuse does not really exist except in the minds of people who are irrationally prejudiced.

The strength of the Hegelers' commitment to moral relativism drives them to a remarkably tolerant view of necrophilia. Necrophilia generally involves the sexual abuse by men of women's bodies. Because women's bodies are in poor supply outside morgues men will murder to supply themselves with such bodies, and necrophilia is the urge behind the mass killings of women. Necrophilia is a male sexual practice which is not in women's interests either in life or in death. The Hegelers do not see a problem with it.

> Necrophilia, necromania, necrosadism: Are all the sexual things people can think of doing with dead persons' bodies. It is not exactly an unknown phenomenon for people whose

sexual urges have not found outlet in the more normal fashion to allow themselves to be tempted by corpses.

These things naturally take place in particular amongst people whose profession causes them to deal with corpses in their daily work. For such people death is not so frightening, and respect for dead persons therefore decreases in the course of daily routine.[11]

Presumably, according to the Hegelers' logic, a feeling of squeamishness at the idea that your body would be used after death as a masturbation machine for the morgue attendant is just another feeling that sexual enlightenment should eradicate.

Lars Ullerstam's book *The Erotic Minorities*, first published in 1964, is another Scandinavian example of the sexual revolution. Ullerstam wrote what he called a 'Sexual Bill of Rights' for these minorities. He wanted the erotic minorities to have easy access to sexual satisfaction and he wanted prejudice against them to end. His minorities included necrophiliacs again, alongside homosexuals. He wanted incest to be legalised. He wanted exhibitionists to be tolerated. Most of his minorities were men who achieved sexual satisfaction through acts of abuse towards women. Exhibitionists, after all, find it necessary to frighten and sexually threaten women in order to achieve satisfaction. Ullerstam was immune to any understanding of the power dynamics that could affect sexual practice. Having made his plea for tolerance and understanding of his minorities he provided a programme of action. The most important step was to establish brothels. He claimed to envisage all members of the population using the brothels. He had no gender analysis and the problem of prostitution being an institution of male supremacy that could not exist in an egalitarian society did not occur to him.

By rational methods the price level of sexual commodities could be reduced considerably; adolescent boys and people without an income should be allowed reduced rates. For the unmarried person the brothel would be a time-saving factor, at least in cases of strong sexual urges, and he would have more time to pursue his education and training. Sexually fatigued wives would find relief by sending their husbands to these houses of joy, and they would not have to worry about any complications.[12]

These state brothels were clearly for men. There should also, he suggested, be mobile brothels to visit 'hospitals, mental hospitals, and institutions, paralysed, housebound patients, and old people, as well as individuals who are too inhibited to visit such establishments themselves'. The employees would provide masturbation and striptease.

THE SEX RADICALS

To many who lived through the 1960s and early 1970s the changes in sexual behaviour that took place would have been imperceptible. But many on the left, those who saw themselves as progressive and avant-garde, believed they were taking part in a sexual revolution. This revolution had its prophets in Wilhelm Reich and Herbert Marcuse. The ideas of these men became the conventional wisdom of a generation of young people who were living out the revolution now through their sexual practice. Their ideas have not died. They may have been reworked a little but they still inform the new 1980s-style sex radical. Paul Robinson, in his study of Reich, Marcuse and Geza Roheim, gives us a definition of the sexual radical. He explains:

> Reich, Roheim, and Marcuse are all convinced of the unparalleled significance of sex, both in individual psychology and in the evolution of civilisation ... What makes them sexual radicals is their unqualified enthusiasm for sex, their belief that sexual pleasure is the ultimate measure of human happiness, and their pronounced hostility to the sexual repressiveness of modern civilisation.[13]

These ideas were not new to the 1960s since such men were all products of an earlier time; but it was in the 1960s that their ideas were taken up. Sex was given an apocalyptic role and these prophets were enlisted to justify it. While mainstream sexologists might believe in the importance of sexual pleasure because it served to reinforce men's power and subordinate women, or simply because they accepted Freudian notions, the sexual radicals gave sex a revolutionary role. Yet if many 1960s students understood that it was in some way revolutionary to 'do it in the road' they may not have been sure how this would help to create the socialist revolution. Those who wanted theory read Reich, whose works were all reprinted in the 1960s and read by an admiring new generation. His decline into ignominy in the 1940s and 50s was forgotten. The new generation were interested in the good Communist Reich of the 1920s and 30s.

Reich saw the orgasm as the measure of health. He believed that neurotics fell ill because they could not achieve a satisfactory orgasm. He took from Freud the hydraulic model and took it to extremes. In this model a biologically given amount of sexual energy wells up and demands release. If all the energy were not efficiently released then illness would result. Reich defined orgasm as 'the capacity for complete discharge of all dammed-up sexual excitation through involuntary pleasurable contractions of the body'.[14] Orgasm had to be of the right type, i.e. heterosexual. Most people, according to Reich, were not having the right type of orgasm with full discharge, and suffering as a result.

In very simple language he explained this model to young members of the Communist party in 1931 in a pamphlet entitled *The Sexual Struggle of Youth*. He stated that 'sexual relations occur under the pressure of sexual tensions and drive . . .' and that 'Nature . . . has arranged things so that a man in good health wants to have sexual relations on an average from once to three times a week'.[15] Reich defined sex as coitus. It is clear that Reich's model is a male one. A discharge theory does not fit women very well. It was women who would have to service the young men's pursuit of revolutionary orgasms and they would be subjected to powerful arguments. Reich asked 'What happens to any organ if its natural activity is obstructed for a long time will happen to the sexual apparatus; it will deteriorate.'[16] What woman would wish to visit such dire consequences upon her boyfriend?

Reich's appeal to the young of the 1960s lay not just in the commandment to do sexual intercourse. He laid out a clear map of the way the repression of sexual intercourse led to such political ills as fascism. Robinson described Reich's message thus:

> The connection between sexual repression and the authoritarian social order was simple and direct: the child who experienced the suppression of his natural sexuality was permanently maimed in his character development; he inevitably became submissive, apprehensive of all authority, and completely incapable of rebellion ... repression existed ... in order to create the character structure necessary for the preservation of an authoritarian social regime.[17]

Reich indicted the family as the institution within which sexual repression created a rigid character armour and the authoritarian personality who would seek a leader. In the 1960s assaults upon the family whether from R. D. Laing or from Reich were all immensely popular. Free love, non-monogamy, communal living all needed their theoretical underpinnings and these Reich supplied. Reich called the family 'a factory for authoritarian ideologies and conservative (character) structures'. This indictment of the family led to a rather uncritical celebration of Reich by feminists too in the early 1970s.

The knowledge that the performance of frequent sexual intercourse was a political duty was a powerful excuse for the sexual demands of young revolutionaries. Reich's injunction to politically necessary sexual intercourse was clear and straightforward.

> The demand of capitalist society that you should live ascetically to protect yourself from the onslaught of your own sexuality, is unconsciously accepted by internally erecting barriers against your own sexual wants ... The Church has its strongest ideological props in the sexual repression of youth: they refuse their own sexuality themselves, and uphold the antisexual capitalist morality which causes them harsh suffering.[18]

Reich stated: 'To define freedom is the same as to define sexual health.'[19] This message is replicated today in the arguments of 1980s sexual libertarians that women's liberation is sexual liberation.

Reich's basic beliefs about sexuality were in tune with the other major sexologists of the twentieth century. He believed that a 'natural' sexuality existed which was perverted by cultural influences into undesirable forms or repressed altogether. Health required the expression of this 'natural' sexuality which turned out to mean frequent sexual intercourse. Kinsey expressed very similar ideas, asserting the need of the adolescent male for sexual 'outlets' because of a biological drive.[20] Women and girls were to be the receptacles and servicers of this drive. Paul Robinson was under the impression that Reich was a feminist. Here is his definition of what being a feminist meant for a sex radical:

> In particular he was an ardent defender of the sexual rights of women. His feminism was as pronounced as Freud's misogyny. He was likewise a severe critic of the traditional ideal of marital fidelity. The compulsive marriage of existing society was to be eradicated, since every individual had the right to seek a new partner whenever his sexual happiness so demanded.[21]

Whether his use of the male possessive adjective in the last sentence was deliberate or accidental it does reveal the limitations of a definition of feminism which simply meant, in practice, that women should be available to service men's need for sexual variety. But this definition of feminism was one in general use during the 'sexual revolution'. Women have, historically, shown less enthusiasm for the opportunity to have sexual variety whereas radical men have always seen it as liberating for women. Radical communities set up by men from the Owenites to the communards of the 1960s and early 1970s have expressed a commitment to sexual equality. Under the guise of liberating women from being men's sexual property they have abolished marriage and turned women into the common property of the men. The experimental Oneida Community in America, which flourished from the 1840s to the 1870s, saw women showing a growing disenchantment with being held in common.[22] Men's power in such communities was never seriously challenged and

103

in such an unequal situation a verbal assertion of the sexual equality of women was nothing but hot air. A greater and more varied sexual access to women has traditionally been a revolutionary perk for men and a dubious advantage for women.

The other great inspirational thinker behind the sexual revolution was Herbert Marcuse. Marcuse, like Reich, saw sexual repression as necessary for capitalism and the elimination of this repression as revolutionary in its implications. According to his analysis pleasure and the kind of work required by the capitalist system were not compatible. Therefore it was necessary for capitalism to repress pleasure including sexual pleasure.

> The unsublimated, unrationalized release of sexual relations would mean the most emphatic release of pleasure as such and the total devaluation of work for work's sake. The tension between the innate value of work and the freedom of pleasure could not be tolerated by the individual: the hopelessness and injustice of working conditions would strikingly penetrate the consciousness of individuals and render impossible their peaceable regimentation in the social system of the bourgeois world.[23]

Marcuse reinterpreted the bleak and apparently sexually conservative message of Freud that civilisation depended on the repression of the destructive force of sexuality. Marcuse proposed that a certain amount of repression might indeed be necessary to civilisation but that a large amount of repression over and above this necessary amount was imposed in order to facilitate a political system of domination. This 'surplus repression' could and should be eliminated with no chance of society falling into barbarism and chaos. It is hard for feminists to sympathise with this idea. It is clearly based upon a male model. Feminists do not see male sexual aggression as 'natural', or as lacking full self-expression, but as socially constructed to maintain male power. In such a context the concept of repression is meaningless.

Marcuse differed from Reich in some crucial respects. He did not concentrate on genitality but called for a 'resexualisation of the body'. He considered that capitalism concentrated sexuality and pleasure in the genitals so that the rest of the body would be free for labour. The whole of the body and its pleasures needed to be released. This belief led him to cite a revolutionary role for sexual deviants and homosexuals in particular: 'The perversions ... express rebellion against the subjugation of sexuality under the order of procreation, and against the institutions which guarantee this order.'[24] Reich regarded homosexuality as an illness which resulted from repression and would fade away. Marcuse was a much more sympathetic prophet for gay liberation.

The publisher Maurice Girodias provides us with a good example of how such ideas were translated into sexual revolutionary ideology. He imbibed the ideas of the sex radicals whole and used them to justify his pornography business.

> As moral censorship is really nothing but political censorship in thin disguise, so is the sexual revolution the one true, central reality of the political revolution. Imagine that the freedom to read sex books should be granted tomorrow ... to the people in Russia, Spain, China, Portugal, Greece and a dozen other countries: the current authoritarian regime would be toppled overnight. Why? Because civic discipline begins with the educated reflex of sexual restraint.[25]

How exactly would this mechanism work? Girodias explains that once someone stopped believing 'it is wrong to read erotic books' you might 'think twice before going to Vietnam to do your duty' because 'it is the same not-so-abstract Big Brother who tells you what to do in bed and out of bed; in love, and in war'.[26]

EROTICISING THE SINGLE WOMAN

One significant change in 1960s sexology was in the attitude towards sex outside marriage. Sex-advice literature before the 1960s was addressed to respectable married persons. The unmarried were instructed to sublimate the sex instinct through creativity or good works. This changed dramatically in the 1960s when the value of virginity was hotly debated. Whether or not more girls became persuaded that they should lose their virginity and acted upon it, the sex-advice literature showed a change. Writers gave up telling unmarried women or men to sublimate. Books were written specifically for single women instructing them how to act sexually. The most famous is Helen Gurley Brown's *Sex and the Single Girl* of 1962. Brown later became editor of *Cosmopolitan* magazine. *Cosmopolitan* symbolised the new single woman of the 1960s. With new opportunities for education and career, young women had more money and independence than ever before. They were flatsharing and conducting relationships with men quite independently of their families. Potentially this new generation of women was a threat to traditional patriarchal patterns. There was now a considerable gap in women's lives between leaving the control of the family home and coming under the wardship of a husband. During this interregnum they had money and independence.

The solution to the problem of this freefloating population of young women who were out of the control of men, was to eroticise the single woman. The single woman was to acquire a role in the heterosexual institution. She was expected to join in the sexual servicing of men previously reserved for her married sister. She was enjoined in liberated magazines to divert her energies into acquiring a suitable male and keeping him by making him happy. The assumption was still there that she would want to marry him in the end, but even if she did not she was at least occupied putting her energies into a man or men rather than into women or revolution.

Sex and the Single Girl was a chaste little book compared with what would emerge in the late 1960s. The book resembled previous advice to young women on how to get a husband but was groundbreaking in its concentration on sex. It instructed girls on how to use specifically sexual lures to hook men and assumed that sexual activity might take place before marriage. Gurley Brown pitched her book at women who wanted to acquire a husband with status and money. She told them that they did not need to be beautiful or brainy, just wily and sexy. She urged them to follow her example so that they might catch a millionaire at the age of 37 as she did. She provided instruction

106

in how to be sexy. She assumed considerable ignorance in her audience about what was sexually attractive to men and offered very specific nitty-gritty advice.

> Clean hair is sexy. Lots of hair is sexy too. Skimpy little hair styles and hair under your arms, on your legs and around your nipples isn't. Lovely lingerie is sexy ... Girdles aren't sexy. I know they are a necessary restraining wall against wavy buttocks but they are *not* magnetic ... Being able to sit very still is sexy. Smiles are sexy ... Talking all the time about *anything* is unsexy. Sphinxes and Mona Lisas knew what they were doing.[27]

Girls who obeyed such advice would be turned into the ultimate in sexual objects, moulding their appearance, body and behaviour to appeal to men who were assumed to be interested in nothing but sex. This was not much of a liberation of single women. Whereas the spinster in the 1950s might at least take comfort in her intelligence and her woman friends, the 1960s single woman was given only one function in life, the stimulation of the male sexual appetite. This construction of the single woman which was the stock in trade of the new and supposedly 'progressive' women's magazines of the 1960s was precisely the straitjacket that women revolted against in creating the women's liberation movement of the late 1960s. Such narrowing of mind and body could no longer be tolerated as women gained a real taste of their new independence. But this prescription has not departed and still dominates magazines for young women. Such magazines existed and still exist to exploit the new market provided by the single woman's income. They sell a need for beauty aids, make-up and corsets, which the advertisers can exploit.

Gurley Brown stressed over and over again that intelligence in a woman was not sexy, and any kind of independent sense of self was unsexy too. Girls wanting men should appear ignorant and totally besotted with any man who spoke to them. She gave the following instructions on 'how to flirt':

A man is talking to you, nothing very personal. Look into his eyes as though tomorrow's daily double winners were there. Never let your eyes leave his . . . Never interrupt a man when he is telling a story. Not for all the rugs in Persia. This is a terrible habit of girls, even with other girls.[28]

She instructed women to seem deliberately 'softer and less self-sufficient' by going on a 'helpless campaign'.[29] Women who found such advice difficult to accept were derided. They were told that they needed 'professional help' if they 'secretly envy [men] their "superior advantages", their jobs, their ability to exploit'.[30] Such embryo feminists who might have been developing self-respect were told 'Manhaters may secretly envy men's penises', in a crude reduction of good old-fashioned Freudianism.

Gurley Brown's is a careers book for women in the style of the inspirational mid-nineteenth-century English classic from Samuel Smiles, *Lives of the Great Engineers*. As Smiles told average Englishmen that anyone could make it to be an engineer, so Gurley Brown told women that any one of them could marry well, even if, like herself, they were not endowed by nature or inheritance with any advantages. The principle is the same but the difference in ambition is rather glaring.

In 1969 another 'how to' book appeared which demonstrates the progress of the sexual revolution during this period. J., author of *The Sensuous Woman*, tells us that she has 'heavy thighs, lumpy hips, protruding teeth, etc.', and yet had achieved the career opportunity she dreamed of. 'Through intelligence and hard work' she had become 'a Sensuous Woman'.[31] J. did not offer the prize of gaining a high-status husband if women followed her advice. Her career ambition was simply to be sexy and a 'marvellous bitch in bed'. This is a new development in sex advice for single women.

One of the demands of the British women's liberation movement of the 1970s was a 'self-defined' sexuality for women. J. was not concerned with such niceties. Women were to learn to have orgasms simply to fit in better with men's sexual interests. She instructed women to masturbate because they would then be able to have orgasms more efficiently during sexual intercourse. She explained:

The reason *you* have to teach yourself to come alive is that men don't have the patience to explore your body thoroughly while they are sexually excited themselves. They want to get on with the action, not play laboratory.[32]

Women were instructed that they would need to use fantasies in masturbation and that these could be culled from pornography such as *The Story of O*. Masochistic fantasies were fine, such as 'being kidnapped and raped'.[33] The libertarian feminists of the 1980s who believe they are inventing a new sexuality for women simply replicate many of these instructions so it is worth looking at the 1969 version which made no pretence to be feminist. J. was demanding in her requirements that women should become no more than objects and servicers for men. She explained that women had been selfish in the past in demanding to be satisfied in bed rather than simply servicing men. Women had forgotten their biological role: 'We were designed to delight, excite and satisfy the male of the species.'[34] The sexes had different roles in sex, she explained. 'Men conquer through aggressive and skilled passion and love; women surrender to and are swept up in passion and love.'[35] Woman's aim should be to 'joyfully, tenderly and lustfully offer up every square inch of yourself for him to feast upon' and 'to use sweetly your erotically skilled body as a sensual instrument to satiate his appetite'.[36]

J., like other sex-advice writers of the 'sexual revolution', told women they must perform oral sex on men. She explained that she had had 'revulsion' at the idea at one time but she had come to love it. Women must do it, she said, whether they liked it or not because 'your man will love you for it'.[37] J. recognised that two-thirds of women, supposing they had got over their revulsion at fellatio, didn't want men to ejaculate in their mouths. At this point she became a stern schoolmistress figure and reminded women of their duty:

Apparently when it comes to this, a lot of pretty sensuous women desert the ship, or would like to. Oh no you don't! No skipping out for you! I bet you never even tried it. Don't say, 'This isn't for me.' You don't know yet. Make a fairly long-term effort to feel the pleasure in this highly sensual adventure.[38]

J. told women that they must engage in sexual intercourse even when they didn't feel like it, because they must not disappoint their man. They should try to feel some interest but if they couldn't they should fake orgasm. She asserted 'no woman of any sensitivity would refuse to make love to a man she cares for, just because she "doesn't really feel like it" '.[39]

The sexual revolution completed the sexualisation of women. Both married and unmarried women were expected now to become experts in sexually servicing men, and to get over their own tastes and interests in order to become efficient at this task. Where once a large group of single women might have escaped the destiny of servicing men and concentrated upon their own life work, they were now conscripted into compulsory heterosexuality. That group of women who retained primary ties with women and refused their new role were labelled lesbians. The spinster disappeared. The spinster, whether she sexualised her relationships with other women or not, had been able to live a reasonably independent life, free from the scrutiny and management of the sex regulators. Now there were no spinsters. Single women were divided into lesbians and active heterosexuals. Sexual activity was mandatory and backsliding was unforgivable.

HOMOSEXUALITY

The sexual revolution was heterosexual. Even the most progressive of sex-advice writers was unable to conceive of homosexuality in women or men as a reasonable alternative to heterosexuality. Sexual liberals like the Hegelers tried hard to be nonjudgmental about homosexuality and devoted a good few pages to the issue in the *ABZ of Love*. They saw homosexuals as worthy of tolerant understanding and as having the right to a sexual life. It would have been difficult to take a different line when they were liberal about everything else from paedophilia to necrophilia. But Alex Comfort, self-proclaimed sex radical, remained unaffected by this liberal urge, though he too waxed enthusiastic about group sex, anal sex and many other activities which carried serious taboos. He claimed to cover all varieties of sexual behaviour in *The Joy of Sex* but did not include homosexuality. He has a section on 'bisexuality' which positively warns readers not to treat sex with their own gender as anything other than a way to jazz up their heterosexual relationships.

Comfort had to mention 'bisexuality' because of his proselytising approach to group sex. At group-sex parties same sex desire was likely to arise and be acted upon, particularly by women. J. found herself forced to mention lesbianism for the same reasons. She gave a list of rules of etiquette for orgies and included this at number six: 'There are sometimes lesbians at orgies who may make passes at you. If you realize this in advance, you should be able to handle the situation gracefully when it arises.'[40]

Another popular sex-advice book which was infamously hostile to lesbians and gay men was *Everything you ever wanted to know about sex but were afraid to ask* from 1969. David Reuben is described on the jacket as a 'noted psychiatrist' but his book is written in colloquial language and sold 400,000 copies in the first four months. We are told that he 'answers all questions with wit, style and authoritative candour' whilst 'avoiding any moral judgement'.[41] Reuben's scruples let him down over homosexuality. Lesbianisn is discussed in the section on prostitution. In answer to the question 'What do female homosexuals do with each other?' Reuben answered, 'Like their male counterparts, lesbians are handicapped by having only half the pieces in the anatomical jigsaw puzzle. Just as one penis plus one penis equals nothing, one vagina plus another vagina still equals zero.'[42]

Reuben tells us that, 'No matter how ingenious they are, their sexual practices must always be some sort of imitation of heterosexual intercourse.'[43] He explained that lesbians either used dildoes or, 'Occasionally a woman may have an unusually large clitoris which reaches as much as two or more inches in length when erect.' Such women, if lesbians, 'may penetrate the vagina'.[44] It is not hard to imagine where Reuben got such astonishing information. Male pornography for centuries has

111

attributed imitation penises to lesbians, either because such an idea has satisfied a particular erotic whim of males or because sex with no penis in existence has always been unthinkable to men. Lesbian culture does not mention the two-inch clitoris and makes little reference to dildoes.

The sexual revolution was heterosexual but in the heady atmosphere of the revolution it was possible for lesbians and gay men to organise and use the precepts of sexual liberalism to their advantage. In Britain and the US lesbian and gay organisations proliferated. But the greater tolerance which allowed such organising did not signify a fundamental change in attitudes towards homosexuality. The 1967 Act in Britain which decriminalised male gay sexual behaviour in private with partners over 21 helped the development of gay pride and confidence. A change of ideology was evident in the Act but this change did not concern attitudes to homosexuality directly. The 1957 Wolfenden Report into homosexuality and prostitution, which laid the groundwork for the new legislation, established the principle that private sexual behaviour was not a legitimate area for the law to concern itself with. The decriminalisation of some forms of male homosexual behaviour and the increased penalties imposed on street prostitutes were both applications of this principle. This separation of the public and the private is a fundamental premise of sexual liberalism. In the short term it was helpful for gay liberation. But the idea that whatever takes place between consenting adults in private should be seen as exempt from politics has led to a sexual libertarianism in the 1980s which is in direct opposition to feminism. The 1988 legislation in Britain which forbids the promotion of homosexuality by local government, known as Section 28, and the level of public support for that legislation, underlines the extent to which tolerance never meant acceptance.

FORUM *MAGAZINE: FLOWER OF THE REVOLUTION*

In 1968 *Forum* magazine was founded. This magazine demonstrates the extent to which the heterosexual agenda was changed in the 'sexual revolution'. It was meant to appear authoritative and the material was either written by doctors or with their

112

advice. *Forum* was cuddly and respectable. The Patriarchy Study Group who analysed twelve years of *Forum* in 1981 found that the magazine had 'fifty-two *Forum* groups around the country and abroad, an Advisory Clinic in London and a doctors' seminar group: it was fighting censorship cases and running private training courses for sex therapists'.[45] *The Times* praised the way that '*Forum*'s sustained full-frontal assault on sexual ignorance had contributed to its readers' peace of mind and quality of life'.[46] From 1974 it was on sale in the British chain of booksellers, W. H. Smith, which refused to stock *Spare Rib* or *Gay News*.

Both married and unmarried women were to receive an uncompromising message from *Forum* that all male sexual interests were to be indulged in the name of sexual freedom. *Forum* was dedicated to getting rid of 'repression' and that meant tackling the agent of repression, the inhibited woman. The articles promoted all kinds of activities which women might have been expected to have inhibitions about as normal and healthy. Starting with anal intercourse and progressing through incest to deep throat, which involved the use of a woman's throat as a substitute vagina, *Forum* set out to persuade its massive audience in 40 countries that anything goes. The readers' letters are particularly revealing about the way in which women struggled to reconstruct themselves under the strictures of the magazine into uncomplaining sexual servicers of their men. The following letter expresses a woman's attempts to overcome her revulsion at swallowing a man's semen. Rather than showing us any delights that the sexual revolution had to offer, this shows us the stark reality of a new form of women's subordination:

... I like to suck my husband's penis during love play, but was always afraid to have him climax in my mouth. But after reading some of the letters from other women on how they overcame this fear I decided to try it. I fortified myself with a few drinks to get me in the mood and then proceeded to give my husband the best blow job he ever had ... I don't mind swallowing his semen ever since I read in *Forum* the trick of keeping enough saliva in my mouth so that the taste is hardly noticeable ... I hope this letter will help other women who read *Forum* to overcome their guilt feelings so they can enjoy true sexual feelings with the guy they love.[47]

Through letters women gave each other tips on how to make their situation bearable. Resourceful as women have always been at making do and helping each other to cope with their oppression, so these women caught up in the 'sexual revolution' struggled to survive. They advised each other on how to swallow semen in the same way in which they would advise each other on how to remove red wine stains from the carpet in another kind of women's magazine. Fellatio was a new kind of housework.

The practices that male *Forum* readers expected their wives to suffer could reach remarkable extremes of abuse. One reader described a sadomasochistic ritual he carried out on his wife.

> I made my wife put on the very tight rubber corset over the large pad of long blunt nails, as these can cause quite severe pain after a time . . . I never let her off without the spiked heel pads as these can be exquisitely uncomfortable after a short time . . . I put the two obdurators, the long wide one into the vagina, and the smaller one into the rectum. I use toothpaste as it causes an intense burning feeling in the anus for some hours . . . I put on her head the black rubber bathing cap and then put the thick rubber head mask on. This one has an inflatable bag that goes in the mouth, and flaps over the eyeholes so that she is in complete darkness and zips from the crown down to the back of her neck. Over this I put the stiff neck collar and then I blow up the rubber balloon in the mouth . . . I then tied some thread round her nipples and crossed her wrists and . . . tied her thumbs to her nipples.[48]

One development of the sexual revolution was the appearance of respectable sex shops like Ann Summers in which men could buy such sadomasochistic equipment to use on their wives. Readers like this one relied on *Forum* to educate women in their duty to accept and pretend to enjoy such practices. Some of the letters in *Forum* may be hoaxes or deliberately constructed by the editor to validate some new sexual practice, but they purported to be real and had an educative function.

114

The more detailed case studies that follow are included in order to demystify the ideology of sexual liberalism. *The Joy of Sex* represents the apogee of sexual revolutionary propaganda. 'Swinging' is an example of sexual revolutionary practice. Sex therapy, especially its famous 1960s exponents, Masters and Johnson, shows how the new revolutionary prescription for maintaining male power was to be taught to reluctant or incompetent participants.

THE JOY OF SEX

Alex Comfort's *The Joy of Sex* is probably the most famous and popular sex manual of recent time. It stands in relation to the second sexual revolution of the twentieth century as Marie Stopes' *Married Love* did to the first. *The Joy of Sex* was first published in 1972, at the zenith of the sexual revolution, and can be seen as the quintessential expression of the values of that revolution. It purports to be scientific. Alex Comfort, who calls himself the book's editor, is a doctor and sex researcher. He introduces the book as 'the first sex counselling book to be properly researched'.[49] It is such a respected book that 'medical colleagues' in America and Canada 'are leaving it in the waiting-room or giving it out on prescription'.[50]

Comfort describes *The Joy of Sex* as 'an unanxious account of the full range of human sexuality – resources, novelties, jokes, problems'.[51] It is for those who know the basics and are interested in 'gourmet sex'. The practices described are arranged under 'main courses', 'sauces and pickles' and 'problems'. Homosexuality is not covered by the book. There is but half a page on 'bisexuality'. Presumably Comfort sees heterosexuality as the 'full range' of human sexuality. The book was seen as shocking at the time of publication because it described in detail, in a jolly, unjudgmental way, sexual practices previously regarded as perversions, such as bondage, anal intercourse and so on, as a normal part of sex, with drawings to illustrate the practices. When looked at from the perspective of the 1980s, it doesn't look quite so daring and adventurous. Comfort makes it clear that the practices described are only to supplement that

115

which must always form the heart of sexual interaction, sexual intercourse in the missionary position. As the introduction states, 'The *pièce de résistance* is the good old face-to-face matrimonial . . . with mutual orgasm.'[52]

The word 'unanxious' occurs again and again in the preface and introduction. Not only is the book an 'unanxious account' but it 'deals with sex as unanxious, self-actualising people play it'.[53] The word 'unanxious' is important, and not just because it seems to be a new and rather dubious invention. It helps us to understand the function of the book. Where 1920s sex manuals had sought to make their readers unanxious about the 'old face-to-face matrimonial', this book seeks to make readers unanxious about practices which, the text makes plain, many of them would find distasteful. The 1960s sexual revolution revived the myth that 1920s and 30s sexologists had propagated, that sexual problems and incompatibilities existed because of the impact of Victorian morality. Where 1920s sexologists could make out that they were bravely combatting Victorianism, because of its nearness in time, writers like Comfort have a more difficult task in identifying the bogey which has caused 'people', but quite obviously women, to be afraid of sex. The section on what is 'normal' explains where anxiousness comes from.

> . . . sex, for reasons built into the species, makes us uniquely anxious compared with other divergencies of need or taste and our culture is coming out of a period of moral panic into a re-awareness that there is nothing to fear. Accordingly, a lot of people are, in their sexual assumptions, like the generation of Victorian children brought up to believe that green sweets were poisonous and rice pudding was good for you because it was unpalatable: they need reassuring.[54]

When we look in detail at the practices described, it becomes clear that women, in particular, have very good reason to be anxious. Women's anxiety is not just some unnecessary vestige of a past morality but a realistic response to most, if not all the practices and ideas about sex in this book. *The Joy of Sex* shows women to be rather unregenerately 'Victorian' in attitude to sex, never quite catching up to what is modern. Women's backwardness was the problem in all sexual-revolution advice literature. In such literature a range of practices was being normalised which women were seen as having particular problems with. Women are instructed on how to find the taste of semen pleasant lest they feel reluctant to let men ejaculate in their mouths, how to delight in being tied up, how to enjoy being spanked and anal intercourse. Not surprisingly it is women, not men, who have resistance to such practices and need reprogramming. This literature instructs women to turn themselves into willing and enthusiastic sexual objects and servicers of male sexuality even to the detriment of their health, pride and self-respect. Women are told in The Joy of Sex that they should cheerfully accept every variant form of sexual interest or fantasy that their male partner might suggest and act it out joyfully. The woman should be joyful even though the fantasies consist of degrading and humiliating her.

> Most wives who don't like Chinese food will eat it occasionally for the pleasure of seeing a Sinophile husband enjoy it, and vice versa. Partners who won't do this over specific sex needs are usually balking, not because they've tried it and it's a turn-off (many experimental dishes turn out nicer than you expected), but simply through ignorance of the range of human needs, plus being scared if these include things like aggression . . . [55]

In theory the book is free of gender bias. It sets out to suggest that both men and women could act out any of the practices, but the pictures and text give the lie to this apparent gender neutrality. The superficial friendliness of the book breaks down when women's resistance to men's sexual demands is under discussion and naked threat shows through. In the section for women on what male sexuality consists of, women's anxiety about having to dress up in corsets or black vinyl is addressed directly and a lecture on fantasy delivered. Women are warned that failure to find out and act upon their men's fantasies 'lands people in the divorce court for incompatibility'.[56] This is serious.

Behind the velvet glove of this 'fun' sexual-revolution bible lies the iron fist of male power and punishment.

The book offers a very useful definition of male sexuality. The definition is precise, narrow and prescriptive. If feminists were to describe male sexuality in this way they would probably be called manhaters, hostile, biased against men and extreme. But this advanced sexual-revolution manual is unembarrassed in its prejudices. In the section entitled 'Men (by him for her)' Comfort remarks:

> Prof. Higgins was right – men wish that women's sexuality was like theirs, which it isn't. Male sexual response is far brisker and more automatic: it is triggered easily by things, like putting a quarter in a vending machine. Consequently, at a certain level and for all men, girls and parts of girls are, at this stimulus level, unpeople. That isn't incompatible with their being people too. Your clothes, breasts, odor, etc., aren't what he loves instead of you – simply the things he needs in order to set sex in motion to express love. Women seem to find this hard to understand.
>
> Second, most though not all male feeling is ultimately centered in the last inch of the penis . . . [57]

All that women find most inconvenient or distressing about male sexuality is described here as natural and inevitable. Men, we are instructed, cannot 'be passively "taken" in a neutral way'.[58] The implication here is that women can be. The extra emphasis given by inverted commas to the word 'taken', which is a word associated with capture and enslavement, suggests an alarming aggression. Though the book claims gender neutrality, such slip-ups give the lie to this. Sexuality is viewed as a male-dominant and aggressive, and female-passive and submissive, activity throughout.

Not only are women told to accept and adjust to the given form of male sexuality, i.e. all those things they find most difficult, but they are instructed to service men's sexual interests in advance of them being voiced whether they like it or not. Women must learn what turns their men on and provide the appropriate stimulus. This is the sexual revolution. No longer may women lie around reluctantly tolerating sexual practices and interests they find objectionable. They must anticipate and turn themselves into a willing object and sexual servicer to the male.

> ... the most valued thing from you, in actual lovemaking, is intuition of these object reactions and direct initiative – *starting* the plays, taking hold of the penis, giving genital kisses ahead of being asked – being an initiator, a user of your stimulatory equipment ... what the male turn-on equipment requires is the exact reverse of a virgin or a passively recipient instrument – not a demand situation, because that in itself can threaten a turn-off from inadequacy feelings, but a skill situation ... [59]

We notice that women must not demand sexual servicing from men lest the men feel threatened, but they must initiate sexual servicing of the men. Male and female sexuality are very different, we are told, because 'male turn-ons are concrete, while many female turn-ons are situational and atmospheric'. None the less women are instructed to try to develop male sexual responses in order to be the 'ideal lover'.

> You can't of course control your turn-ons any more than he can, but it helps if a woman has some male-type object reactions, like being excited by the sight of a penis, or hairy skin, or by the man stripping, or by physical kind of play (just as it helps if the man has some sense of atmosphere).[60]

So clearly sexual behaviour is not natural or inevitable. It can be learned where this serves the interests of male-dominant heterosexuality, and is only disconcertingly recalcitrant where such learning might serve women's interests.

The section on 'Women (by her for him)' does not have a similar format. It is not devoted to telling men exactly what women's sexuality is like and demanding that men learn to anticipate women's sexual interests and service them. It starts with a warning to men not to make a 'direct grab for the clitoris' but to concentrate on 'breasts and skin first'.[61] Then it moves on to a lengthy apology to men that women aren't programmed

119

suitably for men, but assures men that women will do their best to please them. It claims that the penis is a 'shared possession, rather like a child' for a woman. Men are warned not to use clumsy brutality which would result in large bruises or twisted fingers. They are told that women enjoy a 'tough-tender' mixture. But men have to get it right and not let the toughness become brutality, which of course it easily can. There is a paragraph on sadomasochism in which we are told that women have difficulty in 'reifying', i.e. objectifying, and men can help them learn to do this. 'Role-swapping', it is stated, is general and women are no more masochistic than men and 'good sex can be wildly violent but still never cruel', except for the twisted fingers of course. We are told 'a little frightening helps some people sometimes'. Perhaps we are really expected to imagine sexual scenarios in which it is the women who are frightening men, but this seems unlikely. Suddenly there is a message which contradicts the import of the section on male sexuality.

> As to the Women's Lib bit, nobody can possibly be a good lover − or a whole man − if he doesn't regard women as (a) people and (b) equals.[62]

But we have earlier been told that 'all men' regard women as 'unpeople' sometimes and women just have to accept this! Clearly there is a small contradiction of interest between women and men revealed here.

The section on women's sexuality, then, turns out to be an apology for inadequacy, together with some instructions for men on what not to do and what would be absolutely gross. Men are not instructed in what women's sexuality inevitably is because, fortuitously, women 'can be less rigid and more experimental'. Men are told that women will adapt. They are not told to learn female sexual response. Men are told to help women to please them. The dramatic difference between these two sections reveals the real purpose of the book. It is a handbook which will teach women their new role in the sexual revolution, the servicing of male sexuality actively and not just passively.

Discussed in detail in the book are the ways in which women

are advised actively to service male desires. They must pay attention to manipulating their body image through the use of clothes and other apparel, including black leather, cosmetics, and adornments, including 'sadistic-looking buckles' and 'slave bangles'. They must learn to like playing with semen and to like smelling, tasting and swallowing it. They must learn not to be frightened of bondage, gagging or other 'aggressive symbolism'.

The section on 'gagging' reveals a wonderful confusion of language.

> Gagging and being gagged turns most men on – most women profess to hate it in prospect, but the expression of erotic astonishment on the face of a well-gagged woman when she finds she can only mew is irresistible to most men's rape instincts.[63]

The 'but' is wholly inappropriate. The fact that most men delight in seeing a woman whimper with fear, called here 'erotic astonishment' in no way contradicts the fact that women profess to hate gagging. It might in fact explain why women are not keen on being gagged. 'Because' would be a more appropriate conjunction. The writer's own excitement at the idea of gagging and perhaps raping a woman has overwhelmed his articulacy at this point. There are instructions on how to gag someone safely and a safety code for bondage in general with handy hints like, 'Ropemarks usually go in a few hours if you've been gentle.'[64]

The Joy of Sex is ill informed about prostitution in every way. It offers as the 'commonest motive' for becoming a streetwalking prostitute 'an active dislike of males'. This is a bizarre notion. The prostitute has to get closer to more males than other women. The commonest motive according to any modern studies of prostitution is, as a woman would expect, the need for money. Women working as prostitutes may well develop a strong dislike for males. Indeed it is surprising if they do not, but dislike is hardly likely to form a motive for their job.

'Sexual freedom', the writers maintain, is 'likely to displace monetary sex altogether'. It would do this by turning all women into surrogate prostitutes:

121

'Any women who herself is ready to enjoy and understand sex, and meet her partner's needs as fully as a professional but with love, can outclass anyone hired. . .

She can learn from periods and cultures in which the courtesan was a repository of the art of pleasing, but what we call whores' tricks ought to be called lovers' tricks. A woman who can make love with love and variety needn't fear commercial competition.[65]

This demand that a woman not working in prostitution act like a 'professional' is incompatible with women's freedom, though it may indeed sum up very well what men such as the writers of this book wanted from the sexual revolution. Prostitute women do sex to get paid, not for their own pleasure. They devote their energies totally to the man's pleasure and ego. A free woman in a love relationship with a man could not do this without serious threat to her sense of self. She would have to become a doormat and sex slave. It is because men have such difficulty in imagining a kind of sex not organised around dominance and submission that they can confuse what a prostitute does with what they want their girlfriends to do so disastrously. It is understandable that they should want total sexual maid service combined with devotion because use of prostitutes must sometimes lack necessary ingredients such as genuine adoration. But in a world in which women are supposed to be men's equals in terms of human rights and dignity, this is not possible.

There is another problem with this ambition of sexual-revolutionary men. One reason men go to prostitutes is to get the sort of sexual servicing they cannot get at home. Where once this was simply fellatio, it now includes some quite heavy sadomasochism and in some cases death. In snuff movies 'professionals' are actually killed on screen. This is not a service which many women would wish to provide for their husbands, though some have no choice and do get killed. In average sadomasochistic movies women get quite badly hurt. Peter Sutcliffe, the Yorkshire Ripper, went to 'professionals' so that he could kill them. Prostitutes have to suffer the worst extremes of womanhatred. It is not in women's interests to have to service all those sexual needs which men feel they want serviced. It should seem reasonable to suggest that women do not engage in any practices which cause them the least anxiety, because that anxiety is a good guide to what is a degrading practice. But our sexual-revolutionaries take quite a different viewpoint. They are prepared to threaten women who will not emulate prostitutes that their husbands will visit prostitutes if they do not comply.

In the context of a discussion of prostitution it is worth looking at another practice covered in the book, one that is called 'buttered bun'. This term, with which many women will probably be unfamiliar since it is certainly male sexual argot, refers to a 'woman who has recently had relations with another man'.[66] We are told that this is a 'carry-over from a fairly general ape behaviour, where sharing a partner is a form of bonding between males'. Notice that the writers do not mean 'general ape behaviour' here but male apes, even supposing this to be an accurate and not anthropomorphic interpretation of ape behaviour. They suggest that the attraction of the 'buttered bun' lies in her being an outlet for homosexuality and that this is what draws men to wife swapping and to the prostitute who is a 'shared woman'. What is revealing about this practice and the jovial way it is described in *The Joy of Sex* is that the use of a human being simply as a receptacle in which men can make contact with each other through their ejaculate can be regarded as unremarkable and morally neutral.

Exhibitionism, or indecent exposure, is a form of sexual harassment in which men follow or wait for women in order to intrude their penises on the women's attention. It is usually experienced by women as frightening and offensive because the harasser means it to be frightening and offensive. It is from women's shock and fear that he gets his thrill. *The Joy of Sex* is totally sympathetic to the harasser and treats women's fear as something they should just get over.

This would be a harmless but unrewarding activity (these timid characters are by definition not rapists) if people weren't shocked or frightened by it, though it's a disability to the fellow who can't get further than that. Under our extraordinary system, we reward them with public disgrace, imprisonment, etc. No woman need be scared if she meets one.[67]

The approach to rape is equally lighthearted and dismissive of women's pain. We are told that the 'surefire way a woman can resist rape, armed or not, is by suddenly emptying her bowels'. Is this serious? Women are instructed, 'Don't get yourself raped – i.e. don't deliberately excite a man you don't know well, unless you mean to follow through.'[68] Rape, then, is something women cause by tempting strange men sexually and then not wanting to engage in sexual intercourse. This bears no relation to what rape actually consists of.

The Joy of Sex may be liberal about many sexual practices but homosexuality is not one of them. 'All people,' we are told, 'are bisexual.' The problem is being homosexual, i.e. wanting to relate solely or mainly to persons of the same sex instead of being basically heterosexual with a bit of same-sex activity on the side. Homosexuality is described unflatteringly:

> All people are bisexual – that is to say, they are able to respond sexually to some extent towards people of either sex. Being 'homosexual' isn't a matter of having this kind of response, but usually of having some kind of turn-off towards the opposite sex which makes our same-sex response more evident or predominant.[69]

Homosexuality, therefore, is narrow and limited. Bisexuality isn't, though the only occasions on which 'bisexuality' might take place during the normal heterosexual lifestyle are said to be 'threesomes and group experiences'. In fact the bisexuality section seems designed to reassure anyone who feels tempted towards the same sex during such group scenes that there is no chance that this means they are homosexual: 'a great many people worry . . . because they are scared afterwards that they will become "queer" '.[70] They are told, 'There is not much risk of this.' The reason is that people with a 'strong counter-sex bias usually recognise it early (and might be better not to cultivate it, if straight sex has satisfied them so far)'. This is an exercise in heterosexual gatekeeping. Comfort and others want to legitimise group sex and are seeking a way around the problem that this might lead to destabilisation of heterosexuality through same-sex attractions.

124

After giving us the interesting information that women are much more likely than men to engage in same-sex activity in a group-sex scene, the section concludes with a statement clearly hostile to homosexuality.

Straight man-woman sex is the real thing for most people – others need something different, but their scope is usually reduced, not widened, by such needs.[71]

Comfort was a 'sexual radical' as long ago as the 1940s. A fascinating pamphlet from 1948, entitled *Barbarism and Sexual Freedom. Lectures on the sociology of sex from the standpoint of anarchism*, gives us a glimpse of his political philosophy. It might be a surprise to us to learn, after reading his later work, that he abjured 'power' and considered it undesirable. But he tells us in 1948, 'I write as an anarchist, that is, as one who rejects the conception of power in society as a force which is both anti-social and unsound in terms of general biological principle.'[72] He explains that he sees it as the responsibility of 'psychology and medicine . . . to initiate the process of sociological change by prescribing conscientious, intelligent and responsible disobedience and resistance by individuals towards irresponsible power-institutions such as war, military service, and other forms of coercion . . .'[73] He saw his political duty as an anarchist to fight against the constraints which 'every contemporary state' placed upon sexuality. Sexuality had to be freed and it was a problem that women, as he learned from comments in a gynaecological department, did not like it enough.

He expressed a hostility towards feminism and saw it as causing sexual repression. He considered, as have virtually all sexologists this century, that flashing was a harmless male hobby that women should not be alarmed by unless they were 'conditioned by a wholly bogus modesty'. The severity of the law, he explained, was a 'residue of the excessive and frigid feminism of a previous century'.[74] His attitude towards prostitutes shows a hostility towards women which might look rather illiberal coming from a sexual anarchist. He said that English prostitutes were 'largely recruited from the psychopaths and mentally defective'.[75]

125

The similarity between Comfort's earlier and later work lies in his contempt for women and his cheerful acceptance that, though the abuse of power might be a bad idea in some areas, the abuse of women by men was simply nature. Sex, for this 'anarchist', was a zone in which abusive power relationships could be allowed full rein, and were even necessary in the name of countering repression and defeating state power.

SWINGING

Swinging epitomises what was seen as most advanced and most liberated about the sexual revolution. It was an activity which many of the sexual revolutionaries whose work is examined in this book took up with great enthusiasm and promoted vigorously. Alex Comfort for example was a devotee.

Edward Brecher, populariser of the work of Masters and Johnson and an important translator of sexological literature for a mass audience, was also a swinger. He describes, in his book *The Sex Researchers*, the development of the 'sexual freedom movement' and the 'swinging scene'. He explains that the direct antecedent of swinging was a phenomenon called wife swapping which first received public mention in 1957 in a men's sex magazine called *MR*. The theme of group sex was then taken up by numerous other pornographic magazines which, as well as carrying promotional articles, would feature advertisements by aspirant practitioners alongside photographs of the wife to be swapped. Brecher points out that the photos resembled the magazines' regular models rather too closely and suggests that this early promotional work was really a scam. Soon, though, male readers caught on and started to send in ads and photos of their wives. Pornographic magazines began to organise parties at which the potential swappers could meet. The pornographers had invented a cult, and swinging is a useful example of the influence of pornography on culture.

Apparently the term 'wife swapping' occasioned some embarrassment among its new and liberated clientele. Even the term 'mate swapping' did not suffice though it had the advantage of being gender neutral. Though the group sex of the sexual revolution has retained the character of wife swapping throughout, so that the term is accurate and helpful to our understanding, it was important to blur the crudity of the abuse of the women involved. 'Mate swapping' was rejected in favour of 'swinging' in the 1960s because it 'involved much more than swapping' and single people took part.[76]

Sandstone Mansion in California was the site in the early 1970s of upmarket swinging. It was here that Brecher, Comfort and the Kronhausens swung. It helps an understanding of the gender dynamics of swinging to look at the development of the Sandstone experiment. It is described in detail in Gay Talese's journalistic but interesting survey of the sexual revolution, *Thy Neighbour's Wife*, subtitled *The sensational odyssey through sexuality in our time*. Talese was also an active participant in Sandstone.[77]

The inspirer of Sandstone was an engineer named John Williamson, a follower of Wilhelm Reich. Talese describes the nobility of Williamson's ideals thus:

> . . . he wanted to go further than Reich's followers in altering the sociopolitical system through sexual experimentation – he hoped to soon establish his idealized community for couples wishing to demolish the double standards, to liberate women from their submissive roles, and to create a sexually free and trusting atmosphere in which there would be no need for possessiveness, jealousy, guilt, or lying.[78]

Williamson, then, was one of those men possessed of their own vision of women's liberation, a vision tailored to their own interests, which they sought to persuade or educate women into. This male-designed and inspired version of women's liberation consisted in getting rid of women's hangups about sex and their need to associate sex with emotion. Women were to become sexually enthusiastic on demand about any male initiatives. They were to overcome jealousy. The campaign against 'possessiveness' which formed such an important plank of sexual-revolution ideology, tended, like any other supposedly 'liberating' strategy in a society in which men and women were far from equal, to benefit men resoundingly. Women were to be trained to accept that their male partners would be sexually active with other women. Let us see how Williamson put this training into effect.

In the summer of 1966 Williamson married Barbara Cramer. Shortly after their marriage the training began. Williamson planned a weekend break. As they were about to leave he told Barbara that they would be accompanied by an ex-lover of his, a woman who worked in his office. Barbara realised that John and Carol had planned the weekend between them. On arrival at their cabin John and Carol went into a bedroom and began to make love. At this stage Barbara was not fully trained and was unable to join them. She spent the night miserably in the other bedroom, no doubt castigating herself for her backwardness. In the morning John and Carol came in to comfort her. Later that day a male guest, invited by John, joined the party and was clearly intended as a sexual contact for Barbara. Barbara acquiesced and when John and Carol went into their room that night she took the new arrival to bed. Does this sound like women's liberation? The episode forms a useful model for our understanding of the Sandstone experiment when it was finally set up. The initiative, control and vision lay with men, particularly the guru of the enterprise, Williamson.

The experiment began in the house the Williamsons lived in before Sandstone. They held nude gatherings and group-sex evenings. Talese was a participant in Sandstone and is in total sympathy with its philosophy. He describes the behaviour of Williamson in the element he had created thus:

> Sitting in the centre of the room, surrounded by a small circle of people who seemed to be listening raptly to his words, was the burly figure of John Williamson, broad-chested with a potbelly and small penis, a blond Buddha whose right foot was being massaged by the dazzling olive-skinned Oralia, a nude Nefertiti whose perfect body . . . was the envy of every woman in the room.[79]

Williamson's power was exercised over men as well as women. He used brutal techniques to overcome the 'ownership problems' of both sexes, such as exposing to a woman her husband's infidelity, forcing her to witness her husband going to bed with another woman and then taking the wife for his lover. Through such shock techniques, it seems, he was able to acquire emotional control of his flock.

Sandstone was set up as a commune and a business proposition. The acolytes of both sexes would live in the grounds and work on improving the property. Guests would pay $250 per year to come to use the facilities and join in the group sex, which took place in the 'ballroom'. Participants were well-off members of the bored American middle class, performing meaningless jobs and seeking something to give purpose to their lives. Williamson sought to gain acceptance for Sandstone in the scientific and sexological community in order to establish its credentials. Well-known sexologists were invited to associate their names with the venture and to take part. Talese points out that Sandstone was in the tradition of American communal experiments like the Oneida community, in which women were held in common under the leadership of a guru figure who had sexual access to them all.

An example of the way in which Sandstone 'liberated' women is the behaviour of Barbara Cramer on seeing a man trying to rape a woman at the side of the road.

Barbara pulled her own car off the road, jumped out, and fearlessly approached the man, shouting: 'Let her alone! If you want to fuck somebody, you can fuck me.' The man, astonished, was quickly intimidated, and retreated.[80]

This response, seen as admirable by Sandstone residents, symbolises the attitude of such sexual revolutionaries to sexual violence. Rape was to be ended by all women being prepared to offer themselves sexually to men, the assumption behind such logic being that men rape because they do not have access to women. That is not in fact the case. Men rape because they intend to inspire fear and exercise power. A willing alternative victim would not suffice. Cramer, here, was acting fully in consonance with sexual-revolution ideology. Instead of going to the woman's aid in fighting off the attacker she offered herself to him.

Participants at Sandstone included, besides Comfort, the Kronhausens and Edward Brecher (described as a 'close friend of Masters and Johnson'), 'the marriage counsellors William Hartman and Marilyn Fithian, often referred to as the Masters and Johnson of the West Coast', Daniel Ellsberg of Pentagon Papers fame, Betty Dodson, 'artist and feminist', the editor Kent Carroll of Grove Press, the American equivalent of Girodias' Olympia Press and publisher of the banned books of the 1960s, and Art Kunkin of the Los Angeles Free Press, an alternative-culture publication. So Sandstone brought together all engines of the sexual-revolution propaganda machine: sex therapists and radical sexologists, the alternative press, an early feminist prophet of sexual liberation, and pornography publishers. Comfort's role in Sandstone, according to Talese, was that of voyeur as well as participant:

Often the nude biologist Dr Alex Comfort, brandishing a cigar, traipsed through the room between the prone bodies with the professional air of a lepidopterist strolling through the fields waving a butterfly net, or an ornithologist tracking along the surf a rare species of tern. A grey-haired bespectacled owlish man with a well-preserved body, Dr Comfort was unabashedly drawn to the sight of sexually engaged couples and their concomitant cooing, considering such to be enchanting and endlessly instructive; and with the least amount of encouragement – after he had deposited his cigar in a safe place – he would join a friendly clutch of bodies and contribute to the merriment.[81]

In Comfort's follow-up to *The Joy of Sex, More Joy of Sex*, he is, not surprisingly, enthusiastic about Sandstone. Its importance is expressed as follows:

Sandstone was many straight people's first and only encounter with genuinely open sexuality in a structured setting, and the fact that it recreated an intense experience of infantile innocence in hung-up adults makes many who went there

130

nostalgic or overenthusiastic about it. But allowing for this its capacity to facilitate the sort of growth at which individual psychology aims was pretty remarkable.[82]

The growth resulted from the overcoming of 'the custodial anxieties of conventional marriage'. It took place as follows: '. . . both sexes found that the sight of a lover relating sexually to someone else – often while still holding their regular partner's hand – was moving, exciting and finally immensely releasing.'[83]

Before swinging, the only opportunity for men to have access to large numbers of women was in brothels. *The Joy of Sex* claimed that prostitution would disappear as women in general imitated prostitutes and were prepared to perform free all the functions of a prostitute. It would be a reasonable extrapolation then to see swinging as the substitute for the brothel. The writers of *More Joy of Sex* are clearly worried that such an association might tarnish the image of swinging and are anxious to point out that Sandstone in no way resembled a brothel, but they had clearly made the association themselves.

> The essential point is that, in spite of enthusiastic sex on all sides, it was wholly unlike a brothel, and wholly like a relaxed home, the keynote not being excitement or lasciviousness but innocence, once the freakout produced in strangers by its openness was over.[84]

More Joy of Sex has a section on swinging as well as a section specifically on Sandstone. While wholeheartedly enthusiastic about Sandstone, the writers sound notes of caution about swinging either with strangers or with close friends. Swinging is best done, they seem to suggest, as members of a club or community. The introduction to the swinging section illustrates the gender dynamics of the practice very well, though the authors are apparently innocent of any gender imbalance in the joys of swinging. They explain that, 'In primitive societies . . . people exchange wives and husbands.' Then they proceed to talk about lending wives only. They explain that lending wives can be a gesture of hospitality and can increase the number of kin. Presumably the bonding that occurs, since it is wives who

131

are lent, is between men. This, they suggest, is one of the motives in swinging too. Men bond with each other through the exchange of women, or, as these writers maintain, 'people' acquire more 'kin'. The section on 'Threesomes' gives another clear example of the male-dominant gender dynamics. After using the gender-neutral language of 'permanent couple' and 'third party' the writers lapse into an example which is clearly male dominant, when describing how a 'loving couple' might invite another to join them.

> The relationship is a rather subtle, two-way gift – the woman who invites another that her man fancies is giving him a present (not least the feeling that she is totally secure and doesn't need to be jealous), and both are giving the third party the gift of sharing their secure intimacy – and their sexual knowhow. The same applies when the man does the same for his woman.[85]

Here the duties of the sexual-revolutionary woman have increased from the need to anticipate the male's sexual desires while they are alone to anticipating his sexual desire for someone else and arrange his satisfaction. The illustration shows a man being sexually serviced by two women.

Brecher, in his chapter on the swinging scene, gives the findings of three research projects into swinging being undertaken in the late 1960s by sociologists and psychologists who seem mainly to have been participants themselves. Some of the findings he includes give a glimpse of the gender dynamics of swinging in settings other than Sandstone. Comfort gives no indication that there was a gender imbalance in the joys of swinging. Swingers quoted in the Brecher chapter give the lie to this. The first indication that there might be a gender imbalance lies in the difficulty of achieving a mix of sexes in swinging. Brecher explains that, 'All over the country, swinging attracts far more males than females', which meant that swinging parties had to introduce rules that only couples could attend. 'Most men,' he writes, 'dig the scene' on their first exposure to it; many women, in contrast, are 'turned off'.[86] One respondent said she could 'gain nothing' from the parties. She liked the

' "relationship" of a sexual experience' and could 'gain nothing from just the sex act in itself'. Another spoke of swingers having to pay special attention to the problem of the 'unwillingness of most women – even "swinging" women – to have sex with strangers'. Swinging in Chicago seems to have been particularly brutal in its implications for women who got involved.

> At some Chicago parties, for example, the doors are locked at 10 p.m. and every girl or woman staying after that hour is expected simply to say yes or no immediately upon being approached and propositioned.[87]

It is not difficult to imagine the sort of pressure which a man who knew he could not get access to a swinging party without bringing his partner might exert. One woman reported, 'Before we were married, my husband talked me into it (sufficiently) to enjoy them.'[88] Threats of the withdrawal of love, in a society in which a woman's status and feelings of self-worth are dependent on attachment to a male, would be enough to encourage some reluctant women. The words of one female swinger illustrate the lengths to which a wife is prepared to go to keep her husband happy.

> I find, being a woman, that my opportunities for sexual encounter are more easily found than for my husband, being a man and having to be the initiator of encounters. I feel my primary responsibility is to him. I am watchful and attentive of his mood; rather than leave him alone to sulk and feel sorry for himself (and angry at me), I would forgo sexuality.[89]

What were the results of swinging? For some wives swinging had helped their marriage keep together by stimulating the husband's sexual interest in his wife. One woman reported that swinging had:

> ... relieved the boredom my husband had been feeling; after attending one party our sexual relationship improved greatly for a while ... Of course I hope that I remain his sexual object too.[90]

In swinging we have an example of sexual revolution precepts taken to their logical extreme. According to the enthusiastic sexologists, it was a liberating practice based upon the noblest of ideals of overcoming possessiveness and of pursuing 'open' sexuality, the obvious relinquishing of Victorian prudery and sexual hangups gained from repressive childhoods. Swinging was good for all 'people'. Swinging in operation, however, shows that its joys were not gender-neutral. It looks indeed as though a process of often brutal manipulation and brainwashing was used to persuade women to swing. Women seem, from their reluctance to swing, to see through the ideological baloney to what the experience of swinging would mean for them. Swinging women were required to act out with enthusiasm the role of brothel prostitute, turning themselves into objects of consumption, learning to suspend self-respect. Brecher, who was a convert to swinging, was still prepared to state that, 'In many cases . . . it is the husband who initiates swinging contacts and then either persuades or browbeats his wife into "going along".'[91] But, he is swift to point out, it was possible to find women who were keen on swinging.

Some women doubtless tried to win in the swinging game and that could only be achieved by being more sexually aggressive than the men and flinging themselves with enthusiasm into the role. A subjection willingly embraced can seem more tolerable than a subjection unwillingly borne. Why, our enthusiastic sexologists would ask, should it be the women who lose dignity, self-respect and personhood from swinging when men are equally naked and also taking part? But the ability to ask such a question would presuppose innocence of the power dynamics of heterosexuality in which there are still what are called double standards. A double standard represents the difference in political meaning attached to male and female sexual behaviour. Nakedness in a man and in a woman have different meanings under male supremacy. Similarly men's sexual use of women is imbued with quite different meanings from women's use of men. When women feel shame and anxiety at situations such as swinging it is because they sense the loss of status they undergo and the gain in status that accrues to the male. They are not suffering from hangups but are experiencing an instinct for self-protection.

MASTERS AND JOHNSON AND SEX THERAPY

William Masters and Virginia Johnson are seen as responsible for a revolution in sex therapy in the 1960s. Their work was hailed by feminists because they concentrated attention on the clitoral orgasm, apparently disproving once and for all, through their research, the Freudian notion that the healthy woman should have a vaginal orgasm. Edward Brecher, author of *The Sex Researchers*, was a personal friend as well as an admirer of their work. With his wife he wrote a popular companion guide to Masters' and Johnson's first book *Human Sexual Response* which, he proudly tells us, sold 500,000 copies. Brecher tells us that their study 'made it possible to follow the entire human sexual cycle from the first stirrings of erotic desire through to ultimate subsidence as objectively as nineteenth-century physiologists had followed the digestive cycle'. Their study was 'authoritative' because it was based on 'direct laboratory observation of more than 10,000 male and female orgasms'.[92]

Masters and Johnson applied the findings of their research in the laboratory to sex therapy and created a form of therapy which is based upon technique rather than psychotherapy or surgery. They have acquired a progressive veneer but the underlying purpose of the sex therapy they advocate remains the maintenance of male dominance. Brecher cites an example of successful sex-therapy treatment to illustrate the 'significance' of their clinical achievement. In this case a man who was a premature ejaculator and could not consummate his marriage was cured and became capable of penetration. Brecher expresses Masters' and Johnson's conclusion about this case as follows:

They add that the husband's ability to perform effectively and securely in the sexual sphere has also profoundly affected his ability to play the male with confidence in the other spheres of his life, and has revolutionised the marriage relationship.[93]

135

Efficient and frequent wielding of the penis was indissolubly linked with male dominance for individual men. We can assume from all we know of sexology that to 'play the male' means the exercise of power as playing the woman, the parallel goal of therapy, would mean submission.

Brecher tells us that Masters began his research by interviewing 'at length and in depth' 118 female and 27 male prostitutes. The use of prostitutes as a pilot-study group helps us to understand the politics of his kind of sex therapy. Brecher tells us how 'remarkably perceptive' or 'exceedingly lucky' Masters was to turn first to prostitutes. They were, he said, the best-informed experts on human sexual response. They were such useful experts because they had developed the skill of bringing a bored and uninterested man who did not even fancy them to orgasm. He explains that the clients of prostitutes had routinely eaten and drunk too much and were up long past their bedtimes. Often they were assailed by guilt and, to add to their difficulties in sexual responsiveness, they were likely to be with women for whom they had no affection or sexual passion.

> Despite many such obstacles, the prostitute is expected to and in almost all cases succeeds in arousing her client erotically and triggering his orgasm in as short a time as possible – often within a few minutes. Even a moderately competent and intelligent prostitute, after a few hundreds of thousands of such encounters, is surely a worthwhile informant concerning sexual response patterns.[94]

The prostitute-client relationship reveals the naked power politics at play in heterosexual exchange under male supremacy. Women who work as prostitutes service male sexuality for the sake of money. The relationship has all the inequality of any servicing occupation and powerfully symbolises the sexual oppression of women. Masters ignored the political dimension of prostitution and saw it as a representative sexual interaction particularly suited to form the foundation of his work. Prostitutes, through servicing the male erection, serve male dominance. They, like sex therapists, help men to be 'men'. Masters based his sex-therapy techniques on the techniques the prostitutes taught him about from their experience. Their 'methods for elevating or controlling sexual tensions' and 'variations in stimulative technique' had 'been integrated into the clinical research programs'.[95]

An example of such techniques is that prescribed for premature ejaculation. To take premature ejaculation seriously we have to assume that prolonged sexual intercourse is a necessary and desirable practice and important for women who wish to achieve orgasm. Masters and Johnson did believe this. The recommended therapeutic technique required the active co-operation of the wife in the role of prostitute, in a direct, hands-on approach. The technique was based on that introduced by James Semans. Semans taught the technique to men to practise on themselves. Masters and Johnson believed it could only be effective if practised by the woman. They prescribe a correct position for the procedure and describe the 'squeeze technique' thus:

> ... the female partner's thumb is placed on the frenulum, located on the inferior ... surface of the circumcised penis, and the first and second fingers are placed on the superior ... surface of the penis in a position immediately adjacent to one another on either side of the coronal ridge ... As the man responds to sufficient pressure applied in the manner described, he will immediately lose his urge to ejaculate.[96]

The wife thus has to use techniques derived from practice in prostitution to cure her husband. We are told that this is in her own interests. The purpose was ostensibly to enable the husband to penetrate long enough for the woman to orgasm with the penis *in situ*. Once ejaculatory control was established, the wife had the task of gradually introducing the penis into her vagina while still using the squeeze technique and in a female superior position so that appropriate control during sexual intercourse could be learned. The original treatment programme would take two weeks but the wife was required to give the husband refresher courses for at least another year. Masters and Johnson propose that such refresher courses take place when the woman is menstruating in order to 'provide at least one session of 15 to 20 minutes devoted specifically to male sexual stimulation'.[97]

Such an instruction makes short shrift of any idea that Masters and Johnson sex therapy was supposed to be in the woman's interest. If a woman wanted penetration with the penis, menstruation would not necessarily deter her. If menstruation interfered with the desired penetration, and particularly if she did not desire penetration above all things, then surely other sexual practices could be engaged in. In fact she is expected simply to practise, irrespective of her own pleasure, for a time when penetration with the penis could be employed. The woman is expected to put time and energy into a procedure she may well find repellent or irksome so that the male may dominate her more effectively. The wife's part is equally onerous if the man's complaint is that of ejaculatory incompetence, i.e. difficulty in ejaculating at all. This time the wife must employ an opposite technique and masturbate the man to orgasm, then masturbate him to just short of orgasm and get him to penetrate. Again it is a long-drawn-out process.

Treatment of supposed sexual inadequacies in women is rather different. The male is not expected to bear the burden of servicing the woman in quite the same way. There is no male equivalent of the female prostitute to service women, so the male has no model of subservience to emulate. Vaginismus, which is described as a muscular spasm preventing entry of the penis to the vagina, is treated by the insertion of dilators of graduated sizes into the woman's vagina by the husband. This practice coincides with an active pornographic model of male sexuality in which various unlikely objects are inserted into women's orifices. It could therefore be seen as offering some satisfaction to the male practitioner. But the woman is expected to turn herself into an object and behave like the heroine of a masochistic pornographic story. Masters and Johnson remark that:

After the larger-sized dilators can be introduced successfully, it is good policy to encourage intravaginal retention of the larger dilators for a matter of several hours each night.[98]

What mind could have invented such a distressing, humiliating and essentially pointless treatment save the pornographic mind?

138

It reveals the pornographer in the heart of the male sex therapist. If such treatment were to train the woman for anything it would be the role of useful and uncomplaining hole.

In some cases, where there was no wife to play the part of prostitute, Masters and Johnson would provide 'partner surrogates'. There is little obvious difference between partner surrogates and prostitutes except that partner surrogates were volunteers and did not get paid. They were seen as infinitely more useful than actual prostitutes because they would provide more than simply a physical performance. They were to 'approximate in so far as possible the role of a supportive, interested, cooperative wife.'[99]

Masters and Johnson did not provide surrogates for women who were unable to provide their own partners. They were anxious that this might seem to be a reinforcement of the double standard in sexuality, as indeed it was. They rationalise this implication thus:

> Refusing to make a male partner surrogate available to a sexually inadequate woman, yet providing a female partner surrogate for a dysfunctional man, seems to imply application of a double standard for clinical treatment; such is not the case. As repeatedly described, psychosocial factors encouraged in this method of psychotherapy are developed from the individual's existing value system.[100]

In other words, because a double standard exists in the construction of male and female sexuality, Masters and Johnson feel they should continue it because it facilitates treatment. Using a surrogate fits with men's sexual-value system and will be useful to them. It doesn't fit with women's sexual-value system and would be contraindicated therapeutically for women. This is the application of a double standard of course. Women were to be trained to be efficient in their prescribed subordinate role and men in a dominant one.

There was one sexual practice which was specifically proscribed. This was the insertion of fingers into the vagina. Masters and Johnson have a reputation for sexual liberalism and fulminated often against the destructive effects of sexual negatives, so why would they exhibit disapproval of this particular sexual practice? They phrase their disapproval thus:

> A further dimension of sexual excitation is derived from manipulation of the vaginal outlet when lubricating material is acquired for clitoral spread by superficial finger insertion. There is usually little value returned from deep vaginal insertion of the fingers, particularly early in the stimulative process. While some women have reported a mental translation of the ensuing intravaginal sensation to that of penile containment, few had any preference for the opportunity.[101]

At first sight this might seem very puzzling. We are told that women have to imagine that fingers are penises in order to be able to come to terms with them being in their vaginas at all and still don't really like the experience. Women, they say, only like penises in their vaginas. Masters and Johnson make a clear value judgment in saying that fingers in vaginas are of 'little value' and the only possible reason for fingers to be anywhere near vaginas is to make the approach to the clitoris easier. Similar warnings about the use of fingers in vaginas are issued by other sexologists. The possibility of digital penetration was clearly a source of concern. The Japanese sexologist Sha Kokken, in a 1960 sex manual, gives us an explanation which might help to explain such sexological anxiety.

> Many men who realise the need of preliminary play tend to overdo it. This is not advisable from the medical viewpoint, particularly when the fingers are inserted deep into the vagina, for it may cause infection. The use of fingers should be limited to the entrance to the vagina. Fingering the cervix or the vaginal wall should be avoided for another reason: The woman may develop deeper satisfaction from these caresses than from sexual intercourse itself. Man should not forget that the vagina should normally be reserved for the penis.[102]

There may be a clue here. The sexologists are afraid that women will prefer fingers in their vaginas to penises. They have sound reasons for their concern. Fingers are flexible and sensitive

compared with the blunt instrument of the penis. The sex therapists acknowledge that they are good for the clitoris and other
parts of the body. How are they to explain why they suddenly
cease to be efficacious at the entrance to the vagina? Were
women to discover the delights of fingers in their vaginas they
might abandon sexual intercourse and thus undermine heterosexuality by spurning its sacred institution. They might also, of
course, question why they need to be with men. A woman's
fingers are likely to be as sensitive, or because of their greater
familiarity, more sensitive than those of a man.

Masters and Johnson provide a fairy story to justify the need
for penises and not fingers in the vagina. They tell us that
women come to regard the penis in the vagina as their own little
toy to play with. We can almost hear the woman's disbelief as
they tell her this:

> Frequently, it is of help to assure the wife that once the marital
> unit is sexually joined, the penis belongs to her just as the
> vagina belongs to the husband.

Women are then told what they will feel and do in the manner
of a child-development textbook.

> When conceptually she has a penis to play with, usually the
> woman will do just that. If she will allow the vaginally con-
> tained penis to stimulate slowly and feelingly in the same
> manner she enjoyed sensate pleasure from body stroking or
> the manipulation of her genital organs under her controlled
> directions, she will find herself overwhelmed with sexual
> feeling.[103]

Masters and Johnson justify their belief in male-dominant sexuality by advancing sociobiological arguments. Men, they
explain, have to be active and dominant in sex for the purpose
of reproduction. They believe in some higher plan constructed
by nature which supersedes the arguments of feminism.

> A man places primary valuation on his capacity for effective
> sexual function. This is both valid and realistic. His sexual

effectiveness fulfills the requirement of procreation and is honored with society's approval, thereby providing support for the cultural idiosyncrasy of equating sexual function with masculinity.[104]

Woman's sexual response is described as depending upon 'real indentification with the male partner', a sentiment in which the male supremacist values shine confidently through.

Their discussion of the causes of sexual dysfunction omits any reference to an inequality of power between men and women or to the role played by sexuality in the maintenance of women's oppression. The main problem causing sexual dysfunction in women, they state, is sexual ignorance. There may be all kinds of different factors operating in individual cases, such as being handicapped by 'religious orthodoxy' or 'unexplained dyspareunia' or 'aging constriction of the vaginal barrel', but all sexually dysfunctional women have 'one thing in common'.

They all exhibit almost complete lack of authoritative information from which to gain some degree of objectivity when facing the psychosocial problem evidenced by the symptoms of their sexual dysfunction.[105]

These women were to receive the objective truth from the expert sexologists instead of relying on their own judgment. They might, after all, be persisting in subjectively not liking sexual intercourse or wanting something quite different sexually from what the sexologists were prescribing as healthy.

In their 1970 book *The Pleasure Bond*, Masters and Johnson spell out their philosophy of sex in rather more detail. Collaboration with a journalist is helpful to the intelligibility of their ideas. It is described as 'a landmark book on the ways in which the loving and caring sexual relationship of a couple can be strengthened and intensified as time goes by'.[106] By this time they had become aware of the existence of the women's liberation movement. The book seeks to hijack the WLM in order to harness its energies to the task of greater heterosexual fulfilment, primarily for men. They redefine women's emancipation as sexual emancipation. They explain that up to the middle of the twentieth century sex was seen as something that husbands did to wives with little consideration of female pleasure. The sexologists are credited with creating a change in consciousness such that sex became something a husband did 'for' his wife and with her pleasure in mind. Masters and Johnson saw the period of sexological history in which they were living as one in which sex was to be something that husband and wife did 'with' each other. They expressed this remarkable progress thus: 'So woman's role has accomplished a hundred-and-eighty-degree turn – from that of sexual servant to sexual equal, all in the last ten to twenty years.'[107]

One chapter in the book is devoted to 'What men stand to gain from women's liberation'. It is headed by a Virginia Johnson quotation in which she asks whether a couple 'can make progress toward sexual equality without undermining the sexual relationship itself?'[108] This central anxiety is the theme of the chapter. Uneasily the writers remark that 'feminism today is moving forward with all the fervour of a fad'.[109] They ask whether women will pursue 'sex equality' if it threatens 'emotional fulfilment in their private worlds' because, they tell us, 'fulfilment for the overwhelming majority of women requires as enduring relationship with a man'.[110] Their hostility to women's liberation is revealed in their comment: 'Militant Women's Liberation advocates may deplore that fact, but a fact it remains.' They reassure themselves with a recitation of statistics to demonstrate the popularity of married and unmarried heterosexual coupling and include a dire warning to 'liberationists'.

> If some of the leaders of the women's movement make the strategic mistake of attacking marriage as part of a male plot to keep women under control, they will almost surely find themselves out of touch with most other women.[111]

They optimistically identify women's liberation with sexual liberation. This sexual liberation would entail women participating with real enthusiasm in the sexological prescription for male dominance and female submission. Women's emancipation would mean that woman's last vestiges of reluctance would

143

disappear as she sought willingly to service the male. Emancipated women would become sexually responsive and exciting partners, initiating sexual activity and new stimulating varieties of sexual practice.

Chapter 4

THE FAILURE OF GAY LIBERATION

It might seem to heterosexuals that lesbians and gay men would have a great deal in common and that a movement for the liberation of gay people would clearly benefit lesbians. This chapter looks at why gay liberation failed lesbians and women in general. Gay liberation, I suggest, after an initial heady commitment to feminist principles, became a movement for male gay liberation, incorporating principles which are at total odds with the concept of women's liberation. To understand the way in which the gay liberation movement developed it is necessary to look at the form historically taken by gay male sexuality.

Heterosexual ideology teaches that sex is eroticised dominance for men and submission for women. This sexual model reflects and enhances the real power imbalance between men and women in the world outside the bedroom. It is not unreasonable to expect that since such a power imbalance is not built into the relationships of gay men, they might provide a model of mutual, non-exploitative, non-objectifying sexual practice. Unfortunately the history of male homosexuality shows that, in general, male gay sexual practice has only provided an analogue of male heterosexual practice. The absence of built-in inequality between gay men seems to have necessitated the creation of deliberate inequality in the form of class or age or sadomasochism. If we understand sexuality as being socially constructed then this is not surprising. As men gays receive the same socialisation as do heterosexual men. Dominance and submission are eroticised for them too.

A few examples from male gay history show how middle-class gay males worked out this problem.

Today's political gay men see themselves as the heirs of a tradition starting with Walt Whitman in the mid-nineteenth century and carried down, through the pioneers of gay male sexual freedom he inspired, to gay liberation. All these respected forebears eroticised power difference around class, age or race. Whitman, esteemed poet of an American literary establishment which manages to teach him without mentioning the homosexuality which is such a potent force behind his poetry, writes with passionate enthusiasm about working-class men, particularly young ones.

> The young fellow hoeing corn, the sleigh-driver driving his
> six horses through the crowd,
> The wrestle of wrestlers, two apprentice-boys, quite grown,
> lusty, good-natured, native-born, out on the vacant lot at
> sundown after work,
> The coats and caps thrown down, the embrace of love and
> resistance,
> The upper-hold and the under-hold, the hair rumpled over
> and blinding the eyes;
> The march of firemen in their own costumes, the play of
> masculine muscles through clean-setting trowsers and
> waist-straps, . . .[1]

Whitman's work inspired the gay socialist and sex reformer of the late nineteenth and early twentieth century, Edward Carpenter. Carpenter took not just inspiration and ideas from Whitman's homoeroticism but also his literary style. He also, in the prose work *Towards Democracy*, writes lists of working-class male types. Like Whitman he intersperses female types, perhaps to throw readers off the scent of his homosexuality. A male example from one of Carpenter's lists is 'The thick-thighed hot coarse-fleshed young bricklayer with the strap round his waist'.[2] Carpenter's personal preference for virile working-class men was lived out in his long partnership with George Merrill.[3]

Such socialist gay sex reformers were able to integrate the passion for working-class men into their politics. There is no doubt of Carpenter's passionate enthusiasm to eliminate class. In *Towards Democracy* he adopts Whitman's habit of starting sentences with 'of' and never finishing them, to declaim against the iniquity of class distinction. A small fragment will serve to show the drift:

Of exclusiveness, and of being in the swim; of the drivel of aristocratic connections; of drawing-rooms and levées and the theory of animated clothespegs generally;... of being a parson and afraid to be seen toping with Christ in a public [bar]; a barrister and to travel in a third class carriage; an officer and to walk with one of your own men ...[4]

Whitman and Carpenter believed that their egalitarian sexual interests and politics could be blended together; homosexual love could overcome class barriers. Carpenter explains:

Eros is a great leveller. Perhaps true Democracy rests, more firmly than anywhere else, on a sentiment which easily passes the bounds of class and caste, and unites in the closest affection the most estranged ranks of society. It is noticeable how often Uranians of good position and breeding are drawn to rougher types ... [5]

E. M. Forster was not a public campaigner for homosexual rights in his lifetime but did leave many male gay stories and a novel to be published on his death. Forster seems to have been a typical middle-class gay man of his time in being sexually attracted to working-class youths. He was inspired by being touched on the bottom by Carpenter's lover George Merrill, so it is not surprising that his eroticism should take a form similar to Carpenter's. In 1935 Forster wrote: 'I want to love a strong young man of the lower classes and be loved by him and even hurt by him. That is my ticket, and then I have wanted to write respectable novels ...'[6] The description of the milkman who has a sexual encounter with a middle-class man in Forster's short story 'Arthur Snatchfold' demonstrates the working-class qualities that such an eroticism found attractive. Working-classness meant sensuality and down-to-earthness.

. . . he was a very proper youth. His shoulders were broad, his face sensuous and open, his eyes, screwed up against the light, promised good temper . . . Seen at close quarters he was coarse, very much of the people and of the thick-fingered earth; and a hundred years ago his type was trodden into the mud, now it burst and flowered and didn't care a damn.[7]

Christopher Isherwood was inspired in his early writing by the novels of E. M. Forster. Isherwood, in both life and art, demonstrated a devotion to working-class German boys. The power difference between the middle-class Englishman and the German youths at a time of economic distress at the end of the Weimar Republic, was exacerbated by the fact that Isherwood paid for the boys. They were prostitutes. The way he describes Otto in 'On Ruegen Island' and 'The Nowaks' has much in common with Forster's description of the milkman above.

Otto is his whole body; Peter is only his head. Otto moves fluidly, effortlessly; his gestures have the savage, unconscious grace of a cruel, elegant animal.[8]

His brand new brown suit was vulgar beyond words; so were his lilac spats and his pointed yellow shoes. On his finger was an enormous signet-ring with a square chocolate-coloured stone.[9]

Again working-classness is seen as sensual and primitive, elemental but also essentially vulgar. There is no doubt that the relationships middle-class Englishmen engaged in in Berlin were exploitative and objectifying. Auden introduced Isherwood to a boy bar where boys offered themselves for sale and could be handled by prospective purchasers through cut-off pockets at the tables.[10] Isherwood met Bubi there who was a heterosexual and practised homosexuality for money. Isherwood, who writes autobiography in the third person, described the fantasy he projected on to Bubi thus:

Christopher chose to identify himself with a black-haired British ancestor and to see The Blond as the invader who comes from another land to conquer and rape him. Thus The Blond becomes the masculine foreign yang mating with Christopher's feminine native yin . . . [11]

The above examples of middle-class male gay behaviour are selected from the histories of those men who have served as admired exemplars to the male gay reform movement in the twentieth century. Why did such men not relish the opportunity that being homosexual gave them, particularly when they saw themselves as democrats and socialists, to abandon dominance and submission sex in order to have mutual and equal relationships with men of their own class and tastes? It appears that men of their own class were not erotically attractive to them. For men whose eroticisim depended upon power difference homosexuality presented a real problem. It is possible that not being aroused could only be avoided by structuring sexual relationships around a power difference created by age, class, race or payment. It would be reassuring to see such men simply as products of a very different historical period and to expect middle-class gay males of today to exhibit an altogether more egalitarian approach to sexual practice. Unfortunately, as we shall see, eroticised power difference remains the bedrock of gay male practice, though there are a good few gay men today who will criticise this model.

A FALSE DAWN

Gay Liberation got under way in Britain in 1970. The auguries were good for a thorough re-examination of sexuality and particularly male sexuality so that it might be transformed in ways which would promote the liberation not just of gays but of peoples suffering from any form of oppression. The principles published in December 1970 state:

GLF therefore sees itself as part of the wider movement aiming to abolish all forms of social oppression. It will work to ally itself with other oppressed groups while preserving its organisational independence.[12]

149

The first ally to be mentioned was the women's liberation movement which was seen to be crucially important because, 'The roots of women's oppression are in many ways close to our own.' The other allies were to be 'black people and other national minorities', 'the working class', 'young people' and 'peoples oppressed by imperialism'.

The 1971 manifesto embraced feminist analysis of gender roles and male power. The commitment to support women's liberation was more than empty words and does seem to have been central to gay-liberation theory. The failure of lesbians and gay men to adopt traditional gender roles was seen to be a cause for celebration and the basis of a more liberated lifestyle.

> We are already outside the family and we have already, in part at least, rejected the 'masculine' or 'feminine' roles society has designed for us. In a society dominated by the sexist culture it is very difficult, if not impossible, for heterosexual men and women to escape their rigid gender-role structuring and the roles of oppressor and oppressed. But gay men don't need to oppress women in order to fulfil their own psychosexual needs, and gay women don't have to relate sexually to the male oppressor, so that at this moment in time, the freest and most equal relationships are most likely to be between homosexuals.[13]

In the early days this analysis of gender roles was reflected in the writings in the gay liberation magazine *Come Together*. Male gay sexuality was subjected to the searchlight of a feminist analysis. It was not simply role playing that was rejected. The critique extended to sexual behaviour, and cruising, the search for casual sexual partners, came under scrutiny. One writer describes cruising as 'searching for fulfilment of their adolescent sex fantasy (their "type"). Engaging in the "hunt". Cruising each other. Playing "games" with each other. Games of destruction. Prick teasing.'[14] He sees cruising as the result of 'Guilt at being homosexual . . . shame at being unable to be proud of his sexuality . . .' He describes the role players of male homosexuality as the 'ultra-butch, camp bitch' who 'betray fear and loathing' as 'tenderness, sensitivity are frozen out'. The cruising

150

ground of the public lavatory, called the 'cottage', is described as a 'coffin'. Gay men are invited to 'come out and live' with the lesbians and gay men who are 'proud and love one another'.

It was common for gay liberation men at this time to explain cruising, a practice with which they felt uncomfortable politically, as a result of gay oppression. Either this oppression could induce guilt and shame which would incline its victims to seek furtive contacts, or gay oppression could be seen as making sexual contacts, in any but the furtive way of cruising, difficult for gay men.

This argument cannot be sustained when we look at the sexual behaviour of lesbians. Lesbians are as oppressed as gay men and as likely to suffer guilt and shame. One might argue that the invisibility of lesbians would make cruising an even more necessary practice. But lesbians do not cruise. It is difficult to get accurate information on lesbian and gay sexual practice, but the 1978 Kinsey Institute survey shows up the differences dramatically. The study found that nearly all the male respondents had cruised in the past year. Half had sought sexual partners on the streets, in baths, or at private parties, less than a third at public parks and beaches and even fewer in public toilets and cinemas. Less than 20 per cent of the lesbians had cruised in the past year and none in any place but bars and private parties. The researchers comment: 'Because such a small number of the lesbians had done any cruising, no attempt was made to analyse these data further.'[15] The difference is even clearer when we look at the number of sexual partners lesbian and male gay respondents reported in the course of their homosexual careers. Almost one half of the white men and one third of the black men had had at least 500 sexual partners. Most of the women had had fewer than ten sexual partners in their adult lives and all of these had tended to be substantial interactions or relationships rather than cruising contacts.[16]

The gay liberation critique of cruising did not last long. A piece in the April 1972 edition of *Come Together* gives us a clue as to what went wrong. Men from Camden Gay Liberation went to Hampstead Heath with a coffee trolley to make contact with cruising gay men and 'offer them an alternative' to 'impersonal anonymous sex'. To give the author, Mike, his due, he did realise that they were being 'heavy missionaries'. This seems to have been the result of his discovering that he enjoyed cruising. He joined in and was entranced.

> [I was] fascinated with the ritual of the place, and I wandered off away from our group and joined in with the cruising in another part of the woods. It was very strange, scary and exciting, a sort of stalking game with a lot of special patterns . . . It was only when I left our group and started cruising myself that I could stop thinking in terms of categories of 'us' and 'them' and start relating honestly.[17]

Mike's conclusion was that his group should go to the park again 'to add something, without destroying what is there. We can learn too'. What Mike had learned was that cruising turned him on and he decided that something which turned him on could not be entirely a bad idea. This is the problem that seems to have emerged with other aspects of the gay liberation critique of sexuality. When gay men discovered that practices they had not been familiar with before could be sexually enjoyable they threw out the political analysis. They fell prey to the prevalent sexual libertarian delusion that whatever turns you on must be good and positive. They had plunged into their impressive political analysis of gender roles and sexuality assuming that they were somehow born anew and quite separate from the general run of their gay brothers.

John Shiers gives an explanation of how this deradicalisation worked in his case in an article entitled 'Two steps forward, One step back' published in 1980 in an anthology called *Homosexuality: Power and Politics*. The first part of the article is called 'Coming out six years on' and describes Shiers' feelings and political beliefs on coming out into gay liberation. He was committedly pro-feminist. 'Understanding sexism and the oppression of women seemed like the key which unlocked the prison gates.'[18] He shared all the visionary desire of early GLF days to remake sexuality and the world, but he suffered from acute crises of confidence about his own desirability. He found that such personal matters as the fact that your sexual interests did not necessarily match your ideals, were not discussed. He found himself drifting back to the commercial gay scene of which GLF had had such a cogent critique. Like Mike with the Hampstead Heath coffee trolley, this voyage into the subculture was justified as an attempt to bring the values of GLF to the scene but, 'It wasn't me who was changing the gay scene, but the gay scene which was changing me.'[19] Shiers started to go cottaging, i.e. engaging in anonymous sex in public toilets. He was not happy about this development. He considered it to be a serious problem that he wanted anonymous sex and did not seem able or inclined to have sexual relationships which lasted more than a few weeks.

Shiers' analysis of the reasons why such a split between the personal and the political arose in himself and others who were committed to the idea that the personal is political, is very useful in understanding the failure of gay liberation. The first is that there was no understanding of the difficulty of transforming emotions and sexual feelings which had taken a lifetime of construction. It was expected that the newly liberated gay man would be born again overnight in a new and perfect form with feelings corresponding to political ideals. Thus no machinery was set up to help in the personal transformation. '(GLF) assumed that a lifetime of conditioning could be magically whisked away by one simple act of coming out.'[20] There was a need, Shiers explained, to 'really take account of the deep barriers, both personal and social, which we have to confront, and to examine ways of gradually chipping them down'. He suggests 'new kinds of groups which do seek to reach that underlying psychic structure'. This failure to reckon with the difficulties of transforming inner life seems the most useful way to explain the retrogressive developments of the 1980s in the sexual practice of gay men and of lesbians and heterosexual women.

Another explanation Shiers offers is the failure to advance an alternative form of relationship toward which those involved in gay liberation should be striving. There was no clear idea of the 'kinds of social/sexual relations which advance the development of a gay liberationist consciousness and way of life'.[21] The third explanation is the impact of the commercial gay scene: 'the capacity of capitalist enterprises to colonise gay life'. The alter-

153

native culture was not as exciting as the commercial bars and clubs and did not exist in large parts of the country.

The second part of the article, entitled 'Moving into the 1980s', is very different in tone. Whereas in the first article Shiers politically rejected cruising and cottaging, though he felt personally unable to live up to his ideals, in the later piece he elevates that kind of sexual practice into a politically revolutionary act in its own right. This is quite a change. He explains that cruising is revolutionary because:

> ... gay men's capacity to have casual genital sexual relations with one another does pose a challenge to the heterosexual moral order and thus to patriarchal sexuality, where power defines the sexual relationships made by men and women. Gay men encounter one another as reciprocally acknowledged equals ...'[22]

Shiers has reconciled himself with his contradictory desires by redefining those desires as revolutionary. This is convenient but a real problem politically. It is at this point that lesbian feminism and male gay liberation part company most dramatically. Many lesbians left gay liberation early on because of the sexist behaviour of the men and because they found they had more in common politically with heterosexual women than with gay men. But the theoretical shift contained within the redefinition of practices which had been seen as needing reconstruction into revolutionary practices, tolled the death knell for any obvious compatibility between male gay liberation and lesbian feminism. Shiers reasserts his 'commitment to making the links between gay liberation, feminism and socialism that I did in the days of the Gay Liberation Front ...' but there is now a proviso. The proviso is the acceptance by feminists and socialists of gay male sexuality, presumably the unregenerate variety, without criticism or challenge.

> Unless, however, those of us who believe the links must be made are prepared to affirm as gay men what we are most oppressed for (our sexuality), then any acceptance either by

154

the feminist movement or the socialist movement will be on their terms not ours.[23]

Shiers is aware that this approach sets for gay men a sexual agenda that is quite different from that of lesbian feminists and one that lesbian feminists cannot but criticise politically. But he is prepared to help other gay men to validate precisely that form of sexuality, casual sex, of which lesbian feminists have been critical. The lesbian feminists have been deluded and have not really understood male gay casual sex, he argues. It is different from male heterosexual casual sex because it is 'equal'.

> It is very different, too, from the pattern of relating which lesbian feminists are developing, and it is tempting for gay men who identify with the feminist movement to define our sexuality in a negative way in contrast to theirs. Some feminists have also been highly critical of the way in which they see gay men apparently aping straight male sexual patterns.[24]

He believes that there is some kind of essential male gay sexuality and explains that gay men 'need to feel confident enough to defend our right to define our own sexuality'. But he does not make it clear where this essential sexuality comes from. If it came from biology it could not be changed, but the heart of Shiers' argument is that gay male sexuality will eventually change. It just happens to be necessary to any revolutionary change in the area of sexuality that gay men should act out objectifying, anonymous sex or as Shiers describes it, 'gay male promiscuity is the reverse side of the coin from compulsive monogamy'. He explains the revolutionary nature of gay male sexuality thus:

> The 'radical kernel' in our sexual lifestyles may be that we are debunking the mystique which surrounds sex and placing it where it had to be placed if we are ever to begin to move towards a less genitally fixated, more sensual society, that of a fun activity we have with others who also feel like having it with us.[25]

According to this analysis gay men's casual sex is very important indeed. It has become the transforming element which will create the revolution. The only way to create change is for gay men to act out their genitally fixated promiscuity so as to explode straight complacency and break through the boundaries into a new sexual future. This would be more credible if it was not so convenient. Precisely that which lesbians criticise gay men for has become a revolutionary force which will in the end do lesbians no end of good when the revolution comes. Meanwhile, promiscuous gay men are the saviours, cottaging not just because it is fun but because it is their duty for all our sakes.

The idea that male gay cruising is a revolutionary activity is perhaps most perfectly expressed in John Rechy's *Sexual Outlaw*. Rechy is a writer from the beat generation, but he is able to continue to promote what Stephen Adams calls 'beat delinquency' under the new mantle of gay liberation without missing a beat. Rechy calls his book a 'documentary' and claims to be 'presenting a true spectrum of the promiscuous experience', his own.[26] Rechy has little passages of social comment and political commentary in between the descriptions of sexual activity. 'Public sex,' he says, 'is revolution, courageous, righteous, defiant revolution.' Here is Rechy's description of the promiscuous homosexual as hero.

> Promiscuous homosexuals (outlaws with dual identities – tomorrow they will go to offices and athletic fields, classrooms and construction sites) are the shock troops of the sexual revolution. The streets are the battleground, the revolution is the sexhunt, a radical statement is made each time a man has sex with another on a street.[27]

Where do lesbians fit into all this? It seems that their role is just to wait patiently until gay men have created the revolution. Having long been told that women must wait until after the socialist revolution for our demands to be taken seriously, we now must wait until after the male gay revolution and try not to complain too much while we wait. The only other possibility is that lesbians transform their 'old-fashioned' sexual practice and adopt the gay male sexual agenda as their model too. That

156

way we can be part of the solution instead of the problem. This is the approach being taken by libertarian lesbian theorists in the 1980s.

FEMINISM AND GAY LIBERATION

Liz Stanley was active in gay liberation in the same town as John Shiers, Manchester, from 1971 until 1977. She has written about why she left the mixed gay movement in the anthology *On the Problem of Men* (1982). To underline the significance of her disillusionment she emphasises that, 'Once upon a time I experienced my relationships with gay men as a paradigm of what "liberated relationships" between women and men might be like.'[28] Liz Stanley was in a Campaign for Homosexual Equality group rather than a GLF group because, she explained, 'GLF, like most other revolutionary organisations, attracted predominantly young, white, middle-class, well-off people. It didn't attract ordinary everyday people.'[29] But, she makes a point of explaining, she does not consider that CHE was any more sexist than GLF. She set out to be Women's Organiser in the local CHE. The womanhating responses she received were not the main reason she left, though they included the following:

> Persistently I and other women in the WCC received complaints that the women in local groups smelled. This was a feature of all women who, literally, stank. Women's cunts were suppurating wounds, full of crawling worms. They should not be permitted in the same rooms with men. Lesbians didn't want to have sex with men, this meant they hated men, all men, including gay men, and wanted to castrate them. Attempting to get women involved in CHE was an attack on the gay movement, which belonged to men. All women should be barred from it.[30]

Along with these routine insults Stanley cites numerous examples of gay male sexual behaviour and ideas about sex which finally formed the theoretical base for her political severance from the mixed gay movement. One example is the attitude of her gay male friends to the obscene phone calls which lesbians

157

womanning the advice phone service received from, presumably, heterosexual men.

> The content of the obscene phone calls, and the reactions of gay and straight men to talks and papers given about them, were remarkably similar. The obscene phone callers, gay men in the gay movement, and straight men in academic circles and in left groups all found the calls arousing. What they found arousing was the phallic imagery, the violence, and the insistence on 'doing' sex to other people. It was nothing, or only peripherally, to do with anything about women in the calls – instead it was the cock, the almighty penis, that they all reacted to.
>
> What, in particular they found arousing was the power the penis gave them, its centrality in the lives of all people, its ability to be used so as to impose their will on other people.[31]

Another example is the behaviour of men involved in the FRIEND befriending group who were meant to help people coming out. The organisation had a rule that, because of the power relationship involved in the befriending situation, it would be abusive to make sexual approaches to the befriended. Stanley found that whatever the gay male befrienders said about their ideals, what they actually did was regularly to exploit sexually the men they were supposed to be befriending.

Stanley concluded that gay men would not and did not pay any attention to the demands or ideas of lesbian feminists if such attention would interfere with the satisfying of what they saw as their sexual needs.

> What I suggest that this means, in relation to gay men, is quite simply this: if it cuts down on the amount of time and opportunity they have for fucking each other, then gay men won't do it. In other words, I feel that the only possible interpretation of 'maleness', the 'needs of men', is purely and simply sex. And sexual 'needs' of a very particular kind . . . these are the needs to behave in sexist, objectifying, unemotional and entirely phallocentric ways.[32]

158

The oppression of lesbians, Stanley recognised, 'is quite different from the oppression of gay men'.[33] Lesbians were threatening to both heterosexual and gay men because their lives were not organised around the penis, and the penis is in no way necessary to lesbian existence. Feminism was a problem for gay men because the success of the feminist project would inevitably interfere with the sexual lifestyle of gay men. In a feminist society the 'essentials of phallocentrism are challenged and dismantled' and the lifestyle of the 'average' gay man would come to an end.[34]

Some gay men are well aware that lesbians and gay men have different and contradictory sexual agendas. Andrew Hodges, who lives in London, had an article called 'Divided we stand' published in the Toronto gay paper *Body Politic* in 1977, about the difficulties of lesbians and gay men working together. Hodges is convinced that they cannot and the reason is the difference in sexuality, but he is sanguine about this. He identifies the feminist programme as 'removing sex from public life'.[35]

This is a misrepresentation of feminist aims. Feminists want to free all women from the threat of harassment in the street through the reconstruction of male sexuality. To eliminate harassment, feminists argue, men would have to abandon objectifying exploitative sex and redefine altogether what they saw as sexuality. Hodges can see no problem with the shape of gay male sexuality and is quite unable to sympathise with feminist demands. He explains that 'it is not possible for gay men honestly to do what they are often expected to do, namely, to give unreserved support to the women's movement'.[36] Gay men, he explains, enjoy and seek precisely the kind of sexual contact that the feminists find a problem.

On the streets of Syracuse, New York, where I have been living, there are large posters which show a woman kicking a man in the balls, with the words: *Men! Next time you whistle at, hassle, ogle, rape, approach . . . may be your last!* How can gay men honestly accept the idea that making eyes is as bad as rape and deserves castration or death? They spend most of their waking hours looking and being looked at; they have to do a great deal of fending off of unwanted attention

159

themselves, and find it hard to imagine that women are such delicate creatures that they cannot do the same. Of course, their more sanguine attitude is due to the fact that they are not objectified as inferiors by those who look at them. The fact remains that it is hard for gay men to consider non-violent sexual approaches as intrinsically evil and dangerous.[37]

Hodges thinks that this form of male sexuality should be the model for all sexuality. Women are encouraged to catch up by adopting this model. Feminists, it seems, are rather backward. Hodges does not see toilet sex as objectifying. His attitude to sexuality he defines as 'sex-positive'. He explains:

> Gay sex can be mutual and unexploitative; if it were not for sexism then so could heterosexuality. Heterosexuality, in which women are allowed only the roles of victim or prostitute, should not be allowed to give all sex a bad name.[38]

Hodges does not consider that the social construction of sexuality in the whole of male supremacy might be deformed by 'sexism'. Sex, in its unregenerate male supremacist form, is seen as sacred and true. Sexism is a shadowy emanation rather than a form of behaviour carried out by men. Thus Hodges is able to sympathise with heterosexual men who are unable to get sexual satisfaction from women.

> I think gay men should also be allowed to feel some sympathy for non-gay men, whose need for sexual release is just as great, and who do not have the same opportunity for achieving it in a decent way.[39]

Hodges, like the majority of gay men, casts his lot with the sex class of men whether straight or gay rather than with women. Hodges is an example of what is probably the dominant gay male attitude to sexuality and to the demands of lesbian feminism. He expresses his politics less ambiguously than most and his anger at feminists overcomes the normal caution that might advise dissimulation.

160

There are gay men who adopt a pro-feminist approach to sexuality and are prepared to launch a thorough critique of the gay male sexual agenda. John Stoltenberg wrote this analysis of the failure of gay liberation in a forum on sadomasochism published in 1978. He asserts that the male-dominated gay liberation movement 'betrayed its revolutionary potential' soon after its inception. He explains that, instead of understanding that their own oppression comes from male supremacy,

> . . . most gay male activists have chosen a completely reactionary strategy: seeking enfranchisement in the culture as 'really virile men', without substantially changing or challenging even their own misogyny and male-supremacist convictions. There are many ways in which gay liberation has become a full-fledged component of the backlash against feminism . . . Gay men do not simply like other men; they are like other men, as their antifeminism makes clear. Licensed by their movement which brought homoerotic sadism out of the closet (but which has not changed much else), the gay male subculture now abounds with neo-Nazi uniforms, torture toys, orgy bars, piss-and-shit shows, fist-fucking shows, films and periodicals portraying torture and mutilation – all of which is tantamount to spitting in the faces of women who are struggling to be free.[40]

Stoltenberg goes so far as to maintain that it is not possible 'for anyone seriously committed to feminist principles to maintain an alliance or affiliation with gay men as a group, except by compromising and deceiving women as a group'.[41] He reaches this conclusion 'as a result of the prevalence of eroticised violence (sexual sadism) among male homosexuals and male heterosexuals alike'. His agenda for men, straight and gay, is quite the opposite of male apologists for male supremacy like Hodges above. Stoltenberg believes men must dismantle the male sexual identity, not defend it against feminists.

> All males who are fully men got that way, gay or straight, by committing crimes against women; they are therefore obstacles to women's freedom and dignity. Any genital male

161

who decides not to live as such an impediment would not equivocate about that fact – he would instead take a stand against male sexual identity itself.[42]

SEXUAL IDENTITY POLITICS

One kind of sexual politics which survived the failure of gay liberation is the politics of sexual identity. It is the politics adopted by today's radical gay men and taught in British college courses on sexuality. It is even taught as if it were feminist theory on women's studies courses, where the works of gay men are routinely studied in preference to the works of feminists.

Sexual identity politics are based upon the idea that a homosexual identity was necessary to any movement for homosexual rights. Gay male historians see this identity as developing in the late nineteenth century as a result of the categorisation of sexuality by the sexologists and the Criminal Law Amendment Act of 1885. This Act made male homosexual behaviour specifically illegal for the first time and ushered in a stigmatising of the homosexual which caused him to be aware of his difference from heterosexuals and encouraged the development of a homosexual subculture and separate lifestyle. Before the Act the sexual practice of sodomy was illegal but was not seen as a specifically homosexual practice, so that no laws penalised homosexuals *per se*. The lines between normal heterosexual behaviour and outlawed homosexual behaviour were now drawn, and against this background both a homosexual identity and a homosexual reform movement based upon such an identity could develop[43] The Gay Liberation Front developed when this homosexual identity took on a proud and self-confident form in the 1960s, as a result of the rapid progress of a supposed sexual revolution and the 1967 Sexual Offences Act which decriminalised sexual activity between consenting males over 21 in private.

Lesbians do not fit well into this model. Lesbians have had to ride as fellow travellers, trying to fit themselves into the form and content of male homosexual reform movements until the 1970s, when lesbians created their own quite distinct movement. Gay men's main concern may be to seek rights on the basis of a sexual identity, but lesbianism was always about more than this. Lesbians as women have to fight the power of men as a class. Gay men are part of the class of men. The fight for lesbian liberation requires the dismantling of male supremacy and the self-assertive 'sexual identity' of gay men must be dismantled too if it reproduces the characteristics of ruling-class sexuality. Unfortunately the clear voice of lesbian feminism is constantly eroded. Lesbians have always been and are now under constant pressure to accept gay male categories and concepts and to fall in with male gay liberation even when this is patently against our interests as women. Lesbian feminism as a movement is subject to growing encroachment from the gay male commercial scene, gay male media, and the gay male hegemony in the field of whatever is seen as progressive or radical in the theory of sexuality.

The sexual-identity politics which have survived the failure of gay liberation to realise its pro-feminist potential form the basis for what Jeffrey Weeks calls 'movements of affirmation'.[44] These are movements organised by different sexual minorities based on a concept of sexual identity, promoting their rights and the revolutionary nature of their project. The politics of sexual minorities has quite a long pedigree. Jeffrey Weeks explains that sexual-minorities politics appeals because it fits into a liberal political tradition. Minorities, national or religious, have traditionally campaigned for, and won, rights to toleration and the practice of their own culture. The idea of 'sexual minorities' can be seen as drawing upon this tradition to further the rights of those groups generally included in the list of sexual minorities, i.e. transvestites/transsexuals, paedophiles and sado-masochists.

As early as 1964 Lars Ullerstam took this approach in his book *Erotic Minorities* which was first published in Sweden, seen at that time as a pioneer nation for sexual freedom.[45] Ullerstam argued for toleration of incest, exhibitionism, paedophilia, saliromania (use of dirt and faeces), algolagnia (sadomasochism), homosexuality, scopophilia (voyeurism) and other less popular minority interests such as necrophilia. These activities mainly involved the humiliation or abuse of women either dead or alive. None the less, Ullerstam felt, toleration was not enough.

163

It was necessary to be really positive about them. Such practices 'allow considerable chances to achieve human happiness,' he felt, 'the "perversions" are in themselves good, and therefore they ought to be encouraged'.[46]

Male gay theorists such as Weeks proclaim that the sexual minorities are radical and that the leaders of such minority groupings are radical sexual theorists. 'Radical' is a word which does not necessarily mean politically progressive in the context of the 1980s. In Britain the media describe as 'radical' the gradual destruction of local government, the welfare state and the state education system, and the Tory theorists effecting this change are pleased to assume the cloak of the radical. 'Radical' is thus being applied to a movement to overthrow all the gains which socialist and feminist campaigners have won in the last century. It is in this way that I think we should interpret the word 'radical' as used about the sexual minorities. Weeks means the word to be positive, and is clearly enthusiastic about the movements of affirmation he describes, but when we look at the nature of these movements it should be fairly clear that they are antithetical to the aims of women's liberation and lesbian feminism.

Weeks supplies us with two lists of sexual minorities. The first is: 'Transvestites, transsexuals, pedophiles, sado-masochists, fetishists, bisexuals, prostitutes and others – each group marked by specific sexual tastes, or aptitudes, subdivided and demarcated into specific styles, morals and communities, each with specific histories of self-expression – have all appeared on the world's stage to claim their space and "rights".'[47] Later he provides another list of 'erotic groups' as follows: 'sado-masochists, pedophiles, transvestites, prostitutes come to mind'.[48]

Prostitutes are clearly out of place in a list of sexual minorities. Prostitution is a job, an occupation. Prostitutes do not take up their occupation in order to exercise their sexual tastes. Indeed, the job has nothing to do with their sexual self-expression except inasmuch as it may damage it. Female prostitutes use their bodies and minds to service male sexuality. There might be more room for arguing that male prostitutes are pursuing sexual fulfilment in their job since some kind of sexual response is

164

usually required, but the main motivation is certainly money. So why is this form of work included in a list of groups organised around the pursuit of their pleasures and sexual fulfilment? It can't be an oversight since it occurs twice. It can be explained in terms of traditional male-supremacist assumptions about women and sexuality. A dip into any of the literature, medical, sexological or sociological, on prostitution in the past hundred years will turn up the assertion that women either choose to be prostitutes because they are seeking sexual kicks or that they at least enjoy their jobs because of the sexual pleasure they receive. More recent literature by prostitutes themselves and by feminists shows up this arrogant and self-serving male assumption for the nonsense that it is.[49] Men have promoted this myth because it justifies male use of prostitutes and out of the belief that contact with the male organ must be pleasurable in any form. Weeks perpetuates this myth by including prostitutes in his list.

Transvestites/transsexuals, paedophiles, fetishists and sado-masochists are overwhelmingly, and in the case of paedophiles, solely male. It may be that the clear male bias of the list caused Weeks to seek dilution by adding a category that is overwhelmingly female. But it won't do. What this very transparent sleight of hand shows up is that sexual-identity politics is an over-whelmingly male concept quite unsuited to women whose relationship to sexuality is fundamentally different from that of men. Men are, under male supremacy, the active agents of an aggressive, exploitative sexuality organised around dominance and submission or gender fetishism. The sexual minorities organise to promote and protect the sexual interests of ruling-class males. Women are most often the objects of this male sexuality. Women simply cannot be included in a list of sexual minorities. Weeks' clumsy attempt to do so shows how little serious attention he has given to understanding women's relationship to sexuality.

A reading of Weeks' most recent work reveals that he excori-ates throughout that variety of feminism which has undertaken a critique of male sexuality. Radical feminists are impugned by associating them with moral purity movements of the New Right; he says that, 'the flirtation of some radical feminists with New Right moralists over issues such as pornography is fundamentally more problematic than it ever was in the early twentieth century'.[50] No evidence is presented to show radical feminists sympathising with or working alongside the New Right. These are slur tactics.

Weeks claims that the sexual minorities are revolutionary. He is a follower of the French gay male theorist Michel Foucault and argues that the movements of affirmation can shatter the assumptions and controls of the sexual tradition and help to create a new sexual universe in which people can concentrate on what Weeks sees as their proper project: 'the body and its potentialities for pleasure'.[51] 'The starting points for the political movements around sex were the categorisations of the sexologists,' he says, but they go on to challenge the norm and, 'in the inventiveness of the radical sexual movements in creating new ways of life lies the ultimate challenge to the power of the definition hitherto enjoyed by the sexologists and the sexual tradition.'

This is a very convenient logic for gay men like Foucault and Weeks. They manage to elevate to a revolutionary role precisely those sexual practices that feminists most object to and with which such gay men identify or have strong sympathy. While feminists seek to explain to gay men why they and heterosexual men must transform their sexual practice, gay men proclaim that the exaggerated forms of what feminists see to be a problem, such as objectification and gender fetishism, are revolutionary and will bring sexual freedom to everyone. Feminists are asked to realise that the sexual rights and opportunities of women depend upon allowing gay men to pursue their sexual interests unhindered.

The argument makes no sense for feminists and lesbians. Rather than seeing the sexual minorities as the radical weapon that will break down the barriers to women's liberation, it is more plausible that the 'movements of affirmation' will actually affirm, strengthen and validate gender fetishism, eroticised dominance and submission and exploitation, and help shore up the construction of a form of male sexuality dangerous to the interests of all women. Moreover an argument that these movements can explode the sexual tradition must be based upon some notion that they are indeed inimical to that tradition rather than the mainstays of it. A feminist analysis would argue differently. The sexual minorities are seen simply as exaggerated versions of damaging aspects of male sexuality. Feminists find it difficult, for instance, to see how a movement to affirm sado-masochism would challenge what American radical feminist theorist Mary Daly calls the sadosociety, i.e. male supremacy. Gender fetishism, so central to gay male culture, exploits the trappings of socially constructed gender inequality to provide erotic excitement. It is difficult to see how the gender fetishism of transvestites/transsexuals could do anything but reinforce the construction of the whole of male-supremacist culture around the concept of gender difference.

A male theorist whose pro-feminist credentials were in order, rather than constructing a theory of how to create major sexual change through the affirmation of damaging aspects of male sexual behaviour, would surely take feminist theory about sexuality seriously. There is a vast body of theory from lesbian feminists and radical feminists which stands in utter contradiction to the male gay agenda, theory which Weeks dismisses as not his kind of feminism. Foucault spares not a thought for lesbians or feminists. His sexual map of the world is simply a male gay map.

A close look at the three most commonly quoted sexual minorities, i.e. transvestites/transsexuals, paedophiles and sado-masochists, shows how they represent aspects of male sexuality dangerous to women's interests. An analysis of their relationship to male gay liberation shows why so many male gays are prepared to see their futures linked to the success of these sexual minorities and are prepared to defend them against any feminist lack of enthusiasm. All three sexual minorities can be explained as arising from internalised oppression on the part of the men (and in the case of sadomasochism, men and women) involved, so that the linkage with a movement for gay liberation is, to say the least, ironic. Sadomasochism will be explained here partly as being the wreaking of gay self-hatred upon the bodies and organs which represent the despised sexuality. Transvestism/transsexualism is important because, in the days when a radical gay liberation movement was giving its last gasps, it was the affirmation of drag, the wearing of clothes normally associated with the feminine gender, that seems to have put the most significant nail in the coffin.

TRANSVESTISM, TRANSSEXUALISM AND GAY LIBERATION

TRANSVESTISM

Dressing in 'women's' clothes, commonly called transvestism by heterosexual practitioners, is called drag by gay men. Drag is an issue which had splintered the pro-feminist platform of gay liberation by 1973. For that reason it is the first of the 'sexual minorities' to be dealt with here. Drag is a phenomenon deeply rooted in gay male consciousness, so deeply rooted indeed that one might be persuaded to see it as the foundation of gay male culture. Men in gay liberation had adopted drag in the belief that this made them 'radical feminists' and that it expressed their solidarity and identification with women's liberation. Aubrey Walter explains the political context in which such a stance was taken, as follows:

> We were searching for something that was basically gender-free ... We had ourselves been conditioned by the gender system. The way round this dilemma was to upgrade the identification we had with our mothers, and so to push the more feminine qualities in our psyches and hence in our outward images and social behaviour.[52]

The desire to be gender-free is a reasonable aim and Walter pursued it without adopting 'radical drag'. But an important group of men did adopt what they called radical drag and Walter describes their politics thus:

> In GLF the butch image was seen to be really bad and oppressive for gay men. From a certain reading of radical feminism, many gays felt that in order to struggle against male privilege, they must do everything possible to show that they were prepared to give up this privilege in themselves. One way of

doing so was to give up clothes which they termed as masculine, such as jeans and trousers, shirts and jackets, in favour of frocks, heels and make-up.[53]

The radical queens would do battle with the butch gay men in meetings in heterosexual women's clothes while 'pointedly . . . knitting and chatting through some person's big ego-trip speech'.[54]

This behaviour in meetings must have been extremely offensive and alienating to the lesbians present. Lesbians are women who have usually experienced considerable stress and difficulty in casting off the effeminate behaviour and clothing expected of them as women. That they should then have to watch gay men adopting such behaviour in order to duel with other gay men at meetings was an unfortunate irony. But gay men even of supposedly radical politics have great difficulty understanding the attitude of most lesbians to drag. When I taught a mixed gay studies class I covered the topic of transvestism. Most of the men present expressed an interest in wearing 'women's clothes'. I pointed out that all the women in the room were wearing jeans and shirts, like the men. Clearly, then, they did not mean women's clothes but stereotypically effeminate clothing that the lesbians present had all rejected. It proved extremely difficult to communicate the idea that the clothes they hankered after wearing were not 'women's' clothes at all but simply the symbols of oppression.

'Women's clothes' are those which a male-dominated culture considers appropriate for females. They are not necessarily the clothes that women choose to wear. Over the last twenty years the women's liberation movement worldwide has challenged the notion that women should be required to wear clothes which cripple and distort their bodies, which are designed to exaggerate women's physical characteristics and are generally restrictive and impractical for everyday use and the work which women perform. They are also usually inferior in quality to men's clothes at similar prices. Such clothing includes high-heeled shoes, low cleavages, corsets, frilly underwear, tights and stockings, and the sort of dresses or skirts which restrict movement. Such clothes make it difficult for women to relax and sprawl their limbs as men do, and make women constantly careful lest men observe their thighs or genitals. The cumulative effect of these forms of clothing are that women cannot run, defend themselves or perform manual labour. Women are thus dependent on men's protection against other men and the clothing acts as a form of social control, as well as reducing the women to fetishised consumer objects for men's delight. Feminists rejected the fetishised image of woman in pursuit of a woman's right to full human status, physical freedom and independence.

Men, straight and gay, have very different reasons from women for wearing 'women's clothes'. To understand the meaning of these clothes for men it is illuminating to look at transvestite pornography. The story line is always similar in this genre of pornography. A man is dressed in fetishistic 'women's' underwear and clothing by women. The following quotation is from a story entitled 'When the Girls made me a Girl'. The young man in the story, while spending a social evening at a friend's house, finds himself in the bedroom being 'dressed' by two women.

'You'll have to put this on next.' A wonderfully boned black waspie, with red ribbons on the bones and dainty red ribbons on the tops of the suspenders, was handed to me. 'I – I don't think I could get into that!' I cried, fondling the proffered garment.

'Of course you will!' said Lorraine, and she stepped behind me, took hold of the waspie, placed it around my waist and proceeded to do up the hooks and eyes. The coolness of the black material and feel of suspenders dangling down my bare thighs, coupled with the sensuous restriction of the garment made me catch my breath! Never had I received such exquisite sensations from a garment before . . .

'Now, young lady, stop admiring yourself in the mirror and let's go downstairs to show you off to the men! I'm sure they'll like what they see!' said Janet.

With trepidation in my beating heart, I walked between the two girls as we entered the dining room downstairs.[55]

Here the young man was forced by the dominating woman to

170

don the undergarments despite his protestations. It is clear that part of his pleasure comes from the fact that he feels the garments to be restrictive. We can get a clue to the symbolic meaning of such clothing in transvestite pornography from a quite similar story in a collection of lesbian sadomasochistic pornography. In this story a dynamic lesbian, heavily involved in political organising, visits her lover for the weekend. The lover decides to enact a sadomasochistic ritual which consists of forcing Meg (the dynamic political character) to be powdered, corseted and ribboned in a fetishistically feminine way.

> Carole loved threatening Meg with lace or anything of that order. Meg worked so damned hard at being noble and unflappable. Carole knew that frills would almost always break Meg's tight composure and get to her in a way that explicit pain would not. Over the years they had played all sorts of sex games together, but after days of tough manoeuvring, she knew the last thing Meg needed was a torture scene . . .
> 'I said put them on,' Carole repeated.
> 'Uh uh, no. Don't make me do it, hon. I'll feel like a fool.' . . .
> 'Yes, Mistress,' Meg said, looking soberly at Carole. She turned and knelt on the floor to open the bottom drawer. In it she found a skimpy hot pink G-string, little more than a small triangle of lace in front and back with narrow ribbons on either side to fasten it together . . . [56]

In this scenario the 'women's' clothing is used to degrade and humiliate a strong and independent woman who would never have worn such garments in her everyday life. If the very same kind of garments can be used by both men and women in rituals of sexual humiliation it would suggest that these clothes represent not 'women' but the crippling, restrictive and inferior role which has been assigned to woman in the gender role system. Attached to fetishistic 'women's' clothing are meanings of powerlessness and submission.

The politics which gay male apologists for drag espouse do not mention the masochistic satisfactions to be obtained. They stress the radical potential of drag. Kris Kirk's book for the Gay Men's Press, *Men in Frocks*, according to its cover blurb, 'explains the development of the drag scene over a whole generation, from the Soldiers in Skirts through the Sea Queens and Radical Femmes to the nouveau drag of 1984'.[57] Kirk and some of the drag queens interviewed in the book express the view that radical drag was and is revolutionary and pro women's liberation. So certain were the proponents of radical drag within GLF that they were pro-feminist that they called themselves 'radical feminists'. Kirk writes:

> But with the advent of the Seventies and GLF, a new strain of drag queen was to appear – the Radical Feminist. Frocks and politics made a heady mixture.[58]

An interviewee in Kirk's book who calls himself Bette Bourne is described as a 'die-hard radical Feminist during his GLF days'.[59] So GLF drag queens parodied not only women but feminist politics as well. The male tendencies within GLF which claimed an allegiance to feminism set themselves up in a kind of butch/fem role playing romance. The radical feminists played fem to the Marxist-feminist butch. This is of course an ugly caricature of feminist politics. Radical feminism is a political philosophy which places the elimination of gender roles at the foundation of its politics. Gay men distorted this idea into an excuse to pursue their predilection for femming-up under the guise of political correctness. Some exponents of radical drag were prepared to assert a leadership role in women's liberation and were extremely scathing about those feminists who dared to question them. One such shared his vision of a women's liberation movement led by men who imitated a sexist notion of women.

> Think how much more inspiring and beautiful the women's revolution will be when it joyously includes all women. Think of a Holloway demo with transvestite, transsexual and drag-queen women, gay women and heterosexual women, black, yellow, brown and white women, mothers, daughters, poor women, rich women, working women, housewives and career

women. Certainly, whatever course we take as transvestites, transsexuals and drag queens, we must first destroy the trap wherein regular women set up standards by which they accept or reject us.[60]

The sheer arrogance of this piece is astounding. The male writer is simply sweeping aside the reasonable political principle that it is the oppressed people themselves who should decide how to fight for their liberation rather than members of the ruling class. Men who choose to imitate their version of women, we are told, have the right to set the agenda for feminists. This ploy did not work. There was some genuine confusion on the part of feminists in the early years of women's liberation about the role of male impersonators of women. But by the late 1970s in Britain women were more confident about setting their own priorities and deciding who had the right to call themselves women, enjoy the right to enter the hard-won women-only space and take part in the construction of women's culture. Women's liberation and women-only space, it was felt at last, were for women and not male impersonators.

The situation in the 1940s is described in *Men in Frocks*. The straight men were called 'hommes'.

Naturally the queens had a different perspective on their homosexuality than is current today. If you asked a queen then what a homosexual man was, he generally had a pretty clear idea. This was not very far removed from the old idea of Third Sex. The one thing the queens were certain of was that they were not real men, or 'hommes' (pronounced 'omies') as they were called in polari, the camp argot. One might well fancy an homme, but it was not something one wanted to be.[61]

With the advent of gay liberation there was, in theory, to be the dawning of a new age of pride in homosexuality. The hommes could come out and admit they were gay, dropping the façade of heterosexual virility, and those gay men who had seen themselves as queens could drop their effeminacy. Gay men could now relate to each other simply as men who loved men

173

rather than as femme men who loved virile men and butch men who loved female impersonators. This new era did not last long. Certainly GLF ushered in a period in which gay men could relate to each other but the hoped-for transcending of roles did not happen.

Effeminacy became, understandably, a symbol of pride at the dawning of GLF because it was precisely for effeminacy that gay men had been traditionally reviled. Moreover it was effeminate gay men who had been the visible standard-bearers of gay male culture. The butch gays had 'passed' as heterosexual and hidden behind their virility. Effeminacy could be associated with anti-sexism because it was the opposite of the masculinity of the ruling class of men. But this crude analysis needed refining. Though feminists might be enthusiastic about the rejection of aggressively male-supremacist traits by some gay brothers, the imitation of femininity was no solution. The radical gays failed to find a way to be men that was not either masculine or a parody of women.

Several of the inverviewees in *Men in Frocks* state that there are varieties of drag which are politically unacceptable because they do mock and caricature women. Some varieties of drag, they assert, do not do this and could cause no offence to women or feminists. If we accept that any validation of gender fetishism is unacceptable then drag cannot have good and bad varieties.

A closer look at the content of drag shows and the way the gay male audience responds to them should make us critical of the idea that any drag is politically harmless. Nicky, of the drag act 'Lick, Stick and Promise', describes the reaction to their performance thus: 'Apart from the occasional cry of "stagnant fish" because we were women, there wasn't much outright hostility.'[62] 'Fish' is an epithet applied to women by gay men to illustrate their horror at the way that they believe women's genitals to smell. It seems likely that some of the enthusiasm that gay male audiences have for drag acts stems straightforwardly from hatred of women. In many if not most such acts the impersonators humiliate and deride women and revel in women's inferiority. In their act, Lick, Stick and Promise gave a 'blow-job' to a 'blow-up rubber doll'.[63] Drag queens show a subservient devotion to the male organ in the way that women are portrayed as doing in heterosexual male pornography. The poses, facial expressions and accoutrements of the drag queens in the pictures in *Men in Frocks* resemble precisely the females constructed by men in heterosexual male porn. The queens pout, simper and look through half-closed lids while draping themselves about uncomfortably. This is not the way real women behave unless posed by men in pornography.

Drag has a very long history and is engrained in male gay culture. It is necessary for much more theoretical work to be done on disentwining the elements of drag from male gay sensibility, understanding the complexity of drag in order to move beyond it. Drag and gay identity are still so strongly interlinked, even for political gay men, that it may be necessary for women and lesbians to do this theoretical work. Gay men like Kris Kirk are unable to construct a critical analysis of drag because they are too involved in it. Feminist critics will be accused of approaching drag simplistically. It is about much more than an imitation of women, we will be told. After all, many of the queens in Kirk's book reject the idea that they wish to resemble women. But at the root of drag is the sex-gender system. Drag would have no meaning in a world beyond male supremacy.

TRANSSEXUALISM

Gay male theorists list transsexuals, the victims of sex-reassignment surgery, alongside transvestites as radical sexual revolutionaries. It is extremely rare for a gay man to venture into print in criticism of the phenomenon of transsexualism. The drag queens interviewed in *Men in Frocks* were mostly keen to establish that they had never had a desire to be other than male, but at the same time expressed sympathy with those who chose surgery. Tish, who operates under the stage name of Fay Presto, identifies as a pre-operative transsexual. He states unequivocally that the dividing lines between transvestism, drag and transsexualism are very blurred and that there is overlap between the categories.

TVs and TSs identify very closely with the gender they aspire to whereas most drag queens don't, though I know some drag queens who are a cigarette paper away from being TV or TS. People often drift round the areas. For me it was all a gradual process – I didn't just wake up one day and say, 'Yesterday I was a TV, today I'm a TS.'[64]

Such sentiments would be heresy to the medical profession which fosters the belief, in order to justify the savagery of surgical intervention, that it has discovered a unique and discrete, identifiable disorder in transsexualism. The doctors find it necessary to assert that there are people who can be classified as 'true' transsexuals. This blurring of distinctions would be anathema too, to most of those very numerous gay men who like to wear women's clothes. But for a feminist analysis the idea of there being a continuum between all these forms of gender fetishism makes most sense.

Janice Raymond's brilliant radical-feminist analysis, *The Transsexual Empire*, shows that transsexualism is not consonant with lesbianism or women's liberation.[65] Raymond identifies the cause of transsexualism as the rigid gender stereotyping of male-supremacist society. This dictates that if a person feels uncomfortable in the gender that has been ascribed to them on the basis of their sex organs, then they have no choice but to switch organs.

I would suggest that a patriarchal society and its social currents of masculinity and femininity is the First Cause of transsexualism. The organs and body of the opposite sex that the transsexual desires merely incarnate the 'essence' of the desired role. Within such a society, the transsexual only exchanges one stereotype for the other, thus reinforcing the fabric by which a sexist society is held together.[66]

Those in the medical profession, Raymond argues, benefit from the 'transsexual empire'. They are able to further their sexual knowledge and techniques, they make money and they receive the ego satisfaction of acting as male 'fathers' able to give surgical birth to remade human beings. It is in their interests therefore to explain the causation of transsexualism in ways which justify the continuance of surgical intervention. They offer two main forms of explanation, biological and psychological, and sometimes a combination of the two. The biological explanation seeks an answer in genes and hormones. Unfortunately for the biologists there is an absence of scientific proof to support this approach. Transsexualism bears no relationship to hermaphroditism. Transsexuals do not have ambiguous genitals but possess the genes and sexual characteristics of the sex they wish to evacuate. Where evidence is lacking there is relief to be sought in a kind of scientific mysticism. Thus John Money argues that something goes wrong in the prenatal period which causes inappropriate neural pathways to be set up in the brain. Masculine or feminine socialisation then fails to take because of the defective biological programming. He has no proof of this either but he does have faith.[67]

Robert Stoller is a sexologist who uses the psychological approach. He attributes transsexualism to 'mother-smothering' by women who suffer from penis envy.[68] Sexologists and psychoanalysts who believe in the psychological approach none the less feel able to recommend surgery which might seem anomalous considering they do not subscribe to any biological cause. There are some psychoanalysts who seek to cure transsexuals of their desire for sex change through psychotherapeutic techniques designed to make them functioning heterosexuals. There are a tiny number who believe that the correct treatment for transsexuals is to help them to come to terms with their homosexuality.

There is a good deal to be learned from male-to-constructed-female transsexuals about the social construction of gender roles in western male supremacy. Gender identity clinics, such as that at the Charing Cross Hospital in London, to which transsexuals are referred to assess their suitability for surgery, require aspirants to cross-dress and live publicly as the desired gender for a specified period of time prior to the operation. This checks out the degree of their motivation. The time ranges from six months to two years in different clinics. During this period they must learn and practise feminine traits. Not surprisingly they choose to imitate the most extreme examples of feminine behaviour and dress in grossly stereotypical feminine clothing. It would be much harder for aspirants to imitate the behaviour of women who had shrugged off unnecessary feminine attributes and dressed in jeans and T-shirts. Indeed it would defeat the object, since transsexual males want to become their image of what women can and should be, not a liberated or feminist version.

Early transsexual autobiographies are most rewarding for readers who wish to understand the transsexual view of woman. Such literature is written in the form of the religious confessional. The transsexuals write of their lives before and after the supreme transformative experience, surgery, in which they are 'saved'. Recent autobiographies, though full of gross gender stereotyping, tend to be more muted about glorying in women's inferiority. Feminism has been a little confusing for transsexuals. *Roberta Cowell's Story* is the autobiography of Robert Cowell, who was the first man in Britain to undergo the operation.[69] Cowell's birth certificate was officially amended to register his change of sex in 1951.

As soon as Cowell seriously started hormone treatment prior to the operation he claims that certain behavioural changes became evident which demonstrated the nearness of the approaching apotheosis. Cowell had been a racing driver and an automobile engineer. He changed his occupation to the management of an haute couture business, though he had terrible trouble learning about raglan sleeves and peplums. One of the first changes was in his handwriting. Then there were more dramatic changes in personality.

> A definite change in the functioning of my mentality began to become apparent. This showed itself in two ways. My mental processes seemed to be slightly slowed up, and I also showed signs of greatly increased powers of intuition . . . Sometimes when the telephone rang I would get a feeling that I knew who was calling, and I was right . . . For the first time in my life, I found I could read stories and novels with sustained interest . . . My nature was becoming milder and less aggressive, and I found it much more difficult to summon up will-power when required.[70]

These psychological changes apparently happened automatically along with a discovery that, according to the woman friend who supported him through the surgery, the ex-racing driver no longer drove nearly as well as he used to. But some forms of behaviour needed learning.

> Lisa was a wonderful help. She would watch me closely, and comment on any small mannerisms which needed correcting. I used to stroke my face occasionally, a gesture which a man often uses, but a woman never. Standing back to the fire and going upstairs two at a time had to be avoided sedulously . . . I never had the slightest difficulty in managing my skirts, and have never once instinctively buttoned my coat the wrong way round, as a man does.[71]

A more recent and famous transsexual in Britain is Jan Morris, ex-Everest climber and *Times* journalist. His autobiography was published in 1974. Like many other contemporary male-to-female transsexuals he gained all the privilege and advantage that life as an upper-class male could give him before he abandoned his male identity. He went to Oxford and was for a while in the Ninth Lancers. He had a wife and five children. Only in middle age when his reputation and social status were assured, did he choose transsexualism.

Like Cowell he experienced miraculous changes as a result of his operation, but in his case they seem to have occurred 'naturally' rather than being learned. He discovered after the operation that his body language had changed and he now moved in a 'woman's way'.[72] He found that he was less 'forceful' generally.

There were other psychological changes too. He suggests that the notion of 'penis envy' is based upon an accurate assessment of the personality characteristics consonant with possession of the penis. The mere presence of the penis, he claimed, was 'positive' and 'stimulating' and when he had had his removed he was not merely more 'retiring', 'ready to be led' and 'passive', but found that his whole body now felt ready to 'yield and accept' instead of feeling as if it should 'push and initiate'. He found that he was more 'emotional' and 'cried very easily'.[73]

From being a journalist commenting on world affairs he now found himself interested in what he saw as 'small' affairs and started to write about people instead of places. He found that he now had a 'simpler vision' which was nearer to that of a child.

It is surely reasonable for women to feel rage at this monstrous presumption on the part of a man about women's natural infantilism and narrow-mindedness.

Male transsexuals really do believe that they carry within themselves some kind of essence of womanhood. Cowell writes, 'in the frame of a man I had the sexual mind of a female'.[74] Morris states that he realised that he had the wrong body and should have been a girl when he was three or four.[75] He tells us that this realisation took place under the piano on which his mother was playing Sibelius. When we examine the evidence for this essence we see it manifest itself in culturally specific, socially learned behaviour and the adoption of fetishistic feminine clothing.

Morris describes what gender means to him. It is something very different from what gender means to sociologists or feminists. While sociologists would generally agree that gender was socially constructed, though perhaps functional and inevitable, feminists argue that gender is constructed with the purpose of maintaining male supremacy. For feminists, gender is not simply about the acquisition of random different characteristics but, for women, the result of oppression. Women acquire certain ways of behaving because they will be punished if they do not, by social disapproval, verbal or physical violence. Correct feminine behaviour demonstrates subservience to the male ruling class. The ultimate conservatism of transsexualism is revealed in the comments from newspaper reviews of *Conundrum* that appear at the beginning of the book. *The Tablet* called the book something for which 'society should be truly grateful' and the *Catholic Standard* called it 'remarkably sensitive'. It is difficult to imagine the pillars of male supremacist religion celebrating the life story of a feminist, particularly a lesbian feminist, who had challenged gender roles.

Morris's view of gender is free of feminist political insights. To him gender was 'insubstantial', composed of 'soul', 'talent', 'taste', 'inner music' and such other more spiritual things. The difference between masculine and feminine he compares to the difference between 'rhythm and melody' or between the 'clasped hand' and the 'open palm'.[76] Gender here is something magical.

It is a kind of personal religion for Morris. In his desire to imitate women we can see the same kind of impulse that drove sensitive and homosexual Oxbridge male graduates to convert to Roman Catholicism. They were in camp pursuit of sensuality, the irrational, the extreme, something to raise life above the humdrum plane and allow an indulgence of feeling. There is a strong element of sexual masochism in both impulses. Morris further reveals that he 'collated' gender with the 'mediaeval idea of soul'. The transsexual urge he explains was more than a 'social compulsion', it was an 'essentially spiritual one'. He considers that 'in the persons of kind, intelligent and healthy women past their menopause' humanity approached nearest to perfection.[77] It was the same Oxford University which had inspired in others the impulse to Roman ritual in the nineteenth century, which crystallised in Morris the desire to be a woman. His life at Oxford started in the choir school of Christ Church college. There, he tells us, he acquired a 'virginal idea' composed of a 'sense of sacrament' and 'fragility' which he later decided was 'femaleness'.[78]

There would be little point arguing with Morris about what is really a matter of religious faith. To those who wish to believe in transsexualism political arguments carry little weight. But upper-class Englishmen are not the only ones to opt for sex change. It is difficult to believe that the very poor young men in Brazil and Bangkok who self-administer latex into their breasts, survive through prostitution and are now suffering the ravages of Aids, experience their mission in quite the same way. There are undoubtedly common threads, but cultural and class differences will influence the way the transmogrification is interpreted.

TRANSSEXUALISM AND HOMOPHOBIA

Transsexuals are motivated by dissatisfaction with their assigned gender role, mysticism, faith in an essence of womanhood. But none of these impulses seem enough to account for men or women choosing to pursue a path of such suffering and effort as surgical mutilation and hormone therapy. There is a simpler explanation which is rejected out of hand by the practitioners and their medical advisers and by most of the apologists for the phenomenon. This is that transsexuals are people who have grown up in a homophobic society but are attracted to others of their own sex. Such is their aversion to homosexuality that these men and women are unable to accept that they are simply gay. In order to relate to people of their own sex they need to transform their bodies so that they can convince themselves that they are really heterosexual. This explanation is vigorously denied by transsexuals, who invest a great deal of money, time and suffering in an effort to establish that they are heterosexual. The vast majority of male-to-female transsexuals relate to other men after the operation. All female-to-male transsexuals relate to women after the operation.

Cowell expressed his aversion to homosexuality in terms which seem very extreme even for the red-blooded male of the 1950s.

> My inclinations, as they developed, were entirely heterosexual. I hated and loathed any boy who showed the slightest sign of being a 'sissy'. I treated any homosexual overtures made to me with complete horror and dislike. Although I made friends with other boys, I could not bear any form of physical contact with a male. Even shaking hands was unpleasant, and it was quite impossible for me to stand having someone link his arm in mine.[79]

When in the RAF 'homosexuals always took it for granted that I was one of their number'.[80] But Cowell was swift to disillusion them. During his treatment he maintained his 'instinctive dislike of the "pansies" '.[81] Cowell married and fathered two children. This part of his life receives only a paragraph in his story. After the operation Cowell discovered to his surprise that he was attracted to men. This is convenient because it could now be said to be a natural and heterosexual impulse.

> Now that my body had developed into womanhood, I slowly began to be a little less asexual. At the theatre or cinema I found I tended to identify myself with the heroine. For the first time in my life I found it possible not only to start reading a love story, but to finish it. I had no desire at all to kiss a

girl, the idea struck me as being almost as unthinkable as it would have been in my previous existence had I an urge to kiss a man. When a man showed interest in me I ceased to regard it as a rather insulting nuisance.[82]

Morris's aversion to homosexuality was less pathological. He had plenty of experience of homosexuality at school but did not see his part in these escapades as homosexual. Homosexual sex 'seemed wrong' to him because 'Nothing fitted', boys' bodies 'did not cleave'. Morris seems to have meant by this that he felt the absence of a vagina which would allow his body to 'open itself'. More importantly, he felt that homosexuality was not 'what the fanvaulting expected of me.'[83]

Morris married and fathered five children. He gives slightly more space than Cowell does to this part of his life and praises the support and friendship of his wife throughout. After the operation Morris, too, magically developed a desire for men and this time he felt comfortable with these feelings. He was able to admit to himself 'without embarrassment how attractive men could be' and he realised that it could be a 'pleasure' to be 'cherished' by them.[84] Morris discovered that he enjoyed being grabbed and kissed by burly taxi-drivers, an experience women might be inclined to call sexual harassment. Neither Cowell nor Morris devote more than a couple of paragraphs to their sexual feelings after the operation. Sex was officially not an important element in their quest.

If we do not accept that it is really possible to 'change' sex, then whatever the transsexuals say, their sexual impulse after the operation is undoubtedly homosexual. In some accounts that are less guarded the homosexual motivation of transsexuals is more obvious. A *Guardian* newspaper article on the Charing Cross Hospital Gender Identity Clinic provides such material.

Nicky telephoned the Samaritans last June. 'I did not feel I could carry on as a male. I wanted to die.' He is 28, tall, blond, pretty, tired of going with men as a male body ... 'I've known since I was eight that I was mentally female. My mother had lots of boyfriends and I used used to take them tea in bed. I wanted to be in bed with them ...'[85]

How did this man know he was a transsexual? It was because he wanted to have sex with men. That is pretty clear. The case where female transsexuals are concerned is even clearer. There do not seem to be cases in the literature in which women who have pursued happy heterosexual careers suddenly decide to change sex and discover to their surprise that they are attracted to women. Female aspirants are generally heavily involved in loving women when they seek surgery, but do not see themselves as lesbian.

> Robby is a tall, 19-year-old West Indian girl with an Afro hair style . . . She arrived at the Charing Cross Hospital with a very feminine girlfriend who accepts Robby as a boyfriend . . .
> 'I've always played football with the boys. I buy clothes from men's shops. I'm definitely not lesbian but I would go to bed with a woman if she considered me male.'[86]

Robby's reasons for seeing herself as a man rather than a lesbian aren't terribly convincing. It is very common for lesbians to buy clothes in men's shops and not uncommon for heterosexual women to do so. Playing football is also common among lesbians and becoming rather more acceptable for heterosexual girls.

Information about female transsexuals is not easy to come by. Little has been written by the sexologists and, until recently at least, they had few cases to work from. In 1983 the first whole book devoted to female transsexuals was published in the US.[87] Leslie Lothstein worked for eight years as co-director of a gender identity clinic. Out of 200 patients seen in that time, 50 were women. Lothstein preferred to use a psychotherapeutic approach to his patients and to guide them away from a surgical solution. He sought to reconcile patients to being heterosexual women. He claims to have been guided by Robert Stoller and saw transsexualism as developing from the failure of mothers to develop the femininity of their daughters who then identified with a male figure. He states that: 'The most prominent view, that all female transsexuals are stigmatised homosexuals, is, at best, an exaggeration of a partial truth.'[88] Transsexualism, he asserts, is not a sexual disorder but 'primarily a disorder of the self-esteem'. Transsexuals should not be seen as homosexual because, 'Once they are mislabelled as homosexuals or sexual deviants, they are further isolated from needed support systems.'[89]

Though Lothstein is unwilling to give much credit to the idea that homosexuality is the main if not the only motivation of female-to-constructed-male transsexuals, this is an explanation not uncommon in the sexological literature. In 1953 Hamburger reported on 108 women who requested surgery. All had homosexual desires and none reported being attracted to men. He concluded, '... in women who feel like men the wish for a change of sex does not seem to manifest itself or become dominant until the person in question falls in love with another woman; this happens in the great majority of cases'.[90] Harry Benjamin, the sexologist who had been working on transsexualism since the 1930s, reported that the characteristics of women wanting the operation included lesbianism combined with 'a dislike for lesbians and an anti-homosexual attitude'.[91] One sensible sexologist suggested that the correct treatment for patients requesting surgery was to use therapy to reconcile them to their lesbianism so that they could live happily loving women. He wrote:

> Some homosexuals, because of societal proscription, have developed such phobic reactions regarding expression of homosexual interests that they believe themselves transsexuals and would rather give up their gender than face a life of homosexual behaviour.[92]

All the women in Lothstein's case studies were sexually involved with women before they sought the operation. This involvement was extensive and usually started in childhood or early teens. There are many indications in Lothstein's book that the women seeking surgery resembled those lesbians who have historically played the butch role in the lesbian community. Of course they were different in that they sought surgery, whereas the vast majority of those who have seen themselves as butch had no desire for surgery. But there are undoubtedly characteristics in common. Cross-dressing is one and breast binding to conceal breast development is another. Merrill Mushroom's article on role playing in the lesbian community in 1950s America describes such characteristics as part of the butch role.[93] She also describes the phenomenon of stone butchness. Some butch lesbians would not allow their lovers to touch them sexually, often explaining this in terms of feelings of discomfort with their bodies.[94] The sexologists Sorenson and Hertoft list two characteristics of women seeking treatment: 'transsexual women play an active and domineering part in sexual relations; they do not usually allow their partners to make contact with their genitals'.[95]

An interview in *Gay News* with Lou Stothard, a female-to-constructed-male transsexual makes some of the differences in motivation for men and women seeking the operation clear. Lou is a lesbian and describes her development thus:

I didn't like boys and felt positively attracted, emotionally and sexually, to girls but I was also aware that it wasn't just lesbian feelings I had towards them.[96]

In many ways her experience in childhood was typical of girls who realise early that they are lesbian. She writes: 'I thought I looked like a boy and was pleased when mistaken for one', 'I was a loner at school.' The difference from typical lesbian development is that Lou was 'aware' at the age of five 'that I would eventually live as a male'. None the less at 16 Lou 'came out as gay'. Her development was in another important respect also very different from that of the average male-to-female transsexual. She doesn't like men and does not wish to be one.

... I don't want a penis which is partly why I would describe myself as living as male rather than as living as a man; I don't like men generally and have no wish to participate in their rituals, back-slapping camaraderie or to be connected with any form of macho ethic.[97]

This indifference to the acquisition of the genitals of the opposite sex would be unthinkable to the male transsexual. Lou's motivation seems to have stemmed more from hatred of her female-

186

ness than from a fetishistic interest in male anatomy. She wanted to eliminate all that was female about herself.

> I felt revolted by periods and was extremely distressed when I started to menstruate at sixteen, by which time I thought of myself as male . . . At nineteen, without telling my parents, I consulted a doctor, was referred to a psychiatrist and . . . had a complete hysterectomy.[98]

Lou took hormones with the effect that her waist thickened, skin grew coarser, hair thinned out and voice broke, her clitoris enlarged and she grew a moustache. She still has a vagina and uses it sexually which, as she admits, would be anathema to the sexologists who define transsexuality. She relates sexually to women who see themselves as heterosexual or bisexual rather than lesbian. Lou's transsexualism seems to stem simply from an extreme dislike of the restrictions of femininity combined with love for other girls. In both respects she resembled many other young lesbians. In her case the dislike of femaleness went as far as the need to physically excise some, but not all, of the primary sexual characteristics. She exhibits none of the fetishistic and objectifying behaviour of the male-to-constructed-female transsexual who desperately seeks to acquire 'female' physical characteristics and to be a perfect 'woman'. What is amazing is that she managed to get a hysterectomy and hormones at all considering that she fails so markedly to conform to sexological classifications.

It has only been necessary to invent the transsexual since the availability of sex reassignment surgery. Such surgery is awesomely painful and irreversible so the sexologists who have accepted it as a reasonable treatment have needed to sharpen up their diagnostic powers and decide who is and who is not a genuine transsexual. Before the surgery was available sexologists cheerfully included within their homosexual category men and women who would now be considered by most sexologists to be transsexual. Cross-dressers were seen as homosexual by Krafft Ebing, and the sexologists to a man identified homosexuals as having behaviour appropriate to the opposite sex. The founding fathers of sexology believed that homosexuals were biologically a third sex. When we read their case studies it is striking how similar the sentiments of the patients are to the modern transsexual. The men asserted that they had female minds in male bodies.

It is not surprising that radical gay men fail to see the sexist nature of transsexualism. There has been little enough evidence that gay men are prepared to support the feminist project if this challenges their pleasures. Gender fetishism in the form of drag is fun and excitement to gay men, as well as being the basis of transsexualism. What is most surprising is the care with which most radical gay men avoid recognising that transsexualism derives from gayhating. Gay men, if they were really concerned with gay liberation, would be determined, as feminists are, to create a world in which transsexualism could not be imagined. Meanwhile a self-confident campaign to assert gay pride could considerably lessen the number of gay men presently choosing surgery over liberation.

PAEDOPHILIA

In Britain, the massive feminist campaign against the sexual abuse of female children was getting under way in 1980. There was little dissension amongst feminists about the centrality of sexual abuse to feminist concerns. Meanwhile the Criminal Law Revision Committee was taking submissions from the public on revising the law relating to sexual offences. Groups campaigning on behalf of paedophiles advised the committee that the age of consent for sexual offences should be drastically lowered or abolished. Paedophile organisations or their apologists demanded the support of gay liberation and of feminists for paedophiles. At the same time as we were just realising the seriousness of child sexual abuse, we were being told that paedophilia was a radical, progressive, socialist, and even a feminist issue. The first principle of the Gay Youth Movement's Charter from this period states that the 'liberation of lesbians and gay men' requires the liberation of women and 'all other oppressed groups, including sexual minorities such as transsexuals, transvestites, and paedophiles'.[99]

Parts of the left were swayed into thinking that paedophilia was a progressive issue as the paedophile activists did their best to show the links between paedophilia and socialism even if these links seemed completely obscure to their listeners. Keith Hose, a former chairperson of the main paedophile organisation, Paedophile Information Exchange (PIE), was interviewed in the *Leveller*, a radical left journal. He was asked to explain the links between socialism and paedophilia. He asserts that, 'In Britain before capitalism one gets the impression that things were more free for paedophiles' and suggests that paedophilia is only condemned because it 'threatens some of the basic institutions of capitalism, such as the nuclear family . . .'[100]

This is thin stuff, but we must remember that the libertarian left of the 1970s believed that the nuclear family was a construct of capitalism and was sexually repressive, and it believed in the idea of children's liberation. The rhetoric of paedophile liberation was designed to appeal to such libertarians. *Peace News* published *Indecent Assault* by Roger Moody, a former *Peace News* editor, about his arrest and trial and subsequent acquittal on four charges of indecent assault and buggery with a 10-year-old boy.[101] *Peace News* announced proudly inside its back cover that '*Peace News* has for many years been one of the few forums open to discussions of paedophilia, by Roger Moody and others'. Eric Presland, another British apologist for paedophilia, claims that he seeks the 'incorporation of children's and paedophiles' liberation into the broad alliance of the sexual left'.[102]

The Paedophile Information Exchange consisted of adult males who wanted sex with children. One might be forgiven for thinking that the paedophile movement was simply a movement of men demanding sexual access, without legal hassles, to the territory of children's bodies. But the paedophile lobby did not put their politics across this way. In a political context in which feminists had for a decade been demanding an end to male sexual aggression and exploitation, paedophile liberation could look like more of the problem rather than the solution. So the paedophiles gave out that they were selflessly striving for the sexual liberation of children. Children were deprived of most important rights, they argued, under the authoritarian rule of the family and the parents sanctified by the state. The most onerous aspect of such a regime was the sexual repression of children which had begun with the invention of childhood as a category in the nineteenth century.

The paedophile movements in the US and in Britain have some different characteristics. PIE purported to be an organisation for adult paedophiles of either sex interested in children of either sex. Though there were rumours that there was a woman in the organisation none such ever appeared and heterosexual paedophiles, interested in female children, were not numerous. But in theory PIE was a catch-all paedophile group and included in its brief sex with children of any age. In contrast the American group, NAMBLA, or North American Man Boy Love Association founded in early 1979, was, as its name implies, for men interested in pubertal boys. It was more directly a homosexual organisation. Some British paedophiles claimed ungenerously that NAMBLA was taking the easy way out and abandoning its convictions to win over the public while the British organisation was fighting for the more radical cause.

Both groups argued for children's liberation. Daniel Tsang edited a collection of articles putting the American paedophile case at the time that NAMBLA was founded. He writes:

> The primary issue, it should be made clear, is not the right of men to have sex with boys. Were that the entire focus, proponents of man/boy love would not gain many supporters. Rather the real issue is the liberation of young people, so that they are empowered to make their own decisions regarding all aspects of their lives, including their sexuality.[103]

Warren Middleton of PIE shows a consummate use of this euphemistic language. He starts his introduction to a 1986 anthology by detailing what he sees as the Draconian sentences handed out to sex offenders against children and men who photograph children in the US. The actions of these men are described as 'childhood sexuality'. He writes of the 'hysteria which invariably accompanies reports of childhood sexuality and the witchhunt against those who show a sexual interest in children or young people'.[104] The sexual activities of adult men with children are described as 'childhood sexuality' to give the impression that paedophiles exist to serve the interests of children rather than the other way round, and Middleton performs this sleight of hand audaciously. He asks:

> Why does the Establishment condemn with such vigour any attempt to examine the issues dispassionately, not only of childhood sexual self-expression and its cross-generational manifestation, but of the other, more general yet equally important issues of the rights and freedoms of youth? Why does society put down children, and try to crucify any adult who dares to meet them on their own terms?[105]

In the US it could more easily be argued that NAMBLA represented the interests of youth since there were two teenagers along with 32 adult men amongst the founders of the group. PIE did not include children. The determination of adults, who are in a relationship of power towards children, to speak for them should cause alarm. We have historical examples of this principle in operation. In nineteenth-century Lancashire the mill owners panicked when moves were afoot to outlaw child labour. They produced eloquent speeches showing that their employment of children was actually a humanitarian gesture aimed at relieving the poverty of whole families who would otherwise have no income. They produced other arguments, too, such as the value of work discipline for the child. It is now clear to us that naked self-interest was speaking. In the absence of child labour the mill owners would have had to pay adult wages and would have had a less quiescent workforce. Slave owners in the southern US in the nineteenth century marshalled arguments as to how slavery was beneficial to slaves. Men for centuries have claimed that what was in their interests as a ruling class was what women really wanted. The paedophile movement is quite clearly about the demand by adult men for sexual access to children, whatever spurious arguments are put forward to gain radical support.

If the main interest of paedophiles was that children should be allowed sexual self-expression, an aim which is scarcely contentious, then there would be more enthusiasm from paedophiles for children expressing themselves with each other. There would be no need to assert that adult males would or should be the necessary beneficiaries of children's burgeoning sexuality. But the paedophiles are not enthusiastic about children having sex with each other. Presland asserts that children are better off relating sexually to adults than to other children because children are '... corrupted very early on. Children pick up the prevailing prejudices of those around them, like burrs ...'[106] Paedophile males, we must assume, are on the contrary free of such prejudice.

The definition of paedophile practice is difficult because, despite the efforts of the paedophile lobby to categorise, actual practice by paedophiles tends to slip out of the categories. The sexperts and the paedophiles themselves seem to agree that heterosexual paedophiles prefer girls from 6–11 years whereas homosexual paedophiles prefer boys of 12–15.[107] This does not, of course, account for those paedophiles whose interest in children is not restricted by gender or the boylovers who choose younger children. The idea that paedophiles are distinct from the rest of the male population does not account for the occasional sexual abuse of children by men who relate at other times to adults and simply like variety.

Roger Moody describes paedophile sexual practice.

... a paedophile is a man or woman who loves a girl or boy (i.e. under 16) emotionally and/or physically ... But one of the things paedophiles assert is that, from all they know of each other ... most of what they do with the young confines itself to fondling, sexual play and mutual masturbation. By and large little else 'happens' but if it does, it's because the kids really want it.[108]

Daniel Tsang explains 'gay men fuck and suck teenage boys regularly. It happens daily in every city or rural rest stop'.[109] This is not the same thing as paedophilia, he says, because it involves the use of pubescent boys rather than children. It is not child molestation either, he says, because that would imply 'physical or psychological coercion'. Tsang explains his sexuality thus:

My own sexuality is as little concerned with children,

however, as it is with women. It is self-consciously homosexual, but it is directed at boys at that time in their lives when they cease to be children yet refuse to be men. I celebrate with them their act of rebellion, their genuine emotion and authentic, self-originating actions and ideas.[110]

Some paedophiles have a rather sweeping definition of their proclivity. Tom Reeves, at the Boston conference at which NAMBLA was founded, declared that a third of all male workers with boys were paedophile in inclination. Speaking of boy scout leaders, teachers and boys' club leaders he said, 'the motivation behind that work [has] a sexual and erotic content'.[111] Presently, Reeves lamented, these men were repressed and felt unable to express themselves sexually with the boys. This led to the creation of boy prostitution and even violence against boys. Similarly, male apologists for the abuse of women have tended to argue that prostitution and rape would disappear if only women would loosen up and be more accommodating to men's sexual demands. An even broader definition is offered by Gerald Hannon who wrote the notorious piece, 'Men loving boys loving men', which led in 1978 to the prosecution of the Canadian gay paper *Body Politic*. Hannon declared that the founder of his local YMCA was a paedophile. The man is dead, it seems, and Hannon has no more evidence for his assertion than the painting of the founder in the foyer which portrays him as most respectable. Hannon explains:

I don't know for sure, of course . . . But I do know what he did. I know, at least, why he was celebrated. He loved boys. He had dreams for them. He made them his life's work. If you are what you do, C. J. Atkinson, benefactor and 'leader in boy's work', was very much a paedophile.[112]

Paedophilia is being defined here as selfless humanitarianism without even a sexual content, unless we must assume that any humanitarian instinct is really sexual. It is a broad brush stroke of a definition and enables the paedophiles to declare that paedophilia is as common in women as men and to cite as evidence the fact that women are often fond of children and hug and kiss them. It creates a smokescreen which can hide the gender-specific nature of child sexual abuse. Even the sexperts are prepared to propagate this deliberate confusion. Maurice Yaffe explains the lack of female paedophiles as arising from women's greater opportunity to satisfy themselves sensually with children.

> Virtually all paedophiles are male, and one reason why there are so few women may be that the sensuous expression of paedophilia in females is socially approved as a vital and necessary function of all maternal caring, and provides sufficient fulfilment.[113]

For the paedophiles and their apologists it is useful to be able to cast doubt upon the motives of anyone who likes children.

When we look at what paedophiles actually do, it does not indicate a disinterested desire to take young boys to the pictures and play trains with them, or even to give them lots of hugs. It certainly doesn't encompass the caring tasks of housework, washing and cooking which fall to the mother. We'll look first at Hannon's description of paedophile practice from the famous *Body Politic* article. Hannon's first example is Simon who is 33, a primary school teacher and a member of several social service organisations which deal with children including Big Brothers, a befriending organisation which provides caring adults for boys who are likely to fall foul of the law and who suffer from deprivation. He has taught in four schools and in each of them and in all the social service organisations he had sexual relations with children. His current lover was a 12-year-old in his class. Simon says he has only 'bumfucked' two boys. 'One of them asked me to, and the other indicated that he wanted it. They didn't like it all that much . . .'[114]

Peter is a 48-year-old rich businessman, who doesn't have access to boys in his job. He meets boys by demonstrating money and glamour.

> With boys you have to impress them at first, you have to call attention to yourself. I do it with a big car, or a deep tan, or an ability. I used to be quite skilled at diving and I would have all eyes on me all summer. It's not the only way, of

course. I've picked up boys in theatres. You sit down beside them and start making comments about the movie, and then you might say 'here's a quarter' – now it would have to be a dollar – 'why don't you get us both a coke.'[115]

Simon had the advantage of having positions of responsibility and authority over the boys he approached, as well as age. Peter selected boys desperate for affection who were disadvantaged in class and education.

Peter has a special interest in the detritus of heterosexual relationships, the unwanted or unloved boys, the boys from homes where the father is dead or has deserted. 'It seems the more disadvantaged the child, the more he needs some stable, mature human being. And they're looking for love as well. Typically, they are not very articulate and not very well educated, and I think I am often a very positive influence.'[116]

Of one of his boys Peter writes, 'He's a professor now, married, two kids, divorced. I began having sex with him when he was twelve.'[117] Peter, like Simon, claims he doesn't do much anal intercourse with the boys. 'My sexual needs are very simple. I don't very often fuck somebody, though I like it once in a while. Most of the time it would be mutual masturbation, with some sucking. I prefer to be sucked: sucking doesn't interest me that much, though I do it if I think it gives someone else pleasure.'[118]

Peter does not confine his sexual interests to the pubescent age group. He has sexually used a boy as young as seven. This boy, like the others, was used to service Peter's sexuality rather than the other way round, despite the claims of paedophile literature to the contrary.

The youngest? Seven, I think. He wasn't a very bright little fellow, but he just loved sucking. He used to come up to the apartment, and as soon as he got in he'd say 'I want some wine.' That meant he wanted to suck me off. And he learned that reference from a policeman in the neighbourhood and the policeman told him that this was wine . . . He'd suck me to orgasm and swallow it.[119]

The boys that Simon and Peter used grew up to be heterosexual. This is a source of pride to the adult abusers. Simon and Peter felt that they had given the boys sex education and smoothed the way to their adult heterosexuality. It may be unclear what this has to do with gay liberation. If there is a connection, and the pro-paedophile lobby constantly reiterate the indissoluble links between the two, it consists in the fact that male gay liberation is dedicated to serving the sexual demands of adult gay men whether they are for adults or children, straights or gays, and at whatever cost. About the adult abusers, Hannon concludes, 'They are the heirs of Mr Atkinson, "Leader in Boys' Work", community workers who deserve our praise, our admiration and our support.'[120]

Eric Presland is a British example of the paedophile who exploits the needs of a child to satisfy his sexual interests. He describes a sexual relationship with a 13-year-old Asian boy from his neighbourhood. Presland negotiated with the mother so that the boy could come to live with him. But responsibility for making this a sexual relationship was apparently nothing to do with Presland. A female friend suggested he take Saleem to bed because the boy was anxious for sex.

> Saleem was thirteen when I met him, small for his age and thin, with the uncertain, ingratiating smile of someone who is used to being clobbered both physically and emotionally. His whole manner seemed to scream out, 'Like me, please,' and to expect the opposite . . . My house represented an escape from home – an overworked mother and four children in a three-bedroomed crumbling council flat . . . It was Marilyn who pushed us into a physical relationship. I had held back, scared witless by thoughts of under-age sex, and unsure of whether Saleem merely craved my approval.[121]

Presland also masturbated much younger children he baby-sat for lesbian friends, such as a six-year-old he masturbated because this helped the child to go to sleep.[122] Presland was the campaign worker for the National Campaign for Legislation on Lesbian and Gay Rights. At the National Conference in May

1987 lesbians had difficulty opposing demands by some men in workshops for the abolition of the age of consent.

The language of these descriptions and the sentiments expressed are difficult for women to sympathise with. Paedophile literature is probably meant to be a conversation between men. The crude manipulation of children towards the genital satisfaction of adult males is disturbing. But the descriptions we have seen are of what the paedophiles see as mutual, caring, non-exploitative relationships. This, however difficult for women to read, is the acceptable, really carefully massaged face of paedophilia. For paedophile lobbyists trying to make themselves look like the selfless saviours of children the existence of a massive industry of child pornography, child prostitution and international sex tourism in children can be an embarrassment.

Robin Lloyd's book *Playland* describes boy prostitution in the US and in Britain in the late 1970s.[123] Playland is the name of an amusement arcade in the sex industry heartland of New York to which teenage runaways, many the victims of incestuous abuse in the family, gravitate to find clients. Prostitution and pornography are the only avenues for survival open to boys below working age. A similar amusement arcade was the focus for boy prostitution in London. The male clients are called chickenhawks and the boys, chickens.

Female prostitutes, in wigs and tight clothes, blatantly pace their territories or lean against doorways. In contrast, boy prostitutes are not as easily recognisable though they outnumber female hookers five to one . . . Among the chickens, there are slightly more Puerto Ricans than blacks; the population of white chickens is significantly smaller than both. Most of the boys come to midtown Manhattan from slums in the Bronx and Brooklyn; a few come from nearby towns in New Jersey . . . By the time the chicken and chickenhawk start to undress, the man knows just what he's going to get for the fifteen dollars he must pay . . . A fledgeling, inexperienced chicken permits himself to be the passive partner in an act of oral sex. Soon he will provide other services and eventually play the active role in anal intercourse.[124]

Boy prostitution is an international industry. Lloyd explains that in major cities like Beirut, Calcutta, Mexico City and Bogotá, the boys service tourists as well as local males and, 'The world's poverty centres become an international harem for the travelling pederast.'[125]

Lloyd writes like a journalist. His style is anecdotal and gives no clear picture of the extent of boy prostitution or pornography. Guides to international boy prostitution do circulate in paedophile circles and the Philippines is currently a favoured area, but when the Lloyd book is mentioned in the paedophile literature it is denied and disparaged. This is because Lloyd sees prostitution as exploitation. The campaigning paedophiles find themselves enmeshed in difficulties over the sex industry. At the same time as claiming that paedophiles want mutual caring relationships in which the main interest is less sex than love they are unable to reject the use of boy prostitutes or pornography.

Richard Green in *The Betrayal of Youth* devotes a whole chapter to 'Child Pornography and Erotica'. He cites evidence that pornography can be good for children as sex education. This is a necessary contention since many of the paedophile campaigners openly admit they use pornography to teach and suggest to boys what they should be doing. But Green shows his understanding that pornography is contentious by attempting to be both positive and negative about it at the same time. 'Pornography, which I have to admit is also an undesirable element in our society, can be introduced to children in an understanding way.'[126] He goes on from this to tell us that the use of children in the creation of pornography is harmless good fun for the children.

> So what of children's involvement in pornography itself? . . .
> Children generally enjoy being photographed and, if they are
> extrovert, will be happy for other people to see pictures of
> them, perhaps even naked pictures . . . No, the mere taking
> of erotic pictures of a youngster will not generally cause
> harm.[127]

Green suggests a solution to the exploitation that can happen in the sex industry. He proposes the plan of Tom O'Carroll, pioneering and crusading PIE member, 'a monitored, legitimate erotica . . . industry in which all participants – like stage actors – whether they be adult or child, should be able to claim a minimum wage and other working standards'.[128] Green adds a justification for freely available child pornography that is more generally used to justify the use of women in the industry. The unavailability of porn, might, he warns, lead to 'kidnapping and forcing children into sex against their will'.[129] The apologists of the sex industry have always argued that a certain number of women must be abused in order to protect the rest. Here we have the same argument being used of children.

Presland also bewails the unavailability of child pornography. This leads to what he sees as the unfortunate result that paedophiles are reduced to masturbating over family snapshots never actually intended for that purpose. This is apparently undesirable because the 'grinning child . . . may be totally unaware of the purpose to which his/her picture may be put'.[130] This drawback could, he suggests, be relieved by more freely available child porn in which the models did know the use to which the pictures would be put because they were familiar with adult male masturbation.

Since both kiddie porn and erotica are rigidly suppressed in this country, there is an acute shortage of erotic visual stimulus for paedophiles, already an emotionally and sexually starved group.[131]

The first line of defence put forward by the paedophiles when their practice is impugned, is to say that it is the children who approach and initiate sex with them. This has long been a popular explanation of child sexual abuse in the sexological literature. The sexperts have made a practice of demonstrating that the abused children participated in or precipitated their abuse. In a study of the literature on child sexual abuse in 1979 I found that the evidence used to prove participation or even precipitation comprised such things as accepting sweets or talking to strangers.[132] The writers who sought to show that abused children had particular personality characteristics which made them liable to abuse, described these characteristics as 'attention-seeking', friendliness and affectionate behaviour. My conclusion on this kind of research was and remains:

> Does this explain their victimisation? It may explain why some children are in more danger than others and why it is necessary to destroy a child's trust and interest in male adults. It does not explain why the adult male offenders make sexual advances to children in the first place.[133]

Studying the victims of crime to explain how they came to be victims, rather than the study of the criminal, is called victimology. When used to prove how women and children precipitate their own sexual abuse it is more properly called victim-blaming. Victim-blaming has the advantage of diverting attention from the adult male offender and preventing any political analysis of sexual assault in terms of male domination. For the paedophiles this approach serves the same function. The fact that children who have not yet learned to be wary seek affection and attention from adults does not mean that they are seeking to service adult male sexuality. The analyst Sandor Ferenczi pointed this out in a sensitive paper in 1932 entitled 'The confusion of tongues between the adult and the child'.[134] The paper was suppressed by his psychoanalytic colleagues because it undermined the Freudian orthodoxy that sexual abuse was rare and mostly fantasised by the child. As Ferenczi points out, children have a gradual sexual development. There is little likelihood of their being familiar with adult male sexuality unless they have already been abused or 'educated' by men through pornography. What they cannot conceive of they cannot fantasise or seek out.

A description by O'Carroll of typical and supposedly 'sensitive' paedophile behaviour makes this clear. It should be remembered that O'Carroll is writing a paedophile manifesto seeking liberal support. It is amazing that he cannot do a better public relations job to make paedophilia look even minimally mutual and non-exploitative.

> Typically, in the formation of a paedophile attachment, as in those between adults, the actual behaviour of either party develops not precipitately, but step by step: each stage is

'negotiated' by hints and signals, verbal and non-verbal, by which each indicates to the other what is acceptable and what is not. In our example, the man might start by saying what pretty knickers the girl was wearing, and he would be far more likely to proceed to the next stage of negotiation if she seemed pleased by the remark than if she coloured up and closed her legs. Despite being 'wrong' about her intentional sexual seductiveness, he might nevertheless be right in gradually discovering that the child is one who thinks it great fun to be tickled under her knickers . . . [135]

The model paedophile here is pursuing his sexual objective ruthlessly with a complete disregard for what the child wants. He does not use overt violence but he does use pressure and does not respond to her negatives. The child's interests are not only not central to this picture, they aren't even in the margin. This is a good example of what Ferenczi called the 'confusion of tongues'. The paedophile would expect the child to know adult codes of sexual modesty appropriate to a particular culture. If the girl did not know that remarks about knickers should make her close her legs then she was held to be willing to engage in an activity she could not even imagine.

It is in this context that we must look at the issue of consent. Paedophiles all argue for the abolition or drastic reduction of the age of consent which currently stands at 16 for sexual intercourse with and indecent assault on girls and at 21 for homosexual males. Confusion is created by paedophile lobbyists when they agitate for the rights of boys over 16. There is no justice in having an age of consent for male homosexuality set higher than that for heterosexual sex. The homosexual age of consent needs to be lowered to 16. When that happens some of the confusions around the paedophile argument will be cleared up. The issue will become more clearly one of adults pursuing sex with boys rather than one of young men being forbidden to pursue their chosen sexual path.

The Gay Activists Alliance proposed the abolition of the age of consent altogether and the decriminalisation of paedophilia.[136] The Paedophile Information Exchange proposed that the age of consent should be four. For feminists the abolition of the age of consent is completely unacceptable. The paedophiles claim that the age of consent was raised in the late nineteenth and early twentieth centuries as a result of puritanical campaigners wanting to repress children's sexuality and engaging in a moral panic. In fact this is not the case. There was a massive feminist campaign to protect children from men's sexual violence and concern over the age of consent was but one part of it. Feminists then as now saw age-of-consent legislation as a political, feminist demand, necessary because of male domination and men's aggression towards women and children.[137] For paedophiles abolition is crucial and the motivating force behind their coming out. They want access to children without legal penalty. Between paedophiles and feminists there is not just a little misunderstanding but a head-on collision.

Those paedophiles with the sophistication to be aware that non-paedophiles will never find it reasonable to allow men sexual access to young children claim, as does NAMBLA, that man/boy love is quite different from paedophilia. Man/boy love is about equal, caring relationships between men and pubescent boys, to whom the demands of adult male sexuality would not come as such a surprise. It is quite reasonable to assume that pubescent boys do gain sexual satisfaction in such interaction. But is this a sufficient reason to drop feminist objections to man/boy sex? The issues of exploitation of vulnerability and poverty, and the abuse of positions of trust and responsibility, still create indigestible political problems.

Since I knew nothing from personal experience about the sexuality of adolescent boys I was prepared to give paedophiles the benefit of the doubt here in relation to pubescent boys, despite the fact that the voices of boys in favour or disparagement were noticeably silent. Then I went to speak at a Gay Workshop in London in 1982 on paedophilia. Linda Bellos and I presented the feminist case against paedophilia to an audience of men. In the discussion that followed a middle-aged Dutch paedophile dominated and spoke of the positive benefits to boys of man/boy love and the sensitivity of paedophiles. A young man burst out in a rage when he could contain himself no longer, that the Dutch paedophile reminded him of the man who had sexually used him when he was a boy. The characteristic that reminded him and brought back distressing memories was the man's dominating, unchallengeable arrogance. Another young man joined in to challenge the paedophile from his own experience. Suddenly the voices of the boys were being heard. Why had they been silent? Until the contemporary wave of feminism, women had not spoken out about their experience of abuse in childhood. Women's Liberation is a supportive consciousness-raising movement that makes such phenomena as incest survivors' groups possible. For young men it is much harder. They live in a male culture in which it is a heresy to speak against the religion that sex is always good and positive. There is little space in such a discourse for the voices of abuse victims. It would be sissy indeed to protest in a world in which macho sexual enthusiasm is the currency of survival.

Flame, who was sexually used by adult men from 12 onwards and became a teenage prostitute, describes in his autobiography, *Flame: A Life on the Game*, many incidents of sexual violence and threat in his early teens. At 13 he was raped by his mother's ponce.

> I was in bed when I suddenly felt there was someone in my room. My mum was out working. It was Micky. He was naked. He walked over to my bed, reached out and nudged me, as though to waken me. Then he put his arm under the blankets, grabbed hold of my hand and placed it round his cock. Then he climbed into bed and screwed me. I enjoyed it. Not liking him as a person somehow made it more erotic. If I'd struggled, I don't know what he would have done – that added more spice. I've always liked a bit of an angle to sex, a twist.[138]

In another incident at age 13 he was raped in a toilet while dressed as a girl.

> But one afternoon I went into a ladies' toilet in town and a man followed me into the cubicle. He pushed me against the wall, lifted my fox-fur coat and my skirt, pulled down my tights and fucked me. He didn't ask if I was animal, vegetable or mineral, though presumably he realised I was male. Then

he walked straight onto the street. At that time I would have had sex with just about anybody, and I found the incident quite amusing. But I thought later that it would have been a traumatic experience if I had been a woman who didn't want to get fucked.[139]

Flame claims to have 'enjoyed' both these incidents, although a gang rape in a remand home he describes as merely painful. If there was a different way of describing sex in the male gay culture, if abuse of power and the problem of how the oppressed eroticise their subordination were topics on the agenda, then Flame might choose to reinterpret his experience. The young men in the Gay Workshop were able to do this because feminists had forcefully presented a different analysis and a language existed in which to make sense of their experience.

In seeking to enable young gay men to develop a different discourse on sexuality we are confronted with a serious obstacle in the profound and tragic masochism revealed in so much gay literature, which is one of the motivating forces of camp. The masochism reveals itself in Flame who rationalises being used as a waste-disposal chute as pleasure. It is evident in the work of many other gay writers too, such as Quentin Crisp. Crisp accepts actual beating up and attempts to excuse the heterosexual young male aggressors. Of the men who attack him in the street Crisp writes:

They were only slightly concerned with forcing me to accept their superiority. If this latter was their whole aim, then all those street brawls were a waste of time. I regarded all heterosexuals, however low, as superior to any homosexual, however noble.[140]

His approach to life in his youth he describes as follows:

My outlook was so limited that I assumed that all deviates were openly despised and rejected. Their grief and their fear drew my melancholy nature strongly. At first I wanted to wallow in their misery, but, as time went by, I longed to reach its very essence. Finally I desired to represent it.[141]

204

This masochism could emerge from the necessity of gay men to reconcile themselves to their oppression, a survival ethic, and from a pulverised sense of self resulting from growing up gay. But there is not such a strong maudlin element in lesbian culture. Gender clearly plays a part. There must be particular problems involved in learning a sexual orientation which in itself is composed of love for the ruling class of men and the masculine principle. This is a problem for heterosexual women too, but women do not have an expectation of status and privilege born of membership of the ruling class which they must sacrifice in pursuit of their desire.

The feminist campaign against the sexual abuse of girls has created something of an embarrassment for the paedophiles. Feminists see the abuse of children by men as a political crime of the powerful against the powerless. Feminists do not accept that there is some harmless form of sexual use of children called paedophilia. Between all adults and children there is a huge imbalance of power which is further exaggerated between men and female children.

The issue of power imbalance caused a furore at the Boston conference at which NAMBLA was formed. Some men argued that the issue of power was important and had not been much addressed at the conference. Tom Reeves argued that not only was the man not dominant over the boy but that it was actually the other way around. The boy, he said, had power over the man.

> He argued that the boy 'has the dominance' in physical, emotional, and spiritual terms and 'has the power over the man'. A woman from the audience swiftly told Reeves that it was 'bullshit' to say the child had more power 'given the way we're structured in this world and the fact is, it's not your right to say it'.[142]

But Reeves did say it and went on to found NAMBLA. There is a contradiction in the paedophile argument here. Paedophile lobbyists put forward their sexual interests under the guise of children's liberation and paedophile literature makes much of children's lack of power and self-determination *vis-à-vis* adults in order to argue for their right to sexual self-determination. PIE even campaigns against corporal punishment in schools as its token gesture towards children's rights. But paedophiles can't have it both ways. Either children lack power in relation to adults or they do not.

Paedophiles who recognise that the feminist argument needs answering seriously produce more sophisticated ways of getting round the issue of power imbalance. Eric Presland accepts that inequality of power is an issue. His solution is that paedophiles give up their power as men and adults, which they can do simply by labelling themselves paedophiles and so becoming part of an oppressed group. He explains,

> Paedophiles who define themselves as such are giving up their power in an immediate and dramatic way. They are placing themselves in the category of the most despised and powerless in our culture.[143]

This does not, on examination, seem like a real solution. The fact that a man defines himself as a paedophile is not likely to outweigh the difference in age, money, social and sexual experience which he would have over any boy.

The paedophiles do not have a good answer to the problem of power imbalance. The incorrigible obtuseness of the paedophile lobby on the issue of power should cause us to realise that the theorists of gay liberation, whether paedophile or supportive of paedophiles, simply have no conception of power or the abuse of power in the arena of sexuality. Radical gays have a libertarian position on sexuality. They take a free-market approach and condemn laws in restraint of trade. They choose to assume that all players are equal. Male gay literature does not usually mention women. Where women are mentioned the writers have real difficulty in grasping that gender difference is about power difference, and a power difference which might mean that women and men are not all free and equal agents in the market of sexuality. To such writers children and slaves are included in the free market as free agents too.

An example of this kind of writing is the gay historian John Boswell's *Christianity, Social Tolerance and Homosexuality*.

This study of male homosexuality in Europe in the early mediaeval period covers material which should provide fascinating
insights into gender, power and sexuality. Boswell avoids any
such insights scrupulously. He writes, 'The Arabic language
contains a huge vocabulary of gay erotic terminology, with
dozens of words just to describe types of male prostitutes.'[144]
The prostitutes in question were slave boys. To someone with
a consciousness about issues of gender and power the abuse
of slave children in prostitution would not be confused with
eroticism. Boswell not only confuses the two, he elides them, by
seeing words for sexual slave as 'erotic terminology'.

Jeffrey Weeks is another gay theorist who has this moral
and political myopia. We have already seen that he includes
paedophiles in the ranks of radical and progressive sexual minorities. He is hostile to those feminists who dare to question the
connection of paedophilia with women's liberation. In October
1980 the national conference of the American National Organisation of Women passed a resolution aimed at distinguishing
lesbianism from any association with 'other issues (i.e. pederasty, pornography, sadomasochism and public sex) which have
been mistakenly correlated with Lesbian/Gay rights by some gay
organisations and by opponents of Lesbian/Gay rights who seek
to confuse the issue'.[145] Weeks' comment on this action is to
condemn the prudery and sexual repressiveness of the feminists.

It marked the acceptance by a significant body of feminists
of an absolutism which attempts to prescribe appropriate
behaviour as the test of legitimate incorporation into the army
of the good.[146]

Another approach taken by paedophiles to neutralising the
embarrassing inequality problem is to state that since all sexual
relationships are unequal by their very nature, then it is not a
problem that adult/child ones are too. Warren Middleton states
that we must all work towards a society where people have
greater equality, and need to break down sexism, racism, class-
ism and ageism in order to do this. But there will always be
'built-in inequalities', he says:

207

> Like it or not, inequality is, and will always remain, a true
> fact of life; from inequalities of size, shape and strength, to
> those of education, experience, capacities and needs. Since life
> will go on regardless, people have to learn to live with such
> inequalities. All of us must continue to have experiences,
> interactions and relationships with others, for if we didn't
> everything would soon grind to a halt . . . None of this should
> stop – nor can it stop – simply because of inequality.[147]

Middleton seeks deliberately to confuse structural inequalities
of power with accidental differences such as size.

Gay male sexuality is not different in kind from heterosexual
male sexuality. All men are trained to be members of and experience the delights of being members of the ruling class. They
develop a ruling-class sexuality in which power and dominance
are eroticised. This is considered absolutely the norm in heterosexuality. It seems almost too obvious to be worth saying that
men are expected to choose sexual partners who are younger,
poorer and educationally disadvantaged, smaller. The social
comment and disapproval that results when this pattern is not
followed tell us the strength of the injunction. It is not considered acceptable for men to marry women older than themselves even by a few years, let alone a generation. Men are
not expected to marry women who are financially secure and
professionally advanced further than their mates. Paedophilia is
then simply a routine facet of male sexuality. Inequality of age
is eroticised for men. Children represent the powerless in every
way and as such are the most appropriate sexual objects for
men whose sexuality is constructed according to the extreme of
normality for their gender. Paedophilia is more understandable
in homosexual men since inequality of power is not necessarily
built into adult male gay relationships. Indeed there is a fair
chance of equality. Paedophilia ensures that such equality does
not intrude.

There is another explanation which makes the support for
paedophilia by gay men seem particularly inappropriate. Tom
O'Carroll describes the development of his sexual preference
in his book *Paedophilia*. O'Carroll maintains that he is not
homosexual and his account suggests, if we read between the

lines, that his interest in children stems from a determination not to become a homosexual. O'Carroll participated happily in sexual romps with boys at school until the other boys started getting interested in girls and showing great hostility to queers. At this stage O'Carroll transferred his attention to younger boys.

Only when I reached the fifth and sixth forms did things become difficult for me. Whereas other boys talked more and more about girls, and interested themselves less and less with each other, I gradually realised that I was not developing as they were. Girls, especially grown-up ones, held little interest; nor did boys of my own age any more, for I remained attracted only to the prepubescent ones, especially each year's new 'fuzzers', the eleven-year-olds in their little grey shorts, who seemed ever more appealing. Not just in a sexual way, either, as it had been with my pals in earlier years. It was a sort of cross between a tender wish to protect and look after them – a 'maternal' feeling, if you will – and a romantic, chivalric even, extension of this feeling into something which I could identify as masculine. Nowadays I couldn't give a damn whether my feelings are 'masculine' or 'feminine', so long as they have a broad human validity, but in my youth I would have died with shame at the thought of being in any way effeminate. I even supposed I would eventually turn on to girls, and gradually became puzzled and anxious that it was not happening.[148]

Here it seems that O'Carroll's fear of losing face and status by following a sexual interest in boys his own age was assuaged by developing an interest in younger and less powerful boys who could not cause him any loss of power. This is a familiar problem in the male gay subculture. It could be solved by relating to youths or working-class men by middle-class intellectuals in the nineteenth or early twentieth centuries or by the use of slave children in the case of early mediaeval Arabs, or as in this case, by the use of children. Tom Reeves reminds us of this dishonourable tradition by claiming that gay liberation was founded by 'boy-lovers'.

The original gay liberation was fostered by boy-lovers who flaunted it or at least defended it as the epitome of their own freedom: Wilde, Gide, Forster, Genet, Isherwood, Goodman, Burroughs.[149]

This is a fascinating use of the concept of freedom and throws light for us on how gay men can describe as radical and progressive and in pursuit of sexual freedom practices which so clearly negate the freedom of others. Freedom here means the right of these men to maintain social acceptability, power, privilege and status, or simply their own ego privileges based on masculinity, whilst pursuing their sexual hobbies.

For women, feminists, lesbians and for gay men themselves, there are obvious dangers in supporting the right of men to maintain at all costs their masculinity and male power and reject equal and acknowledgedly gay relationships. This is what the support of paedophiles would entail.

SADOMASOCHISM

Sadomasochists are the third of the 'sexual minorities' espoused by gay male libertarian theory. Jeffrey Weeks quotes lesbian rather than male gay theorists of sadomasochism and mentions only lesbian sadomasochism in his book, *Sexuality and its Discontents*. In the 1980s some lesbians have set up promotional groups and written promotional literature on s/m, but s/m as a practice and an idea was well embedded in male gay culture long before. Gay men have not produced much theory about s/m. They have simply practised it and taken it for granted. Lesbians were impelled to theory by their uncomfortable feeling that s/m ideology is in contradiction to the most cherished precepts of feminism. This sense of contradiction forced them into print and justification, which has been convenient for gay men who support or practise s/m, who can hide from the flak of feminist criticism behind the barricade of 'lesbian' sadomasochism. Lesbian practitioners and theorists are quoted by gay men in every argument so that they do not have to take feminist challenges seriously or state their own position.

But such gay men are not at all neutral on the issue. The only 'feminist' theorists quoted with real enthusiasm throughout Weeks' book are the two best-known American lesbian proponents of s/m, Pat Califia and Gayle Rubin. Those radical feminists who oppose s/m politics are pilloried throughout. On occasion his political sympathies for s/m are expressed more straightforwardly. In the tenth anniversary issue of the old *Gay News* in 1982, Weeks asserts that there are two approaches to sexuality among feminists and gays: 'one is working towards redefining the nature of sexual relations; the other towards defending the importance of sexual choice'.[150] It is not immediately clear why there should be any conflict since both seem to be unimpeachable aims. Then when Weeks describes those who are so bold as to suggest redefinition his prejudice becomes clear. These are lesbian separatists, 'some of whom are very hostile to gay male lifestyles', and 'paradoxically . . . the more purist male survivors of early gay liberation'.

These tend to stress the importance of the overall relationship and to downplay the genital and orgasmic aspects of sex. At its best this gives rise to a pleasant emphasis on such desirable pleasures as caressing, touching, holding hands and affection and so on – what has been nicely termed bambi-sexuality. At its worst it can arouse the worst excesses of moralism as other forms of pleasure get denounced as 'male' and therefore by definition bad.[151]

Weeks is clearly supportive of the second approach, which happens to focus on s/m. He describes it as 'more concerned with defending our ability to choose our sexualities, whether gentle and bambi, or heavy duty and s/m'. For a sexual radical such as Weeks, change is anathema. Feminists are a problem because they insist on demanding change. 'Choice' has become the new grail for sexual radicals as it has for radical Tories. He describes the feminist position as a 'new absolutism' and the pro-s/m position as 'radical pluralism'. Radical pluralism consists in seeing the sexual minorities as the bearers of sexual freedom to all. He defines the revolutionary role of such minorities thus:

211

So, willy nilly, the defence of choice and sexual freedom is falling to those who until recently seemed on the outer fringes of the sexual spectrum: s/m-ers, lesbians and gay men into role-playing, paedophile activists, as well as the more conventional libertarian socialists and radicals.[152]

Weeks concludes with warnings against the danger that feminists will in the 1980s 'ally with the old absolutism of evangelical Christian morality'. Mary Whitehouse would then appear 'as the prophetess of a sexless feminism'. Weeks' hostility to feminism because of its threat to the sacred absolutes of the male gay sexual agenda is profound.

Sadomasochism is described by one exponent, Ian Young, as 'sex involving pain, either physical (such as slapping or spanking) or symbolic (such as enacted domination or restraint of one partner by another)'.[153] More generally, s/m has come to mean such practices as those designated as 'unusual sexual activities' in the Spada report, a survey of gay male sexuality compiled from 1,000 questionnaires and published in 1979. Spada includes in this category 'fistfucking (active or passive), sadism and masochism, bondage and discipline, humiliation, watersports (sex involving urination), scat (sex involving defecation)'.[154] All these activities are routinely included beneath the generic umbrella of s/m in contemporary lesbian s/m literature. It turns out that these practices were not all that unusual among Spada's respondents, who covered a wide cross-section of the gay community. Nearly 30 per cent of respondents engaged in one or more of the activities.

It would be wrong to see s/m as a bizarre practice quite unconnected with everyday sex. An examination of routine male gay practice shows that dominance and submission and gender role playing are fundamental to male gay eroticism. The Spada report is very useful in forming a picture of standard gay male sexual practice. The questionnaires were open-ended and respondents were encouraged to express their feelings and motivations towards a range of everyday practices at length.

Anal intercourse was enjoyed by 76 per cent and disliked by 12 per cent and is therefore a standard sexual practice. There is no reason to assume that anal intercourse is inherently linked with sadomasochism any more than other sexual practices might be. What is clear from the Spada respondents is that they invest the practice with emotional loadings of eroticised dominance and submission. One question asked: 'During anal intercourse, are you usually "top" or "bottom" man? If both, what determines which it will be – your partner, your mood, or what?' The language is revealing. 'Top' and 'bottom' are the words used for the active and passive roles in s/m. Many of the respondents quoted were unequivocal that anal intercourse is about dominance and submission. As a Spada respondent points out, 'the combination of emotional domination-submission and the closeness it provides between the two people, mixed with the animal sensations and orgasm, are almost inseparable'. [155] In answer to a question about whether emotions differed according to whether they were on the top or the bottom, one man replied revealingly:

> When I am on top I feel strong, in command, and like a mighty stallion. When I see and feel that I am giving pleasure to him, then I feel proud and revel in the sensuous feeling that I am a great lover – that just inspires me further and he senses and enjoys it even more. When I am on the bottom for a man that I feel deeply about, I feel very lovable and am delighted that I am turning him on so. I also feel vulnerable for some reason.[156]

Many of the respondents go so far as to describe anal intercourse as a grotesque parody of what they imagine vaginal intercourse to be like. One man described himself as feeling when 'on top' like 'the all-penetrating male! I am the man'. His role he describes as being to 'gently impale his partner'. He treats his partner 'as I would a woman when he is in that vulnerable position' and sees himself when being penetrated as being in the same position, 'When I am on my back with my legs thrown over the shoulders of my partner', as 'the vulnerable woman'.[157] Another respondent saw anal intercourse as 'a great way to express the masculine and feminine parts of your personality'.[158] The top role represented the 'traditional male role' and vice versa.

Clearly a decade of gay liberation had not had much impact on gay men's conflation of effeminacy with homosexuality, or on their concept of the 'real man'. One respondent spoke of the advantages of the practice in bolstering the masculinity and heterosexuality of his partner. For this man the act allowed the acting out of the couple's internalised self-loathing.

> The emotional character of it [anal intercourse] permits my partner to keep his masculine identity and perform almost as though he were with a woman. I suppose it is the ultimate act (for me) in acting out a same-sex act, yet keeping the ingredients of my partner's heterosexuality intact. [159]

Some respondents seemed to attach no meanings of domination and submission to anal intercourse, whereas others rejected the practice altogether because of the meanings which clung to it. The redefinition of sexuality in terms of equality and mutuality was not yet, in the US in 1979, a dead issue, and one man pointed out, 'I see no real domination here, but a mutuality that makes two people closer.'[160]

A cursory glance at any gay male publication will reveal an obsession with uniforms and leather. On the commercial gay scene the leather clone image of hairy chest with leather waistcoat and chaps, leather cap and the whole bestrewn with chains, sells massage, prostitution, poppers, clubs and bars. Particular bars and magazines are devoted exclusively to uniform or leather fetishists. In the Spada report 59 per cent of men said they didn't get aroused by uniforms and leather but 25 per cent found uniforms sexually exciting and 18 per cent found leather so. Spada comments: 'Most of the men who find these things arousing do so because they heighten masculinity and sexuality.'[161] Typical responses were:

> I like men. Likely, if they are in leather, a uniform, and/or have a masculine odor, their masculinity is enhanced.

> I think I associate black leather with manhood of which I seem not to have too much in my own personality.

To me a uniform is a definite sign of power, strength, and dominance. Instant arousal.

I am turned on to levis, flannel shirts, tight-fitting T-shirts, tube socks (white), and work shoes. Although these are gay stereotype garments, they represent (in fact or fiction) my current image of being masculine.

. . . soldiers are the epitome of masculinity.[162]

One respondent expressed his negative feelings towards uniforms and leather succinctly:

The 'butch drag' syndrome puzzles me. Ask any of those guys what they think of drag queens and they'll probably tell you they can't stand guys who pretend to be women. So why is it that they have to 'pretend' to be men?[163]

The achievement or imitation of masculinity is so important to gay men and to their sexual practice that it is worth looking at responses to the Spada report question, 'How would you define masculinity?' One respondent defined masculinity as virility, courage, strength, muscles, a prick and balls', another as 'Males boot-tough and wolf-mean'.[164] One defined masculinity simply as 'Leather'.[165] One described masculinity as 'being straight'.

For feminists these definitions are chilling in their implications. The respondents were not asked to define femininity but it is not difficult to work out what the opposite of the above would entail. Male gay theorists tend to be indulgent towards the worship of masculinity by gay men. It is explained as being a reaction to the fact that gay men have always been defined and looked down on as effeminate. They are thus getting their own back. It is not easy to be so indulgent as women and lesbians. The worship of masculinity and the attempt to construct a sexuality and a culture which reflects this is a direct threat to the possibility of women's liberation. Spada remarked upon the connection his respondents made between masculinity and performance with the penis so that sex in general between two men 'is the epitome of masculinity'.[166]

Even the most radical and politicised of gay men fall prey to the worship of masculinity and seem unwilling to change. Martin Humphries writes in a collection on *The Sexuality of Men* by writers from the British anti-sexist men's magazine *Achilles' Heel*. He describes the impact of the shift to masculinity which has overwhelmed the early gay liberation aim to break down 'the social distinctions between femininity and masculinity', in order to create 'an androgynous world ... within which gender would no longer be relevant'.[167] These politics succumbed to a cult of machismo. Humphries describes the subsequent gay scene thus:

> Walking into practically any gay pub or club, you can see construction workers, truckers, men in overalls who could be plumbers or electricians, men in bikers' leather, cowboy denims or soldiers' fatigues.[168]

Humphries says he is implicated in this climate. He has fantasies focused on men who conform to 'current images of masculinity' and looks for 'butch-looking' men when cruising. Humphries, not surprisingly, does not wish to eliminate such role playing but merely seeks ways of 'widening the realms of desire in such a way that we are not trapped into rigid and highly delineated patterns of behaviour suggested by these images'. He wants roles to 'become only a part of sex' and not a 'straitjacket'.[169] Roles would enable gay men to act out masculinity or to worship it according to their mood. Roles, then, would remain, but gay men would seek to swap roles more routinely. He does not question the very construction of desire around the heterosexual s/m romance, nor believe that 'roles' can be eliminated.

The s/m scenario that many gay men are able to make of their whole sexual practice, based upon fetishised masculinity and femininity, should make clear, supposing any doubt remains, that the traditional heterosexual system is an s/m romance. Through the exaggeration of the characteristics of gender roles, the naked, eroticised power dynamic which fuels heterosexuality is laid bare.

John Rechy describes in *The Sexual Outlaw* the extent to which s/m had pervaded gay culture and social life by the mid 1970s.

The manifestations of the growth and power of S&M in the gay world are many: gay leather bars are jammed nightly from Los Angeles to New York. Classified columns in gay publications are cluttered with exhortations for 'masters' and 'slaves' – and for humiliation ... A significant part of the content of gay magazines is taken over by advertisements for 'toys' – a revealing euphemism, evoking childhood, for implements of 'torture': steel clamps, branding irons, whips, straps, even handcuffs ... Increasingly, gay bathhouses feature at least one room constructed to evoke a dungeon, or a jail cell, replete with chains.[170]

Since most gay men in the Spada survey interpreted a routine gay sexual practice such as anal intercourse to constitute dominance and submission, expressed in the form of parodied male/female heterosexual gender roles, we should not be surprised to discover that 30 per cent of gay male respondents engaged in s/m-related practices. It could be argued that not all the practices labelled 'unusual' in the report involve s/m. Some men, for instance, reported that watersports, i.e. urinating into each other's mouths and over other parts of the body, were engaged in simply for sensual delight. But practices like fistfucking and scat are fairly clearly about power and humiliation and therefore deserve to fall under the umbrella of s/m. Fistfucking is not a rare activity. Of the Spada respondents 14.5 per cent had engaged in active fistfucking and 8.2 per cent in passive fistfucking. This practice, in which the whole of the active partner's forearm is inserted *per anum* into the passive partner's body, is commonly carried out in public before crowds of sexually aroused onlookers in clubs.

Fistfucking is a dangerous activity because of the fragility of the walls of the colon and the possibility of sudden death or severe damage if poisons go directly into the bloodstream. One respondent in the Spada report who had negative feelings about fistfucking commented, 'I worry about what people's assholes will be like after forty years of fistfucking.'[171] Some of the Spada respondents criticised s/m on the grounds that it was dangerous: 'I have heard too many stories about people injured or permanently disabled by such activity, most of the times accidentally.'[172] Others saw it as quite the opposite of the way they wanted to relate to other people and especially gay brothers.

> I am lukewarm to hostile on these activities, since they tend to involve degrading or humiliating the other person. In my normal life at work and in my relationships with people outside work, I like to support, encourage, and build up people. These types of sexual activities go counter to that for me.[173]

Another respondent exclaimed, 'Humiliation? No way! Isn't that what we're fighting?' and another asserted, 'This is the kind of sex that keeps the yoke on gays.'

S/m sex, whether top or bottom, serves a very important purpose for the average gay man. It shores up masculine identity. As one 'role switcher' explained, 'only a real man can dish it out and take it'.[174] This concept of macho masochism is useful to an understanding of male s/m. Men invent all kinds of rituals to test each other's masculinity through torture and ordeal, such as the rigours of army training camps and school initiation rituals. Those who survive such ordeals have their masculinity strengthened.

Piercing is an s/m practice which is interesting for the light it sheds on the motivation behind s/m. In Los Angeles I visited The Gauntlet, a shop run by a gay man which sold jewellery to put in body piercings. The proprietor, Jim Ward, carried out the piercings, mostly on gay men and lesbians, in a back room. It is not ear piercing that Jim does but piercing of nipples, clitoris, labia, scrotum, penis, belly and chest. Jim produces a glossy magazine entitled *Piercing Fans International Quarterly* which is addressed to both a straight and gay audience. Sexual orientation is not mentioned, except where some heterosexual readers became suspicious about gay content and sounded off angrily in the letters column. The magazine carries photos of piercings, instructions on how to pierce and some heterosexual pornographic stories on a piercing theme. It is clear from the magazines that male-supremacist power dynamics are involved in piercing. Gay men and lesbians get themselves pierced, heterosexual men get their girlfriends pierced or do it themselves to their girlfriends.

Much of the material is directed at gay men. One issue contains excerpts from 'DungeonMaster: A newsletter of male S&M equipment and techniques', from Chicago. An excerpt describes a piercing session in which a gay man nailed his penis to a block of wood with a steel needle straight through it and then proceeded to nail three other men's penises to the same block.

So Ed proved that it wasn't all that bad by calmly flipping his own cock onto the block and hammering a large sterilised, stainless steel needle through his cockhead and into the wood. Then, with his cock still firmly attached, he leaned across and tacked down Jim's foreskin with two needles. Soon three needles similarly impaled Lee's scrotum. And finally Mark allowed Ed to nail his cockhead to the block. [175]

Lest this episode should strain our credulity photos are provided of the impaled organs. Piercing is a dangerous practice and copies of the PFIQ are littered with safety warnings. The instructions for piercing male genitals are as follows:

Foreskin, cockskin, scrotal skin: In all places on the male organs take care to avoid the several large blood vessels that run near the surface.

Cockhead: piercings such as those depicted on the first page of this issue are best done with the cock as soft as possible to reduce the amount of bleeding.[176]

There are detailed instructions, photos and descriptions of testicle piercing. This can apparently be much more dangerous than simply piercing the scrotum because it can leave the player neutered. Participants are advised not to mix 'scat or golden showers' with piercing and to use sterile equipment on clean skin.

The frequent repetition of safety instructions and their sense of urgency suggests not just the grave dangerousness of the practice but the frequency with which the rules are ignored.

219

There are particular warnings against piercing while under the influence of drink or drugs. 'Safe' piercing requires a good deal of very specific equipment. There are instructions on types of needles and piercing guns to be used, on anaesthesia, and after-care. Nipple piercing alone takes many weeks to heal and will, like any piercing, go nastily septic without great care. I asked Jim about the problem of hygiene. I suggested that gay men who lived a hectic social and sexual life in a context of drink and drugs might not take safe care of themselves and their piercings. He failed to reassure me and simply stressed the personal responsibility of piercers and piercees to take care.

The degree of self-mutilation that gay male s/mers are prepared to seek is very remarkable. Penises are not just tortured, they are even cut off for s/m kicks. This seems shortsighted in the short term because it cuts short the pleasures of torturing the offending organ, but in the long run presumably affords a permanent masochistic satisfaction. A correspondent to PFIQ requested stories and photos about his particular hobby, which was castration.

> Some years ago when I first subscribed to PFIQ, I ran an ad having to do with castration and penectomy. The response I received was very large and devoted to those subjects. Several had collections of stories and/or photos. My guess is that this represents an area of great interest to a considerable segment of your subscribers.[177]

The editor replied that he could not publish such material without falling foul of the law. This s/m interest in castration may help to shed light on motivations for transsexualism and the extreme 'body modification' required for sex-change surgery.

There is little interest in understanding motivation in any s/m literature, but it is possible to pick up some clues from PFIQ. The connection of piercing with sexual arousal is constantly reiterated.

> . . . for those into piercing *per se*, it is the actual penetration of the body that is the turn on. For the most part they like the feeling and the sight of the sharp shaft of steel entering

their body and piercing their flesh. The piercing Top has the same interests, and he uses piercing in the same way he would use whipping, ball squeezing, or anal stretching. For both the pain produced by the piercing is important, as is the psychological rending of flesh. The small amount of blood produced may or may not be a part of the turn-on for one or both parties.[178]

But showing that sexual satisfaction is linked to piercing does not really lead to an understanding of it. Piercing, particularly in the realms of castration, is the s/m activity that takes us nearest to the elision of sex with death. Self-strangulation, which sometimes does result in death when practitioners are unable to cut themselves down in time, is a comparable practice. The fact that so much trouble is taken by gay men to punish the genitals might indicate a hatred of the body and sexuality born of gay oppression. Heterosexual males do not seem to go in for piercing themselves much. They prefer to write, read about and practise the piercing of women. The women are pierced by men, whether straight or gay, and occasionally by each other. Gay men pierce each other. If the ruling class of heterosexual males disdain this practice then it is tempting to see it, along with alcohol and chemical abuse, particularly by needle, suicide attempts and self-mutilation such as wrist slashing, as reflecting the self-hatred of the oppressed.

Gay men have produced very little theory about why s/m exists. S/m proponents perceive questions about motivation as hostile. For those who see s/m as natural, inevitable and good there is no need for explanation. Explanation, they argue, is only required for practices which are disapproved of, and which hostile interrogators would like to bring to an end. As an example they cite homophobes who seek to explain homosexuality and see heterosexuality as 'natural'. For libertarian gay male theorists all forms of male sexuality are valid, natural and inevitable. Paedophilia and transsexualism require no more explanation than s/m. They direct their energies to justifying the practices, explaining why they are positive and why all progressive, radical people should support and defend them.

The Lavender Culture's *Forum on Sadomasochism* consists

of written replies by two gay men and two lesbians to ten questions on sadomasochism. The questions force the respondents to apply themselves to explanation. Ian Young, who is pro-s/m, offers the argument that s/m is natural.

> Everyone has erotic fantasies. People into S&M are simply more aware of their erotic imaginations in this respect and have found ways to externalise their fantasies in agreeable ways, to act on them. As far as the dominance-submission aspect of S&M goes, and this is what is most upsetting to outsiders – we all have a need for aggression and a need for submission in our lives . . .[179]

Young also argues that s/m is a superior form of sexual practice to non-s/m sex. Only 'creative and highly imaginative' people, he says, have the capacity for s/m because s/m 'is a pretty sophisticated and complex mode of behaviour'.[180] He concludes that s/m is 'a more evolved form of sexuality, higher on the human evolutionary ladder' than reproductive sex. Young's sentiments are in the mainstream sexological tradition. Havelock Ellis, founding father of sexology, made the same argument.[181]

Young goes on to congratulate himself further by stating that s/mers are anarchists and libertarians devoted to ending oppression. S/m, he argues, enables practitioners to understand, through ritualised dominance and submission, how power and powerlessness really work in the world beyond the bedroom. It empowers its disciples to more effective political action. Opponents of s/m are portrayed as powermongers who are politically dedicated to maintaining political inequality. He explains that s/m 'tends to take away a person's "need" to oppress and be oppressed', and those who oppose s/m are described as 'political power-trippers'.[182] Young suggests that s/m can be 'outright rebellion' and that this is why so many 'anarchists and libertarians' are involved. The cynicism and the bankruptcy of the politics expressed here are breathtaking.

John Rechy is no libertarian and will not accept the idea that what goes on inside people's heads is quite different from 'real' politics. He points out that gay s/m is defended by 'nouveau chic heterosexuals' because we live in a time when fashion decrees the acceptance of absolutely anything.

> I hear, increasingly, intellectualised defenses of Manson, even of Hitler. From there the defence of S&M is easy. We are not confounded by the paradox of opposing (correctly) police S&M and government S&M in genocide and yet supporting its charade. We find it difficult even to differentiate between speaking out against what is destructive, though willing, and legislating against it – no mutual consenting sex act should be outlawed. But the right must be held to decry what is destructive, in one's own sexual, social, or racial group, or in another's.[183]

Rechy states unequivocal condemnation of s/m, asserting that the 'proliferation of sadomasochism is the major threat to gay freedom'.[184] Rechy sees the self-hatred of male gays as the main reason for s/m. He describes the oppression that anyone gay experiences from the straight world as they grow up. The ritual of s/m, he says, follows from this and 'embraces the straight world's judgement, debasement, hatred, and contempt of and for the homosexual'.[185] The male homosexual grows up ashamed of his love for other men, according to this analysis, and only feels able to practise sex with men when forced to do so in s/m ritual, or while receiving punishment for 'desiring homosexual sex acts'.[186] The 's' is included in this explanation. Rechy explains that 'he is transferring his feelings of self-contempt for his own homosexuality on to the cowering "M", who turns himself willingly into what gayhaters have called him'.[187] The result is that the 's' says, 'You are the queer now, not me, and I'll punish you for it, just as I was punished for it . . .'[188] According to Rechy, 'Gay S&M is the straight world's most despicable legacy.'[189]

This is a persuasive argument. It really seems to explain the attack made, in s/m practice, upon the flesh, the apparent hatred of sexuality. It helps to make sense of the violent attacks made in piercing practice upon the male genitalia, even to the extent of castration. Such an explanation indicates the destructiveness of male gay support for s/m. So powerful is the support that there is censorship of any dissenting voices. Rechy's anti-s/m remarks were heavily edited or omitted in an interview in what he describes as a 'gay liberation' newspaper. It is a real irony that theorists of gay liberation should espouse and promote as sexual freedom a practice which results from and recycles among gays the hatred and oppression they experience from the straight world.

This explanation feels right and doubtless helps to explain gay male s/m, but one vital ingredient is missing. It doesn't explain the differences between male gay and lesbian sexual practice. Where there are differences related to gender it is necessary to look for a feminist explanation. Rechy has no understanding of gender politics. He makes this clear in *The Sexual Outlaw* partly through the great incongruity of his ability to condemn s/m so fiercely in the context of what looks to be a paean of praise to s/m practice. Half of the book, described as a 'documentary', details the cruising adventures of the hero Jim on beaches, in alleyways, and in abandoned buildings. The hero 'pumps', i.e. bodybuilds, before going out on the street. He flexes at prospective sexual contacts who flex back at him. The whole 'sex-hunt' is described in terms of conquest and defeat. It is about dominance and submission and the assertion of masculinity. One brief description of an encounter should give an idea of the s/m elements of this brand of cruising. Jim has gone home with a pickup.

Two beautiful male bodies lie side by side naked. They don't touch. Neither moves. Each looks straight ahead, away from the other. Used to being pursued, each waits for the other to advance first. Both are severely turned on, cocks rigid. Now they glance at each other, each wanting the other even more now. But they look away. Their cocks strain in isolation. Nothing.
Nothing.
Jim jumps off the bed, the other reaches for his clothes simultaneously. Looking away from each other, both dress hurriedly each cut deeply by regret they did not connect.[190]

These men could not perform sexually because neither would

initiate contact. To initiate contact was to admit defeat and allow the other to gain a victory. Jim cruises to assure himself of his power and desirability. One rejection is enough to destroy his confidence and happiness. Yet the gay men who do this macho posturing, this terrifying and brutal battle in which silent men, seeking to look like thugs, struggle to immolate themselves in masochistic tribute to a 'masculine' body or to win victories by being constantly worshipped in the act of fellatio, are called by Rechy the 'shock troops of the sexual revolution'.[191] Rechy seeks to make a clear and absolute distinction between this activity he sees as so positive and s/m, which he sees as such a threat. It is difficult to know where the line could be drawn. Rechy is not prepared to do less than eulogise about cruising. To be consistent he should see male gay s/m as simply the tip of an iceberg. When mainstream male gay sexual practice eroticises dominance and submission then male gay s/m has to be explained in the context of the construction of male sexuality.

John Stoltenberg sees s/m as the inevitable result of a 'social structure of male-over-female sexual domination'. 'For the genital male,' he explains, 'eroticised violence against women results in male sexual identity reification.'[192] How can this work between two men? Stoltenberg sees the top as embodying 'the cultural norm of male sexuality' and identifying with 'male-supremacist values and behaviours'. The bottom shores up his male sexual identity, his masculinity, by absorbing into himself either the body fluids of the real man or his violence.

> For this partner, gratification consists in the fact that he ingests the sadist's semen and/or absorbs the sadist's violence. These mythic residues of the sadist's virile presence stay in his body, and he assimilates potency like a battery getting charge.[193]

Spada respondents bear out Stoltenberg's insights into the ingestion of masculinity by bottoms in sexual encounters. Their comments on fellatio are particularly relevant. One fellater remarked: 'I always feel I am draining a bit of male power from my partner's body to mine.'[196] On the swallowing of ejaculate one man commented: 'It makes me feel like I have the seed of

225

superman if my partner is a real turn-on.'[195] Others described semen as 'mysterious, potent . . . the beginning of life and creation', and 'the most vital part of his [the partner's] manhood'.[196]

The difference between male gay s/m and lesbian s/m is clarified by such statements. Lesbians cannot ingest ruling-class power by serving as bottoms since no women have that power. Stoltenberg explains that the urge to s/m practice is quite different in men and women 'because the male homosexual drive to incorporate manliness functions as a means of dissociating himself from the inferior status of the female, while the masochism of a woman functions to fix her in that state'.[197] It may be that to understand the importance of s/m in male gay culture we need to combine explanations based on gay oppression with explanations based on gender oppression. Sexual acting out is crucial to male sexual identity and a main source of ego enhancement. For gay men this is complicated by self-hatred and the fact that the object of their desire is the male ruling class. The worship of the masculinity principle can be carried out in either active or passive roles in s/m.

Chapter 5

FEMINISM AND SEXUALITY

THE DAYS OF INNOCENCE

In the first few years of women's liberation the precepts of sexual liberation were adopted quite uncritically by the heterosexual mainstream of the movement. However, from as early as 1970 some feminists were mounting a wide-ranging critique of heterosexuality itself and developing lesbian separatist theory, which was quite distinct from sexologic. Heterosexual feminists tended to acknowledge the great extent of their debt to Masters and Johnson. They expressed their belief that the enormous power of women's sexuality as evidenced in women's ability to achieve multiple orgasm could, if released from bondage, liberate women. The enthusiasm for the fulfilment of women's sexual potential went so far that some feminists confused sexual liberation with the political liberation of women. Like Masters and Johnson they saw women's liberation as synonymous with sexual liberation. Such feminist ideas on sexuality were at a very early stage of development. Experience was to show their limitations and it is these limitations which now need careful consideration. When looking at the incredible excitement felt about those ideas, it is important to understand the great feeling of liberation that women experienced when they were suddenly able to talk about sex with other women and see themselves as sexual actors. The contrast with the isolated angst experienced by many who were sexually active in the 1960s was strongly felt.

An article in the British women's liberation newspaper, *Shrew*, from 1972, shows the extent to which sexual liberation ideology became conflated with feminism. *Shrew* was not regularly published but circulated between different women's liberation groups. A group with something burning to say would simply take responsibility for an issue. The issue entitled 'The Suppressed Power of Female Sexuality' was produced by the Bromley group. The front page article started by explaining the notion common to feminist discussion of sexuality at this time, that women had a true and authentic sexuality which had been suppressed or stolen from them by men.

> Women have a capacity for sexuality far in excess of that of men. But thousands of years of patriarchal conditioning has robbed us of our sexual potential and deceived us about the true nature of our sexuality. Women are forbidden to own and use their sexuality for themselves, as a means of personal self-expression. Our authentic sexuality has been taken from us, subjected to a process of distortion and mutilation, and then returned to us as a passive submissiveness which is held up as 'true' female sexuality.[1]

This was an essentialist notion which suggested that women had a true and natural sexuality which would be released when all the adverse conditioning had been overcome. Women's sexual essence turned out to be a replica of what the sexologists of the 1960s were prescribing, a constantly responsive, multi-orgasmic woman who was enormously enthusiastic about sexual intercourse with men.

The enthusiasm to recover women's authentic sexuality derived from the excitement women felt at Masters' and Johnson's findings. Susan Lydon in her 1970 article 'The Politics of Orgasm' expressed these feelings.

> But if the Masters and Johnson material is allowed to filter into the public consciousness, hopefully to replace the enshrined Freudian myths, then woman at long last will be allowed to take the first step toward her emancipation, to define and enjoy the forms of her sexuality.[2]

The writers of the *Shrew* article saw the work of Masters and

Johnson as very positive: 'Their findings have been particularly significant for women, especially the discovery of the vastly superior sexual capacity of women to that of men.'[3] This superior capacity was the ability to go on having orgasms until physical exhaustion intervened. They were equally happy with the work of Mary Jane Sherfey, who was inspired by Masters and Johnson to demonstrate women's superior capacity and found that women could, with an electric vibrator, achieve up to fifty orgasms at a time.

It is difficult now to see why Sherfey's work was greeted so positively. She writes about women as mindless, uncontrollable sexual animals. Women could never be sexually satiated, she argued, because their capacity for orgasm was so infinite. She described this capacity as 'the universal and physically normal condition of women's inability ever to reach complete sexual satiation [even] in the presence of the most intense, repetitive orgasmic experiences'. A woman usually 'willed' herself to be satisfied 'because she is simply unaware of the extent of her orgasmic capacity'.[4] Sherfey's analysis did not challenge the sexological assumption of the centrality of sexual intercourse. She recommended extended sexual intercourse. She wrote: 'On the basis of these observations, it seems that the vast majority of cases of coital frigidity are due simply to the absence of frequent, prolonged coitus.'[5] She was delighted by Masters' and Johnson's horrific techniques for training women to have orgasms. She explained that 'daily sessions were instigated of marital coitus followed by prolonged use of the artificial phallus (three to four hours or more)'.[6]

Sherfey's theory about women's sexuality and history was clearly anti-feminist. She considered that women's sexuality was 'too strong, too susceptible to the fluctuating extremes of an impelling, aggressive eroticism' and that women's 'inordinate' sexual demands had had to be forcefully suppressed as a 'pre-requisite to the dawn of every modern civilisation'. Women, she concluded, had to be controlled by men in order to make ordered 'family' life possible.[7] The sexuality she described was a male model and it was this male model that women caught up in 'sexual liberation' sought to emulate. Sherfey's view of women's sexuality was not very positive and yet the *Shrew* article, in line with other feminist writings of that time, called her analysis 'brilliant'.

The *Shrew* writers saw a vital connection between the realisation of 'women's erotic potential' and women's liberation. Women must recover the power of their sexuality, they argued, not just because it would be fun but because women could only challenge the restrictions on them in any other sphere by first achieving their sexual power. They expressed the connection thus:

> Denying women their full sexual autonomy, then, is one of the ways in which male society ensures that women experience themselves as powerless and unable therefore to change the conditions of their lives. By robbing women of their powerful sexuality, male society effectively robs them of their power.[8]

It did not occur to the members of the Bromley group, as it did not to most of us in those days, that enthusiastic following of the sexological prescription might not be in women's interests. Feminists who were heterosexual at that time tended to throw themselves into sexual activity in pursuit of their 'authentic' sexuality. This meant more sexual intercourse, in more positions, and more initiating of sexual activity. The liberating effects were not immediately obvious.

In their conclusion, the *Shrew* writers criticised 'sexual liberation' which had meant for women 'a freedom to be a more readily available sexual object'. They wanted 'real sexual liberation' which would only be achieved when women 'have totally redefined sexuality, and in so doing have redefined themselves'.[9] But the redefinition was going to prove very difficult. There was a great deal of sexological baggage to be thrown overboard first. Woman, they said, was no longer to be told 'that she is inherently passive, essentially masochistic, and that she will only find true fulfilment in submission to a man'. She was to be initiatory and enthusiastic about sexual intercourse. But this was precisely the course recommended by Masters and Johnson in order to counter the challenge posed by feminism. It was a course recommended too in *The Joy of Sex*.

The other aspect of Masters' and Johnson's work which

appealed to feminists, apart from the apparent proof of amazing orgasmic capacity, was the proof that woman's orgasm was clitoral. Sexological writings had been proclaiming throughout the twentieth century that women must achieve a vaginal orgasm during sexual intercourse in order to be healthy. Some sexologists had questioned this before Masters and Johnson but they put the nail in the coffin of the vaginal orgasm through their laboratory experiments. The experiments seemed to prove that however the orgasm was experienced and wherever it appeared to come from, the seat of sensation and the trigger of the mechanism lay in the clitoris and not the vagina. Feminists seized upon this with delight. The most famous valediction to the vaginal orgasm was the American feminist Anne Koedt's 1970 article 'The Myth of the Vaginal Orgasm'.

Koedt interpreted Masters' and Johnson's findings on clitoral orgasm as challenging the idea that women must engage in sexual intercourse. This was not at all what the sexologists had intended. Koedt concluded that men had only maintained the myth of the vaginal orgasm and the concomitant necessity of sexual intercourse because this was the practice which gave them most convenient sexual stimulation. Men had suppressed the truth about the clitoral orgasm, she argued, because 'Men fear that they will become sexually expendable if the clitoris is substituted for the vagina as the centre of pleasure for women.'[10] Koedt was positive about lesbianism and suggested that if clitoral orgasm was accepted then 'it would indicate that sexual pleasure was obtainable from either men or women, thus making heterosexuality not an absolute, but an option'.[11]

But in their enthusiasm about the clitoral orgasm and the idea of woman's amazing sexual potential, feminist writers adopted sexological ideas which did not necessarily match women's experience. Koedt asserted that the vagina was utterly insensitive and incapable of feeling in order to support her idea that the clitoral orgasm liberated women from the necessity of vaginal sex. She stated that 'women need no anaesthesia inside the vagina during surgery, thus pointing to the fact that the vagina is in fact not a highly sensitive area'.[12] She described the vagina as being very 'insensitive' and wrote: 'Even the importance of the vagina as an erotic centre (as opposed to an orgasmic centre)

231

has been found to be minor.'[13] Lesbian writers did not necessarily agree with this. Jill Johnston satirised the insensitive vagina theory in her 1973 book, *Lesbian Nation*. She explained that she had never found the vagina insensitive and suggested that heterosexual feminists found it necessary to assert this in order to justify avoiding fucking. They had only experienced penises in the vagina she guessed and had no idea how sensitive this organ could be to hands.

> I have a record entry June 18, 1970: 'find out what they mean by the myth of the vaginal orgasm.' Subsequently I asked a few 'feminists'. They informed me, in effect, that I don't experience what I say I feel or feel what I say I experience or any combined way of being a liar. And their chief authority was Masters and Johnson. Studying the feminist literature I decided that the feminists had found the perfect rationale for their frustration and excuse for not being required to fuck with the man any more ... It seems actually amazing that what they were asserting was a stubborn refusal to submit to conventional intercourse on grounds of an insensitive vagina. (No mention of hands or bananas or dildoes.)[14]

Another puzzling idea adopted from male sexology was the crucial necessity of the orgasm to health. The sexologists all spoke of the serious health problems women would suffer if they did not have orgasms. Pat Whiting asserted as fact that 'Women who are constantly exposed to intercourse without having orgasm over a long period often develop chronic congestion of the pelvic region which leads to gynaecological disorders.'[15] Mary Jane Sherfey supported this notion. She said women could be 'emotionally satisfied' without orgasm but 'such a state would rarely persist through years of frequent arousal and coitus without some kind of physical or emotional reaction formation'.[16] It was a classic technique of the sexologists to threaten women with nonspecific but alarming forms of physical or mental illness if they failed to meet the sexological specifications in sex.

The feminists we have been looking at adopted a male model of what constituted sexual liberation. Women were to imitate male sexuality and become efficient, aggressive sexual per-formers. Betty Dodson's work is a good example of this approach. Dodson made a great impact on early feminist ideas on sexuality through her bodysex workshops, her book *Liberating Masturbation* and her slides of female genitals shown at a women's liberation sexuality conference. Dodson, more than any other feminist writer of the period, had an unregenerate sexual revolution agenda. In the section on swinging Dodson was noted as one of the guests at Sandstone, the swinging academy of the US. Dodson explains that after a conventional marriage she began an affair in 1966 which introduced her to 'good sex' and to swinging.

Learning how to live without owning another person went in stages. First, Grant and I stopped going steady. We started dating other people and exchanged information about our successes and failures. Sharing sex in a group setting helped us to overcome any remaining jealousy. We discovered the joy of having our cake and eating it too by sharing erotic love with each other and several other people at the same time. Sexual abundance drove us sane. We no longer expected or even wanted our sexual exchange to last 'forever'. Now we could simply enjoy it for as long as it was good.[17]

Dodson 'went public' in 1968 with her erotic art. Her illustrations of female genitals and sexual exchanges between women and between men and women were used not just in her own works but in books such as the influential and respectable Helen Singer Kaplan's *The New Sex Therapy*.[18] When she mounted an exhibition of drawings of masturbation there was such a shocked reaction that she became convinced that 'sexual repression related directly to the repression of masturbation. It followed then that masturbation could be important in reversing the process of sexual repression.'[19]

In 1970 she set up a consciousness-raising group. Dodson decided that sexual liberation was central to women's liberation. She advocated 'power that was based upon pleasure. Economic power was not enough. Without sexual liberation, which freed the human spirit, we would misuse power the same as men.'[20]

She was disappointed with the women in her second CR group. They were professional women who were 'trapped in false modesty and very uptight about their bodies' and 'they all had drippy romantic attitudes about sex'. Dodson set out to educate them about sex. '[I] raved about guilt-free masturbation and showed them different pelvic movements and positions I used with my vibrator'.[21] Before she left the group she distributed electric vibrators to all its members.

Dodson decided that she had to become a sex teacher. In 1973 she joined a group of feminists to plan the National Organisation of Women's sexuality conference in New York. For the plenary session she decided to present 'a slide show of "split beaver" for feminists so women can become "cunt positive" '. She photographed the genitals of twenty women at the conference. Dodson was not the only feminist to be photographing genitals. Anne Severson's film of female genitals, including tampon strings and yeast infections, was shown at the Edinburgh Festival in 1972.[22]

In 1973 Dodson inaugurated the first of her bodysex workshops. She would open the door naked to the participants and ask them to disrobe immediately. The workshops took place in a circle and nude. Dodson would demonstrate how she masturbated to orgasm and all the women would be encouraged to show their genitals to each other. Dodson writes: 'I always went first. Using both hands, I spread my outer vaginal lips, exposing my cute little wattles . . .'[23] They performed anal self-massage and group masturbation. Dodson waxes mystical about the masturbation which she called the 'Guided Masturbation Ceremony'. She came to realise, she says, that she was a 'Tantric master' who was 'teaching sex by doing sex'. She had 'guided nearly five thousand women through orgasm rituals. These women were all my divine lovers.' The ceremony took place as follows:

We began the ritual by standing in a circle dancing to music with our vibrators. It was an overwhelming vision of female erotica. I guided the group through different kinds of genital stimulation, pelvic movements, and breathing patterns. Then we got on top of our vibrators which were placed on pillows and experimented with pelvic thrusting . . . We were bringing masturbation out of the nuclear family's darkest closet and putting self-sexuality into the Temple of Pleasure . . . The ecstasy came when I looked around the circle of masturbating women and nearly swooned from the erotic image.[24]

Yet interestingly Dodson never identified as a lesbian, despite the satisfactions obtained from her 'divine lovers', and women were not encouraged to touch each other in these sessions.

Despite Koedt's assertion that the validation of the clitoral orgasm could validate lesbianism and lead to women feeling that they did not need men at all for their sexual pleasure, most of these feminist theorists of sexuality did not choose for women. They seem to have used the new insights about sexuality to make themselves better bed partners for their boyfriends. Dodson kept her impulses towards women firmly under control. She explained to her consciousness-raising group one night how she felt about women:

I was a sexual feminist who was willing to celebrate women loving women, not with the idealised romantic pairbond, but in a happy playful way. In the groupsex setting, I had experienced the joy of being with women physically and sexually. I also believed that sexual labels would soon be obsolete.[25]

It is not lesbianism that Dodson is talking about here. Within the swinging scene men were happy to encourage women to do sex with other women because it turned them on and was not seen as threatening. She does not, from her own account, seem to have entered into sexual and emotional relationships with women but directed her energies to enabling women to be sexually more efficient with men. Her remark about labels shows that she did not see sexual orientation as political. In a society in which heterosexuality is a political institution lesbianism and heterosexuality were not going to become equally valid sexual preferences.

Many of those things which Dodson and other British and American feminists of this time were promoting seemed really revolutionary. It was true that women's genitals had been regarded in male culture as disgusting or dangerous and that female children had been brought up to ignore their genitals or feel ashamed of them. Girls and women had been brought up to deny the importance of their own sexual pleasure, ignorant of the existence of the clitoris and guilty about masturbation. In such a climate the naked group masturbation sessions, which bring consternation or hilarity to young women of the 1980s, did bring a breath of fresh air. It was, and is, very important for women to feel that they have a right to their own bodies, to look at them, to feel them and to care for their health and pleasures. But the ideas and practices of these feminists were locked into a sexual revolution agenda which was not premised upon women's interests, but on the maintenance of male supremacy.

These early feminist thinkers saw sex as something that women had been shut out of. Women had not been allowed the delights that men had taken for granted. Sex was an equal rights issue. Male sexuality was taken as the model which women were to emulate. Feminists did not realise that the male model could not be emulated by women because, rather than simply being 'sex', it was a ruling-class sexuality which the powerless class could not adopt. But heterosexual feminists in the early 1970s believed women could be more successful at that model than men. Pat Whiting explained how this would occur: 'Given the right psychological and erotic stimulation, the female can respond to sexual pleasure and orgasm in the same way as the male and has a greater potential of response.'[26] Anne Koedt likened the clitoris to the penis. She wrote: 'the clitoris is almost identical to the penis'; and 'the clitoris is a small equivalent of the penis'.[27] The ideal form of male sexuality in the sexual revolution was potent, continuously capable of sex and always desiring, capable of separating sex from loving emotion and making use of all sexual opportunities. It was based on a boom-slump model. The parameters of sexual activity were set by engorgement of the penis caused by sexual attraction, which was to lead directly to greater and greater engorgement until orgasm and deflation. Sex was goal-orientated. The goal was orgasm and sex ended when the orgasm was achieved.

The female version of this male model was the Erica Jongstyle 'zipless fuck'. It was felt that women should be able to experience attraction to strangers, immediate arousal, swift progress towards orgasm – preferably through intercourse – and a cheerful, guilt-free promiscuity without jealousy. Whiting, for instance, attacked the 'myth that women have to be "in love" to enjoy sex'.[28] Dodson, as we have seen, promoted swinging, the overcoming of jealousy and vigorous non-monogamy. Women were to be potent, preferably superpotent, with endless orgasms.

Though one motive behind the obsession with masturbation and orgasm was undoubtedly that women should be able to have sexual pleasure independently of men, another important motive seems to have been to speed up women's sexual response so that they were more suited to the male response cycle and men's preferred practice of sexual intercourse. Dodson uses this as an inducement to doubtful women to use vibrators and masturbate. 'I assured them that a sexually turned on feminist was a joy to a man, not a threat.'[29] If women masturbated and learned quickly and efficiently to have orgasms it would enable them to blend in with the boom-slump model of male sexuality without men having to change their practice in the slightest.

The main problem for women trying to emulate male sexuality is that as a ruling-class sexuality, it is constructed around the fact that they have a subordinate class on whom to act sexually. Women are that subordinate class. The elements that constitute male sexuality depend upon the possession of ruling-class status such as objectification, aggression, and the separation of sex from loving emotion. Women are bound to be unsuccessful in seeking to acquire a form of sexuality which depends upon the possession of ruling-class power. It might be possible for some lesbians to seek a close emulation of ruling-class sexuality because they are able to practise on other women. Heterosexual women cannot practise ruling-class sexuality on men because they are not the ruling class. All that heterosexual women are in a position to do is to accommodate male sexual interests while feeling inadequate for not being able to accomplish such feats as the elimination of jealousy. Not surprisingly, the 'zipless fuck' did not usually lead to feelings of powerfulness. In male supremacy men's sexual access to women gives them power and status. It does not make much difference who initiates the act, the men still gain the advantage.

In the early days of the development of feminist theory on sexuality there was little questioning of the content of female desire. Dodson saw it as quite laudable for women to utilise rape fantasies in order to acquire orgasms. One woman who was questioning the construction of her sexual feelings was told by Dodson that her rape fantasies were fine.

> I assured her that all fantasies were okay. Whenever she gets stuck or is in a hurry, she brings out the rape scene with the five Irish cops and always reaches orgasm quickly. Fantasies about rape can turn us on in our minds because we are masturbating with pleasurable sensations in our bodies. For me, there is no such thing as 'feminist fantasies' or 'feminist sex' . . . There will never be one 'right way' to have fantasies and orgasms.[30]

This section of Dodson's book seems to be part of the revision done for the 1983 edition rather than the 1974 edition. She shows considerable hostility to radical feminists whom she sees as wanting a revolution. Dodson urges women to replace 'radical feminism' with 'erotic feminism' and pursue 'personal liberation'. She concludes: 'It's time for us to support sexual pleasure in whatever form it takes and to get on with life, liberty, and the pursuit of happiness. An orgasm is an orgasm is an orgasm.'[31] For Dodson it was sex that would make women free and she has not changed her mind.

The discussion of the construction of female desire to which Dodson alludes happened in the 1980s and will be looked at in detail in Chapter 6. Suffice it to say that at this early stage feminists were not dissecting their fantasies. Fantasies were necessary to many women for masturbation to take place. In a male-supremacist world, where the content of male and female fantasy life tended to be as opposite as gender roles in every other aspect of life, it could not long remain unproblematic that women were using fantasies of their own humiliation to get turned on.

But the early feminist theorists saw sex as good, positive and innocent, a magic garden of delights that women had been unfairly locked out of. There was no understanding that men and women existed in a power relationship and that male and female sexuality were constructed through material relations of power and powerlessness such that they could not be changed easily by an effort of will. Individual men were seen as exempt from the power structure of male supremacy, as if men and women could caper as free and independent individuals in the bedroom once their consciousnesses were raised. The sexologists had always said that women suffered from sexual ignorance and repression and that they needed to experience pleasure in sex with men. But, as a study of the development of sexology makes clear, the eliciting of an enthusiastic heterosexual response from women was seen as an efficient way to maintain male power. The early feminist theorists adopted the same aim, believing that it would liberate women. It was unlikely that both could be right.

This state of innocence and acceptance of the sexual-liberation agenda lasted until feminists began to work on the problem of men's sexual violence to women. Starting with rape, feminists dragged into the public arena plentiful evidence that sex was not an unproblematic joy for women. The result of uncovering the huge but hidden amount of abuse that women and girl children suffered in the form of sexual harassment, sexual abuse in childhood and marital rape, was that the sexual-liberation agenda had to be submitted to critical scrutiny. Not only was sex not always a positive good, but it looked as if women's fabled sexual repression and ignorance, and the double standard, were not the only culprits in preventing women from having a wonderful and abandoned time in bed. When women and girls experienced throughout life such systematic sexual aggression from men it was realistic and reasonable for women to be resistant to and suspicious of male sexuality. The focus moved away from women as the problem to a critique of male sexual behaviour and an analysis of the ways in which men's sexual violence sustained their power. Feminist theory on sexuality developed through the 1970s and 80s to encompass a wide-ranging critique of male sexuality, male violence and its effect on women, and the construction of female desire.

THE DAYS OF EXPERIENCE

As early as 1971 Susan Griffin's article, 'Rape: the All-American Crime', set out the framework of the feminist analysis. She stated that rape was learned behaviour, and a product of the way male-supremacist culture constructed male sexuality.[32] Aggression was expected from the male and passivity from the female. She attacked the myths developed by male-supremacist culture to legitimise rape such as that 'all women secretly want to be raped' and that 'most or much of rape is provoked by the victim'. She pointed out the lack of any clear dividing line between rape and sexual intercourse, evident in the difficulty courts have in distinguishing between 'mutual' and 'forced' copulation. She stated that 'the basic elements of rape were involved in all heterosexual relationships' since 'in our culture heterosexual love finds an erotic expression through male dominance and female submission'. She rejected the idea that rapists were men who were simply overenthusiastic or tactless in the pursuit of sexual pleasure. Rapists, she said, raped because they enjoyed the power it gave them; they 'clearly must enjoy force and dominance as much or more than the simple pleasures of the flesh'. The 'professional rapist' was separated from the 'average dominant heterosexual' only by a quantitative difference. Even 'good boys' raped.

She described the effect of rape on the construction of women's sexuality as the inculcation of fear: 'Each girl as she grows into womanhood is taught fear.'[33] The result of such fear was that she must 'learn to distrust her own carnality. She must deny her own feelings'. The sexologists, as we have seen, had long denounced women's 'inhibitions' as the result of 'ignorance' and 'repression'. Griffin made it clear that 'inhibitions' resulted from the concrete reality of men's sexual violence. Feminists could no longer accept that women suffered from quite unfounded anxieties and needed simply an effort of will to get over them. It was clear that women's fear was not the result of malign propaganda and false consciousness but of something that really existed and was genuinely frightening.

This basic analysis was developed in succeeding years but the nuts and bolts remained unchanged. Rape was a political crime committed by men against women in order to assert their power. It was an act of terrorism by which, as Susan Brownmiller expressed it, 'all men keep all women in a state of fear'.[34] Moreover it was not 'exceptional' but totally understandable in terms of the construction of male sexuality around the eroticising of dominance and violence. From this understanding feminists derived the slogan: 'All men are potential rapists' which has always brought forth howls of protest from men who wanted to disassociate themselves from rape.

The slogan simply means that if male sexuality is constructed in such a way that men associate sex with aggression then every man is capable of rape. The slogan also means that women are not in a position to know whether the men they meet are likely to rape or not. Some men may feel entirely innocent but it is not possible for women to treat them differently. To a woman in a train carriage or on a street every man is a potential rapist. The judicial system expects her to act on that assumption and will hold her responsible for her own victimisation if she treats a man who subsequently rapes her, with ordinary human politeness.

The outrage engendered by the slogan shows us the conflict that faces women who are aware of the shape and extent of men's sexual violence. Women are expected to know and to protect themselves while retaining love and respect for individual men and men in general. If their love and respect break down they are accused of being 'man-haters', 'castrators', initiators of a sex war. Women's love and respect is the homage expected by the ruling class of the oppressed class. It must be constantly evidenced by smiling and enthusiasm, not mere politeness, by the expenditure of time and energy in servicing. Women who fail to pay homage are pounced upon and branded as 'uppity' if not actually as 'lesbians'. A distancing from men which might be seen as entirely realistic in view of the evidence is viewed as unacceptable treachery to the political structure of the sex-gender system. This painful contradiction of being required to love despite all their understanding of men's sexual violence is the rock against which heterosexual women and particularly heterosexual feminists keep stubbing their toes.

Feminist analysis of rape started with stranger rape. Stranger rape is the only kind of rape that the judicial system and the other institutions of male supremacy, such as the media, have been prepared to define as rape. The notion of stranger rape, though threatening to the dominant ideology which seeks to make women loving, trusting, friendly and polite towards men in general, can be made to serve men's interests. Women are forced to seek protection from boyfriends or husbands from the quite exceptional freak rapist who attacks women in the street. The protection racket Griffin calls 'chivalry' works to men's advantage. Women are propelled into the arms of men they label 'nice' lest they fall victim to men who are 'nasty'. When feminist analysis moved on from stranger rape to the much more likely possibility in a woman's life of rape by a man close to her, the male establishment and heterosexual system suffered a more serious challenge.

The issues of incest and marital rape strike blows at the fundamental institution of male supremacy itself, the heterosexual family. The serious contradiction faced by heterosexual women became much more pronounced as the prevalence of child sexual abuse and relationship rape was revealed. How could the trust and innocence required to get women to love and marry men, and produce children with them, be sustained in the context of this knowledge?

Since feminists first started to discuss the issue of incest and sexual abuse in articles such as Florence Rush's 'The Sexual Abuse of Children: A Feminist Point of View' it has become clear that rape of girls by fathers, brothers and other adult males is vastly more common than the sexological literature estimates.[35] Year by year, as women and girls learn that they will be believed and we learn to look for sexual abuse, we become aware that the real extent of such abuse surpasses any estimates we are bold enough to make. If indecent exposure, various forms of abusive touch and the use of pornography are included in our definition of sexual abuse, then it is unlikely we will discover many women who have survived childhood without experiencing it. In trying to understand the effects of the abuse it is useful to have an idea of what such abuse can entail. One woman whose older brother started raping her when she was 10 describes the practices included in her brother's arsenal:

. . . he made me go into the toilet and lie on the floor, while he pissed and shat all over me, on my stomach . . . That was what he called 'initiation' . . . I felt more like a *thing*, then, more like I had less to me in terms of feeling, than any other time. Just a *thing*. Then he shoved the loo paper at me, and said, 'Here. Wipe it off.'[36]

She describes the confusion around sexuality that her brother's abuse caused her: 'there were times when my brother would touch me and I enjoyed it'. This made her feel 'very bad' and 'as if I was worse than he was. Like I could no longer say that I was being raped.'[37] She never wanted the abuse, she explains, but her body sometimes reacted automatically.

It is not unusual for abused girls to experience sexual response during episodes of abuse. The implications for women's learning of sexuality in this way are several. If a girl responds sexually to her own degradation, when she is being used as a 'thing', sexual arousal is unlikely to be a positive experience for her. Sex and self-loathing are linked. A distrust of sexual response is likely to develop from an unwillingness to experience the feelings which are associated with shame. A further possibility is that, once sex and degradation have been efficiently learned as one package, ritualised or actual degradation will be necessary in the future to elicit sexual response. Here lies the basis for sadomasochism.

But of course some girls do not respond sexually to abuse and their future experiences of sexuality will be different. One girl's grandfather abused her whenever she played at the work-bench in his toolshed.

What he did was to pull my knickers down, to round my knees. He used to position me so that I couldn't see him. I would be doing something at the bench, and he would be standing behind – and he'd put his penis between my legs and he would hold me in that position. When he finally ejaculated, he would just wipe between my legs with his handkerchief, and that was it. I was never ever facing him; he was always behind me.[38]

This woman 'was frigid until I was thirty: I married at twenty ... I couldn't bear to be touched sexually.'

Another girl was abused by her stepfather who 'kissed me on the lips, on the breasts, on the vagina ... everywhere ... He'd make me kneel in front of him. And then he'd start pulling himself off and then he'd make me lick him ... Once he ejaculated into my mouth ...'[39] She, too, explains that she felt like an object as a result of his attentions and this led to her being permanently divorced from sexual interest.

The way you feel after that sort of thing has been done to you – you don't feel a person, you feel like a thing. You just don't feel a human being, you feel like an object that they've done what they like with, and that you haven't got any feelings ... I've got no physical feelings about sex which has really got me ... Why? I don't feel as though I've got any sex drive at all ...

It takes away all dignity from your body, and from your soul. It is the ultimate invasion of privacy. There is nothing private left. Your whole body – and all your feelings too – have been displayed against your will.[40]

After sexual abuse of children the issue which brought home to feminists most powerfully the dramatic impact of sexual violence on women's lives was that of marital rape. A better term would doubtless be relationship rape, since this would cover rape by lovers as well as husbands, but researchers have confined themselves to looking at rape within marriage. Finkelhor and Yllo found that 10 per cent of the 323 Boston-area married women they studied had been sexually assaulted by their husbands. The definition of sexual assault they used was that the husbands had 'used physical force or threat to try to have sex with [their wives]'.[41] Not all the assaults, as we shall see, involved intercourse. Diana Russell surveyed 900 women in San Francisco. Twelve per cent of the married women had had experiences that would qualify legally as rape in that state, i.e. sexual intercourse using force or physical threat or when a woman was unable to consent. She found another two per cent had been forced into other practices such as oral or anal sex. One in seven women then, according to Russell's study, had suffered unwanted sex effected by force or threat of force from their husbands.

An acknowledged problem with these statistics is that many women would be unwilling to recognise that they had been raped even though their experiences were identical to others categorised as rape in the studies. Women would so demur because of a reluctance to accept what an acknowledgment of rape would imply about their marriages, husbands or themselves in a culture in which women routinely see themselves as failures or responsible if husbands behave badly.

One woman in the Finkelhor and Yllo study was badly beaten and threatened by her husband. 'In the context of such abuse,' Finkelhor and Yllo remark, 'it is no surprise that sex stopped being enjoyable.' He wanted sex three times a day and would hit her, abuse her verbally or throw her out of the house if she did not comply. Mostly she did comply to avoid violence or further abuse and because 'she believed it was her duty'. Four times he forced her to have sex, in one instance to fellate him, in front of her child. One night he 'took a pair of pliers out of the drawer and told her, "I'm gonna rip out your vagina". He made her get on her hands and knees and beg him not to, but then he put the baby on the kitchen counter and said he was going to kill them both.'[42] When asked by the interviewers if she had ever been raped, this woman said, 'No.' Clearly then, the survey findings can be expected to underestimate considerably women's actual experience of sexual violence. Marital rape is vastly more common than stranger rape. Of the women in the Finkelhor and Yllo study, only three per cent reported rape by a stranger, 10 per cent marital rape and 10 per cent by a 'date'. More than twice as many women in the Russell study had been raped by a husband than by a stranger.

Finkelhor and Yllo point out that women's real experience of marital rape is very different from the conventional wisdom which would define marital rape as being a slight disagreement about when to have sex. They explain that they found three different varieties of marital rape. One variety, which usually took place in the context of a battering relationship, seemed to be 'capricious expressions of anger and resentment' and had nothing to do with sexual disagreements. These rapes were very brutal, and would follow beatings or the hitting and punching would continue throughout the sex. Many other practices were forced on wives in this group besides simple vaginal intercourse.

Wives are raped with objects. For instance, one woman's husband tried to rape her with a broomstick and several husbands had their wives insert things into their vaginas and then took pictures of them. Wives are raped anally and their genitals are mutilated. One woman said that her husband would bite her genitals until they bled, and another said she was burned with cigarettes. Wives are forced to have intercourse with their husbands' friends. Two of the women we interviewed said that their assaults had occurred when their husbands ganged up on them with some of their friends.[43]

One third of the women had been subjected to forced anal intercourse, one fifth to forced oral sex and nearly a quarter to sex in the presence of others, usually their children. These were deliberate sexual humiliations in which the rapist husbands forced their wives to do those things which the husbands would know were most horrifying to them. The victims of anal rape reported much pain and long-term damage as a result. In the case of one women the injuries took five years to heal. Anal rape was particularly effective in humiliating the woman because the act emphasised the 'passivity, subservience, and impersonality of the victim'. The man was not in a vulnerable position and did not have to face the woman's feelings as he would have to in face-to-face rape.

The two other categories of rapes that they identified were the 'force-only' rapes which would happen in relationships in which women were professional, apparently 'liberated' and even feminist. A small category of rapes were bizarrely brutal and humiliating but separate from the context of battering. This category was called, by the researchers, 'obsessive rape'.

Finkelhor and Yllo point out that the consequences of marital rape are likely to be rather different from those of stranger rape.

246

Some would be the same, they suggest, such as the 'humiliation, the physical injuries, the guilt and self-reproach', but the victims of marital rape suffer some special traumas in the form of 'betrayal, entrapment, and isolation'.

> They have been violated by someone they loved. Many have been subjected to on-going abuse, sometimes as virtual hostages in their own homes. And they have no one to commiserate with in their pain . . . When you are raped by a stranger you have to live with a frightening memory. When you are raped by your husband, you have to live with your rapist.[44]

One particular difference that a victim of relationship rape faces is that she will be expected to continue a sexual relationship with the rapist. Victims of stranger rape often find it difficult to pick up a sexual relationship with a lover. The raped wife has to continue sex with the husband who has raped her or perhaps continually rapes her. Astonishingly some of the wives told the interviewers that they enjoyed sex with their husbands on the occasions that they were not being raped.

Shirley is a battered woman who was continually raped by her husband, usually in the middle or at the end of beatings. He peeped on neighbour women during their marriage and 13 of them complained to her about it. He had many affairs with other women and got three pregnant. None the less, Finkelhor and Yllo tell us:

> In spite of the violence, Shirley reported that for the most part their sexual relationship was very good. Even after all the pain he caused her, she still looks back favorably on the sex. She thinks that it may have been the only thing that kept the relationship going at times.[45]

Should we interpret this as a triumph of the human spirit or a tragic example of the limited choices available to women under male supremacy? What could the word 'good' mean in this context? This woman's response is an example of what is required of women in general by sexologists. Despite women's experience or knowledge of sexual violence, despite whatever is going on in their marriages and how their husbands behave, women are expected to engage with enthusiasm in sex. Shirley's experience is simply a graphic example of what is expected of and achieved by many woman all the time. They have to make a separation between the sex in which they 'let go' and become enthusiastic and the rape they experienced last night or the pornographic advert they saw on the underground this morning. What is required is either a mind/body split or an eroticising of the oppression itself.

Two women actually learned to extract sexual satisfaction from the abusive sex they experienced and were able to have orgasms. Finkelhor and Yllo call this 'a practical adaptation to painful and difficult circumstances'.[46] Another woman reported involuntary arousal during the violent sex on occasion when her body seemed to be acting autonomously to her considerable distress.

More commonly the experience of rape caused women to have difficulty feeling enthusiastic about sex again even with other men. One woman whose husband ripped open her vagina with his fist had sexual difficulties in two subsequent marriages. The women experiencing such difficulties in new relationships with men were very distressed that they were unable to show wholehearted sexual enthusiasm. But they are expected, and expect themselves, to make such adjustments. Finkelhor and Yllo do not think to question whether such adjustments might be worthwhile. They do not question heterosexuality as an institution and if the institution is to be upheld it is necessary for women to get themselves back in working order.

Finkelhor and Yllo did not include in their statistics for marital rape experiences of sexual abuse which were not consensual but did not include force or its threat. They did not include sex agreed to as a result of 'social expectations or conventions', and as a result of 'duty'. They did not include sex agreed to in the face of threats 'that were not violent in nature' such as being deprived of money or help, or the threat of affairs, or to avoid conflict. If these categories of coercion had been included then the figures for rape would have been a great deal higher. Certainly the unwanted sex that women get forced into must be much vaster than rape statistics from such surveys would indicate.

Inevitably an awareness of the extent and effects of male sexual violence has complicated feminist analysis of sexuality. At first feminists were able to interpret women's difficulties at relaxing into sexual pleasure with men as resulting from the 'repression' of women's sexuality, or men's lack of consideration and poor technique. Now it was clear that there were other more pressing reasons for women's lack of enthusiasm.

Jane Caputi, in her compelling book *The Age of Sex Crime*, points out that the rate of serial sex killings is increasing rapidly. In serial sex killings individual men kill a number, sometimes a very large number, of women and in some cases men, over a period of time. Her analysis of the FBI statistics shows that there were 644 such murders in the US in 1966 and an estimated 4,118 in 1982. She points out that the Justice Department estimated in 1987 that there were at least 35 and possibly as many as 100 such killers operating in the US at that time. Caputi defines serial sex murder as 'gynocide, sexually political murder, an extreme form of terrorism in the service of the patriarchal state'.[47] The result of this and other acts of sexual terrorism is that 'women are supposed to accept it as a "normal", unavoidable consequence of modern life that we must conduct our lives in constant vigilance and fear, restricting our movements, staying inside at night'.[48]

A woman who has experienced rape or sexual harassment in childhood or adulthood, who knows about the rape and murder of women from the media, who has seen the sexual values of men portrayed in their pornography and on billboards, has a difficult choice in the area of sex with men. She can choose to treat her man as being quite different from other men and as being in no way implicated in men's sexual violence. This is not easy and requires an awkward split in her mind. She is still unlikely to escape having her sexual and emotional responses affected by her experience and knowledge. The woman who associates the man with whom she is sexually involved with the rest of the male gender because of his behaviour and values, or because of an embryo feminist understanding, is in a great dilemma. She is likely to experience intolerable conflict.

To clarify the dilemma women have about sexual enthusiasm for men, it is helpful to contrast it with men's situation. It is unlikely in the extreme that men will have experienced actual sexual violence from women or its threat. Men do not live in cultures where the degradation and brutalisation of men at the hands of women is the stuff of pornography, entertainment and advertising. Men do not live with the consciousness that they are being hunted by women who would take sexual delight in dismembering them simply on account of their gender. They do not live in a society in which their degradation through sex is the dominant theme of the culture. They do not have to approach women sexually in fear or with distressing images or associations with their own oppression. The images they are likely to carry with them are those of women degraded and brutalised by men. In fact they are likely to have practised sexual arousal with such images, extensively, through pornography and fantasy. It is not surprising, then, that sexologists have identified women's 'inhibition' as the main sexual problem of this century. They have identified as healthy sexual feelings those which the male ruling class experiences and have chosen to avoid recognising the political reasons why women might feel differently.

PORNOGRAPHY

One result of the 'sexual revolution' was that pornography was 'derepressed'. The pornography industry exploded into growth in the late 60s and early 70s and became a massive, multi-billion-dollar industry. It also became visible in a way that it had not been before. Pornography no longer had to be under the counter, but appeared on news-stands and at supermarket checkouts. The content changed too. Gay Talese's book *Thy Neighbour's Wife* describes the transformation that took place in the pornography industry in the late 50s and early 60s. In the 1950s American girlie magazines relied upon drawings of scantily clad women since use of photographs and nakedness could invite wholesale repression. A changing climate towards sexuality was necessary before the pornbrokers felt brave enough to experiment with photographs of women in veils of wispy clothing and then entirely naked. In the 1960s the porn industry made great strides. Decensorship, which was based upon the derepression of sadomasochism and womanhatred, allowed pornography to come in from the cold. Hiding at first behind the protection of 'great works of art' which differed little in their values from high-street porn, the pornbrokers built their empires.

The sheer visibility of the porn industry had a consequence which the pornbrokers may not have intended. Women were able to look at pornography and for the first time had at their disposal a panoramic view of what constituted male sexuality. During the 1970s pornography became more and more concerned with sadomasochism and much more brutal in its portrayal of women. Where once whole bodies or parts of bodies constituted the staple of pornography, women were now being shown simply as available holes. The first London anti-pornography group was formed in 1977 because we saw double-page spreads of women's genitals, called 'split beaver' or 'salmon sandwich', in shop windows and being perused by young boys in corner newsagents' shops. We decided we needed to study pornography, to see exactly what was in it and understand what it told us about men's attitude to women, about male sexuality and about the construction of heterosexuality. As daughters of the sexual revolution we had to overcome feelings of guilt at not liking pornography. Reprogrammed by our experience in the 1960s to see 'explicit' sex in movies and books as a positive good and nakedness as desirable, we had to overcome some powerful conditioning through consciousness-raising sessions before we could articulate our rage. Women can only seriously critique any expression of sexuality when they have thrown the junk of psychoanalytic notions of inhibitions and repression out of the window.

Women formed feminist anti-pornography groups in Britain and the US with a sense of horror and rage. Pornography gave the lie to any idea that women were gradually achieving equality. Pornography made it clear that what constituted sex under male supremacy was precisely the eroticised subordination of women. Inequality was sexy and the sexiness of this inequality was the grease that oiled the machinery of male supremacy. The sexiness

251

of inequality, it became clear, was the unacknowledged motor force of male supremacy. Through sexual fantasy men were able to reinforce the sense of their power and of women's inferiority daily and be rewarded for every thought and image of women subordinated with sexual pleasure; a pleasure acknowledged to be the most valuable form of pleasure in male-supremacist culture.

Pornography could not be ignored by feminists who were concerned to end male violence. An examination of pornography revealed that all the varieties of male violence against women were depicted in pornography as pleasurable to men and to women too. Women raped and tortured in pornography claimed to love and seek their abuse. Incest was shown as harmless and good fun for all the family. It became clear that pornography provided a textbook for and justification of such violence. The defenders of pornography have always most consistently denied any link between pornography and male violence. They have claimed that pornography was a privileged exception to other media in that it had no effect on the way its users felt about the world. But feminists could not see pornography as an exception.

The campaigns against pornography were a logical extension of earlier 1970s campaigns against sex stereotyping in school textbooks such as Janet and John readers. Feminists challenged the sexism in the representation of girls as helping Mummy with aprons on while boys helped Daddy to clean the car. This campaign inspired no howls of rage from publishers, civil liberties unions, other feminists, and men in general. Certainly no special organisations of women on the left were formed to protect the sexism of school reading materials. Such organisations are being set up to protect pornography.

Feminists have been forced to use men's research on the effects of pornography to support their argument that pornography could affect attitudes and behaviour. The pornographers and their supporters have demanded proof that sex offenders use porn immediately prior to committing acts of violence. No such evidence is required of the effects of sex stereotyping in textbooks. Indeed, the argument about textbooks has been nearly won. Without any direct evidence that women need to read

Janet and John books just before each occasion on which they don an apron, publishers and libraries, schools and education authorities have moved towards using less obviously prejudiced material. Why then is such a different degree of proof required of pornography's consciousness-lowering potential? The sex stereotyping in pornography is blatantly obvious. Indeed it is not contested by its defenders. Pornography is much used by adolescent and teenage boys and now seen by children as never before because of the burgeoning of porn videos which men use on the living-room television. Why is pornography seen as a privileged category of representation?

The big difference between sex stereotyping in children's reading material and sex stereotyping in pornography is that the use of pornography offers positive reinforcement to its users. Girls playing with toy vacuum cleaners do not have the same orgasmic potential as women shown as holes in pornography. Sexual response to pornography is possible for both men and women. The protection of this 'pleasure' makes the defence of pornography more important for male supremacists than the defence of Janet and John books. Another reason for the rush to defend pornography, despite the conflict with logic required for its defence, is that at this stage in the history of western male supremacy the sexualising of inequality might have taken over from the division of labour as a bastion of male power.

Feminists were outraged at the way pornography justified and promoted sexual violence but the feminist critique has never been limited to violent pornography. Feminists have always asserted that all pornography teaches the inferiority of women as a class. Andrea Dworkin describes the ideology of male sexual domination that pornography revealed:

The ideology of male sexual domination posits that men are superior to women by virtue of their penises; that physical possession of the female is a natural right of the male; that sex is, in fact, conquest and possession of the female, especially but not exclusively phallic possession; that the use of the female body for sexual or reproductive purposes is a natural right of men; that the sexual will of men properly

253

and naturally defines the parameters of woman's sexual being, which is her whole identity.[49]

New York Women Against Pornography describe the process involved in making women an inferior class in pornography as 'objectification'. They define objectification as:

> . . . [a] process through which a powerful group establishes and maintains dominance over a less powerful group by teaching that the subordinate group is less than human or like an object. This precludes the powerful group from identifying with or sympathising with the less powerful group.[50]

They explain that objectification is the 'precondition for violence against oppressed groups' and provide two historical examples of objectification being deliberately used to facilitate such violence, in Hitler's Germany against the Jews and by the American army in Vietnam. The difference between such objectification and the objectification of women is that the latter is sexualised.

Defenders of pornography assert, as Comfort does in *The Joy of Sex*, that men want to be sex objects too. This shows a failure to grasp the politics of the process of objectification. There have been a couple of attempts by the male pornography industry to create analogous magazines for women such as *Playgirl*. The problem with objectifying men for the consumption of women is that it is not sexy. In heterosexuality the attractiveness of men is based upon their power and status. Objectification removes that power and status. Naked beefcake is not a turn-on for women because objectification subordinates the object group. Pornography is not egalitarian and gender-free. It is predicated upon the inequality of women and is the propaganda that makes that inequality sexy. For women to find passive, objectified men sexy in large enough numbers to make a pornography industry based upon such images viable, would require the reconstruction of women's sexuality into a ruling-class sexuality. In an egalitarian society objectification would not exist and therefore the particular buzz provided by pornography, the excitement of eroticised dominance for the ruling class, would be unimaginable.

Pornography apologists engage in special pleading and insist that pornographic images, unlike any other kind of images in our culture, have no effect on the way anyone thinks. Evidence provided by feminists, however, shows the connection between pornography and abuse. Rather than concentrating on trying to connect pornography with one-off attacks on women by strangers, it is useful to look at the more common forms of abuse within ongoing relationships. There is evidence that pornography has led to new forms of abuse. The pornographic imagination might have thought of these abuses before, but for the averagely slow learner in the area of sexuality, the less-creative male mind, pornography undoubtedly educates. An example of this is 'throat rape'. Dworkin explains: 'We see an increase since the release of *Deep Throat* in throat rape – where women show up in emergency rooms because men believe they can penetrate, deep-thrust, to the bottom of a woman's throat.'[51] Throat rape can lead to death through suffocation as well as other forms of physical damage. Dworkin provides an example of throat rape from pornography. The woman suffers violence and considerable pain but ends up loving it.

> He could kill me with [his cock], she thought. He didn't need a gun in his hand.
>
> As his hot organ filled her mouth and throat, Sandy felt him beginning to thrust his hips forward. The shiny cockhead crammed into the back of her throat. She tried to take as much of his cock into her mouth as possible, but it filled her throat so full that she couldn't at first get it down. She swallowed and swallowed at each of his forward thrusts, but her throat wouldn't stretch large enough to accommodate him. It wasn't until he grabbed her hair with his left fist and held her head against the force of his tool that she was able to relax her throat muscles enough that his cock raped its way over her tongue and buried itself in the passage to her stomach.
>
> Pain seared through her throat like she had swallowed a hot branding iron as her throat stretched to its maximum capacity . . . She nursed greedily at his body.[52]

Feminists began to amass evidence of the ways in which pornography directly educated men in how to abuse women, for presentation in Minneapolis in support of the anti-pornography ordinance. This ordinance, constructed by Catharine MacKinnon and Andrea Dworkin, would have allowed women to take action against pornographers under civil rights legislation to get recompense for the injuries pornography had caused them. Shelter workers told of cases in which pornography was implicated in the torture of wives. One woman's husband acted out a scene he had discovered in a magazine. 'She was forcibly stripped, bound and gagged. And with help from her husband, she was raped by a German Shepherd.'[53]

One woman, in the Minneapolis evidence, explained that her husband used pornography 'like a textbook' when sexually abusing her.

In fact, when he asked me to be bound, when he finally convinced me to do it, he read in the magazine how to tie the knots and how to bind me in a way that I couldn't get out. And most of the scenes that we – most of the scenes where I had to dress up or go through different fantasies were the exact scenes that he had read in the magazines.[54]

The Minneapolis evidence contains many examples where pornography has clearly inspired particular instances of sexual abuse. One woman told of being gang raped by hunters in the woods when she was 13 and camping with the girl scouts. She came across three deer hunters reading pornography magazines in the afternoon.

I turned to walk away and one of the men yelled, 'There is a live one.' And I thought they meant a deer and so I ducked and tried to run away . . . two men held their guns at my head and the first man hit my breast with his rifle and they continued to laugh. And the first man raped me and when he was finished they started making jokes about how I was a virgin and I didn't know how they knew I was a virgin but they did . . . The second man raped me . . . When the second man was finished, the third man was not able to get an erection and they, the other men, told me to give him a blow job and I didn't know what a blow job was. The third man forced his penis into my mouth and told me to do it and I didn't know what I was supposed to be doing.[55]

An Assistant County Attorney gave evidence of the links between pornography and sexual abuse that he had found in hundreds of cases of abuse of adults and children. He explained that the police did not look for pornography but found it 'often' in cases of assault on women and in 'very close to the majority of cases' of sexual abuse of children. The pornography would be found in the home of the abuser.

A native American woman gave evidence of the way in which the pornographic teaching manuals led to the racist targeting of particular women of colour. The two white men who raped her were inspired by the video game 'Custer's Revenge' in which a native American woman is attacked. She explains that they let her know from the beginning that they hated her people and 'they screamed in my face as they threw me to the ground. "This is more fun than Custer's Last Stand".'[56]

Evidence from a group of women who had worked as prostitutes showed how pornography had been used on them in the course of their work, providing the model scenarios for gruesome rapes and assaults. They explained that, 'Women were forced constantly to enact specific scenes that men had witnessed in pornography.'[57] The young women entering prostitution would be trained and accustomed by the use of pornography, '... the man would show either magazines or take you to a movie and then afterwards instruct her to act in the way that the magazines or films depicted.'[58]

Pornography, then, educates the male public. It would be very surprising if it did not.

PORNOGRAPHY AS A PRACTICE

The publication of Linda Lovelace's *Ordeal* drew feminist attention to the experience of the women used in the production of pornography. Apologists argue that pornography is simply 'fantasy'. But live women are used and abused in the production

257

of pornography. Their experience is fact and not fantasy. Linda Marciano was the prisoner of a violently abusive pimp who sexually tortured her and used her in prostitution and pornography. She is famous for having been the apparently enthusiastic star of the porn movie *Deep Throat*. Marciano was forced to engage in sex acts with a dog by three men who threatened her with a gun. This was filmed to make a porn movie. When Marciano did eventually escape her pimp she became involved in the anti-pornography struggle and sought ways of achieving legal redress for the fact that such vicious pornography, made while she was a slave, was still being watched all over the world. Out of her search for redress and the efforts of her lawyer, Catharine MacKinnon, the anti-pornography ordinance was born.

Pornography is not just produced for strictly commercial reasons. Amateur pornography is produced when women are filmed or photographed as part of abuse they are being subjected to. The attack upon the woman is turned into pornography, introducing, as Andrea Dworkin points out, 'a profit motive into rape'.[59] Many witnesses at Minneapolis gave examples of being filmed during sessions of abuse either by husbands or, in the cast of prostitutes, by pimps and by clients. Valerie Heller, in a description of how she was sexually abused routinely in childhood by three male members of her family, explained how her 28-year-old stepbrother made pornography out of his abuse of her.

> What I remember most about Carl taking pictures of me is that I was not allowed to do 'certain things' while the pictures were being taken. I could and in fact had to do those same 'certain things' when pictures were not being taken. I recall thinking, how come Carl does not want my mouth touching his cock while pictures are being taken? Today I know why: because actual physical contact was considered hard-core porn and hard-core was not as easily sold as soft-core porn was.[60]

The filming of sexual assault, particularly in the case of child sexual assault, gives the attacker lasting satisfaction as well as offering the possibility of profit.

There has been a concentration in feminist organising on opposing 'violent' pornography but it is pornography itself that feminists need to oppose and not just 'violence'. Catharine MacKinnon provides an analysis of the relationship between pornography of any kind and male supremacy. She asserts that what is sexual under male supremacy is the subordination of women. Therefore there is no possibility of separating OK porn from porn which is violent. Pornography, she explains, is necessarily hierarchical, with women on the bottom, because if it was not it would not be sexy.

> Under male dominance, whatever sexually arouses a man is sex. In pornography, the violence *is* the sex. The inequality is sex. Pornography does not work, sexually, without hierarchy. If there is no inequality, no violation, no dominance, no force, there is no sexual arousal.[61]

She explains why it is difficult for those living in male supremacy, in which the values of pornography are the conventional wisdom, to see the harm that pornography does to women.

> If pornography is an act of male supremacy, its harm is the harm of male supremacy made difficult to see because of its pervasiveness, potency, and success in making the world a pornographic place. Specifically, the harm cannot be discerned from the objective standpoint because it *is* so much of 'what is'. Women live in the world pornography creates. We live its lie as reality . . . So the issue is not what the harm of pornography is, but how the harm of pornography is to become visible. As compared to what? To the extent pornography succeeds in constructing social reality, it becomes *invisible as harm*.[62]

Pornography's significance to male supremacy, MacKinnon argues, is that it 'institutionalises the sexuality of male supremacy'. And it is this sexuality, the eroticised inequality of women and power of men, which fuels male supremacy and constructs the gender system.

> With the rape and prostitution in which it participates, pornography institutionalizes the sexuality of male supremacy, which fuses the eroticization of dominance and submission with the social construction of male and female. Gender is sexual.[63]

When the feminist campaign against pornography first got under way it was possible to attack pornography as a male product designed for male consumption. This is not so true in the 1980s. Women are now being won as an audience for pornography. Women are being told – by the libertarian theorists whose work will be examined below – that because 'women are equal now' it is all right for women to enjoy pornography. According to a feminist analysis the conscription of women into the use of pornography is tied to the new opportunities offered to women in the last quarter century, but in order to defeat women's emancipation rather than pander to it. While women may have greater opportunities in work, more money and more independence, they are being pressured by the sex industry, lovers, the therapy profession, and doctors to become complicit in their oppression through the use of pornography. The fierceness and brutality of 1970s pornography was a backlash against feminism which reassured men. The selling of the idea of pornography to women in the 1980s is a more sophisticated and effective way of bolstering male power.

THE BACKLASH

The backlash against radical feminism in the 1980s has come from many directions. The right wing has attacked with attempts at anti-abortion legislation, the sequestering of lesbian books and raids on bookstores. In Britain this culminated in 1988 with the passing of Section 28 of the Local Government Act which forbids the 'promotion' of homosexuality. In the US and in Britain there has been a resurgence of family values with the encouragement of right-wing governments. Women's poverty has increased and funding to women's groups has been cut. The climate for feminism has become hostile, particularly for lesbian feminism. But combined with this onslaught from the right, feminism has been under attack from the left. The attack from the left has focused on the anti-pornography campaign. A good deal of the theoretical basis for this attack, and the applause and publicity that has kept it going, has come from socialist gay male intellectuals. It has been particularly agonising for feminists because it has been fronted by women who describe themselves as feminists and who have been involved in previous feminist campaigns. It has looked as if the Women's Liberation Movement has been tearing itself apart in the throes of what have been inappropriately named 'the feminist sexuality debates'. But the 'debates' are actually between feminist theory on sexuality and theory which does not derive from and is actually hostile to feminism.

The opposition to radical feminist theory about sexuality can be called 'libertarian'. Libertarian theory does not originate in feminism but in the ideas of the sexologists, the ideology of the 1960s 'sexual revolution' and the work of gay male theorists such as Michel Foucault. Sexual libertarians believe in 'sexual freedom'. In Britain libertarian conservatives believe in a completely free economic market even to the extent of decriminalising the sale of hard drugs. The sexual libertarians want freedom of the sexual marketplace. Like the libertarian conservatives they disallow the discussion of power and regard any restrictions on the freedom of the marketplace as vile. In this context laws against incest or pornography are seen as being 'in restraint of trade', as Victorian mill owners once thought of trade union activity.

In such a context feminists are regarded as repressive because of their demands that male sexual behaviour must change. To libertarians the enemies of 'sexual freedom' are the state and other repressive agencies such as the church and the education system. Radical feminists are seen as another class of enemy because of their complaints that complete sexual freedom for the male ruling class leads to the abuse and murder of women. Women who have adopted this theory as their philosophy of

261

sex have engaged in a battle with radical feminists who fight male violence and pornography. Battle has been joined in journals and newsletters, in women's centres, bookstores and conferences. Radical feminist campaigners have experienced grief as they have witnessed the loss of what they had believed to be safe spaces where certain feminist principles would be uncontested. In the 'feminist sexuality debates' all the major developments in feminist thought about sexuality are under frontal attack.

Andrea Dworkin describes the libertarian women as 'collaborators'. She explains:

> And the pornographers have found a bunch of girls (as the women call themselves) to work for them: not the chickenshit liberals, but real collaborators who have organised specifically to oppose the civil rights legislation and to protect the pornographers from our political activism – pornography should not be a feminist issue, these so-called feminists say. They say: Pornography is misogynist but . . . The but in this case is that it derepresses us. The victims of pornography can testify, and have, that when men get derepressed, women get hurt. These women say they are feminists. Some have worked for the defeated Equal Rights Amendment or for abortion rights or for equal pay or for lesbian and gay rights. But these days, they organise to stop us from stopping the pornographers. Most of the women who say they are feminist but work to protect pornography are lawyers or academics: lawyers like the ones who walked away from *Snuff*; academics who think prostitution is romantic, an unrepressed female sexuality. But whoever they are, whatever they think they are doing, the outstanding fact about them is that they are ignoring the women who have been hurt in order to help the pimps who do the hurting. They are collaborators, not feminists.[64]

I call this opposition group 'libertarians' to make it clear that they have a developed theory, and to distinguish them from other women who might want to argue different tactics for fighting pornography, such as those who might disagree with the Dworkin/MacKinnon Ordinance but still intend to demolish pornography. The libertarians actually like pornography. Not all left intellectuals are libertarians, nor even all gay male intellectuals. Certainly women on the left who support feminist anti-porn struggles are probably as puzzled by the development of libertarianism as are other feminists. Libertarianism is a distinct politics. Its proponents provide a useful weapon with which male libertarians can attack and divide feminists. Its impact has been so disruptive that it has become vital to understand the arguments of this group and their motivations.

ANTI-ANTI-PORNOGRAPHY

Certain publications and events mark the development of the libertarian tendency amongst women in the US. One is the publication of the Sex Issue of *Heresies* magazine in 1981. Another is the Barnard Conference in 1982 and the subsequent publication of the papers of that conference as the book *Pleasure and Danger*.[65] In Britain the tendency is less defined and less developed. A body of opposition did develop to feminist anti-pornography campaigners, but this is only just beginning to gel into a consistent and articulate force. Sheba Feminist Publishers look set to provide a focus for this tendency with their recent publication and promotion of the work of Joan Nestle.[66]

The Sex Issue of the magazine *Heresies* was the first intimation that many radical and revolutionary feminists in England had of the development of the libertarian current. It contained articles from several of those whose names would become familiar as theorists of the libertarian tendency, such as Paula Webster, Pat Califia and Joan Nestle, and covered several of the themes which were to be the stock in trade of this new tendency, i.e. an attack on anti-pornography feminists, and a promotion of sadomasochism and of role playing in lesbian relationships. The issues of sexual violence in its many forms and its impact on women, even on women's sexuality, were absent except in the form of an attack on anti-violence campaigners. Sex was defined simply as the possibilities for pleasure. Problems were either avoided or redefined, as in the promotion of role playing and sadomasochism, as positive pleasures. To feminists who had been working for years, immersed in the realities of women's

263

pain at the hands of men in childhood, in marriage and in relationships, this cheerful concentration on an unproblematic 'desire' seemed like a brutal callousness and indifference to the real material situation of women's lives.

This was to be the shape of the libertarian discourse in succeeding years. The British socialist feminist journal, *Feminist Review*, for example, reprinted a classic American libertarian article, 'Talking Sex', which attacked anti-pornography campaigners in its own sex issue in June 1982. What did all this have to do with socialism, let alone feminism? It seemed remarkable that socialists, who might be expected to focus on women's oppression, could, in the area of sexuality, only see 'pleasure' or 'desire'. An issue on housing would not be expected to focus on interior decoration at the expense of looking at homelessness. An issue on women's work would probably not just focus on individual fulfilment but on the issue of exploitation. It is inconceivable that an oppositional group of socialists would set themselves up to say that there had been altogether too much gloom and doom about oppression, now was the time to talk about fashion, interior decoration, eating out and so on. In fact, of course, the phenomenon of 'designer socialism', an adaptation to the material delights of living in Thatcher's Britain, has emerged, but it is only in the area of sexuality that individual pleasure has taken precedence over the ending of oppression.

To understand this concentration amongst socialists on 'pleasure' it is necessary to understand the ambivalence and hostility that has always existed in certain quarters on the left to feminist initiatives against male violence in all its forms. This hostility has not come from socialist women at the grassroots, in trade unions and labour and communist parties, many of whom have been enthusiastic supporters of feminist anti-male violence action, but from the self-styled socialist intellectuals. The issue of male violence has provided a major stumbling block to such theorists, both male and female. It is important to look at why this issue sticks in the craw of socialist intellectuals and designer socialists in particular.

THE ARGUMENTS OF THE LIBERTARIANS ON PORNOGRAPHY

The article 'Talking Sex' by Gayle Rubin, Amber Hollibaugh and Deirdre English was first published in *Socialist Review* in the US in 1981. It was reprinted in the British *Feminist Review* in 1982 because it 'gives a useful insight into the debates as they are developing over there'.[67] Paula Webster's article 'Pornography and Pleasure' appeared in 1981 in the Sex Issue of *Heresies*. Both articles mention the slide shows that anti-pornography feminists were showing to raise consciousness about pornography. The slide shows seem to have been an igniting event for these writers. Webster states that, 'Dogmatism, moralising, and censorial mystifying tended to dominate the anti-porn campaign.'[68] She was enraged by the anti-pornography slide show. She complains that only 'pernicious' meanings were given to the pictures by the presenter. Presumably Webster felt that some of the slides were suited to a positive presentation. The one she selects as her example shows a pubescent girl awaiting anal intercourse.

> Despite the lecturer's claim that all reactions to the slides were encouraged, each slide was interpreted to reveal its implicit pernicious meaning. One viewer, for example, asked why the photo of a young girl about to have anal intercourse was described as 'the violent rape of a child'. The reply was that she was obviously under age, so at the least it was statutory rape. The lecturer added that anal intercourse was 'very painful'; therefore it was unlikely that this 'tiny little girl' could have been anything other than *brutally injured*. I thought this reply indicated certain biases about pain and pleasure and preferred positions.[69]

The actual experience of young girls of being sexually abused and the validation and encouragement such male-constructed photos would give to the male consumer are ignored here. Webster sees a possibly positive representation of consensual sexual activity. It is true that radical feminists have 'certain biases' about sexual abuse of children and that it is very difficult

265

to get these biases any kind of hearing. Pornography, sexology, great art, psychoanalysis constantly trivialise and justify sexual abuse of girls. Yet Webster tells us that the lecturer should have left room for positive interpretation.

The libertarian onslaught upon anti-pornography feminists shows a callous disregard for the abuse of women and the writers show great annoyance that other women do not share that disregard. Gayle Rubin was perplexed that women being taken on a feminist tour of sex shops were particularly horrified by sadomasochistic material.

> When I went on the WAVPM tour, everybody went and stood in front of the bondage material. It was like they had on blinkers. And I said, look, there's oral sex over there! Why don't you look at that? And they were glued to the bondage rack. I started pulling out female dominance magazines, and saying, look, here's a woman dominating a man. What about that? Here's a woman who's tied up a man. What about that? It was like I wasn't there. People said, look at this picture of a woman being tied up![70]

It was surprising to Rubin that women should be most shocked by pictures which showed women suffering obvious forms of violence, but that is surely quite to be expected. Rubin is a proponent of sadomasochism who provides a theoretical justification for the practice in her article in the anthology of sadomasochism, *Coming to Power*.[71] She complains that the women visitors could not understand that s/m images were fantasy and for use in a particular context by practitioners rather than anything to do with violence against women. But the s/m that women were seeing was produced by men for a male audience and used real women in its production. It did not show consensual fun and would not seem amusing to women with experience or knowledge of the actual violence done to women by men in the name of fun and sexual pleasure.

In another example of the inability of the libertarians to see the abuse of women, three writers in the Canadian anthology *Women Against Censorship*, 1985, confuse oral sex with 'deep throat'. Duggan, Hunter and Vance criticise Catharine Mac-

Kinnon for saying that the movie *Deep Throat* was about 'sexual subordination'. In this famous movie Linda Lovelace was coerced by the violence of her pimp to portray the activity of swallowing men's penises as pleasurable. The practice is quite dangerous. Women have to learn to relax their throats lest they gag and find themselves unable to breathe. It is difficult to see how this practice could be confused with consensual oral sex, particularly bearing in mind the circumstances of the film's production. But the libertarians write scathingly of Mac-Kinnon's description of the movie's action.

> These descriptions are very revealing, since they suggest that multiple partners, group sex and oral sex subordinate women and hence are sexist. The notion that the female character is 'used' by men suggests that it is improbable that a woman would engage in fellatio of her own accord . . . it is hardly an unending paean to male dominance, since the movie contains many contrary themes. In it, the main female character is shown as actually directing encounters with multiple male partners.[72]

The motivation of these writers to ignore sexual violence must be unimaginably strong for them to be able to translate throat rape as 'oral sex', but throughout the history of male supremacy there have been women who have been unable to face the knowledge of women's oppression.

Such women see porn as having positive value for women. Duggan, Hunter and Vance see pornography as serving to 'flout conventional sexual mores, to ridicule hypocrisy and to underscore the importance of sexual needs'. It is difficult to see pornography, which is a mainstream massive industry, as radical and countercultural, but these writers do. It has all kinds of radical messages, they explain, besides 'womanhating'. It does, they say, advocate 'sexual adventure, sex outside of marriage, sex for no reason other than pleasure, casual sex, anonymous sex, group sex, voyeuristic sex, illegal sex, public sex'.[73] The implication is that feminists have been unable to recognise these supposedly positive messages because they were so fixated by the minor problem of womanhatred. Gayle Rubin describes the porn district as a 'zone of freedom' which provides people with 'a range of experiences they can't get in a suburban family'.[74] Webster explains that pornography 'contains important messages for women'.

> As Angela Carter suggests, it does not tie women's sexuality to reproduction or to a domesticated couple or exclusively to men. It is true that this depiction is created by men, but perhaps it can encourage us to think of what our own images and imaginings might be like.[75]

So the message of the libertarians is that women should learn from porn about their sexuality. They see it as brave, exciting and rebellious to use pornography and Ellen Willis says that a woman, if she 'enjoys pornography (even if that means enjoying a rape fantasy) is in a sense a rebel, insisting on an aspect of her sexuality that has been defined as a male preserve'.[76] They acknowledge that pornography is produced by men for men and that some of it is sexist but overall they see it as useful.

Though the libertarians call for the most obvious sexism of pornography to be cleaned up, they do not object to pornography *per se*. It is not surprising then, since they see pornography as positive for women, that they have no sympathy with feminist anti-pornography campaigners. Having, apparently, no way of understanding the feminist project, they show great anger and contempt for feminists who see pornography as a problem. They seem mystified as to why feminists should object to pornography and direct considerable energy to offering psychological explanations for such a phenomenon.

Rubin offers the explanation that the anti-porn campaigners are caught up in a Victorian anti-sex heritage. Taught that sex is violence by their mothers they have somehow not been able to get over this. She explains that 'the notion that sex itself is violent is very much with us. The woman who raised me was raised by a Victorian. We're not very far from that system . . .'[77] It would be interesting to speculate for how many more centuries women's inhibitions will be explained as part of a Victorian heritage. Ann Snitow argues that feminists went into campaigns against pornography out of a loss of heart about their ability in

268

a time of backlash to challenge male power. These feminists decided to stop demanding equality and demand instead 'specific recognition in law and custom of women's special nature and vulnerability'.[78] But apart from loss of heart feminists started to worry about pornography because they 'frightened themselves'. They 'frightened themselves' by looking at the issue of male violence and finding out about its extent. This caused them to exaggerate the problem and become paranoid.

> . . . our movement began to be frightened by what it had brought to light. Visibility created new consciousness, but also new fear – and new forms of old sexual terrors: sexual harassment was suddenly everywhere; rape was an epidemic; pornography was a violent polemic against women. It was almost as if, by naming the sexual crimes, by ending female denial, we frightened ourselves more than anyone else.[79]

Another form of explanation offered is that the feminists who object to pornography are simply middle class and it is a sexological axiom that the middle class has always had a fear of sex, unlike the determinedly raunchy working class.

> As middle-class straight women joined up with those lesbians who hated the more extravagant and stigmatised aspects of lesbianism, lesbian feminism and political lesbianism were born and invented a sexual 'iron maiden' with which every dedicated feminist has had to live.[80]

Hollibaugh puts the feminist objection to pornography down to anti-sex conditioning in childhood. She writes: 'our horror at pornography is often horror at sex itself and reflects a lesson all women carry from their earliest childhoods: sex is filthy.'[81] This sort of name calling is simply sexological dogma recycled. Women, said the sexologists, were ill educated about sex, subject to inhibitions and still under the sway of Victorianism. So say the libertarians too.

To a woman the libertarians describe the anti-pornography feminists as being conservative, right-wing, allied to the moral majority. It is not easy to find evidence of present-day feminists being allied with moralistic right-wing movements, so the libertarians use their own particular interpretation of history to cast guilt by association with a particular set of historical forebears. History is more difficult to challenge for the average feminist who is ill supplied with historical information or who has, as many have, a faith that what is written down by historians is the whole truth, rather than simply an interpretation. The book of published papers from the Barnard Conference on sexuality took its title from the presentation on history by Linda Gordon and Ellen Dubois. Their talk was entitled 'Seeking Ecstasy on the Battlefield: Danger and Pleasure in Nineteenth-Century Feminist Sexual Thought'. Their argument was that nineteenth-century campaigners against aggressive male sexuality were misguided and formed relationships with conservative and moralistic, anti-woman forces. Their main problem, according to Gordon and Dubois, was an inability to be positive about sexual pleasure.

Contemporary feminists have, apparently, not learned from the mistakes of their foresisters and, disappointed by the fruits of the sexual revolution, have become conservative.

In reaction to the profound disappointments of what has passed for 'sexual liberation', some feminists are replicating an earlier tradition, focussing exclusively on danger and advocating what we believe to be a conservative sexual politics.[82]

They provide a definition of 'conservative' which can be compared with contemporary feminist anti-male-violence politics. They say:

We use the term 'conservatism' to characterise strategies that accept existing power relations. We are suggesting that even feminist reform programs can be conservative in some respects if they accept male dominance while trying to elevate women's status within it.[83]

As we shall see, the libertarians make clear that they know anti-pornography feminists are mounting a real challenge to the institution of heterosexuality itself, and this is something that worries them profoundly. What, then, could existing power

270

relations in the field of sexuality mean? Surprisingly it means the family. Anti-pornography feminists are supposed to be pro-family.

> As in the nineteenth century, there is today a feminist attack on pornography and sexual 'perversion' in our time, which fails to distinguish its politics from a conservative and anti-feminist version of social purity, the Moral Majority and 'family protection movement'.[84]

This characterisation of nineteenth-century feminists as conservative and dangerously misguided has become the conventional wisdom of the sexual libertarian camp. It is now repeated over and over again without question as if it is indeed truth. The same idea appears in the Canadian book *Women Against Censorship*.[85] Varda Burstyn talks about the dangerous alliances feminists made with the conservative forces of social purity, and comments:

> According to the recent historical work of Carol Lee Bacchi, while the specific campaigns were different, the pattern of feminist-social purist collaboration was even more pronounced in Canada than in Britain or the US. According to her, only a tiny fraction of women's suffrage leaders were feminist first and foremost; most saw votes for women more as a tactic to hasten the implementation of temperance and social purity ... than as a means to hasten equality for women, though this formed part of their program.[86]

The accuracy of this interpretation can be judged by assessing the reasonableness of the libertarians' characterisation of contemporary feminists. If it seems that contemporary feminists are not promoting pro-family moral majority conservatism then such an interpretation of the work of our foresisters should also be seen as open to question and inadequate since it arises from the same premises.

Most work on the history of sexuality in the nineteenth century up until now has been done by sexual libertarians who have approached it with the preconceptions of the twentieth-

271

century sexual revolution. My book *The Spinster and Her Enemies: Feminism and Sexuality 1880–1930* offers a very different interpretation since I approach the work of the nineteenth-century campaigners as someone who has become interested through my involvement in contemporary anti-male violence campaigns rather than through a desire to discredit them. Not surprisingly I found these feminists to have offered a profound challenge to 'existing power relations' through their critique of male sexual behaviour and, in many cases, their deliberate rejection of marriage and relations with men.[87]

LIBERTARIAN POLITICS

While mounting a savage critique of anti-male-violence campaigners of the last wave of feminism, the libertarians state that there was another tradition of thinking about sexuality within the feminist tradition. Carole Vance points out that while one tradition within feminism emphasised 'danger' the other emphasised 'pleasure'. Women in this latter tradition have been 'expansionist and exploratory, believing that women could venture to be sexual in more visible and daring ways . . .'[88] Gordon and Dubois also state that there was a more liberated tradition which was more positive about sex, which they juxtapose to the conservative tradition which was so dangerous. They criticise this latter tradition for being rather too cavalier about the problem of male sexual abuse, yet it is clear that this is the tradition they empathise with. They call the women in this tradition 'sexual libertarians' and comment:

> We must not make the same mistake as the early twentieth-century sexual libertarians who believed that ending sexual inhibition in itself could save women. Instead, we have to continue to analyse how male supremacy and other forms of domination shape what we think of as 'free' sexuality.[89]

What were the ideas that inspired the sexual libertarians? They were the ideas of the sex reformers and sexologists of the late nineteenth and twentieth centuries, particularly, in Britain, Havelock Ellis. Gayle Rubin is more graphic in her characterisation of the two 'traditions' in feminist thought. She calls the feminist tradition conservative and the sexual libertarians 'pro-sex'.

> The conservative tradition has promoted opposition to pornography, prostitution, homosexuality, all erotic variation, sex education, sex research, abortion, and contraception. The opposing pro-sex tradition has included individuals like Havelock Ellis, Magnus Hirschfeld, Alfred Kinsey, and Victoria Woodhull, as well as the sex education movement, organisations of militant prostitutes and homosexuals, the reproductive rights movement, and organisations such as the Sexual Reform League of the 1960s. The motley collection of sex reformers, sex educators, and sexual militants has mixed records on both sexual and feminist issues. But surely they are closer to the spirit of modern feminism than are moral crusaders, the social purity movement, and anti-vice organisations.[90]

Rubin then goes on to point out that my work 'exemplifies some of these trends' by criticising the pro-sex tradition for its anti-feminism and suggesting that it made a 'great contribution to the defeat of militant feminism'.

Rubin criticises feminism for not having developed any theory of sexuality and for even having blocked the development of theory. She does not expect to get any help from feminism in creating 'an accurate, humane, and genuinely liberatory body of thought about sexuality' because, 'Much of what is available from the feminist movement has simply added to the mystification that shrouds the subject.'[91] Pat Califia is a leading theorist of sadomasochism. In her article 'Feminism and Sadomasochism' in the Sex Issue of *Heresies*, she sees feminists as simply ignorant about sexuality.

> . . . feminist theorists do not do their homework on human sexuality before pronouncing judgement on a sexual variation. Like Victorian missionaries in Polynesia, they insist on interpreting the sexual behaviour of other people according to their own value systems. A perfect example of this is the

'debate' over transsexuality. In its present form, feminism is not necessarily the best theoretical framework for understanding sexual deviation, just as unmodified Marxism is an inadequate system for analysing the oppression of women.[92]

Rubin wishes to distinguish the politics of sexuality from those of gender, i.e. feminism. She explains:

Feminism is the theory of gender oppression. To automatically assume that this makes it the theory of sexual oppression is to fail to distinguish between gender, on the one hand, and erotic desire, on the other.[93]

Rubin is well known and respected in women's studies circles for a groundbreaking anthropological essay entitled 'The Traffic in Women' in which she spoke of a sex/gender system and, by her own admission, failed to 'distinguish between lust and gender'. She has now rejected that earlier approach to sexuality.

It appeared to me at the time that gender and desire were systematically intertwined in such social formations. This may or may not be an accurate assessment of the relationship between sex and gender in tribal organisations. But it is surely not an adequate formulation for sexuality in Western industrial societies.[94]

For validation of her ideas on the autonomy of sexuality, Rubin uses a quotation from Michel Foucault. Foucault is used as the theoretical source of much of that theorising about sexuality which appears even on feminist courses in Britain and the US. Because Foucault is gay, perhaps, he is seen as being appropriate to women's studies courses, though he does not ever mention feminism and rarely mentions women. Some theorists of sexuality see a convergence of interest between gay men and the class of women. His work and that of British gay male theorists such as Jeffrey Weeks, who derive their theoretical inspiration from Foucault, are used on the British Open University Course 'The Changing Experience of Women'. The fact that Foucault offers a theory of sexuality which is independent of feminism and may on examination be found to be in contradiction to it, remains obscure to many women's studies teachers who would not dream of offering feminist or lesbian feminist analysis of sexuality to their students. Or perhaps that is why Foucault is used. His analysis, being independent of feminism, is very safe and is respected by a male academic establishment.

Rubin argues that it is 'essential to separate gender and sexuality analytically to more accurately reflect their separate social existence'.[95] She explains:

> Feminist conceptual tools were developed to detect and analyse gender-based hierarchies. To the extent that these overlap with erotic stratifications, feminist theory has some explanatory power. But as issues become less those of gender and more those of sexuality, feminist analysis becomes irrelevant and often misleading. Feminist thought simply lacks angles of vision which can encompass the social organisation of sexuality. The criteria of relevance in feminist thought do not allow it to see or assess critical power relations in the area of sexuality.[96]

The assertion that sexuality is an area which should be immune from feminist analysis is particularly startling.

But the assertion of the independence of sexuality from feminist analysis is obviously useful to a proponent of sadomasochism. From a feminist perspective there are all kinds of difficulties in accepting sadomasochism as a revolutionary practice for lesbians and other women. The validation of sadomasochism has taken place in gay male thought but is indigestible in terms of feminism. Thus the gay male sexual agenda is adopted. Feminists are told, to the delight of gay male theorists who have always wanted to say this, that they should not apply feminist theoretical tools to the sexual minorities. The whole area of gay male sexual practice and culture is to remain an isolation zone which is immune to feminist enquiry and subject to rules of debate drawn up by gay men and those women who accept their theoretical premises.

So what is the sexual system? According to Rubin, sexuality and particularly the practitioners of certain outlawed sexualities are oppressed by the state. As Foucault would argue, sexuality is not necessarily repressed by the state but 'deployed' or organised by the state and other agencies within society as a technique of social control. The enemies to be challenged are, apart from governments and their restrictive apparatus of laws, police and so on, the church, and the education system. We do not ask why these forces organise sexuality in the ways that they do. Rubin explains the sexual system thus:

> Like gender, sexuality is political. It is organised into systems of power, which reward and encourage some individuals and activities, while punishing and suppressing others. Like the capitalist organisation of labor and its distribution of rewards and powers, the modern sexual system has been the object of political struggles since it emerged and as it has evolved.[97]

Those who are penalised by the 'systems of power' are those who should be in struggle for sexual change and, according to this logic, these will be the despised sexual minorities. The despised sexualities according to Rubin are 'promiscuous homosexuality, sadomasochism, fetishism, transsexuality, and cross-generational encounters'.[98] Crucial to the radical theory of sex she aspires to create, she states, is a 'concept of benign sexual variation'. Such a concept will apparently be found in the work of the male sexologists such as Kinsey, and John Gagnon and William Simon, and, of course, Havelock Ellis, whose attitude to sexual variation was conditioned by his own sexual interest, i.e. urolagnia. She believes classical sexology and modern sex research should be taught in the universities so that students will imbibe a 'concept of benign sexual variation'. Such a concept would mean seeing the sexual minorities as simply there by some mysterious process, all as valid as any other kind of sexual practice.

It is difficult to see how this independent way of seeing sexuality or sexual variation, free of feminist insight, would not conflict with feminist insight in those areas of sexual behaviour which feminists really cannot help getting involved in analysing, try as they might to step around the sensibilities of gay men. Feminists are surely allowed to look at sexual abuse of children.

276

But when we look at the Rubin model we find that sexual abuse of children has disappeared only to be replaced by 'cross-generational sex'. There is bound to be conflict here. In the Rubin model sexual behaviour is judged by the satisfaction it gives to its, mostly male, practitioners. Feminists are forced to consider the harm to women occasioned either directly in the same practices such as in necrophilia or child rape or through the promotion of dominant/submissive sex as a fun sexual variant when it is precisely this model of sexuality that feminists find it necessary to challenge in the interests of preserving the lives and safety of women and children. Rubin's radical sexual politics and those of the gay male theorists on whom she relies and the gay and straight world of sexology, start from the viewpoint of the adult male and his sexual rights and privileges. A politics deriving from this viewpoint must seek to enlarge the scope within which the adult male can seek and act out his pleasures. Radical feminists are aware that women's interests are not served by untrammelled male sexual adventure. This was understood by feminist theorists of sexuality in the last wave of feminism and is understood today.

The pursuit and privileging of pleasure which is embraced by libertarians is bound to find itself in conflict with the realities of the sexual landscape in which women and children live. Libertarian women choose to call the reality of sexual violence simply 'danger', thereby implying that it is foolish of feminists to 'overemphasise' it and 'frighten themselves'. But such feminists understand that 'pleasure' must be subjected to a thoroughgoing reconstruction and that the gender fetishism and dominance and submission model of sex have to be undermined in order for women to have a future. The separate worlds of 'gender' and 'sexuality' can maintain their separation only in the world of gay men.

The other female libertarian theorists may not have worked out so carefully their politics about sexuality but it is clear that their premises rest upon the ideas of sexology and that they are much influenced by contemporary gay male theory. Carole Vance also stresses the need for a 'concept of benign sexual difference'. We can see a familiar Foucaultesque form of analysis here.

Our ability to think about sexual difference is limited, however, by a cultural system that organises sexual differences in a hierarchy in which some acts and partners are privileged and others are punished. Privileged forms of sexuality, for example, heterosexuality, marriage, and procreation, are protected and rewarded by the state and subsidised through social and economic incentives ... Those practising less privileged forms of sexuality – what Rubin calls members of the sexual 'lower orders' – suffer from stigma and invisibility, although they also resist.[99]

Alice Echols fulminates against feminists for being hostile towards the sexual minorities and suggests that this 'reflects their fear that male sexuality as it is symbolised to them in s/m, cross-generational sex, transsexualism and pornography is polluting the "women's community" '.[100] Paula Webster criticises anti-porn feminists for finding ' "Perverse" pleasures, like voyeurism, bondage, s/m, fetishism, pornography, promiscuity, and intergenerational sex incomprehensible'.[101] Amber Hollibaugh includes in her list of women who feel alienated by the feminist movement's intolerance of 'sexual difference': 'the lovers of butch and femme women; who like fucking with men; practise consensual s/m; feel more like faggots than dykes; love dildoes, penetration, costumes ... think gay male porn is hot; are into power'.[102] Hollibaugh does not just adopt a gay male sexual agenda but suggests that some lesbians might quite reasonably consider themselves to be gay men.

HETEROSEXUALITY

The libertarians assert that their feminist opponents are conservative even to the point of supporting, or eagerly accepting the support of, the pro-family politics of the right. But at the same time they savagely indict the anti-porn feminists for being hostile to heterosexuality.

Libertarian sexual politics do not define lesbianism or heterosexuality in political terms. They define them as sexual preferences. This is important to understand since otherwise the constant carping of the libertarians at the 'family' might be understood to imply a political critique of heterosexuality as well. In this way the politics of female libertarians fit with those of gay men who do not criticise heterosexuality. They criticise monogamous marriage and reproductive sexuality. They desire the possibility for all men and particularly gay ones to act out sexually in any way they can imagine, which necessitates a solidarity with heterosexual men against marriage and monogamy. Libertarian theory does, after all, see promiscuity as revolutionary. Thus both gay male theorists and female libertarian theorists reserve their deepest rage for those lesbians who have pointed out that heterosexuality is a political institution and the choice of lesbianism is a form of political resistance. This, they complain, 'desexualises' lesbianism.

An example of such hostility to a political interpretation of heterosexuality lies in the work of Simon Watney, a British gay writer who is more overtly anti-feminist than any other gay male theorists writing at present. Watney urges that lesbians and gay men should not suggest 'that homosexual desire is merely learned, and therefore curable by enforced unlearning'. He comments: 'That no such suggestions have ever been made about heterosexuality, except by the lunatic fringe of the women's movement, remains, however, enormously significant.'[103] This shows one reason why gay men have been chary of accepting the lesbian feminist analysis that sexual orientation is socially constructed. They depend for social acceptance on a 'poor me, I need tolerance because I cannot help myself' model. Lesbian feminist theory threatens this. Who will be tolerant to lesbians and gay men if they say they 'chose' their perversion? But more worrying is that such gay men are able to abandon the social construction analysis to which they mostly pay lip service with so little anxiety and show a clear belief that being gay is somehow biological. This basic essentialism underlies the libertarian approach to other 'sexual minorities' where any attempt at analysis is resisted on the grounds that men simply are paedophiles or sadomasochists, and that this cannot be altered.

So, the suggestion that heterosexuality is an institution and that heterosexual behaviour is learned by women, is 'lunatic' according to this libertarian. His source for these 'lunatic' views is the Leeds Revolutionary Feminist Group paper 'Political Lesbianism: The Case Against Heterosexuality'.[104] The female libertarians represented at the Barnard Conference and in books such as the Sex Issue of *Heresies* and *Desire: the Politics of Sexuality* share this view.

Alice Echols attacks separatists for 'defining lesbianism as a political choice' and condemns the 'heterophobia which is in turn vented in the anti-pornography movement'.[105] Use of the word 'heterophobia' suggests that feminists who challenge heterosexuality are suffering from a psychological disorder which makes them irrationally hostile as in 'homophobia', rather than crediting them with a political analysis. She postulates about the anti-porn movement:

> Perhaps the movement's success in enlisting the support of certain sectors of the lesbian community reflects the extent to which the movement validates lesbianism through its demonisation of maleness and heterosexuality.[106]

What is Echols worried about here? It could tell us a lot about why the libertarians are so concerned at the strength of anti-pornography politics.

It is not noticeable from the writings of anti-pornography feminists in the US that they are hostile to heterosexuality *per se*. Many of them are heterosexual. Lesbian feminists with a political analysis of heterosexuality have played an important part in the movement but are by no means the most visible element. This was slightly different in Britain where revolutionary feminists were the leading movers behind the development of anti-pornography politics in the late 1970s. But even though anti-porn campaigners may make no overt statements about heterosexuality and have no general criticism of it as an institution, it is true that showing pornography to women, and the analysis of the male values and view of women behind it, is profoundly destabilising for heterosexuality. It is hard to look at and think about pornography without experiencing unsettling thoughts about heterosexual love and sex. It is possible that the worries of Echols and other libertarians about anti-porn feminists' critique of heterosexuality may derive not so much from the rhetoric of the campaigners, since such a critique is rarely voiced, but from their own reactions to pornography. It may be that their horror at what porn reveals is being transferred into rage at the feminists who are showing porn because they do not want to have the knowledge that porn provides.

In fact, it is precisely the function that porn serves in illustrating what lies beneath the romanticised notion of heterosexual love that makes it an important object of campaigning effort by lesbian feminists who want to challenge heterosexuality. Pornography is the very best consciousness-raising tool that male supremacy offers to women. For this reason libertarian feminists must constantly assert that pornography is capable of many meanings and that feminists are simplistic or simply wrong to see it as showing womanhatred. Womanhatred on the scale that pornography displays cannot be envisioned by those who do not wish to unsettle the 'existing power relations' of heterosexuality.

The libertarians have accepted the burden of defending heterosexuality and heterosexual desire from the destabilising impact of feminist anti-pornography organising. One might well have thought that heterosexuality was not in serious danger. Feminist anti-pornography politics and the arguments of lesbian separatists are not exactly the conventional wisdom. Observation of an average bar, billboard or television programme would not indicate that heterosexuality is under serious threat of losing its hegemony or becoming in the least self-conscious. But the libertarians do see heterosexuality as being in need of their best energies in its support.

THE ATTACK ON FEMINISM

The libertarians are not simply involved in a massive defence of pornography and a rescue mission on behalf of heterosexuality. They attack the basic premises of feminism and enter into gross and, it would appear, deliberate, distortion of radical feminism in an attempt to disparage feminism. A sample of libertarian writing shows this attack on feminism in action. Ann Snitow expresses horror at the fact that the anti-pornography movement is a uniting force for women and tries to show that there is no basis for women to unite around sexuality.

281

The anti-pornography movement has attracted women from many sectors of women's liberation, but this unity has a high price, for it requires that we oversimplify, that we hypothesise a monolithic enemy, a timeless, universal, male sexual brutality. When we create a 'them', we perform a sort of ritual of purification: There are no differences among men or women – of power, class, race. All are collapsed into a false unity, the brotherhood of the oppressors, the sisterhood of the victims.

In this sisterhood, we can seem far closer than we are likely to feel when we discuss those more basic and problematic sources of sexual mores: ethnicity, church, school and family. We are bound to disagree once we confront the sexual politics implicit in these complex social institutions, but from just this sort of useful debate will come the substance of a nonracist feminist concept of sexual freedom.[107]

The basis of feminist theory and organising was and is the idea that women do have something in common as women, and that however much aspects of their experience may differ according to their different access to racial and class privileges, and their different cultural backgrounds, women share an oppression as women. In the case of male violence and pornography it is particularly clear what women share. All are vulnerable to male sexual aggression. But socialists who are unsympathetic to feminism have always sought to divide women and stress differences between women rather than their commonality. This is what Snitow does here. She refers to the unity that women feel about pornography as 'a premature unity through female outrage'.[108] What would constitute a 'premature unity' in a political struggle? Surely unity is the aim of political consciousness-raising? But any unity between women would be 'premature', in other words undesirable, to an anti-feminist. Snitow uses language carefully. Rather than referring to women's reaction to porn as 'rage' which has a positive sound, she calls it 'outrage' which makes it sound moralistic and misguided. Snitow, in common with other libertarians, shows nothing but contempt and condescension towards women involved in anti-pornography politics. Her sudden mention of the need for a 'nonracist concept of sexual freedom' casts the slur of racism on the feminist anti-porn campaign. Why would it be racist? Simply because it unites women, it would seem from this analysis.

Alice Echols chooses to attack the anti-porn feminists from an angle common to libertarian writings but nowhere so well developed as in her work. Her thesis is that early radical feminists believed in sexual liberation. This apparently got corrupted somewhere along the way during the analysis of male sexual violence. The result was that radical feminism got changed into what she calls 'cultural feminism' or 'femininism'. Cultural feminists, she argues, believe in an essential masculinity and femininity. They see men as naturally evil and women as naturally good and elevate all traditional feminine values, hence 'femininism'. This is an interesting analysis. It may be true that there is a group of women somewhere who hold these views. But when we look at the feminist theorists she indicts as 'cultural feminists' or 'femininists', we discover that she is referring to just about every influential American feminist that women on the other side of the Atlantic have ever heard of.

She includes within her attack Janice Raymond, Adrienne Rich, Mary Daly, Sally Gearhart, Andrea Dworkin, Julia Penelope, Robin Morgan, Ethel Specter Person, Kathleen Barry, Diana Russell. It transpires that Echols is not talking about some obscure feminist tendency she has unearthed, but about feminism itself in America. It will be a surprise to anyone who has read the writings of these feminists that they believe in essential masculinity and femininity. In fact they constantly seek to understand the construction of gender and they desire the end of male supremacy. There would be little point in challenging male sexual violence if it was thought to be innate. The only point in challenging it is the belief that it can be changed. Echols characterises her invented tendency of 'cultural feminism' thus:

> I believe that what we have come to identify as radical feminism represents such a fundamental departure from its radical feminist roots that it requires renaming. To this end, I will refer to this more recent strain of feminism as cultural feminism, because it equates women's liberation with the nurturance of a female counterculture which it is hoped will

supersede the dominant culture. Cultural feminism's polarisation of male and female sexuality and its demonisation of the former and idealisation of the latter has its political incarnation in the anti-pornography movement. By the end of the 1970s, cultural feminism had achieved hegemony within the movement and its celebration of femaleness, which has led some to label it 'femininism', not only informs the anti-pornography campaign, but eco-feminism and the feminist peace movement as well.[109]

While much of the name calling of radical feminists by the libertarians simply replicates the way the sexologists attacked feminists in the early part of this century, i.e. as prudes, puritans, and manhaters, this constitutes a new form of attack. Last-wave feminists were attacked for challenging the separate spheres ideology in which sexologists like Havelock Ellis believed. They were condemned for wanting to do men's work and look like men. Today the emphasis has shifted. Echols attacks radical feminists for promoting old-fashioned sexual virtues. But many aspects of the attack are the same. The Women's Social and Political Union brought down great opprobrium on itself from the left before the First World War for daring to suggest that a 'man-made socialism is not less dangerous to women than a man-made capitalism'.[110] Echols is clearly very angry that 'cultural feminists . . . see capitalism and socialism as equally injurious to women'.[111] Rather than understanding this to be a critique of a male-defined socialism, Echols states that some 'cultural feminists . . . embraced capitalism while repudiating democratic process'.[112] These are big and serious claims which are not really backed up in Echols' article. Probably, as with the detractors of radical feminism before the First World War, any criticism of the male left and male left political practice is seen as so shocking that it is identified with capitalism and hostility to democracy. The male left tends to see itself, after all, as representative of the very spirit of democracy.

'Cultural feminism', according to Echols, is a reincarnation of lesbian separatism. This is quite difficult to credit since femininity is a vice that separatist politics and practice hardly seem to support. But Echols is determined to spin this curious web:

Lesbian separatism's open hostility to heterosexual feminists guaranteed that it would remain a minority view. However, in its reincarnation as cultural feminism, lesbian separatism has been modified and refined in such a way as to make it more acceptable to a wider audience. Whereas lesbian separatists advocated separation from men, cultural feminists advocate separation from male values.[113]

SEX AND POWER

At the basis of the libertarian support of pornography lies the belief that sex is inevitably about eroticised power difference. Feminist arguments that whether pornography is violent or not, it none the less is about the eroticising of power difference, do not cause libertarians to stop in their tracks. They know that anyway and believe that this is the immutable human condition. Alice Echols explains this as her justification for abandoning the idea that sexuality should in any way mirror politics.

> But we must also break with the radical feminist tradition which encourages us to subordinate sexuality to politics in an effort to make our sexuality conform to our political ideology, treating our sexuality as an ugly blemish which with vigilance and time might be overcome . . . we should acknowledge that power inheres in sexuality rather than assume that power simply withers away in egalitarian relationships. Perhaps we might achieve more equality were we to negotiate rather than deny power.[114]

Carole Vance is very doubtful about whether sexuality can be changed.

> Some suggest that if sexuality is constructed at the cultural level, then it can be easily reconstructed or deconstructed at the social or personal level. Not necessarily.[115]

She has to acknowledge that people do seem to be able to change their sexual desires very considerably, as in the example of the thousands of women who have become lesbians through the influence of feminism who might never otherwise have seen themselves as other than heterosexual. Clearly some aspects of sexuality can be changed, but she remains convinced that some areas of sexuality may not be amenable to change. For her, the fact that sexual desire is inevitably built around power difference seems unchangeable.

But why should this be? Echols' use of the word 'inhere' suggests a biological essentialism. Other writers produce a different form of explanation which renders change just as impossible, but which can be seen as lying within a social constructionist model. The libertarians attack the radical feminists for being essentialist and they need an explanation which can pass as constructionist. They do not, of course, choose a feminist explanation. Feminists believe in change and revolution in sexuality as well as in other spheres. The libertarians go back to psychoanalysis. All of those who offer an explanation of why sex is about power rely on some version of childhood influences, stemming from the baby's problems in differentiating itself from the mother, or from frustration. They consider that the child is naturally insatiable and suffers terrible anger at having a mother who sets limits on its suckling and other wants.

There are big gaps in such an analysis for feminists. It avoids, as psychoanalytic explanation routinely does, paying any attention to gender and power difference between the sexes. Material, everyday male power and oppression of women and their effects are considered irrelevant to those who favour psychoanalytic explanations. The earlier the childhood influences they favour, and the less they result from anything mutable like male power, the more they are able to construct a satisfying psychological determinism.

Once the connections between sex, power and aggression have been explained as immutable and harmless, the libertarians are in a position to concentrate on treating 'complex' sexuality as a garden of delights in which the very connections which trouble the prudes and puritans can be mined for the pleasures they can provide. The production of s/m primers, erotic magazines and videos becomes a respectable industry and a service to the community.

286

Chapter 6

CREATING THE SEXUAL FUTURE

HETEROSEXUALITY AS AN INSTITUTION

To many people the word 'heterosexual' would be obscure in meaning. The fact that the social relationships in western male supremacy are organised on a heterosexual principle, i.e. based on the act of sexual intercourse, would seem as little worth comment as the fact that rain falls from the skies. The heterosexual principle is seen as part of nature, requiring neither a particular word to describe it nor, most particularly, an explanation. It was the late-nineteenth-century sexologists who, in the course of stigmatising homosexuality, popularised the word they needed for its opposite. Heterosexuality was named. It was presented as the normal and desirable form for the expression of sexual emotion. The current *Oxford Dictionary* definition derives from this coining. 'Hetero' is defined by the *Oxford Dictionary* as meaning 'other, different'. 'Heterosexual' is defined as 'relating to or characterised by the normal relation of the sexes'.[1]

The sexologists propagated the idea that it was deviant and sick or hereditarily flawed for members of the same sex class to relate to each other. They limited their definition of this deviance to sexual acts and feelings. They did not portray heterosexuality as a political institution. Their limited definition is the one that has been in use until the current wave of feminism. In the last wave of feminism the term was not used in political discussion. Sexological language had not yet become the common parlance save for those women who became followers of the sexologists.

287

This does not mean that our foresisters were not aware of the political implications of heterosexuality. They criticised marriage vigorously and, indeed, all forms of sexual and love relations with men. Many chose to be spinsters or lesbians for political reasons. But the language they used was different from that of today.

In the current wave of feminism, feminist and lesbian theorists have seen heterosexuality as a political institution. They have rejected utterly the idea that it is 'normal' or 'natural' for women to relate sexually to men. They have used the term 'heterosexuality' not just to mean sexual feelings, but to describe a political system. Similarly lesbianism has been defined by feminists not just as a form of sexual attraction, but as a politics, and a strategy for revolution.

In the 1960s and 1970s a new approach to sexuality by psychologists took over from the pathologising of sexual deviation which had dominated the rest of the century. This was the sexual preference model, or what Celia Kitzinger, in her book *The Social Construction of Lesbianism*, calls liberal humanism. Humanistic psychologists challenged the disease model of homosexuality. The humanistic model sees homosexuality and heterosexuality as equally valid and seeks to counter what is seen as irrational prejudice or homophobia towards homosexuals. Kitzinger explains:

> The 'pathological' model has already been widely criticised in the professional literature for its methodological and theoretical inadequacies and its ideological biases, and it no longer represents the dominant psychological approach to lesbianism. In its place is a model of lesbianism (and male homosexuality) as a normal, natural and healthy sexual preference or lifestyle, and the issue of pathology has shifted to the diagnosis and cure of the new disease of 'homophobia' (fear of homosexuals).[2]

Acceptance of this model depends upon accepting that heterosexuality, if not 'natural', is at least inevitable for the vast majority of people. Homosexuals are seen as a harmless minority who should be tolerated and indeed assimilated into mainstream heterosexual culture. There is no challenge to heterosexuality in this approach. Heterosexuality is certainly not seen as a political institution. Heterosexuality and homosexuality are seen as sexual preferences or choices, defined by sexual activities and feelings or even 'lifestyles', but having no more to do with politics than a preference for peas over cabbage. The majority of those involved in the feminist and gay movements have adopted this approach and determinedly resisted a political analysis of heterosexuality. As Kitzinger points out, liberal humanistic research is 'cited enthusiastically by many gay people and, especially in the anti-gay climate encouraged by the AIDS scare, liberal humanistic beliefs about homosexual normality and mental health are often experienced as reinforcing and affirming gay and lesbian culture'.[3] The sexual libertarians take this perspective. The politics of sexuality for them is restricted to combatting the ways in which the free expression of the preference is restricted by repressive agencies. There is no political critique of heterosexuality here.

Why is this depoliticised approach taken by so many feminists, lesbians and gay men? Kitzinger points out that liberalism is the answer of the ruling class to finding its hegemony threatened. It is designed to damp down any serious challenge and smooth out conflict. She quotes Kathie Sarachild on the political role of liberalism:

> Liberal leadership emerges whenever an oppressed group begins to move against the oppressor. It works to preserve the oppressor's power by avoiding and preventing exposure and confrontation. The oppressed is always resisting the oppressor in some way, but when rebellion begins to be public knowledge and the movement becomes a powerful force, liberalism becomes necessary for the oppressor to stop the radical upsurge.[4]

Thus does liberal humanism work to remove any threat to the heterosexual system. Political lesbians and gays are forced into the use of liberal concepts such as sexual preference because such arguments can appeal to the liberal establishment. In an increasingly hostile climate demonstrated by the 1988 anti-gay legislation in Britain, lesbians are forced to conceal the radicalism of their politics in order to gain credibility.

The radical or revolutionary feminist challenge to heterosexuality as a political institution has encountered a hostile response from feminists and lesbians who take a liberal humanistic approach. From the birth of lesbian feminism lesbians have asserted that lesbianism is a fundamental threat to male supremacy. We have asserted that lesbianism is a crucial strategy for women to undertake if they wish to end their subordination. This lesbian radicalism has been carefully tidied away by the new wave of assimilationist, designer dykes but it cannot be expunged from the record entirely. The most famous of lesbian feminist manifestos, the 'Woman-Identified Woman' paper by Radicalesbians, written in 1970, gives an uncompromisingly political definition of lesbianism:

> A lesbian is the rage of all women condensed to the point of explosion. She is the woman who, often beginning at an extremely early age, acts in accordance with her inner compulsion to be a more complete and freer human being than her society . . . cares to allow her.[5]

The Radicalesbian paper asserts that it is necessary for women to become lesbians if they are to develop self-love and work effectively for their own liberation. They explain:

> Our energies must flow toward our sisters, not backwards toward our oppressors. As long as women's liberation tries to free women without facing the basic heterosexual structure that binds us in one-to-one relationships with our own oppressors, tremendous energies will continue to flow into trying to straighten up each particular relationship with a man, how to get better sex, how to turn his head around – into trying to make the 'new man' out of him, in the delusion that this will allow us to be the 'new woman'.[6]

In the early 1970s many radical lesbians all over the western world were stating in various ways that lesbianism was the political strategy necessary for the liberation of women and that heterosexual practice was not consonant with feminism. Jill Johnston stated this particularly clearly in her 1973 collection, *Lesbian Nation*.

> Feminism at heart is a massive complaint. Lesbianism is the solution. Which is another way of putting what Ti-Grace Atkinson once described as feminism being a theory and lesbianism the practice. When theory and practice come together we'll have the revolution. Until all women are lesbians there will be no true political revolution. No feminist *per se* has advanced a solution outside of accommodation to the man . . . Feminists who still sleep with the man are delivering their most vital energies to the oppressor.[7]

Within the lesbian feminist community in Britain this idea was quite widely accepted in the 1970s but was not written down until 1979 by the Leeds Revolutionary Feminist Group, of which I was a member, in the 'Political Lesbian' paper. This was written for the Revolutionary Feminist conference held in September of that year. It was a brief conference paper intended to stimulate discussion rather than to attempt a detailed analysis.

The paper explains that the writers were often asked by heterosexual feminists when they were explaining their political position, whether they thought all feminists should be lesbians. The answer was: 'We do think that all feminists can and should be political lesbians.' A political lesbian is defined as 'a woman-identified woman who does not fuck men'.[8] Up until the time of writing the paper we had felt under pressure to dissemble in order not to cause offence. Now we wanted to set out the politics behind saying that all feminists should be lesbians. The paper explains that sexuality is important because 'it is specifically through sexuality that the fundamental oppression, that of men over women, is maintained'. It states that as the form of the oppression of women changed and 'more women are able to earn a little more money and the pressures of reproduction are relieved so the hold of individual men and men as a class over women is being strengthened through sexual control'.[9]

The role of heterosexuality as a political institution in the oppression of women is described:

The heterosexual couple is the basic unit of the political structure of male supremacy. In it each individual woman comes under the control of an individual man. It is more efficient by far than keeping women in ghettoes, camps, or even sheds at the bottom of the garden. In the couple, love and sex are used to obscure the realities of oppression, to prevent women identifying with each other in order to revolt, and from identifying 'their' man as part of the enemy. Any woman who takes part in a heterosexual couple helps to shore up male supremacy by making its foundations stronger.[10]

The paper went down well at the conference and only became a *cause célèbre* when it was printed, on request, in the national feminist newsletter WIRES some months later. Angry letters flooded in. There were also some in support, but at the time when we were trying to cope with the ferocity of the personal attacks we were receiving, they were not the ones we noticed most clearly. Responses to the paper generally ignored what was being said about the political role of sexuality and heterosexuality and concentrated on the fact that the paper was telling feminists that they should be lesbians. This selection from correspondence indicates the tenor of the hostile response:

> . . . one might think that these women were automatons. Or more exactly one would think that they were trying to be 'cadres' (professional revolutionaries) in the vanguardist Marxist tradition; shining eyes fixed on the glorious future after the revolution, jumpers covered in badges and hearts beating to the rhythm of the right-on line.[11]

> It is . . . the most patronising, arrogant piece of rubbish I have ever read, including orthodox psychology etc. about women.[12]

> Sheila Rowbotham wrote . . . about the Leninist 'vanguard' of the left. It is to get away from this kind of politics that many of us came to the WLM in the first place. Do we really want it here?[13]

The paper and some of the responses were later published by

Onlywomen Press and the paper by itself was included in other collections. It was responsible for many women beginning to think about leaving men. But the analysis of the politics of heterosexuality which we had hoped would develop went no further. It was the style of the paper that was attacked, and the personalities of the writers. The ideas about sexuality were ignored. The Leeds group broke up under the strain of being under such serious outside attack.

At the time we were not able to understand why the paper had provoked such a virulent attack. The protesters accused us of 'telling women what to do' as if we were a powerful authority. But we were a group of five women who wrote a brief conference paper which was published in a very small-circulation feminist newsletter. The characterisation of us as 'cadres', as authoritarian and so on, seemed wholly inappropriate. We had no power and were able only to express an opinion. It was the power of the idea that feminists were reacting to, though they experienced this as the power of the writers.

Respondents did not seek to counter the basic arguments behind political lesbianism. For women serious about working for a feminist revolution they were unimpeachable. It did not make much sense to place women first in your life, to love women and proclaim sisterhood and then to commit all the most important emotional and sexual energies to men. Pouring energy into men when men were the problem and women the solution did look unreasonable. Heterosexual feminists who decried the paper therefore employed liberal humanistic arguments. They spoke of choice. They would not approach the argument that heterosexuality was a political system and that their 'choices' could uphold or threaten that system. They simply spoke of loving or being sexually attracted to men as if these things were given and unchangeable despite years of feminist analysis of the social construction of both romance and sexuality.

The scale of adverse reaction to the 'Political Lesbian' paper taught us how fundamental and sacred an institution heterosexuality is to male supremacy. Women who had been very brave in many other respects could not bear even to hear a serious critique of heterosexuality and their own sexual choices.

293

The tension between the liberal humanistic approach to heterosexuality and the lesbian feminist challenge was starkly revealed. So long as lesbians asked for toleration as a persecuted minority, and the right to exercise their sexual preference, they could receive a hearing within the women's liberation movement, even if no active support. If lesbians challenged heterosexuality, then they would be anathematised.

The most hostile reactions to the paper came from socialist feminists. Anna Coote and Beatrix Campbell are dismissive in their account of the history of women's liberation in Britain. They write: 'Leeds Revolutionary Feminists confounded an already depressed movement with a paper published in 1979' and are congratulatory towards the critics who rejected the 'doctrinaire approach of the Leeds group'.[14] Lynne Segal in her book *Is the Future Female? Troubled Thoughts on Contemporary Feminism* writes of the paper, 'How could such concrete reductionism, such phallic obsession, have got such a hold on feminism?'[15]

Adrienne Rich's article 'Compulsory Heterosexuality and Lesbian Existence' was published in the American women's studies journal *Signs* in 1980. Unlike the 'Political Lesbian' paper it did not ask heterosexual women to make a choice to become lesbian and thus avoided an intensely hostile reaction. The article gives a cogent analysis of the forces employed to conscript women into heterosexuality. It would be difficult for heterosexual readers to claim that they had chosen a 'sexual preference' when faced with this evidence. Rich states:

Feminist theory can no longer afford merely to voice a toleration of 'lesbianism' as an 'alternative life-style', or make token allusion to lesbians. A feminist critique of compulsory heterosexual orientation for women is long overdue.[16]

Rich shows how most literature seen as feminist portrays heterosexuality as a sexual preference and inevitable for most women. This she describes as 'heterocentric'. Rich explains that heterosexuality is enforced on women 'as a means of assuring male right of physical, economical, and emotional access'.[17] She lists the forces which she sees as enforcing heterosexuality as including: 'The chastity belt; child marriage; erasure of lesbian existence (except as erotic or perverse) in art, literature, film; idealization of heterosexual romance and marriage'.[18]

She throws light on the reasons for heterosexual feminists' fierceness in resisting criticism of heterosexuality.

> What deserves further exploration is the double-think many women engage in and from which no woman is permanently and utterly free: however much woman-to-woman relationships, female support networks, a female and feminist value system, are relied on and cherished, indoctrination in male credibility and status can still create synapses in thought, denials of feeling, wishful thinking, a profound sexual and intellectual confusion.[19]

What they are resisting is the idea that 'for women heterosexuality may not be a "preference" at all but something that has had to be imposed, managed, organized, propagandized, and maintained by force'.[20] She describes heterosexuality as being a political system of oppression like capitalism or the caste system designed to produce a class of inferior status which can be exploited for the benefit of the ruler class and maintained 'by a variety of forces, including both physical violence and false consciousness'.[21] Rich's paper was dynamic in its effect on theorising around heterosexuality. Widely used on women's studies courses it has led to the concept of 'compulsory heterosexuality' coming into general usage in feminist theory.

But Rich's paper did not encapsulate radical lesbian theorising on heterosexuality. One criticism of her paper is that by concentrating on a critique of 'compulsory heterosexuality' rather than on heterosexuality *per se*, she has managed to validate 'optional heterosexuality'. If it is only the compulsory nature of heterosexuality that is a problem, then feminists can say they have seen through all the pressures forcing them towards heterosexuality and have still, in the end, chosen it. Ariane Brunet and Louise Turcotte explain:

> Once one has recognised the obligatory character of heterosexuality, she's rid of this same obligation to conform. She

can now, voluntarily, take a new direction, a new understanding of heterosexuality – consensual or optional heterosexuality. Thusly one can move from obligatory heterosexuality to an 'optional' heterosexuality, reducing heterosexuality and lesbianism to a simple sexual choice . . . How can one speak of choosing between the political institution of the dominators and the power of revolt of the dominated? How can one compare the enforced accessibility of women with the sexual autonomy of lesbians?[22]

By writing about compulsory heterosexuality rather than heterosexuality, it is argued, Rich has reinforced the very sexual preference model she was determined to expose.

Janice Raymond criticises Rich for her concept of the lesbian continuum. Rich put women who loved, had friendships with, and worked politically alongside women, on the lesbian continuum, even though they might relate emotionally and sexually to men. Rich defines the lesbian continuum thus:

I mean the term lesbian continuum to include a range – through each woman's life and throughout history – of woman-identified experience; not simply the fact that a woman has had or consciously desired genital sexual experience with another woman. If we expand it to embrace many more forms of primary intensity between and among women, including the sharing of a rich inner life, the bonding against male tyranny, the giving and receiving of practical and political support . . . [23]

Raymond comments that she has a 'gnawing intuition that this affirmation is logically incorrect, morally shortchanging to women who are Lesbians, and patronizing to women who are not Lesbians'.[24] Raymond points out that there is a difference between being woman-identified and being a lesbian and that becoming a lesbian involves a change of consciousness and an acceptance of the risks involved, risks which woman-identified women do not share. 'Woman-identified women who are not Lesbians, while showing courage in the midst of a womanhating society and taking other risks, have not taken the specific risk of choosing and acknowledging Lesbian Be-ing.'[25]

The Rich paper is seen as much less offensive to heterosexual women than the 'Political Lesbian' paper. It seems to allow heterosexual women to continue their relationships with men while feeling politically validated by sharing in a lesbian continuum. Heterosexuality is not indicted, only the force necessary to get women to participate. Neither paper has managed to spark off a debate which asks what role heterosexuality plays in the oppression of women. Radical lesbians in Montreal are asking this question. Brunet and Turcotte define the political role of heterosexuality thus:

> Heterosexuality is the institution that creates, maintains, supports, and nourishes men's power. Without woman's subjugation to heterosexuality, man could not survive on his own, or so he thinks. Women's maintenance of men voluntary or forced, paid or unpaid, is what generates men's power and enables them to continue living on women's energy.[26]

They go further than simply identifying heterosexuality as the structural support of male supremacy. They identify heterosexuality as the root of all other oppressions that exist under male supremacy. Heterosexuality is based on and justified by the concept of difference. Without this concept, rooted in heterosexuality, other systems of oppression could not function.

> From heterosexuality flow all other oppressions. Heterosexuality is the cornerstone on which men have grounded the norm, located the source and the standard for defining all relationships. The concept of difference is inherent to heterosexuality. That concept, as explained by Monique Wittig in *La Pensée Straight*, makes us view the other as different. But to view the other as different one has to consider one's own difference as the norm, for the norm confers power and control . . . The concept of difference, institutionalised as heterosexuality, rests on a value system where one is superior and the other inferior, one is dominant and the other dominated.[27]

297

It is the system of heterosexuality that characterises the oppression of women and gives it a different shape from other forms of exploitative oppression. The extraction of unpaid women's labour for men in the workplace of the home, whether that labour is domestic, sexual, emotional, or reproductive, depends on the heterosexual system. This exploitative relationship is justified by and predicated upon the practice of the act of sexual intercourse. Around the practice of this act family relationships are constructed. The work relationship is disguised under notions of love and family.

From the heterosexual basis of the 'family' a system of what Janice Raymond calls hetero-relations then organises the social relations of the whole of the rest of male-supremacist society. Sex roles originate from heterosexuality. Raymond explains that women and men are constructed so as to necessitate heterosexual union. Sex roles must be created so that no human being of either gender is fully capable of independent functioning and heterosexual coupling then seems natural and inevitable.

> . . . hetero-reality and hetero-relations are built on the myth of androgyny. 'Thou as a woman must bond with a man' to fulfill the supposed cosmic purpose of reunifying that which was mythically separated into male and female. Arguments supporting the primacy and prevalence of hetero-relations are in some way based on a cosmic male-female polarity in which the so-called lost halves seek to be rejoined. In a hetero-relational world view, the overcoming of such polarity requires the infusion of all of life with the comings-together of the separated halves. All of life's relations are then imbued with an androgynous energy and attraction that seeks to reunite the selves divided from each other, forever paired in cosmic complementarity. All of life becomes a metaphor for marriage. Every social relation demands its other half, its cosmic complement. The two – female and male – must become one, whether in the bedroom or the board room. Hetero-relational complementarity becomes the 'stuff of the cosmos'.[28]

Raymond's book shows the ways in which men have sought to

298

prevent women from bonding together not just in lesbianism but in any form of friendship, the ways in which women have been prevented from valuing each other and themselves.

According to a radical lesbian analysis, heterosexuality is constructed by various means, including force, and relies upon the prevention of the bonding of women. This is the missing link in feminist theory. Feminist analyses of love, sex, domestic labour, male violence, sex roles and the division of labour all fall into place coherently when heterosexuality is understood as the system that organises male supremacy. Brunet and Turcotte, like other radical lesbians, call any version of feminist or lesbian theory which does not focus on heterosexuality, 'heterofeminism', i.e. a kind of trade unionism of the oppressed in which the workers get together to improve the conditions of labour with no real attempt to change the system altogether.

The aim of women's liberation and most particularly of lesbian liberation must be the destruction of heterosexuality as a system. It is time we started to envisage how to organise a society that is not structured by heterosexuality. Lesbian separatists are creating such a society and showing that a world beyond heterosexuality is possible.

HETEROSEXUAL DESIRE

Heterosexual desire is eroticised power difference. Heterosexual desire originates in the power relationship between men and women, but it can also be experienced in same sex relationships. Heterosexuality as an institution is founded upon the ideology of 'difference'. Though the difference is seen as natural, it is in fact a difference of power. When men marry women they carry into the relationship considerable social and political power. The organisations of state will back their power through religion, the courts, the social services. Their use of battering and rape within marriage will be condoned through these institutions. The women they marry will generally have less earning power since women's wages are lower than men's. The women will be trained not to use physical strength or be aggressive. They will have been inculcated with social expectations of service, obedience and self-sacrifice. But this is not enough to ensure male power. Means of reinforcing the power differences are employed when men choose partners. They are encouraged to seek in marriage women who are smaller in stature and younger in age. The serious taboos that exist against men marrying women who are taller or older are too well known to need emphasis.

But there are taboos also against men marrying women with the slightest possible advantage in terms of education or earning power. To show the extent to which the ruling male establishment accepts and supports male power in marriage, we need only look at the way that criminologists explain crimes of violence against women. A 1975 study interviewed the wives of rapists and incest offenders to understand why the husbands committed the offences. The authors, Garrett and Wright, found that the wives had, on average, about one year more schooling than their husbands. They suggest that these 'powerful' wives deliberately married men to whom they could feel superior. The men were then driven to their assaults by a feeling of inferiority. The authors conclude that 'for this sample, rape and incest by husbands served as a particularly useful lever by which the wives can further build positions of moral and social dominance'.[29] Male power is so normal to these men that women who happen to be married to less-educated men are credited with a power complex and responsibility for their husbands' sexually abusive behaviour. Presumably the fact that men routinely select less-educated women to marry is seen as unquestionably appropriate behaviour. In support of their conclusions, Garrett and Wright use a study in which educational advantage in wives is said to explain wife battering. The power that men have in marriage, both that which is given them by the sex-role training of a male-supremacist society and that which they individually seek out, is so much part of the fabric of life that it is invisible to male academics. They only notice and object when such male power is not total.

It would be a matter for some astonishment, surely, if, in this carefully engineered situation of inequality, men's sexual desire for women turned out to be egalitarian. It is not of course. Men need to be able to desire the powerless creatures they marry. So heterosexual desire for men is based upon eroticising the otherness of women, an otherness which is based upon a difference of power. Similarly, in the twentieth century, when women have been required to show sexual enthusiasm for men, they have been trained to eroticise the otherness of men, i.e. men's power and their own subordination. The avalanche of sexual advice and 'scientific' sexological literature testifies to the efforts required to construct heterosexual desire. Sexologists over the last hundred years have argued that male sexuality is inevitably aggressive, active and delights in inflicting pain. Female sexuality has been seen as its opposite: inevitably submissive, passive and delighting in the receiving of pain. Sexologists have differed in the form of explanation they have offered for this phenomenon. Havelock Ellis used an evolutionary explanation, Freud used childhood influences in the family but resorted to biology in the final analysis. But they have been united in seeing this system as inflexible.

Feminists in both waves of feminism in this century have opposed this sexological prescription. They have demanded that men change their sexual behaviour and they have opposed the sexological version of women's sexuality. Recently, libertarian gay men and lesbians have proclaimed sadomasochism to be a revolutionary sexuality and have stated that 'power' is inherent in sexuality.

Once the eroticising of otherness and power difference is learned, then in a same-sex relationship, where another gender is absent, otherness can be reintroduced through differences of age, race, class, the practice of sadomasochism or role playing. So it is possible to construct heterosexual desire within lesbianism and heterosexual desire is plentifully evident in the practice of gay men. The opposite of heterosexual desire is the eroticising of sameness, a sameness of power, equality and mutuality. It is homosexual desire.

SEXUAL PLEASURE

Under male supremacy, sex consists of the eroticising of women's subordination. Women's subordination is sexy for men and for women too. For years this was a secret within women's liberation. In order to challenge men's pornography which reiterated that women enjoyed pain and humiliation, and to campaign against sexual violence in a culture which asserted that women enjoyed sexual abuse, feminists denied that women were masochists. Feminist theorists of male violence would acknowledge that women had sadomasochistic fantasies but assert that there was a huge difference between the fantasy and the reality. No women, they said, wanted abuse. The existence of s/m fantasies was not really dealt with as an issue because of its explosive potential. This left the women's liberation movement wide open to attack when a sadomasochist lobby developed.

It should not be a surprise to find that s/m fantasy is significant in women's sex lives. Women may be born free but they are born into a system of subordination. We are not born into equality and do not have equality to eroticise. We are not born into power and do not have power to eroticise. We are born into subordination and it is in subordination that we learn our sexual and emotional responses. It would be surprising indeed if any woman reared under male supremacy was able to escape the forces constructing her into a member of an inferior slave class.

From the discriminating behaviour of her mother while she is still in the cradle, through a training in how to sit and move without taking up space or showing her knickers, how to speak when spoken to and avert her gaze from men, a girl learns subordination. She is very likely to experience overt sexual harassment from men. She will experience unwanted overtures from males and will have to learn to respond positively or negatively. Training of this kind is not geared to creating a strong and positive emotional and sexual personality in any woman. Within women's liberation negative self-image, lack of confidence, worries about appearance, negative emotional patterns in relationships, have all received attention from consciousness-raising groups. The burgeoning of feminist therapy in place of consciousness-raising as the movement has lost its radical edge testifies to the urgency with which women are seeking to overcome our conditioning. But the negative effects of this training on our sexual feelings have scarcely been explored.

Sex has been seen as different. Feminists accepted the basic idea of the sexual revolution that sexual response was an ultimate good. According to sexual revolutionary ideology, how sexual response was achieved was of little or no importance so long as it was achieved. Sex, we were led to understand, was somehow disconnected with the rest of life. It was a pleasurable garden of delights which was unaffected by the outside real world and certainly had no effect on the workings of the real world. Therefore, the fact that women might have sexual feelings which mirrored the undesirable emotional responses they were trying to change was seen as no problem. A sexual problem for a feminist was understood to be lack of orgasm or the correct number of orgasms. Masochism was not on the agenda. The fact that for many women orgasm and masochism, especially in masturbation, were apparently inextricably connected was avoided or positively affirmed.

The construction of women's sexual pleasure only became a subject for serious debate with the development of the feminist challenge to pornography. Campaigners who had sexual responses to the materials they were opposing found themselves in a dilemma. There was a pressure to conceal such responses for fear of disapproval. Campaigners who claimed never to have experienced any kind of response to sadomasochistic material appeared scandalised at those who did. How was it possible, after all, to campaign against something which turned you on? Speakers against pornography would receive hostility from women who felt guilty about their response to pornographic material and turned their anger on to the messengers rather than the material. It became necessary to explain that a sexual response to pornography was not at all unusual, was not a reason for guilt or shame and did not preclude our anger at pornography. It was possible to be even more angry at pornography because it revealed the extent to which our subordination had affected those feelings we had been encouraged to feel were most our own.

To deal with the problem of the eroticising of our subordination we really need a new language, and a new way of categorising our sexual feelings. There is a cultural assumption in a post-sexual-revolution society that sexual arousal is 'pleasure'. This makes it particularly painful to experience pornography, which clearly shows the humiliation of women, as sexually arousing. We feel guilt at having taken pleasure in or 'enjoyed' the oppression of women. The literature of the libertarians has no word or category for sexual response that is not positive, no word that would allow us to describe the complexity of our feelings in such a situation. This is not an accident. Part of the repertoire of techniques for political control is the control of language. It is hard to 'think' about things for which no word is available. Women are not supposed to think in a way which is not positive about sex. In the absence of a word which could distinguish negative sexual feelings or experience the libertarians are able to label feminists as 'anti-sex'. They have a one-dimensional view of sex as inevitably good. Thus only two positions on sexuality are acknowledged, pro and anti sex. A feminist approach to the question of desire requires the invention of a new language. We need to be able to describe sexual response which is incontrovertibly negative.

Linda Gordon and Ellen Dubois give us an example of the confusion felt by some feminists about women's sexual response. They are libertarians and see sexual response as positive and even revolutionary for women. They include women's capacity for orgasm in their description of how nineteenth-century middle-class women engaged in 'resistance that actually challenged' the 'sexual system', i.e. the supposedly repressive morality of the nineteenth century.[30] These women apparently had orgasms, according to a survey of the time. Forty per cent reported orgasms occasionally, twenty per cent frequently, and forty per cent never. Since we can assume that these women were in unregenerately oppressive relationships it is difficult to see how their orgasms were 'resistance'. Their orgasms indicate a remarkable ability to accommodate themselves to their oppression so that they can find in it a source of satisfaction, but that is very different from resistance. The absence of orgasm might more appropriately be seen as a form of resistance in such a situation. It is, after all, lack of orgasm which the sexologists have treated as resistance to male power all this century.

The libertarian feminists, as well as the sexologists from whom they take their inspiration, have seen sexual response as inevitably positive and generally revolutionary, but when we look at the situations in which men and women can experience orgasm, this approach has to be questioned. Men experience orgasms whilst killing women. Girls and women can have orgasms during rape and sexual abuse and then spend years in guilt and shame for 'enjoying' what happened to them. In fact the body is capable of physiological responses quite unconnected with an emotional state of 'pleasure'. Similarly the mind can cause a sexual response in situations where words like 'enjoy' or 'pleasure' are entirely inappropriate. Most women probably have experience of waking from sexual dreams involving rape or abuse, feeling uncomfortable or distressed. This is quite different from the feelings of well-being that can be associated with a positive sexual experience. The sexologists and their libertarian heirs have mandated that women distrust their feelings. In *The ABZ of Love* and *The Joy of Sex*, women are required to overcome their 'inhibitions' and rename their discomfort 'pleasure'. But if we listen to our feelings about sex sensitively instead of riding roughshod over them through guilt or anxiety about being prudes, we can work out what is positive and what is negative. The negative feelings are about eroticised subordination or heterosexual desire.

THE RESURGENCE OF HETEROSEXUAL DESIRE

In the early years of this wave of feminism there was criticism of the dominance and submission roles of heterosexuality. As well as a dominant concern with the possibilities for women's sexual pleasure and how these had been limited in relationships with men, there was a real desire for equality. In the 1980s, in a feminist community which has accepted use of the term 'post-feminism', this search for equality in sex is being vigorously challenged both by some heterosexual women and by some lesbians. The British heterosexual feminist theorist Sheila Rowbotham explained in 1984 why she and some other feminists had given up the attempt to 'democratise' desire. She says that 'moral earnestness' came to grief when confronted with 'lust, romantic fantasy, fear of ageing, sado-masochism'. The most serious reason for abandoning the attempt to democratise desire was the fact that such equality was not sexy. She recounts the experience of an American therapist who encouraged her clients to democratise their relationships. The couples kept returning to her with a new problem, they were 'unable to summon up desire. Love yes, but not desire'.[31]

Feminists have always been uncomfortably aware that men's sexual passion was likely to fade if relationships were democratised. Rowbotham tells us that this is a problem for women too. The sociologist Jessie Bernard's 1972 book *The Future of Marriage* dealt at length with the issue of men's difficulties with democratic desire. She explains that research as long ago as the 1950s had suggested that the search for companionate marriage was destroying marital sex life. Companionate marriages were to be based upon equality.

> . . . Veroff and Feld were beginning to raise disturbing questions about the way an ideology oriented toward egalitarian companionship might affect the sexual component of marriage . . . they were speculating that the conception of the 'traditional marital relationship [as] a friendship relationship may play havoc with the potential that the marital role has to permit sexual and interpersonal activity.' In other words, can you mix companionship and sex? The future of marriage rides on the answer.[32]

In tune with the hopefulness of the early 1970s Bernard answers: 'Can you mix companionship and sex? My own answer, is, Yes, you can.'[33] Bernard did not see men's linking of power and aggression with sex as biological or innate. She saw this linkage as being about status and she was optimistic about change. Women's refusal to accept inferior status was bound to cause men to transform their sexual responses in their own interests.

But Rowbotham's answer is very different. She concludes that the feminists like herself who tried to change had:

> . . . too great a confidence that in altering the outward manifestation, the pattern of relationships in which we experienced desire, our inner feelings would fall automatically into place. There was an incongruity between overt democracy and hidden yearnings.[34]

306

She recommends the abandonment of the task of democratising desire in favour of recognising 'its capacity to surprise, to take us unawares'. She then embarks upon a lyrical description of what she sees as the characteristics of 'desire'.

Desire has the capacity to shift us beyond commonsense. It is our peep at the extraordinary. It is the chink beyond the material world.

The glimpse we still have in common. And in its daftness desire is thus a democrat, not the solemn, public face of democracy, but the inward openness which is prepared like the fool to step over the cliff.

True it can land us down with a bump. Folly, fear, embarrassment, humiliation, violence, tumble about with ecstasy and bliss. Desire is a risk, but so is freedom.[35]

As feminists we might have to ask, as Rowbotham does not, who profits from the undemocratic nature of desire under male supremacy. We might find it worrying that there should be such an asymmetry in the ways that male and female desire are constructed. For all her attempts to provide a metaphysical status for desire, not to be questioned by ordinary mortals, feminists find that desire does not exist beyond the material world but in it, and is formed out of the material inequalities between men and women. What Rowbotham tries to disguise is that the 'risk' of desire lies in the fact that it is based upon the eroticising of women's subordination. To equate the 'risk' of desire with the 'risk' of freedom is a shoddy and quite prestidigitational trick. It may well be that some women, as well as plenty of men, will choose their ability to experience a particular form of sexual passion over the desire to be free, but they are not the same thing. Indeed a feminist approach to sex would suggest that women's freedom cannot be achieved whilst some people who see themselves as radical and progressive place their right to take pleasure from women's lack of freedom before the task of creating freedom.

The defence of heterosexual desire within feminism is associated with a tendency to promote the validity of heterosexuality as a sexual choice and to attack lesbians for questioning it. A spate of writers in the mid 1980s started to talk about the necessity for heterosexuality to 'come out of the closet' on the grounds that lesbians had forced heterosexual women to feel embarrassed about their preferences. It is an astonishingly insensitive choice of term comparing as it does the real oppression of lesbians with the discomfort some heterosexual women who are aware of the incongruity of their 'desire' might feel within women's liberation. Rowbotham uses the phrase and it seems clear from the rest of the article that she defines heterosexuality as eroticised power difference. The resurgence of heterosexual desire, or eroticised power difference, is seen by such women as emerging bravely from a closet that it was never in. In a sado-society heterosexual desire is very 'out' indeed.[36]

Eileen Phillips is another heterosexual socialist feminist who validates the conflict and fear involved in heterosexual desire. She describes 'desire' as:

> . . . unnecessary, irrational, an excess – and also compelling. When going to meet the desired one, we can be sweating, our legs trembling, our heart beating fast – in fact behaviourally we can be exhibiting all the symptoms of fear. Yet it feels exciting as well as scary, the very strangeness producing a peculiar sort of clarity which often eludes us in many other activities of daily life.[37]

It looks as if desire is not being very democratic here either. Phillips provides this description of desire in combination with an attack on lesbian feminism as a 'politics of voluntarism and male banishment' and disparages attempts by both lesbians and heterosexual women to challenge the centrality of sexual intercourse. It seems that Phillips, Rowbotham and other such feminists understand very well that the sexual attraction involved in heterosexuality is eroticised power difference. Since they have rejected the lesbian alternative they have no choice but to attack lesbian feminists who offer a cogent critique of their sexual choice. Lesbian feminists are a problem because they question the necessity for any woman to organise her life around the eroticising of her own subordination.

Rowbotham's retreat from the pursuit of sexual equality is not taking place in a vacuum. Mainstream heterosexual feminism in America gives evidence of a similar phenomenon. In May 1986 *Ms* magazine produced a health issue called 'The Beauty of Health'. The only article on sex in the magazine was an interview with a husband and wife sex advice team called the Mershorers. Entitled 'Going for the Big "O" ', the article advised women how to have multiple orgasms through masochism. It might have been expected that a feminist health magazine dealing with sex would touch on some of those problems that really interfere with sexual well-being for women, such as sexual abuse, pornography and sadomasochism. In fact, far from recognising sadomasochism as a health problem, the sexologists see it as a way to achieve sexual health.

The goal of the Mershorers' advice is how to get not just one orgasm but up to a hundred. The Mershorers' book recounts the ways in which some multi-orgasmic women achieve their success. These ways include various forms of eroticised subordination such as the wearing of gender-fetishised clothing and 'the minister's sister who craves bondage and group sex'.[38] But what they have in common is the ability to 'completely let go'. It turns out that this requires surrender. Here we are back in the 1950s. Marc Mershorer explains:

> The woman is out there, competing with men, used to guarding her vulnerabilities – she has to. But the requirements out there in the world are much different from the requirements for deriving pleasure from making love. And that's a real contradiction today for many women.
>
> But – and this is a very important concept for a woman to understand – when a woman lets go, gives up, she is surrendering herself, not to her partner, but to Nature. She's giving herself to herself.[39]

The Mershorers seem to have been aware that they were being interviewed for a feminist magazine. So though the woman still surrenders in strict conformity with sexological prescriptions she no longer surrenders to the man but to 'Nature' and 'herself'. This slight change does not alter the construction of male and female sexuality though it might disinfect it a little. Men are not being advised to 'surrender'. It is difficult to see how sex as it is constructed under male supremacy could survive if men went in for surrendering. The Mershorers tell us that no matter what changes feminism and changing social realities have wrought in woman's role outside the bedroom, inside it she must continue as before.

An article in *Cosmopolitan* magazine in 1985 has the same themes but pays even less lip service to feminism, though *Cosmopolitan* has a reputation for being sexually progressive. The article 'Sexual Surrender' seeks to instruct women how to achieve 'satisfying sexual surrender'. This is defined as 'when we accept – or surrender to – our deep psychological needs for connection, intimacy, and the full expression of our sexuality'.[40] According to the writer men can and should surrender in sex too, but men's and women's sexuality is different, so obviously they won't be doing so as often or in the same way. She explains:

> In their sincere attempts not to be sexist, both men and women risk overlooking the real differences between them. As George Gilder writes in *Sexual Suicide*, 'There are no human beings; there are just men and women, and when they deny their divergent sexuality, they reject the deepest sources of identity and love. They commit sexual suicide.'[41]

The differences that women should acknowledge are the old-fashioned ones of male aggression and female submission. Men's aggression is largely socially constructed, the article tells us, but none the less unchangeable, because 'centuries of biological and cultural reinforcement have taught men to forge ahead, making, doing, conquering and controlling' with the result that men 'feel aggressive during sexual intercourse'.[42] So women must accept traditional gender roles in sexual behaviour although these may be more apparent than real since in sexual intercourse the man 'appears to control' and the woman 'appears to surrender'.

Like the Mershorers the writer of this article shows an awareness that such a prescription might seem incongruous to women reared in a world of feminism and greater opportunities. Woman is assured that she can be liberated in the public sphere as long as she remains a traditional passive woman in the bedroom.

310

Considering that sexologists throughout the twentieth century have been convinced that 'surrender' in the bedroom did not stop at the bedroom door but spilt over into the whole relationship with a man and other areas of life, then the surrender that is being vaunted must actually be the antidote to feminism. Women may have greater opportunities but while they surrender in bed they will become no real threat to male privilege. Accordingly the *Cosmopolitan* article admonishes women that though 'the freedom to earn equal pay and satisfaction through a career' have been a 'tremendous breakthrough' women should not 'throw out the old-fashioned joys of womanhood in the bargain'. The old-fashioned joys turn out to consist of being the object of male sexual attention in the form of being 'pursued, chosen and adored'. The *Cosmopolitan* article concludes with a warning that is clearly anti-feminist. Women must not try to be too equal.

> Part of those old-fashioned joys is being pursued, chosen, and adored. It's hard to pursue someone who is already pursuing. Although contemporary women are still developing their ability to take charge, being cast in the role of the one who surrenders is potentially a woman's greatest asset.[43]

The resurgence of heterosexual desire within feminism after a brief period in which it was questioned fits into the increasingly sadistic tenor of male-supremacist society. Women Against Pornography in New York point out that men's pornography has become more and more violent and sadistic in the late 1970s and early 1980s. The androgyny and unisex of the late 1960s and early 1970s has given way to a pronounced gender fetishism in fashion and in the entertainments industry. This new gender fetishism focuses much more obviously than that of the 1950s on violence. The language of fashion in the early 1980s has been heavily reliant on black leather, chains and handcuffs. There is a much more prominent sexual aggression in fashion. The mini skirt of the 1960s looks tame and domesticated compared with the tiny clinging, black, late 1980s variety.

How can the increasingly sadistic tone of male-supremacist culture be explained? It cannot simply reflect the right wing turn of politics and the move towards nuclear confrontation of Reaganism and Thatcherism. Certainly masculine values dominate the enterprise culture of the 1980s, but the 1950s too were a time of cold war and McCarthyism, and such overt sadism did not infuse the culture then. This new aggressive masculinity can be explained as an answer to the threat of women's liberation, an answer made possible by the sexual revolution which normalised male sexual aggression. It certainly seems effective, particularly inasmuch as it has percolated through into the women's liberation movement itself.

HOMOSEXUAL DESIRE

The demolition of heterosexual desire is a necessary step on the route to women's liberation. Freedom is indivisible. It is not possible to keep little bits of unfreedom, such as in the area of sexuality, because they give some people pleasure, if we are serious about wanting women's liberation. Male-supremacist sexuality is constructed from the subordination of women. If women were not subordinate then sex as the eroticised subordination of women would not be thinkable. Those who wish to fight feminists in order to retain dominance and submission sex are standing in the path of a feminist revolution. Feminist revolution is not 'sexy' because it would remove those material power differences between the sexes on which eroticised power difference is based. To retain sadomasochism it is necessary to prevent the progress of women's liberation. It should not surprise us, therefore, to discover the libertarians launching vigorous attacks on feminism, lesbian feminism, and lesbian separatism. It should not surprise us that the libertarians have achieved a serious slowing down and in some cases destruction of feminist initiatives against violence against women. The feminist challenge to male violence cannot thrive in harmony with the promotion of sadomasochistic values by women who in some cases call themselves feminists and in others escape challenge through the wearing of a radical veneer.

The feminist fight against male violence requires the reconstruction of male sexuality. The abuse and murder of women and girls cannot be separated from sexual 'fantasy' and pornography. The relationships of power that exist in the world do not exist as a result of nature but as a result of being imagined and created by those who benefit from them. The subordination of women is 'thought' in the fantasy and the practice of sex. The 'thought' of women's sexual subordination delivers powerful reinforcement to men's feelings of dominance and superiority. The liberation of women is unimaginable in this situation since it would disrupt the possibilities of pleasure. But even if men cannot imagine it, it is necessary that we should. If we cannot imagine our liberation then we cannot achieve it.

Male sexuality must be reconstructed to sever the link between power and aggression and sexual pleasure. Only then can women be relieved of the restrictions placed upon their lives and opportunities by male sexual objectification and aggression. Men's pleasure in women's subordination is a powerful bulwark of their resistance to women's liberation. The reconstruction of male sexuality must extend to gay men too. While they vigorously promote eroticised dominance and submission as sex they constitute a serious obstacle to women's liberation. It is not to be expected that men, gay or straight, will voluntarily choose to relinquish the pleasure and privilege they derive from the eroticised subordination of women. Though some are capable of political integrity and of working against their own interests as a class, we cannot expect this to take place on any mass scale.

As women and as lesbians our hope lies only in other women. We must work towards the construction of homosexual desire and practice as a most important part of our struggle for liberation. However important heterosexual desire has been in our lives we will all have some experience of its opposite. We will have experience of sexual desire and practice which does not leave us feeling betrayed, a sexual desire and practice which eroticises mutuality and equality. It is this avenue that we should seek to open up while gradually shutting down those responses and practices which are not about sexual 'pleasure' but the eroticising of our subordination. We need to develop sensitive antennae for evaluating our sexual experience. None of this will be easy. It will take some effort, but then nobody said that the journey to our liberation would be an easy ride. The question we have to ask ourselves is whether we want our freedom or whether we want to retain heterosexual desire. Feminists will choose freedom.

The libertarians are trying to turn feminism into a movement for sexual liberation. Ti-Grace Atkinson described the problem clearly as long ago as 1975 in a speech to the Masochists' Liberation Front, a precursor of the s/m lesbians of the 1980s. She explained:

> Feminists are on the fence, at the moment, on the issue of sex. But I do not know any feminist worthy of that name who, if forced to choose between freedom and sex, would choose sex. She'd choose freedom every time.[44]

She contrasts this with the stated choice of a masochist in an s/m publication: 'if an M has to choose between oppression and chastity, the M considers chastity the worse alternative'.[45] She asserts that 'By no stretch of imagination is the Women's Movement a movement for sexual liberation' and explains that 'That used to be an old Left-Establishment joke on feminism: that feminists were just women who needed to get properly laid.'

It is in the interests of the male ruling class that some women are now asserting that sexual liberation and women's liberation are analogous. This should be particularly clear from the fact that the sexual liberation that such women are pursuing replicates the hopes and dreams of our oppressors. It is the liberation not of 'sex' but of sadomasochism. They are seeking to gain more satisfaction from their oppression in a way which a century of sexological literature has confidently predicted would subordinate women. Masochism, the sexologists believed, would disempower women and render us quiescent. It would cause us to embrace our oppression and cease to struggle against it. The last laugh over the sadomasochism of lesbian or pre-lesbian women must go to the male establishment. Women have been lured into accepting a substitute for their liberation which is designed to ensure that they cannot achieve liberation. The aim of the sexological industry over the last century was that women would be trained to eroticise their subordination. The result they hoped for was that women would then have a stake in prolonging their own oppression and resist any attempt to end it. The resurgence of heterosexual desire among some ex-feminists shows how successful the sexologists have been. They have been successful in a period of backlash against feminism but feminism has not yet completely died out. If we are to revive the movement for our liberation then we must start working towards the construction of an egalitarian sexuality.

Our struggle for liberation does not necessarily require chastity, though many women do choose this path and it is an honourable choice. Such a strategy could only cause disbelief in a male-supremacist society in which sex has been made holy. Sex is holy because of its role as a sacred ritual in the dominant/submissive relationship between men and women. The importance attached to sex defies rationality and can only be explained in this political way. But we can also choose, as many of us have done, to work towards homosexual desire if that suits our lives and relationships. We must remember that homosexual desire will not be recognised as 'sex'. We do not even possess suitable words to describe it. The course of eroticising equality and mutuality has received no prizes from male supremacy or its agents but it is time we shared our wisdom and experience, learned from feminists and lesbians in our history and became proud of what distinguishes lesbian experience from male-supremacist culture.

Psychoanalysts have described lesbianism pejoratively as 'narcissistic regression'.[46] This means that in loving their own sex lesbians are in fact loving themselves and need to mature into loving the other, i.e. men. Narcissism is seen as negative and dangerous. In fact, the psychoanalysts have spotted the basis of homosexual desire. It is heretical in this culture deliberately to avoid the rituals of sadomasochistic sex and to choose to eroticise sameness and equality. Differences of race and class can provide power differences to eroticise even in same-sex relationships. Lesbians committed to the creation of an egalitarian sexuality must be prepared to challenge this too, since same-sex relationships do not automatically ensure a symmetry of power and privilege. It is not surprising that sexologists who have been dedicated to the construction of heterosexual desire and are enthusiastic about lesbian sadomasochism have derided lesbian love. We should value what our enemies find most threatening.

Readers who consider themselves to be heterosexual will probably be wondering whether homosexual desire can fit into an opposite-sex relationship. In a society which was not founded upon the subordination of women there would be no reason why it should not. But we do not live in such a society. We live in a society organised around heterosexual desire, around otherness and power difference. It is difficult to imagine what shape a woman's desire for a man would take in the absence of eroticised power difference since it is precisely this which provides the excitement of heterosexuality today.

Heterosexuality is the institution through which male-supremacist society is organised and as such it must cease to function. It is difficult to imagine at this point what shape any relationship between different sexes would take when such a relationship was a free choice, when it was not privileged in any way over same-sex relationships and when it played no part in organising women's oppression and male power. In such a situation, when heterosexuality was no longer an institution, we cannot yet be sure what women would choose.

NOTES

Introduction

1. Sheila Jeffreys, *The Spinster and Her Enemies: Feminism and Sexuality 1880–1930*, Pandora, London, 1985.
2. Wilhelm Stekel, *Frigidity in Woman in Relation to her Love Life*, Liveright, New York, 1926, vol. 2, p. 1.

Chapter 1
THE FIFTIES

1. David Mace, *Marriage Crisis*, Delisle, London, 1948, p. 11.
2. H. E. Norman, 'Why Marriages Fail – the social aspect', in Neville-Rolfe, Sybil (ed), *Sex in Social Life*, George Allen and Unwin, London, 1949.
3. Ibid., p. 405.
4. Ibid., p. 7; Foreword by Sir Cyril Norwood.
5. Mace, op. cit., p. 14.
6. Ibid., p. 13.
7. Kathleen Bannister *et al.*, *Social Casework in Marital Problems*, Tavistock Publications, London, 1955, p. 3.
8. Joseph Brayshaw, 'The Stability of Marriage', *Eugenics Review* vol. 44, no. 2, July 1952, p. 85.
9. Ibid., p. 88.
10. Ibid.
11. Ibid.
12. Ibid.
13. Mace, op. cit., p. 41.
14. Ibid., p. 28.
15. Bannister, op. cit., p. 48.
16. Ibid., p. 49.
17. Ibid., p. 82.
18. Mace, op. cit., p. 41.

19. Eustace Chesser, *Sexual Behaviour: Normal and Abnormal*, Roy Publishers, New York, 1949, p. 64.
20. Eustace Chesser, *Love and Marriage*, Pan Books, London, 1957 (first published 1946), pp. 88–9.
21. *Eugenics Review*, vol. 38, no. 2, 1946, p. 117.
22. Ibid., p. 130.
23. Ibid., p. 131.
24. Elizabeth Wilson, *Women and the Welfare State*, Tavistock Publications, London, 1977.
25. John Bowlby, Child Care and the Growth of Love, Penguin, Harmondsworth, 1974 (first published 1953), p. 239.
26. Ibid., pp. 77–8.
27. Eustace Chesser, op. cit., 1949, p. xi.
28. Ibid., p. 201.
29. Ibid., p. 206.
30. Ibid., p. 288.
31. See my book *The Spinster and Her Enemies* op. cit., Chapter 7, 'Antifeminism and Sex Reform before the First World War'.
32. Gertrude Williams, *Women and Work*, Essential Books, New York, 1945, a series written for the citizens of Britain, p. 10.
33. Ibid., p. 33.
34. Ibid., p. 34.
35. Kenneth Walker, 'Why Marriages Fail – the personal aspect', in Neville-Rolfe (ed), op. cit., p. 399.
36. Maxine Davis, *The Sexual Responsibility of Woman*, Fontana Books, London, 1965 (first published 1957), p. 85.
37. Marie Bonaparte, *Female Sexuality*, Imago Publishing Co., London, 1953, p. 175.
38. Ibid.
39. Ibid., p. 1.
40. Davis, op. cit., p.85.
41. Ibid., p. 77.
42. Jeffreys, op. cit., Chapter 2, 'Continence and Psychic Love'.
43. Janice G. Raymond, *A Passion for Friends*, The Women's Press, London, 1986, p. 57.
44. Leni Riefenstahl, *People of Kau*, Harper and Row, New York, 1976, p. 221.
45. Susan Cavin, *Lesbian Origins*, Ism Press, San Francisco, 1985.
46. Edmund Bergler, *Neurotic, Counterfeit-Sex*, Grune and Stratton, New York, 1951, p. 211.
47. Frank Caprio, *The Sexually Adequate Female*, Citadel Press, New York, 1963 (first published 1953), p. 15.
48. Davis, op. cit., p. 33.
49. Caprio, op. cit., p. 102.
50. Ibid., p. 103.
51. Ibid., p. 143.

52. Ibid., p. 79.
53. Chesser, *Love and Marriage*, op. cit., p. 67.
54. Caprio, op. cit., p. 44.
55. Walker, op. cit., p. 342.
56. Caprio, op. cit., p. 79.
57. Walker, op. cit., p. 345.
58. Ibid., p. 358.
59. Davis, op. cit., p. 77.
60. Walker, op. cit., p. 356.
61. Chesser, *Love and Marriage*, op. cit., p. 79.
62. Davis, op. cit., p. 130.
63. Ibid., p. 96.
64. Chesser, *Love and Marriage*, op. cit., p. 66.
65. Davis, op. cit., p. 129.
66. Ibid., p. 72.
67. Leonard J. Friedman, *Virgin Wives: A Study of Unconsummated Marriages*, Tavistock Publications, London, 1962, p. ix.
68. Ibid., p. 20 and p. 27.
69. Ibid., p. 32.
70. Ibid., p. 27.
71. Ibid., p. 22.
72. Ibid., p. 23.
73. Ibid., p. 29.
74. Ibid., p. 55.
75. Ibid., p. 42.
76. Ibid., p. 43.
77. Ibid.
78. Ibid., p. 44.
79. Ibid., p. 45.
80. Ibid., p. 51.
81. Ibid., p. 95.
82. Ibid., p. 97.
83. Ibid., p. 76.
84. Ibid., p. 76.
85. Ibid., p. 15.
86. Ibid., p. 24.
87. James M. Henslin and Edward Sagarin (eds), *The Sociology of Sex: An Introductory Reader*, Schocken Books, New York, 1978, pp. 164–5.
88. Esther Harding, *The Way of All Women*, Longmans Green, London, 1939 (first published 1933), p. 104.
89. Laura Hutton, *The Single Woman and Her Emotional Problems*, Baillière, Tindall and Cox, London, 1937 (first published 1935), p. 3.
90. Ibid., p. 5.
91. Janice G. Raymond, op. cit., p. 3.

92. Ibid., p. 9.
93. Ibid., p. 10.
94. Harding, op. cit., p. 115.
95. Ibid., p. 116.
96. Hutton, op. cit., p. 104.
97. Ibid., p. 103.
98. Ibid., p. 106.
99. Ibid., p. 85.
100. Ibid., p. 109.
101. Ibid., p. 111.
102. Ibid., pp. 119–20.
103. Ibid., p. 121.
104. Hutton, op. cit., p. 27.
105. Ibid., p. 56.
106. Margery Fry, *The Single Woman*, Delisle, London, 1953, p. 14.
107. Ibid., p. 26.
108. Ibid., p. 43.
109. Blanche Marie Smith, *The Single Woman of Today*, Greenwood Press, Westport, Ct., 1974 (reprint of 1951 edition by Watts of London), p. 189.
110. Ibid., p. 47.
111. Ibid.
112. Ibid., p. 49.
113. Ibid.
114. Ibid., p. 64.
115. Ibid., p. 122.
116. Hutton, op. cit., p. 123.
117. Smith, op. cit., pp. 13–14.
118. Sybil Neville-Rolfe, in *Sex in Social Life*, op. cit., p. 465.
119. Thomas V. Moore, 'The pathogenesis and treatment of homosexual disorders; a digest of some pertinent evidence', in *Journal of Personality*, vol. XIV, Sept. 1945, p. 57.
120. Samuel Steward, in James Barr, *Quatrefoil*, Alyson Publications, Boston, 1982, p. xi.
121. Frank Caprio, op. cit., p. 188.
122. Ibid., p. 189.
123. Ibid., p. 190.
124. Edmund Bergler, op. cit., p. 318.
125. Ibid., p. 326.
126. Marie Bonaparte, op. cit., p. 47.
127. Kenneth Walker, *The Physiology of Sex*, Penguin, Harmondsworth, 1969 (first published 1940), p. 157.
128. Ibid., p. 159.
129. Eustace Chesser, *Odd Man Out*, Victor Gollancz, London, 1959, p. 103.

130. Frank Caprio, *Female Homosexuality*, Peter Owen, London, 1957, p. 304.
131. Ibid.
132. Ibid.
133. Walker, *The Physiology of Sex*, op. cit., p. 162.
134. Jeffrey Weeks, *Coming Out*, Quartet, London, 1977, pp. 159–60.
135. Walker, op. cit., p. 153.

Chapter 2
DECENSORSHIP

1. Charles Rembar, *The End of Obscenity*, André Deutsch, London, 1969, p. vii.
2. Ibid., p. x.
3. John Sutherland, *Offensive Literature: Decensorship in Britain 1960–1982*, Junction Books, London, 1982, p. 4.
4. Eberhard and Phyllis Kronhausen, *Pornography and the Law*, New English Library, London, 1967 (first published 1959), p. 4.
5. Rembar, op. cit., p. 12.
6. Kronhausen, op. cit., p. 240.
7. H. Montgomery Hyde, *A History of Pornography*, Four Square Books, London, 1966 (first published 1964), p. 179.
8. Ibid., p. 210.
9. Millett, Kate, *Sexual Politics*, Virago, London, 1977.
10. Ibid., p. 240.
11. Kronhausen, op. cit., p. 205.
12. Wilhelm Stekel, *Frigidity in Woman in Relation to her Love Life*, Liveright, New York, 1936 (first published 1926), vol. 2, p. 25.
13. Kronhausen, op. cit., pp. 206–7.
14. Ibid., p. 155.
15. Ibid.
16. Ibid., p. 227.
17. Suzanne Kappeler, *The Pornography of Representation*, Polity Press, Cambridge, 1986, p. 26.
18. Ibid., p. 27.
19. Michael B. Goodman, *Contemporary Literary Censorship: The Case History of Burroughs'* The Naked Lunch, Scarecrow Press, Metuchen, NJ, 1981, p. 1.
20. John Calder (ed), *A William Burroughs Reader*, Picador, London, 1982, p. 8.
21. Ibid., p. 24.
22. Ibid., p. 7.
23. Ibid., p. 16.
24. Ibid., p. 21.

25. Ibid., p. 28.
26. Ibid., p. 112.
27. William Burroughs, *Cities of the Red Night*, John Calder, London, 1981.
28. Stephen Adams, *The Homosexual as Hero in Literature*, Vision Press, London, 1980.
29. William Burroughs, *The Naked Lunch*, in John Calder (ed), op. cit., p. 105.
30. Calder, op. cit., p. 24.
31. Quoted in Sutherland, op. cit., p. 52.
32. Ibid., p. 53.
33. Ibid., p. 54.
34. Calder, op. cit., p. 28.
35. Goodman, op. cit., p. 221.
36. Calder, op. cit., p. 134.
37. Eric Mottram, *William Burroughs*, Calder and Boyars, London, 1977, p. 153.
38. Ibid., p. 152.
39. Ibid., p. 153.
40. Ibid., p. 152.
41. Hyde, op. cit., p. 156.
42. Kronhausen, op. cit., p. 210.
43. Ibid.
44. Ibid.
45. Russell Trainer, *The Lolita Complex*, Citadel Press, New York, 1966, p. 46.
46. Ibid., p. 73.
47. Ibid., p. 203.
48. Vladimir Nabokov, *Lolita*, Corgi Books, London, 1961, p. 19.
49. Ibid., p. 29.
50. Ibid., p. 81.
51. Ibid., p. 64.
52. Ibid., p. 130.
53. Ibid., p. 139.
54. Ibid., p. 141.
55. Ibid., p. 142.
56. Ibid., p. 149.
57. Ibid., p. 155.
58. Ibid., p. 159.
59. Ibid., p. 173.
60. Ibid., p. 178.
61. Ibid., p. 209.
62. Ibid., p. 175.
63. Ibid., p. 342.
64. Ibid., p. 341.
65. Ibid., p. 340.

66. Ibid., p. 344.
67. Kronhausen, op. cit., p. 210.
68. Nabokov, op. cit., p. 345.
69. Ibid., p. 341.
70. Ibid., p. 343.
71. Ibid., p. 345.
72. Ibid., p. 341.
73. Ibid., p. 331.
74. Ibid., p. 332.
75. Ibid., p. 328.
76. Ibid., p. 329.
77. Kappeler, op. cit., p. 101.
78. Ibid., p. 116.
79. Ibid., p. 111.
80. Ibid., p. 109.
81. Ibid.
82. Sutherland, op. cit., p. 50.
83. Ibid., p. 15.
84. Ibid., p. 4.
85. Kappeler, op. cit., p. 105.
86. Ibid., p. 104.

Chapter 3
THE SEXUAL REVOLUTION

1. Jeffrey Weeks, *Sex, Politics and Society*, Longmans, London, 1981.
2. Inge and Stan Hegeler, *An ABZ of Love*, New English Library, London, 1963, p. 22.
3. Ibid., p. 196.
4. Ibid.
5. Ibid., p. 79.
6. Ibid., p. 80.
7. Ibid., p. 127.
8. Ibid., p. 82.
9. Ibid., p. 83.
10. Ibid., p. 192.
11. Ibid., p. 252.
12. Lars Ullerstam, *The Erotic Minorities*, Grove Press, New York, 1964, p. 151.
13. Paul Robinson, *The Sexual Radicals*, Paladin, London, 1972, p. 15.
14. Wilhelm Reich, *The Sexual Struggle of Youth*, Socialist Reproduction, London, 1972, p. 25.
15. Ibid., p. 23.
16. Ibid., p. 46.

17. Robinson, op. cit., p. 29.
18. Reich, op. cit., p. 48.
19. Robinson, op. cit., p. 48.
20. For a feminist analysis of Kinsey and the ideology of the sexologists in general see: Margaret Jackson, 'Sexology and the universalisation of male sexuality' (from Ellis to Kinsey, and Masters and Johnson), in Lal Coveney *et al.* (eds), *The Sexuality Papers*, Hutchinson, London, 1984.
21. Robinson, op. cit., p. 49.
22. For an fascinating account of the Oneida Community see: Louis J. Kern, 'Ideology and Reality: Sexuality and Women's Status in the Oneida Community', in *Radical History Review*, no. 20, Spring/Summer 1979, pp. 181–205.
23. Robinson, op. cit., p. 144.
24. Ibid., p. 156.
25. Maurice Girodias, 'Obscenity and the Sexual Revolution', in *The Obscenity Report*, Olympia Press, Paris, 1971, p. 23.
26. Ibid., p. 24.
27. Helen Gurley Brown, *Sex and the Single Girl*, Bernard Geiss Associates, New York, 1962, p. 78.
28. Ibid., p. 84.
29. Ibid., p. 86.
30. Ibid.
31. J., *The Sensuous Woman*, Castle Books, Memphis, 1981 (first published 1969), p. 10.
32. Ibid., p. 41.
33. Ibid., p. 45.
34. Ibid., p. 97.
35. Ibid., p. 98.
36. Ibid.
37. Ibid., p. 119.
38. Ibid., p. 125.
39. Ibid., p. 179.
40. Ibid., p. 160.
41. David Reuben, *Everything you always wanted to know about sex but were afraid to ask*, W. H. Allen, London, 1970, jacket blurb.
42. Ibid., p. 215.
43. Ibid., p. 216.
44. Ibid.
45. Lal Coveney, Leslie Kay and Pat Mahony, 'Theory into practice: sexual liberation or social control? (*Forum* magazine 1968–81)', in Lal Coveney *et al.* (eds), op. cit., p. 88.
46. Ibid.
47. Ibid., p. 90.
48. Ibid., p. 92.

49. Alex Comfort (ed), *The Joy of Sex*, Quartet, London, 1979, p. 1.
50. Ibid., p. 2.
51. Ibid., p. 1.
52. Ibid., p. 10.
53. Ibid., p. 1.
54. Ibid., p. 42.
55. Ibid., p. 11.
56. Ibid., p. 24.
57. Ibid., p. 34.
58. Ibid., p. 35.
59. Ibid., p. 36.
60. Ibid.
61. Ibid., p. 63.
62. Ibid., p. 65.
63. Ibid., p. 126.
64. Ibid., p. 129.
65. Ibid., p. 210.
66. Ibid., p. 129.
67. Ibid., p. 193.
68. Ibid., p. 210.
69. Ibid., p. 184.
70. Ibid.
71. Ibid.
72. Alex Comfort, *Barbarism and Sexual Freedom. Lectures on the sociology of sex from the standpoint of anarchism*, Freedom Press, London, 1948, p. 3.
73. Ibid., p. 5.
74. Ibid., p. 55.
75. Ibid., p. 58.
76. Edward M. Brecher, *The Sex Researchers*, Panther, London, 1972 (first published 1970), p. 280.
77. Gay Talese, *Thy Neighbour's Wife*, Pan Books, London, 1981 (first published 1980).
78. Ibid., p. 176.
79. Ibid., p. 186.
80. Ibid., p. 313.
81. Ibid., p. 316.
82. Alex Comfort (ed), *More Joy of Sex*, Quartet, London, 1984 (first published 1977), p. 138.
83. Ibid., p. 143.
84. Ibid., p. 139.
85. Ibid., p. 159.
86. Brecher, op. cit., p. 284.
87. Ibid., p. 285.
88. Ibid., p. 295.

89. Ibid., p. 298.
90. Ibid., p. 299.
91. Ibid.
92. Ibid., p. 312.
93. Ibid., p. 314.
94. Ibid., p. 328.
95. Ibid.
96. William H. Masters and Virginia E. Johnson, *Human Sexual Inadequacy*, Bantam Books, Boston, 1981 (first published 1970), p. 96.
97. Ibid., p. 105.
98. Ibid., p. 257.
99. Ibid., p. 143.
100. Ibid., p. 147.
101. Ibid., p. 294.
102. Sha Kokken, *The Way to Married Love: A Happier Sex Life*, Souvenir Press, London, 1967 (first published Japan 1960), p. 93.
103. Masters and Johnson, op. cit., p. 299.
104. Ibid., p. 147.
105. Ibid., p. 256.
106. William H. Masters and Virginia E. Johnson, *The Pleasure Bond: A New Look at Sexuality and Commitment*, Little, Brown, Boston, 1974 (first published 1970), jacket blurb.
107. Ibid., p. 9.
108. Ibid., p. 78.
109. Ibid., p. 79.
110. Ibid.
111. Ibid., p. 80.

Chapter 4
THE FAILURE OF GAY LIBERATION

1. Robert Creeley (ed), *Walt Whitman*, Penguin, London, 1973, p. 116.
2. Edward Carpenter, *Towards Democracy*, George Allen and Unwin, London, 1921 (first published 1883), p. 69.
3. For the relationship between Carpenter and Merrill see Jeffrey Weeks, *Coming Out*, Quartet, London, 1977, pp. 78–80.
4. Carpenter, op. cit., p. 26.
5. Edward Carpenter, *The Intermediate Sex*, George Allen and Unwin, London, 1921, p. 114.
6. Quoted in the introduction to E. M. Forster, *A Life to Come and Other Stories*, Penguin, London, 1975 (first published 1972), p. 16.
7. Ibid., p. 129 and p. 133.

8. Christopher Isherwood, *Goodbye to Berlin*, Hogarth Press, London, 1960, pp. 127–8.
9. Ibid., p. 207.
10. Brian Finney, *Christopher Isherwood: A Critical Biography*, Faber, London, 1979.
11. Christopher Isherwood, *Christopher and His Kind*, Eyre Methuen, London, 1977, p. 11.
12. Aubrey Walter (ed), *Come Together: The Years of Gay Liberation 1970–73*, Gay Men's Press, London, 1980, p. 48.
13. Ibid., p. 8.
14. Ibid., p. 86.
15. Alan P. Bell and Martin S. Weinberg, *Homosexualities: A study of diversity among men and women*, Simon and Schuster, New York, 1978, p. 75 and p. 79.
16. Ibid., p. 85 and p. 93.
17. Walter (ed), op. cit., p. 185.
18. Gay Left Collective (eds), *Homosexuality: Power and Politics*, Allison and Busby, London, 1980, p. 140.
19. Ibid., p. 142.
20. Ibid., p. 144.
21. Ibid., p. 145.
22. Ibid., p. 148.
23. Ibid., p. 149.
24. Ibid., p. 150.
25. Ibid.
26. John Rechy, *The Sexual Outlaw*, Futura, London, 1981 (first published 1977), p. 16.
27. Ibid., p. 299.
28. Scarlet Friedman and Elizabeth Sarah (eds), *On the Problems of Men*, The Women's Press, London, 1982, p. 190.
29. Ibid., p. 195.
30. Ibid., p. 199.
31. Ibid., p. 203.
32. Ibid., p. 210.
33. Ibid., p. 211.
34. Ibid., p. 212.
35. Ed Jackson and Stan Persky (eds), *Flaunting It: A decade of journalism from* Body Politic, Pink Triangle Press, Toronto, 1982, p. 180.
36. Ibid.
37. Ibid., p. 181.
38. Ibid.
39. Ibid.
40. Karla Jay and Allen Young (eds), *Lavender Culture*, Harcourt Brace Jovanovich, New York, 1978, p. 108.
41. Ibid., p. 116.

42. Ibid.
43. See Jeffrey Weeks, op. cit.
44. See Jeffrey Weeks, *Sexuality and its Discontents*, Routledge and Kegan Paul, London, 1985.
45. Lars Ullerstam, *The Erotic Minorities*, Grove Press, New York, 1966.
46. Ibid., p. 34.
47. Weeks, 1985 op. cit., pp. 186–7.
48. Ibid., pp. 192–3.
49. See Kathleen Barry, *Female Sexual Slavery*, Prentice-Hall, Englewood Cliffs, NJ, 1979; for autobiographical accounts see Claude Jaget (ed), *Prostitutes: Our Life*, Falling Wall Press, London, 1980; Linda Lovelace, *Ordeal*, W. H. Allen, London, 1981.
50. Weeks, 1985 op. cit., p. 251.
51. Ibid., p. 245.
52. Walter (ed), op. cit., p. 20.
53. Ibid., p. 22.
54. Ibid., p. 33.
55. *Glad Rag*, no. 3.
56. Samois (ed), *Coming To Power*, Alyson Publications, Boston, 1982, pp. 233–4.
57. Kris Kirk and Ed Heath, *Men In Frocks*, Gay Men's Press, London, 1984.
58. Ibid., p. 95.
59. Ibid., p. 97.
60. Ibid., p. 20.
61. Walter, op cit., p. 166.
62. Ibid., p. 144.
63. Ibid., p. 143.
64. Ibid., p. 78.
65. Janice G. Raymond, *The Transsexual Empire*, The Women's Press, London, 1980.
66. Janice G. Raymond, 'Transsexualism: The Ultimate Homage to Sex-Role Power', *Chrysalis*, no. 3, p. 15.
67. Ibid.
68. Ibid.
69. Roberta Cowell, *Roberta Cowell's Story: An Autobiography*, Heinemann, London, 1954.
70. Ibid., p. 92.
71. Ibid., p. 109.
72. Jan Morris, *Conundrum*, Coronet Books, London, 1975 (first published 1974), p. 143.
73. Ibid., pp. 144–5.
74. Cowell, op. cit., p. 97.
75. Morris, op. cit., p. 11.
76. Ibid., p. 31.

77. Ibid., p. 156.
78. Ibid., p. 19.
79. Cowell, op. cit., p. 6.
80. Ibid., p. 58.
81. Ibid., p. 77.
82. Ibid., p. 112.
83. Morris, op. cit., p. 29.
84. Ibid., p. 146.
85. *Guardian*, 9 June 1978.
86. Ibid.
87. Leslie Martin Lothstein, *Female-to-Male Transsexualism*, Routledge and Kegan Paul, London, 1983.
88. Ibid., p. 10.
89. Ibid., p. 14.
90. Ibid., p. 24.
91. Ibid., p. 27.
92. Ibid., p. 43.
93. Merrill Mushroom, 'Confessions of a Butch Dyke', *Common Lives, Lesbian Lives*, no. 9, Fall 1983.
94. See my article 'Butch and Femme: Now and Then', in *Gossip*, no. 5, 1987.
95. Lothstein, op. cit., p. 45.
96. *Gay News*, no. 252, Oct./Nov. 1982, p. 32.
97. Ibid.
98. Ibid.
99. Warren Middleton (ed), *The Betrayal of Youth*, CL Publications, London, 1986, p. 190.
100. Interview with Keith Hose, *Leveller*, February 1978.
101. Roger Moody, *Indecent Assault*, Word is Out/Peace News, London, 1980.
102. Presland in Middleton, op. cit., p. 86.
103. Daniel Tsang (ed), *The Age Taboo*, Alyson Publications, Boston, 1981, p. 10.
104. Middleton, op. cit., Introduction.
105. Ibid.
106. Ibid., p. 75.
107. Maurice Yaffe, 'Pedophilia: The Forbidden Subject', *New Statesman*, 16 Sept. 1977.
108. *Outrage*, no. 4, Summer 1978, p. 38.
109. Tsang, op. cit., p. 27.
110. Ibid.
111. Tom Reeves, 'Loving Boys', in Tsang, op. cit., p. 41.
112. Gerald Hannon, 'Men Loving Boys Loving Men', in Ed Jackson and Stan Persky (eds), op. cit., p. 149.
113. Yaffe, op. cit.
114. Hannon, op. cit., p. 153.

115. Ibid., p. 154.
116. Ibid.
117. Ibid.
118. Ibid.
119. Ibid., p. 155.
120. Ibid., p. 159.
121. Eric Presland, 'Power and Consent', in Middleton (ed), op. cit., pp. 63–4.
122. Ibid., p. 72.
123. Robin Lloyd, *Playland: A Study of Human Exploitation*, Quartet, London, 1979.
124. Ibid., p. 25.
125. Ibid., p. 72.
126. Richard Green, 'Child Pornography and Erotica', in Middleton (ed), op. cit., p. 23.
127. Ibid., p. 24.
128. Ibid., p. 27.
129. Ibid., p. 28.
130. Presland, op. cit., p. 86.
131. Ibid., p. 87.
132. Sheila Jeffreys, 'The Sexual Abuse of Children in the Home', in Friedman and Sarah (eds), op. cit.
133. Ibid., p. 64.
134. Sandor Ferenczi, 'The confusion of tongues between the adult and the child', reprinted in Jeffrey Masson, *The Assault on Truth: Freud's Suppression of the Seduction Theory*, Farrar, Straus and Giroux, New York, 1984, pp. 283–95.
135. Tom O'Carroll, *Paedophilia: The Radical Case*, Peter Owen, London, 1980, p. 49.
136. London Gay Activists Alliance, 'Child temptress chased man to bed', *Submission to the Royal Commission on Criminal Procedure*, April 1979.
137. See my book *The Spinster and Her Enemies* for a detailed account of the feminist campaigns concerned with the age of consent.
138. Flame, *Flame: A Life on the Game*, Gay Men's Press, London, 1984, p. 45.
139. Ibid., p. 55.
140. Quentin Crisp, *The Naked Civil Servant*, Fontana, London, 1981 (first published 1968), pp. 66–7.
141. Ibid., p. 33.
142. Daniel Tsang, 'Men and Boys. The Boston Conference', in Tsang (ed), op. cit., p. 43.
143. Presland, op. cit., p. 81.
144. John Boswell, *Christianity, Social Tolerance and Homosexuality: Gay people in western Europe from the beginning of the*

Christian era to the fourteenth century, University of Chicago Press, Chicago and London, 1980, p. 195.

145. Weeks, 1985 op. cit., p. 217.
146. Ibid.
147. Warren Middleton, 'Childhood Sexuality and Pedophilia: Some Questions Answered', in Middleton (ed), op. cit., p. 145.
148. O'Carroll, op. cit., p. 19.
149. Reeves, op. cit., p. 26.
150. *Gay News*, Tenth Anniversary Issue, June 1982, no. 243.
151. Ibid.
152. Ibid.
153. Karla Jay and Allen Young (eds), op. cit., p. 85.
154. James Spada, *The Spada Report*, Signet, New American Library, New York, 1979, p. 126.
155. Ibid., p. 94.
156. Ibid., p. 102.
157. Ibid., p. 103.
158. Ibid., p. 94.
159. Ibid.
160. Ibid., p. 98.
161. Ibid., p. 140.
162. Ibid., p. 141.
163. Ibid., p. 143.
164. Ibid., p. 157.
165. Ibid., p. 158.
166. Ibid., p. 160.
167. Andy Metcalfe and Martin Humphries, *The Sexuality of Men*, Pluto Press, London, 1985, p. 71.
168. Ibid., p. 70.
169. Ibid., p. 83.
170. John Rechy, op. cit., pp. 254–5.
171. Spada, op. cit., p. 133.
172. Ibid., p. 134.
173. Ibid.
174. Ibid., p. 132.
175. *Piercing Fans International Quarterly*, no. 16, p. 7.
176. Ibid., p. 8.
177. Ibid., no. 17, p. 5.
178. Ibid., no. 16, p. 7.
179. Jay and Young (eds), op. cit. p. 90.
180. Ibid., p. 95.
181. Havelock Ellis, *Erotic Symbolism: Studies in the Psychology of Sex*, F. A. Davis, Philadelphia, 1926, p. 114.
182. Ibid., p. 104.
183. Rechy, op. cit., pp. 257–8.
184. Ibid., p. 253.

185. Ibid., p. 257.
186. Ibid., p. 259.
187. Ibid., p. 261.
188. Ibid.
189. Ibid., p. 262.
190. Ibid., p. 65.
191. Ibid., p. 298.
192. Jay and Young (eds), op. cit., p. 92.
193. Ibid., p. 93.
194. Spada, op. cit., p. 83.
195. Ibid., p. 86.
196. Ibid.
197. Ibid., p. 87.

Chapter 5
FEMINISM AND SEXUALITY

1. *Shrew*, vol. 4, no. 6, December 1972, p. 1.
2. Susan Lydon, 'The Politics of Orgasm', in Robin Morgan (ed), *Sisterhood is Powerful*, Vintage Books, New York, 1970, p. 205.
3. Ibid.
4. Mary Jane Sherfey, 'A Theory on Female Sexuality' in Robin Morgan (ed), op. cit., p. 221.
5. Ibid.
6. Ibid., p. 222.
7. Ibid., p. 224.
8. *Shrew*, op. cit., p. 2.
9. Ibid., p. 10.
10. Anne Koedt, 'The Myth of the Vaginal Orgasm', in The Radical Therapist Collective (eds), *The Radical Therapist*, Penguin, Harmondsworth, 1974, p. 141.
11. Ibid., p. 142.
12. Ibid., p. 136.
13. Ibid., p. 138.
14. Jill Johnston, *Lesbian Nation*, Simon and Schuster, New York, 1974, pp. 168–9.
15. Pat Whiting, 'Female Sexuality: its political implications', in Michelene Wandor (ed), *The Body Politic*, Stage One, London, 1972, p. 203.
16. Sherfey, op. cit., p. 221.
17. Betty Dodson, *Self Love and Orgasm*, self-published by Betty Dodson, New York, 1983, p. 15.
18. Helen Singer Kaplan, *The New Sex Therapy*, Baillière, Tindall, London, 1974.
19. Dodson, op. cit., p. 49.
20. Ibid., p. 28.

21. Ibid., p. 29.
22. Anne Severson, 'Don't Get Too Near the Big Chakra', in Marsha Rowe (ed), *The Spare Rib Reader*, Penguin, Harmondsworth, 1982, p. 317.
23. Dodson, op. cit., p. 22.
24. Ibid., pp. 52–3.
25. Ibid., p. 29.
26. Whiting, op. cit., p. 205.
27. Koedt, op. cit., p. 137 and p. 141.
28. Whiting, op. cit., p. 204.
29. Dodson, op. cit., p. 31.
30. Ibid., p. 67.
31. Ibid., p. 68.
32. Susan Griffin, 'Rape: the All-American Crime', *Oz*, issue 41, London, p. 28.
33. Ibid., p. 31.
34. Susan Brownmiller, *Against Our Will: Men, Women and Rape*, Secker and Warburg, London, 1975, p. 15.
35. Florence Rush, 'The Sexual Abuse of Children: A Feminist Point of View', The Radical Therapist Collective (eds), op. cit., p. 186.
36. Elizabeth Ward, *Father-Daughter Rape*, The Women's Press, London, 1984, p. 33.
37. Ibid., p. 41.
38. Ibid., p. 45.
39. Ibid., p. 67.
40. Ibid, pp. 72–3.
41. David Finkelhor and Kersti Yllo, *License to Rape: Sexual Abuse of Wives*, Holt, Rinehart and Winston, New York, 1985, pp. 6–7; Diana Russell, *Rape in Marriage*, Macmillan, New York, 1982.
42. Finkelhor and Yllo, op. cit., p. 28.
43. Ibid., p. 30.
44. Ibid., p. 138.
45. Ibid., p. 20.
46. Ibid., p. 125.
47. Jane Caputi, *The Age of Sex Crime*, The Women's Press, London, 1988, p. 198.
48. Ibid., p. 200.
49. Andrea Dworkin, *Pornography: Men Possessing Women*, Perigree, New York, 1981, p. 203.
50. New York Women Against Pornography, Slide Show Script, 1985, p. 9.
51. Andrea Dworkin, *Letters from a War Zone*, Secker and Warburg, London, 1988, p. 278.
52. Ibid., p. 238.

53. Everywoman (eds), *Pornography and Sexual Violence: Evidence of the Links*, Everywoman, London, 1988, p. 104.
54. Ibid., p. 70.
55. Ibid., p. 60.
56. Everywoman, op. cit., p. 100.
57. Ibid., p. 72.
58. Ibid., p. 75.
59. Dworkin, 1988 op. cit., p. 279.
60. Women Against Pornography, Newsreport, vol. VII, no. 1, 1985.
61. Catharine MacKinnon, 'Not a Moral Issue', *Yale Law and Policy Review*, vol. II, no. 2, Spring 1984, p. 343.
62. Ibid., p. 335.
63. Ibid., p. 326.
64. Andrea Dworkin, 1988 op. cit., p. 321.
65. Carole S. Vance (ed), *Pleasure and Danger: Exploring Female Sexuality*, Routledge and Kegan Paul, Boston, 1984.
66. Joan Nestle, *A Restricted Country*, Sheba, London, 1988.
67. Gayle Rubin *et al.*, 'Talking Sex', *Feminist Review*, no. 11, June 1982, p. 40.
68. Ibid., p. 48.
69. Ibid.
70. Ibid., p. 49.
71. Gayle Rubin, 'The Leather Menace: Comments on Politics and S/M', in Samois (ed), op. cit., p. 195.
72. Lisa Duggan, Nan Hunter and Carole S. Vance, 'False Promises: Feminist Antipornography Legislation in the U.S.', in Varda Burstyn (ed), *Women Against Censorship*, Douglas and McIntyre, Toronto, 1985, p. 139.
73. Ibid., p. 145.
74. Rubin, op. cit., p. 46.
75. Paula Webster, 'Pornography and Pleasure', *Heresies*, Sex Issue, 1981, p. 50.
76. Ellen Willis, 'Feminism, Moralism and Pornography', in Ann Snitow *et al.* (eds), *Desire: the Politics of Sexuality*, Virago, London, 1984, p. 85.
77. Rubin, op. cit., p. 46.
78. Ann Snitow, 'Retrenchment versus Transformation: The Politics of the Antipornography Movement', in Burstyn (ed), op. cit., p. 111.
79. Ibid., p. 112.
80. Esther Newton and Shirley Walton, 'The Misunderstanding: Toward a More Precise Sexual Vocabulary', in Vance (ed), op. cit., p. 248.
81. Amber Hollibaugh, 'Desire for the Future: Radical Hope in Passion and Pleasure', in Vance (ed), op. cit., p. 402.
82. Linda Gordon and Ellen Carol Dubois, 'Seeking Ecstasy on the

Battlefield: Danger and Pleasure in Nineteenth-century Feminist Sexual Thought', in Vance (ed), op. cit., p. 32.
83. Ibid.
84. Ibid., p. 43.
85. Burstyn (ed), op. cit.
86. Varda Burstyn, 'Political Precedents and Moral Crusades: Women, Sex and the State', in Burstyn (ed), op. cit., p. 13.
87. Jeffreys, op. cit., 1985.
88. Carole S. Vance, 'Pleasure and Danger: Toward a Politics of Sexuality', in Vance (ed), op. cit., p. 1.
89. Gordon and Dubois, op. cit., p. 43.
90. Gayle Rubin, 'Thinking Sex: Notes for a Radical Theory of the Politics of Sexuality', in Vance (ed), op. cit., p. 302.
91. Ibid., p. 274–5.
92. Pat Califia, Feminism and Sadomasochism, Heresies, Sex Issue, 1981, p. 30.
93. Gayle Rubin, in Vance (ed), op. cit., p. 307.
94. Ibid.
95. Ibid., p. 308.
96. Ibid., p. 309.
97. Ibid., p. 310.
98. Ibid., p. 283.
99. Vance (ed), op. cit., p. 19.
100. Alice Echols, 'The Taming of the Id: Feminist Sexual Politics, 1968–83', in Vance (ed), op. cit., p. 61.
101. Paula Webster, 'The Forbidden: Eroticism and Taboo', in Vance (ed), op. cit., p. 386.
102. Hollibaugh, op. cit., p. 403.
103. Simon Watney, Pornography, Aids and the Media, University of Minnesota Press, Minneapolis, 1987, p. 56.
104. Leeds Revolutionary Feminist Group, 'Political Lesbianism: The Case Against Heterosexuality', in ed. Onlywomen Press, Love Your Enemy, London, 1981.
105. Echols, op. cit., pp. 55–6.
106. Ibid., p. 62.
107. Snitow, op. cit., p. 113.
108. Ibid., p. 114.
109. Echols, op. cit., p. 51.
110. Elizabeth Sarah, 'Christabel Pankhurst: Reclaiming her Power', in Dale Spender (ed), Feminist Theorists, The Women's Press, London, 1983, p. 273.
111. Echols, op. cit., p. 56.
112. Ibid., p. 54.
113. Ibid., p. 56.
114. Ibid.
115. Vance (ed), op. cit., p. 9.

Chapter 6
CREATING THE SEXUAL FUTURE

1. *Concise Oxford Dictionary*, Oxford University Press, 1964, p. 573.
2. Celia Kitzinger, *The Social Construction of Lesbianism*, Sage Publications, London, 1987, p. 33.
3. Ibid.
4. Kathie Sarachild, 'Psychological Terrorism', in Redstockings (ed), *Feminist Revolution*, Random House, New York, 1975, p. 57.
5. Radicalesbians, 'The Woman-Identified Woman', in Phil Brown (ed), *Radical Psychology*, Tavistock Publications, London, 1973, p. 471.
6. Ibid., p. 479.
7. Jill Johnson, *Lesbian Nation*, Simon and Schuster, New York, 1973, pp. 166–7.
8. Leeds Revolutionary Feminist Group, 'Political Lesbianism: the Case Against Heterosexuality', in Onlywomen Press (eds), op. cit., p. 6.
9. Ibid.
10. Ibid.
11. Ibid., p. 12.
12. Ibid., p. 14.
13. Ibid., p. 16.
14. Anna Coote and Beatrix Campbell, *Sweet Freedom: The Struggle for Women's Liberation*, Picador, London, 1982, p. 225.
15. Lynne Segal, *Is The Future Female? Troubled Thoughts on Contemporary Feminism*, Virago, 1987, p. 97.
16. Adrienne Rich, 'Compulsory Heterosexuality and Lesbian Existence', in Snitow *et al.* (eds), *Desire: The Politics of Sexuality*, Virago, London, 1984, p. 212.
17. Ibid., p. 226.
18. Ibid., p. 220.
19. Ibid., p. 225.
20. Ibid., p. 226.
21. Ibid., p. 227.
22. Ariane Brunet and Louise Turcotte, 'Separatism and Radicalism', *Lesbian Ethics*, vol. 2, no. 1, p. 47. This article is reprinted in Sarah Lucia Hoagland and Julia Penelope, *For Lesbians Only: A Separatist Anthology*, Onlywomen Press, London, 1988 which is an excellent resource for separatist theory on heterosexuality.
23. Rich, op. cit., p. 227.
24. Janice G. Raymond, *A Passion for Friends*, The Women's Press, London, 1986, p. 16.
25. Ibid., p. 18.

26. Brunet and Turcotte, op. cit., p. 46.
27. Ibid.
28. Raymond, op. cit., 1986, p. 12.
29. Sheila Jeffreys, 'The Sexual Abuse of Children in the Home', in Friedman and Sarah (eds), op. cit., p. 61.
30. Linda Gordon and Ellen Dubois, 'Seeking Ecstasy on the Battle-field: Danger and Pleasure in Nineteenth-century Feminist Sexual Thought', in Carole S. Vance (ed), op. cit., p. 36.
31. Sheila Rowbotham, 'Passion off the Pedestal', *City Limits* magazine, no. 126, 2–8 March 1984, p. 21.
32. Jessie Bernard, *The Future of Marriage*, Yale University Press, New Haven, Ct., 1982 (first published 1972), p. 140.
33. Ibid., p. 155.
34. Rowbotham, op. cit., p. 21.
35. Ibid.
36. See Mary Daly and Jane Caputi, *Webster's First New Intergalactic Wickedary*, The Women's Press, London, 1987, p. 94. Daly and Caputi define the 'sadosociety' as: 'society spawned by phallic lust: the sum of places/times where the beliefs and practices of sadomasochism are The Rule'.
37. Eileen Phillips, *The Left and the Erotic*, Lawrence and Wishart, London, 1983, p. 34.
38. Sarah Crichton, 'Going for the Big "O" ', *Ms* magazine, New York, May 1986, p. 86.
39. Ibid.
40. Elizabeth Brenner, 'Sexual Surrender', *Cosmopolitan* magazine, vol. 19, no. 4, October 1985, p. 106.
41. Ibid.
42. Ibid.
43. Ibid.
44. Ti-Grace Atkinson, 'Why I'm Against S/M Liberation', in Robin Ruth Linden *et al.* (eds), *Against Sadomasochism*, Frog in the Well Press, San Francisco, 1982, p. 91.
45. Ibid.
46. See the section on 'Sex and Psychology' in Dolores Klaich, *Woman Plus Woman: Attitudes Toward Lesbianism*, New English Library, London, 1975.

RECOMMENDED READING

Cameron, Deborah and Frazer, Liz, *The Lust to Kill*, Polity Press, Cambridge, 1987.

Caputi, Jane, *The Age of Sex Crime*, The Women's Press, London, 1988.

Coveney, Lal *et al.* (eds), *The Sexuality Papers*, Hutchinson, London, 1984.

Dworkin, Andrea, *Pornography: Men Possessing Women*, The Women's Press, London, 1981.

Dworkin, Andrea, *Letters from a War Zone*, Secker and Warburg, London, 1988.

Faderman, Lillian, *Surpassing the Love of Men*, Junction Books, London, 1980.

Hite, Shere, *The Hite Report*, Summit Books, Sydney, Australia, 1978.

Hoagland, Sarah Lucia, *Lesbian Ethics*, Institute of Lesbian Studies, Palo Alto, California, 1988.

Hoagland, Sarah Lucia and Penelope, Julia (eds), *For Lesbians Only: A Separatist Anthology*, Onlywomen Press, London, 1988.

Jeffreys, Sheila, *The Spinster and Her Enemies: Feminism and Sexuality 1880–1930*, Pandora, London, 1985.

Kappeler, Suzanne, *The Pornography of Representation*, Polity Press, Cambridge, 1986.

Kitzinger, Celia, *The Social Construction of Lesbianism*, Sage Publications, London, 1987.

Linden, Robin Ruth *et al.* (eds), *Against Sadomasochism*, Frog in the Well Press, San Francisco, 1982.

Onlywomen Press (eds), *Love Your Enemy*, Onlywomen Press, London, 1981.

Raymond, Janice G., *A Passion for Friends*, The Women's Press, London, 1986.

Rhodes, Dusty and McNeill, Sandra, *Women Against Violence Against Women*, Onlywomen Press, London, 1985.

Russell, Diana, *Rape in Marriage*, Macmillan, New York, 1982.

WORKS CITED

Adams, Stephen, *The Homosexual As Hero in Literature*, Vision Press, London, 1980.

Atkinson, Ti-Grace, 'Why I'm Against S/M Liberation', in Linden, Robin Ruth *et al.* (eds), *Against Sadomasochism*, Frog in the Well Press, San Francisco, 1982.

Bannister, Kathleen *et al.*, *Social Casework in Marital Problems*, Tavistock Publications, London, 1955.

Barr, James, *Quatrefoil*, Alyson Publications, Boston, 1982.

Barry, Kathleen, *Female Sexual Slavery*, Prentice-Hall, Englewood Cliffs, NJ, 1979.

Bell, Alan P. and Weinberg, Martin S., *Homosexualities: A study of diversity among men and women*, Simon and Schuster, New York, 1978.

Bergler, Edmund, *Neurotic, Counterfeit-Sex*, Grune and Stratton, New York, 1951.

Bernard, Jessie, *The Future of Marriage*, Yale University Press, New Haven, Ct., 1982.

Bonaparte, Marie, *Female Sexuality*, Imago Publishing Co., London, 1953.

Boswell, John, *Christianity, Social Tolerance and Homosexuality: Gay people in western Europe from the beginning of the Christian era to the fourteenth century*, University of Chicago Press, Chicago and London, 1980.

Bowlby, John, *Child Care and the Growth of Love*, Penguin, London, 1974.

Brayshaw, Joseph, 'The Stability of Marriage', *Eugenics Review*, vol. 44, no. 2, July 1952.

340

Brecher, Edward M., *The Sex Researchers*, Panther, London, 1972.

Brenner, Elizabeth, 'Sexual Surrender', *Cosmopolitan* magazine, London, October 1985.

Brown, Helen Gurley, *Sex and the Single Girl*, Bernard Geiss Associates, New York, 1962.

Brownmiller, Susan, *Against Our Will: Men, Women and Rape*, Secker and Warburg, London, 1975.

Brunet, Ariane and Turcotte, Louise, 'Separatism and Radicalism', *Lesbian Ethics*, vol. 2, no. 1.

Burroughs, William, *Cities of the Red Night*, John Calder, London, 1981.

Burstyn, Varda (ed), *Women Against Censorship*, Douglas and McIntyre, Toronto, 1985.

Calder, John (ed), *A William Burroughs Reader*, Picador, London, 1982.

Califia, Pat, 'Feminism and Sadomasochism' in *Heresies*, Sex Issue, vol. 3, no. 12, New York, 1981.

Campbell, Olwen, *The Feminine Point of View: The Report of a Conference*, Williams and Norgate, London, 1952.

Caputi, Jane, *The Age of Sex Crime*, The Women's Press, London, 1988.

Caprio, Frank, *The Sexually Adequate Female*, Citadel Press, New York, 1963.

Caprio, Frank, *Female Homosexuality*, Peter Owen, London, 1957.

Carpenter, Edward, *The Intermediate Sex*, George Allen and Unwin, London, 1921.

Carpenter, Edward, *Towards Democracy*, George Allen and Unwin, London, 1921.

Cavin, Susan, *Lesbian Origins*, Ism Press, San Francisco, 1985.

Chesser, Eustace, *Love and Marriage*, Pan Books, London, 1957.

Chesser, Eustace, *Odd Man Out*, Victor Gollancz, London, 1959.

Chesser, Eustace, *Sexual Behaviour: Normal and Abnormal*, Roy Publishers, New York, 1949.

Comfort, Alex, *Barbarism and Sexual Freedom. Lectures on*

the sociology of sex from the standpoint of anarchism, Freedom Press, London, 1948.

Comfort, Alex (ed), *The Joy of Sex*, Quartet, London, 1979.

Comfort, Alex (ed), *More Joy of Sex*, Quartet, London, 1984.

Coote, Anna and Campbell, Beatrix, *Sweet Freedom: The Struggle for Women's Liberation*, Picador, London, 1982.

Coveney, Lal, Kay, Leslie and Mahony, Pat, 'Theory into practice: sexual liberation or social control?' (*Forum* magazine 1968–81), in Coveney, L. *et al.* (eds), *The Sexuality Papers*, Hutchinson, London, 1984.

Cowell, Roberta, *Roberta Cowell's Story: An Autobiography*, Heinemann, London, 1954.

Creeley, Robert (ed), *Walt Whitman*, Penguin, London, 1973.

Crichton, Sarah, 'Going for the Big "O" ', *Ms* magazine, New York, May 1986.

Crisp, Quentin, *The Naked Civil Servant*, Fontana, London, 1981.

Daly, Mary and Caputi, Jane, *Webster's First New Intergalactic Wickedary*, The Women's Press, London, 1987.

Davis, Maxine, *The Sexual Responsibility of Women*, Fontana, London, 1965.

Dodson, Betty, *Self Love and Orgasm*, self-published by Betty Dodson, New York, 1983.

Dworkin, Andrea, *Pornography: Men Possessing Women*, Perigree, New York, 1981; The Women's Press, London, 1981.

Dworkin, Andrea, *Letters from a War Zone*, Secker and Warburg, London, 1988.

Echols, Alice, 'The Taming of the Id: Feminist Sexual Politics, 1968–83', in Vance, Carole S. (ed), *Pleasure and Danger*, Routledge and Kegan Paul, London, 1984.

Ellis, Havelock, *Erotic Symbolism: Studies in the Psychology of Sex*, F. A. Davis, Philadelphia, 1926.

Ellis, Havelock, *Sexual Inversion*, F. A. Davis, Philadelphia, 1927.

Everywoman (eds), *Pornography and Sexual Violence: Evidence of the Links*, Everywoman, London, 1988.

Faderman, Lillian, *Surpassing the Love of Men*, Junction Books, London, 1980.

Ferenczi, Sandor, 'The confusion of tongues between the adult and the child', appendix to Masson, Jeffrey, *The Assault on Truth: Freud's Suppression of the Seduction Theory*, Farrar, Straus and Giroux, New York, 1984.

Finkelhor, David and Yllo, Kersti, *License to Rape: Sexual Abuse of Wives*, Holt, Rinehart and Winston, New York, 1985.

Finney, Brian, *Christopher Isherwood: A Critical Biography*, Faber, London, 1979.

Flame, *Flame: A Life on the Game*, Gay Men's Press, London, 1984.

Forster, E. M., *A Life to Come and Other Stories*, Penguin, Harmondsworth, 1975.

Friedman, Leonard J., *Virgin Wives: A Study of Unconsummated Marriages*, Tavistock Publications, London, 1962.

Friedman, Scarlet and Sarah, Elizabeth (eds), *On the Problem of Men*, The Women's Press, London, 1982.

Fry, Margery, *The Single Woman*, Delisle, London, 1953.

Gay Left Collective (eds), *Homosexuality: Power and Politics*, Allison and Busby, London, 1980.

Girodias, Maurice, 'Obscenity and the Sexual Revolution', in *The Obscenity Report*, Olympia Press, Paris, 1971.

Goodman, Michael B., '*Contemporary Literary Censorship: The Case History of Burroughs' The Naked Lunch*' Scarecrow Press, Metuchen, NJ, 1981.

Gordon, Linda and Dubois, Ellen, 'Seeking Ecstasy on the Battlefield: Danger and Pleasure in Nineteenth-Century Feminist Sexual Thought', in Vance, Carole S. (ed), *Pleasure and Danger*, Routledge and Kegan Paul, London, 1984.

Griffin, Susan, 'Rape: the All-American Crime', *Oz* magazine, issue 41, London, 1971.

Harding, Esther, *The Way of All Women*, Longman and Green, London, 1939.

Hegeler, Inge and Stan, *An ABZ of Love*, New English Library, London, 1963.

Henslin, James M. and Sagarin, Edward (eds), *The Sociology of Sex: An Introductory Reader*, Schocken Books, New York, 1978.

Hoagland, Sarah Lucia and Penelope, Julia, *For Lesbians Only: A Separatist Anthology*, Onlywomen Press, London, 1988.

Hollibaugh, Amber, 'Desire for the Future: Radical Hope in Passion and Pleasure', in Vance, Carole S. (ed), *Pleasure and Danger*, Routledge and Kegan Paul, London, 1984.

Hutton, Laura, *The Single Woman and Her Emotional Problems*, Baillière, Tindall and Cox, London, 1937.

Hyde, Montgomery, *A History of Pornography*, Four Square Books, London, 1966.

Isherwood, Christopher, *Goodbye to Berlin*, Hogarth Press, London, 1960.

Isherwood, Christopher, *Christopher and His Kind*, Eyre Methuen, London, 1977.

J., *The Sensuous Woman*, Castle Books, Memphis, 1981 (first published 1969).

Jackson, Ed and Persky, Stan (eds), *Flaunting It: A decade of journalism from* Body Politic, Pink Triangle Press, Toronto, 1982.

Jackson, Margaret, 'Sexology and the universalisation of male sexuality', in Coveney, L. *et al.* (eds), *The Sexuality Papers*, Hutchinson, London, 1984.

Jay, Karla and Young, Allen (eds), *Lavender Culture*, Harcourt Brace Jovanovich, New York, 1978.

Jeffreys, Sheila, 'The Sexual Abuse of Children in the Home', in Friedman, Scarlet and Sarah, Elizabeth, *On the Problem of Men*, The Women's Press, London, 1982.

Jeffreys, Sheila, *The Spinster and Her Enemies: Feminism and Sexuality 1880–1930*, Pandora, London, 1985.

Johnston, Jill, *Lesbian Nation: The Feminist Solution*, Simon and Schuster, New York, 1973.

Kaplan, Helen Singer, *The New Sex Therapy*, Baillière, Tindall, London, 1974.

Kappeler, Suzanne, *The Pornography of Representation*, Polity Press, Cambridge, 1986.

Kern, Louis J., 'Ideology and Reality: Sexuality and Women's Status in the Oneida Community', *Radical History Review*, no. 20, Spring/Summer 1979.

Kirk, Kris and Heath, Ed, *Men in Frocks*, Gay Men's Press, London, 1984.

Kitzinger, Celia, *The Social Construction of Lesbianism*, Sage Publications, London, 1987.

Klaich, Dolores, *Woman Plus Woman: Attitudes to Lesbianism*, New English Library, London, 1975.

Koedt, Anne, 'The Myth of the Vaginal Orgasm', in The Radical Therapist Collective (ed), *The Radical Therapist*, Penguin, Harmondsworth, 1974.

Kokken, Sha, *The Way to Married Love: A Happier Sex Life*, Souvenir Press, London, 1967 (first published Japan 1960).

Kronhausen, Eberhard and Phyllis, *Pornography and the Law*, The New English Library, London, 1967.

Leeds Revolutionary Feminist Group, 'Political Lesbianism: the case against heterosexuality', in Onlywomen Press (eds), *Love your Enemy*, Onlywomen Press, London, 1981.

Lloyd, Robin, *Playland: A Study of Human Exploitation*, Quartet, London, 1979.

London Gay Activists Alliance, 'Child temptress chased man to bed', *Submission to the Royal Commission on Criminal Procedure*, April 1979.

Lothstein, Leslie Martin, *Female-to-male Transsexualism*, Routledge and Kegan Paul, Boston and London, 1983.

Lovelace, Linda, *Ordeal*, W. H. Allen, London, 1981.

Lydon, Susan, 'The Politics of Orgasm', in Morgan, Robin (ed), *Sisterhood is Powerful*, Vintage Books, New York, 1970.

Mace, David, *Marriage Crisis*, Delisle, London, 1948.

MacKinnon, Catharine, 'Not a Moral Issue', in *Yale Law and Policy Review*, vol. II, no. 2, Spring 1984.

Masson, Jeffrey Moussaieff, *The Assault on Truth: Freud's suppression of the seduction theory*, Farrar, Straus and Giroux, New York, 1984.

Masters, William H. and Johnson, Virginia E., *Human Sexual Inadequacy*, Bantam Books, Boston, 1981.

Masters, William H. and Johnson, Virginia E., *The Pleasure Bond. A New Look at Sexuality and Commitment*, Little, Brown, Boston, 1974.

Metcalf, Andy and Humphries, Martin, *The Sexuality of Men*, Pluto Press, London, 1985.

Middleton, Warren (ed), *The Betrayal of Youth*, CL Publications, London, 1986.

Millett, Kate, *Sexual Politics*, Virago, London, 1977.

Moody, Roger, *Indecent Assault*, Word is Out/Peace News, London, 1980.

Moore, Thomas V., 'The pathogenesis and treatment of homosexual disorders: a digest of some pertinent evidence', *Journal of Personality*, vol. XIV, Sept. 1945.

Mottram, Eric, *William Burroughs*, Calder and Boyars, London, 1977.

Morgan, Robin, *Sisterhood is Powerful*, Vintage Books, New York, 1970.

Morris, Jan, *Conundrum*, Coronet Books, London, 1975.

Mushroom, Merill, 'Confessions of a Butch Dyke', *Common Lives, Lesbian Lives*, Iowa, no. 9, Fall 1983.

Nabokov, Vladimir, *Lolita*, Corgi Books, London, 1961.

Nestle, Joan, *A Restricted Country*, Sheba, London, 1988.

Neville-Rolfe, Sybil (ed), *Sex in Social Life*, George Allen and Unwin, London, 1949.

Norman, H. E. 'Why Marriages Fail – the social aspect', in Neville-Rolfe, Sybil (ed), *Sex in Social Life*, George Allen and Unwin, London, 1949.

O'Carroll, Tom, *Paedophilia: The Radical Case*, Peter Owen, London, 1980.

Onlywomen Press (ed), *Love your Enemy*, Onlywomen Press, London, 1981.

Phillips, Eileen, *The Left and the Erotic*, Lawrence and Wishart, London, 1983.

Radicalesbians, 'The Woman-Identified Woman,' in Brown, Phil (ed), *Radical Psychology*, Tavistock Publications, London, 1973.

Raymond, Janice G., *A Passion for Friends*, The Women's Press, 1986.

Raymond, Janice G., *The Transsexual Empire*, The Women's Press, London, 1982.

Raymond, Janice G., 'Transsexualism: The Ultimate Homage to Sex-Role Power' in *Crysalis* no. 3.

Rechy, John, *The Sexual Outlaw*, Futura, London, 1979.

Reich, Wilhelm, *The Sexual Struggle of Youth*, Socialist Reproduction, London, 1972.

Rembar, Charles, *The End of Obscenity*, André Deutsch, London, 1969.

Reuben, David, *Everything you always wanted to know about sex but were afraid to ask*, W. H. Allen, London, 1970.

Rich, Adrienne, 'Compulsory Heterosexuality and Lesbian Existence', in Snitow *et al.* (eds), *Desire: The Politics of Sexuality*, Virago, London, 1984.

Riddell, Carol, *Divided Sisterhood*, News From Nowhere, Liverpool, 1980.

Riefenstahl, Leni, *People of Kau*, Harper and Row, New York, 1976.

Rhodes, Dusty and McNeill, Sandra, *Women Against Violence Against Women*, Onlywomen Press, London, 1985.

Robinson, Paul, *The Sexual Radicals*, Paladin, London, 1972.

Rowbotham, Sheila, 'Passion off the Pedestal', in *City Limits* magazine, no. 126, March 2–8, London, 1984.

Rubin, Gayle *et al.*, 'Talking Sex', *Feminist Review*, no. 11, Summer, London, 1982.

Rubin, Gayle, 'Thinking Sex: Notes for a Radical Theory of the Politics of Sexuality', in Vance, Carole S. (ed), *Pleasure and Danger*, Routledge and Kegan Paul, London, 1984.

Rubin, Gayle, 'The Leather Menace', in Samois (ed), *Coming to Power*, Alyson Publications, Boston, 1982.

Rush, Florence, 'The Sexual Abuse of Children: A Feminist Point of View', in The Radical Therapist Collective (eds), *The Radical Therapist*, Penguin, Harmondsworth, 1974.

Russell, Diana, *Rape in Marriage*, Macmillan, New York, 1982.

Samois (ed), *Coming to Power*, Alyson Publications, Boston, 1982.

Sarachild, Kathie, 'Psychological Terrorism', in Redstockings (ed), *Feminist Revolution*, Random House, New York, 1975.

Sarah, Elizabeth, 'Christabel Pankhurst: Reclaiming Her Power', in Spender, Dale (ed), *Feminist Theorists*, The Women's Press, London, 1983.

Segal, Lynne, *Is the Future Female? Troubled Thoughts on Contemporary Feminism*, Virago, London, 1987.

Severson, Anne, 'Don't Get Too Near the Big Chakra', in Rowe, Marsha (ed), *The Spare Rib Reader*, Penguin, London, 1982.

Sherfey, Mary Jane, 'A Theory on Female Sexuality', in Morgan, Robin (ed), *Sisterhood is Powerful*, Vintage Books, New York, 1970.

Smith, Blanche Marie, *The Single Woman of Today*, Greenwood Press, Westport, Ct., 1974.

Snitow, Ann *et al.* (eds), *Desire: the Politics of Sexuality*, Virago, London, 1984.

Snitow, Ann, 'Retrenchment versus Transformation: The Politics of the Antipornography Movement', in Burstyn, Varda (ed), *Women Against Censorship*, Douglas and McIntyre, Toronto, 1985.

Spada, James, *The Spada Report*, Signet New American Library, New York, 1979.

Stekel, Wilhelm, *Frigidity in Woman in Relation to her Love Life, Vol. 2*, Liveright, New York, 1936.

Sutherland, John, *Offensive Literature: Decensorship in Britain 1960–1982*, Junction Books, London, 1982.

Talese, Gay, *Thy Neighbour's Wife*, Pan Books, London, 1981.

Trainer, Russell, *The Lolita Complex*, Citadel Press, New York, 1966.

Tsang, Daniel (ed), *The Age Taboo*, Alyson Publications, Boston, 1981.

Ullerstam, Lars, *The Erotic Minorities*, Grove Press, New York, 1964.

Vance, Carole S. (ed), *Pleasure and Danger: Exploring Female Sexuality*, Routledge and Kegan Paul, London, 1984.

Walker, Kenneth, 'Why Marriages Fail – the personal aspect', in Neville-Rolfe, Sybil (ed), *Sex in Social Life*, George Allen and Unwin, London, 1949.

Walker, Kenneth, *The Psychology of Sex*, Penguin, Harmondsworth, 1969.

Walter, Aubrey (ed), *Come Together: The Years of Gay Liberation 1970–73*, Gay Men's Press, London, 1980.

Ward, Elizabeth, *Father-Daughter Rape*, The Women's Press, London, 1984.

Watney, Simon, *Pornography, Aids and the Media*, University of Minnesota Press, Minneapolis, 1987.

Webster, Paula, 'Pornography and Pleasure', in *Heresies*, Sex Issue, vol. 3, no. 12, New York, 1981.

Weeks, Jeffrey, *Coming Out*, Quartet, London, 1977.

Weeks, Jeffrey, *Sexuality and its Discontents*, Routledge and Kegan Paul, London, 1985.

Weeks, Jeffrey, *Sex, Politics and Society*, Longmans, London, 1981.

Whiting, Pat, 'Female Sexuality: its political implications', in Wandor, Michelene (ed), *The Body Politic: Women's Liberation in Britain*, Stage One, London, 1972.

Williams, Gertrude, *Women and Work*, Essential Books, New York, 1945; series written for the citizens of Britain.

INDEX

210–11, 212–15, 221–6; and transsexuals 187–8; as revolutionary 154, 155–6; Burroughs and 70–1, 72, 75
male homosexuals: and libertarianism 261, 263; and masculinity 214–16; attitudes to women 157–8, 174; misusing befriending groups 158; theorists 215, 261, 263, 274–5, 277, 279–80
male rituals 218
male sexuality 117–19, 154, 155–6, 158, 159–62, 208, 237–8, 305, 306; development 208; necessity for reconstruction 159, 166, 261, 312–13, 313; sexual violence and 240–2, 250
Marciano, Linda see Lovelace, Linda
Marcuse, Herbert 100, 104–5
marriage 5–12, 133, 299–300; and health 48; choice of partners 12, 47, 208, 299; equality in 306; ideology of 8–10, 12; nonconsummation of 32, 35–6; political function 5; power relations in 33–5, 37; rape in 35, 244–9, 299; rate of 92, 93–4
marriage guidance 5–6, 8, 9, 11–12
masochism 66, 109, 181, 204–5, 302, 303, 314
Masters, William 135–44, 227, 228–9, 230–1, 232
masturbation 43, 233, 234–6, 237, 238
Maxwell-Fyfe, David 56
men 19, 30; choice of marriage partners 12, 47, 208, 299; misusing power over boys 193, 194–6, 202–3; prescriptions for sexual behaviour 119–20, 140;

prevalence of homosexual experience 51–2; sharing women 103–4, 123, 129; using prostitutes 70, 122, 123
menstruation 137–8
Merrill, George 147
Middleton, Warren 190–1, 207–8
Miller, Henry 63, 90
Millett, Kate 58, 65
minorities, sexual 99, 163–8, 188, 211–12, 275, 278, 279
Money, John 177
Moody, Roger 189, 192
morality 7, 8, 9, 73, 83, 94–5, 111, 212; relativist 97–100
Morris, Jan 179–81, 183
Morrison, Herbert 56
motherhood 13–18
mothers 194, 302; blaming 13–15, 53–4, 177, 184
murder 70, 74, 79, 98, 122, 249, 305
Mushroom, Merrill 186

Nabokov, Vladimir 83–5, 90; *Lolita* 60, 61, 63, 64, 76–85, 90
Naked Lunch, The see Burroughs, William
North American Man Boy Love Association (NAMBLA) 190, 191, 193, 202, 205
National Organisation of Women (NOW) 207, 234
necrophilia 98–9, 277
Nestle, Joan 263
Neville-Rolfe, Sybil 6, 19n, 39–40, 51
Newton, Esther 269n
Norman, H. E. 6, 7
Norwood, Cyril 7n

objectification 37–8, 253–4
obscene phone calls 157–8
obscenity, defining 62–5, 67–8